AA

EAT OUT
IN BRITAIN FOR AROUND £5

Editor: Penny Hicks
Designers: Ashley Tilleard, Peter Davies

Consultant: Ian Tyers, Manager, Hotel and Information Services
Gazetteer Editor: Pamela Stagg
Maps: prepared by the Cartographic Services Unit of the Automobile Association
Cover photograph: The Old Granary, Wareham

Head of Advertisement Sales: Christopher Heard Tel 0256 20123 (ext 2020)
Advertisement Production: Karen Weeks Tel 0256 20123 (ext 3525)
Advertisement Sales Representatives:
London, East Anglia, East Midlands: Melanie Mackenzie-Aird Tel 0494 40208
Central Southern and South East England: Edward May Tel 0256 20123 (ext 3524) or 0256 67568
South West, West, West Midlands: Brian Thompson Tel 027580 3296
Wales, North of England & Scotland: Arthur Williams Tel 0222 60267

Filmsetting by Vantage Photosetting Co. Ltd, Eastleigh and London
Printed and bound by William Collins, Glasgow

ISBN 0 86145 190 2

Published by the Automobile Association, Fanum House, Basingstoke, Hampshire RG21 2EA

Contents

A New-Style Guide

This year we have had a completely fresh look at the guide and have come up with a new way of presenting the information to our readers. Our purpose is still the same, though – to provide details of pleasant eating places which offer particularly good value for money.

First of all, our team of inspectors have been hot on the trail of lots of new places and we have increased the number of establishments listed by more than 100 from last year. Sadly we have lost a few, but mostly due to closure or change of hands – only a few have failed to keep their prices within our £5 limit. Of course, we recognise that this limit has stood now for a number of years – if only the cost of living would too! – and we felt it only fair to slightly amend our criteria. Although most of the establishments listed can still offer a good three-course meal for less than £5, we only asked them to provide two-course meals within our limits this year and thus avoided losing some good restaurants who might otherwise have just crept over the top.

We have also changed our format – bringing all of the listings into one A-Z gazetteer – and have added a 16-page atlas section and London plans to help you locate the restaurants. If you know which town you are looking for, you can now turn straight to the alphabetical gazetteer; if you are in a strange area and you want to know what's on offer, look at the atlas first where all the towns in the gazetteer are located. London can be a little daunting if you don't know your way around and so we hope our London Plans, with establishments located, will help newcomers to the capital to find a good place to eat.

For our special features this year we have looked at the increasingly popular subject of pub food and have discovered that it isn't just a ploughman's or a pie with your pint. We have also looked at some of the many places around Britain where you can see Food in the Making – mills, cheese farms, honey farms, breweries, distilleries etc. – and if you have ever sat back after a wonderful restaurant meal and wondered where they do their shopping, we have looked for some of those unusual specialist food shops to inspire you to great things in your own kitchens.

Finally, we have included a report form so that you can let us know about your favourite restaurant which offers a good meal for under £5, or tell us what you think of our choices. We will be delighted to hear from you.

Money-off Vouchers

Save £3.50 by using the money-off vouchers opposite. Each voucher, worth 50p, entitles you to money off your bill at many of the establishments in this book. The full list of restaurants which are prepared to accept the vouchers is given on page 200. In addition, each establishment's entry in the gazetteer contains the symbol VS if vouchers are accepted there.

The conditions of use of the vouchers, printed on the reverse side are as follows:

A copy of *AA Eat Out in Britain for Around £5* 1984 must be produced with the voucher.

Only one voucher per person or party accepted.

Not redeemable for cash. No change given. The voucher will not be valid after 31st December 1984.

Use of the voucher is restricted to when payment is made before leaving the restaurant premises.

The Voucher worth
50p
May be redeemed in accordance with the conditions overleaf at any of the 210 establishments listed on page 200 of AA Eat Out in Britain for Around £5 1984 against a restaurant bill.
The Voucher worth
50p
May be redeemed in accordance with the conditions overleaf at any of the 210 establishments listed on page 200 of AA Eat Out in Britain for Around £5 1984 against a restaurant bill.
The Voucher worth
50p
May be redeemed in accordance with the conditions overleaf at any of the 210 establishments listed on page 200 of AA Eat Out in Britain for Around £5 1984 against a restaurant bill.
The Voucher worth
50p
May be redeemed in accordance with the conditions overleaf at any of the 210 establishments listed on page 200 of AA Eat Out in Britain for Around £5 1984 against a restaurant bill.
The Voucher worth
50p
May be redeemed in accordance with the conditions overleaf at any of the 210 establishments listed on page 200 of AA Eat Out in Britain for Around £5 1984 against a restaurant bill.
The Voucher worth
50p
May be redeemed in accordance with the conditions overleaf at any of the 210 establishments listed on page 200 of AA Eat Out in Britain for Around £5 1984 against a restaurant bill.
The Voucher worth
50p
May be redeemed in accordance with the conditions overleaf at any of the 210 establishments listed on page 200 of AA Eat Out in Britain for Around £5 1984 against a restaurant bill.

A copy of AA Eat Out in Britain for Around £5 1984 must be produced with this voucher.

Only one voucher per person or party accepted.

Not redeemable for cash. No change given.

The voucher will not be valid after 31st December, 1984.

Use of the voucher is restricted to when payment is made before leaving the restaurant premises.

A copy of AA Eat Out in Britain for Around £5 1984 must be produced with this voucher.

Only one voucher per person or party accepted.

Not redeemable for cash. No change given.

The voucher will not be valid after 31st December, 1984.

Use of the voucher is restricted to when payment is made before leaving the restaurant premises.

A copy of AA Eat Out in Britain for Around £5 1984 must be produced with this voucher.

Only one voucher per person or party accepted.

Not redeemable for cash. No change given.

The voucher will not be valid after 31st December, 1984.

Use of the voucher is restricted to when payment is made before leaving the restaurant premises.

A copy of AA Eat Out in Britain for Around £5 1984 must be produced with this voucher.

Only one voucher per person or party accepted.

Not redeemable for cash. No change given.

The voucher will not be valid after 31st December, 1984.

Use of the voucher is restricted to when payment is made before leaving the restaurant premises.

A copy of AA Eat Out in Britain for Around £5 1984 must be produced with this voucher.

Only one voucher per person or party accepted.

Not redeemable for cash. No change given.

The voucher will not be valid after 31st December, 1984.

Use of the voucher is restricted to when payment is made before leaving the restaurant premises.

A copy of AA Eat Out in Britain for Around £5 1984 must be produced with this voucher.

Only one voucher per person or party accepted.

Not redeemable for cash. No change given.

The voucher will not be valid after 31st December, 1984.

Use of the voucher is restricted to when payment is made before leaving the restaurant premises.

A copy of AA Eat Out in Britain for Around £5 1984 must be produced with this voucher.

Only one voucher per person or party accepted.

Not redeemable for cash. No change given.

The voucher will not be valid after 31st December, 1984.

Use of the voucher is restricted to when payment is made before leaving the restaurant premises.

Pubs with Good Food

The traditional pub is changing out of all recognition. The beer is much better and more varied than it used to be, thanks to the efforts of the real-ale enthusiasts, and food is available more often than not. Many pubs are opening their doors to families with children, and in all respects the average pub is greatly broadening its appeal. This guide to eating out on a budget includes a large number of pubs where inexpensive meals of two or more courses are available for £5 or less. A full list of these appears on pages 12–13. All of these places provide good food and are recommended by our inspectors. Several of them, though, provide food which is unusual or exotic and well worth seeking out. We take a gourmet's tour of some of these places where good beer, an attractive setting and some interesting food make a visit to the pub a special experience.

Oysters & Seafood

The starting point of our tour is the home of one of Britain's most traditional, but now most uncommon specialities, the oyster. A new entry to the guide this year, *Pearson's Crab and Oyster House* in Whitstable, Kent is a superbly restored old fisherman's pub by the beach, next to the old oyster company building. Oysters are available when there is an 'R' in the month, and can be had in quarter-dozens for those who are cautious. All kinds of seafood is also available, including crabs and lobsters kept in special tanks. The beer is Fremlins, and some tables in the upstairs restaurant look out over the sea. The next stop on our tour is also near the Kent coast, at the little village of Northbourne, near Deal. This is an attractive country pub, *The Hare and Hounds*, where seafood is also on the menu, notably mussels in garlic butter or the prawn and scallop sauce that can accompany the steak. The homemade cheesecakes are also delicious here.

Turning inland now, the *Red Lion* at Appledore is another new entry to this year's guide and features such specialities as Rye Bay Fish, Scallops, or homemade steak and kidney pie. Real ale is available and, interestingly, so is mulled ale. Just across the Kent border into East Sussex is another, very attractive village, Ewhurst Green, with old oast houses and a tranquil village green. *The White Dog Inn*, is actually more than a pub, offering hotel accommodation and an extensive blackboard menu. Among the interesting specialities are venison casserole, moussaka and liqueur syllabub.

Country Cooking

Travelling westwards through the southern part of Britain, we come next to Petworth, near which is the tiny village of Lodsworth where the *Lickfold Inn* can be found. This inn has earned itself a good local reputation for food and also has a splendid selection of real ales. You can sit in the bar here, by the huge open fire and enjoy such delights as fillet of haddock filled with crabmeat and served with Bearnaise sauce. Further west, near Chippenham in Wiltshire is the village of Pewsham, where *The Lysley Arms* is situated. This old coaching inn is new to this guide and has an interesting, varied menu, including tripe and onions, boiled beef and carrots or braised oxtail which are available at the bar. Among the other dishes available is prawns in cream.

Some way off the beaten track in the heart of Dorset is the *Fiddleford Inn* in the village of that name. Among the attractions here, apart from the appeal of the old inn itself, are the homemade Fiddleford savoury pancakes, but Dorset-cured ham is also available and there is a delicious range of desserts. Dorset is a county well-endowed with haunting tales, and *The Marquis of Lorne* at Nettlecombe near Bridport has a splendid one. It also has an attractive menu where generous portions are all home cooked. Especially interesting are the sweets which include pavlova, poached pears and mousses.

Devon Delight

Devon is brimming with pubs offering good food, so this selection is no more than an appetiser. Indeed, although *Ye Old Saddlers Arms* at Lympstone near Exmouth, offers a good, varied menu, it was the range of ice creams that caught our inspector's attention, including special French ice creams flavoured with champagne, or cointreau and raisins. *The Mason Arms* at Knowstone also offers attractive desserts, but we include it here because of their enterprise in offering a wide range of vegetarian dishes, such as baked eggs in onion cream sauce, and parsnip and mushroom casserole. They do some very tempting conventional dishes as well, however, such as Veal Elizabeth and steak and pigeon pie. In the heart of Dartmoor, near Bovey Tracey is *The Rock Inn* at Haytor Vale. This secluded old inn offers some most unusual dishes, including West African groundnut stew and Arabian lamb. *The Nobody Inn* at Doddiscombleigh has its own Nobody soup, and also features such uncommon pub food as lamb sweetbreads. They also say they will prepare your favourite dish on request, which is a brave statement to make. Further down the Devon coast is an unusually named coaching inn, *The Dartmoor Halfway* at Bickington near Newton Abbot. Their menu features a unique starter, 'grotti nosh', which is so filling that you may not be able to cope with the seafood risotto that is also on offer. Across the other side of Dartmoor is the famous Lydford Gorge, and in Lydford village is the historic *Castle Inn*, a charming old building full of interesting curios and with a superb cold table at lunchtime. Curries are a speciality here, but the range of sweets was also most attractive.

Snails & Smokies

Turning back towards the Bristol Channel, our next stop is at Ralegh's Cross in Somerset's picturesque Brendon Hills. *The Ralegh's Cross Inn* has a Cordon Bleu restaurant open in the evenings where, unfortunately, prices put it outside the scope of this guide, but the enterprising bar meals include quite a lot of game, such as local pheasant casserole or Brendon Hill Bobtails (rabbit casserole). Farther west, beyond Bridgwater, is the village of Ashcott and the cosy *Ashcott Inn*, where the bar menu also includes Mendip snails with herb butter. Among the other attractions here are Somerset smokies with white wine and broccoli, stilton and walnut quiche. At Bleadney, near the Mendip Hills, *The Stradlings* offers such exotica as snails in garlic butter and mushrooms Valencienne, while, further north, a new entry, *The White Hart* at Congresbury has a very adventurous menu in their Inwood buttery. This includes cream of smoked trout soup, venison in red wine sauce and Zappion, a Greek dish consisting of macaroni and minced beef with a cheese topping.

Travelling north-east towards the Cotswolds, we travel to the *Compass Inn* at Tormarton where many interesting dishes are served in the Vittler Bar. These can include hot seafood casserole or ham and asparagus in cheese sause as well as a well presented cold buffet. Beyond Cirencester on the road to Stow-on-the-Wold is the *Fossebridge Inn* at Fossebridge, an attractive roadside inn where good inexpensive food is available in the Buttery. Specialities include spicy crab pâté, freshly caught trout and some attractive puddings. Further east in Berkshire, is *The Rowbarge* at Woolhampton where excellent home cooking produces such delicacies as haddock Monte Carlo (with parsley, egg sause, poached egg and saute potatoes), and rissoles in wine gravy which are quite famous locally.

Amersham features a number of interesting pubs included in this book, such as *The Saracen's Head* with several intriguing dishes available in the Bear Pit. These include coquille St Jacques, Mrs Beeton's baked trout and crab salad Louis, as well as a variety of Bear Pit burgers and some tasty sweets. *The Elephant and Castle* also offers some tempting dishes including marinaded anchovies and spotted dick. Moving north again, *The Plough Inn* at Wingfield in Bedfordshire is an attractive 17th century pub where one of the more unusual dishes is venison pie.

Squid & Garlic

East Anglia is not short of good pubs and this guide includes several which it is worth travelling to visit. At *The Eight Bells* in Saffron Walden, steak and oyster pie or hot devilled crab are difficult to resist, while *The Pheasant Inn* at Keyston near Huntingdon offers some even more unusual bar meals. This must be the only pub in Britain to offer fried squid with garlic rolls as a bar snack.

From this point we move west, visiting the famous *Dirty Duck* at Stratford-upon-Avon to sample the braised kidneys before calling at *The Peacock Inn* at Tenbury Wells, where the influence of Malaysia flavours the food available, especially the splendid curry. Not far away, across the Welsh border, is a cosy little pub, *The Radnor Arms* at Llowes in Powys. Among the interesting dishes here are cured herring or mackerel, chicken and lemon terrine and some delectable sweets. Back across the border, in Shrewsbury, the *Dun Cow* is one of the oldest pubs in England. One of its specialities is lamb cutlets cooked with honey and port wine.

Heading North

Crossing the East Midlands to Northamptonshire, *The Falcon Inn* at Fotheringhay, just north of Oundle is a real find. This friendly pub has a tremendous choice of good food, including such delights as fresh asparagus with melted butter, rabbit provençale, as well as creme de menthe frappe and coffee and walnut fudge pie. The beer is good too! *The Chequers Inn*, a new entry this year at Woolsthorpe-by-Belvoir is a traditional old English pub which actually owns its own cricket ground. Not surprisingly, in this area, cheese is one of the pubs specialities, with a different cheese available every day. Among the other dishes are venison with black cherries and baked Alaska. Over in the Peak District, another new entry to the book, *The Shire Horse* at Wyaston near Ashbourne is another unusual pub, since it has a living oak tree growing through the middle of the building. The food is excellent value for money and a wide variety of real ales are always available.

The final leg of this tour takes us to Scotland. On the way, stop at the *Besom Byre* at Longframling-

---

AVON
Bristol
Chequers Inn
Llandoger Trow
Chipping Sodbury
Lawns Inn
Congresbury
White Hart
Tormarton
Compass Inn

BEDFORDSHIRE
Leighton Buzzard
Cross Keyes

BERKSHIRE
Woolhampton
Rowbarge

BUCKINGHAMSHIRE
Amersham
Elephant & Castle
Saracen's Head
Hit or Miss Inn
Aylesbury
Hen and Chickens

CAMBRIDGESHIRE
Keyston
Pheasant Inn

CUMBRIA
Carlise
Malt Shovel

DERBYSHIRE
Sheen
Ye Olde Spinning Wheel
Wyaston
Shire Horse Inn

DEVON
Ashburton
Rising Sun Inn
Bickleigh
Trout Inn
Bovey Tracey
Riverside Inn
Rock Inn
Buckfastleigh
Dart Bridge Inn
Coleford
New Inn
Croyde
Thatched Barn Inn
Doddiscombleigh
Nobody Inn
Dunsford
Royal Oak Inn
Exeter
Ship Inn
Swan's Nest
Exmouth
Ye Olde Saddler's Arms
Fenny Bridges
Palomino Pony
Halwell
Old Lun
Honiton
Monkton Court Inn
Kingsbridge
Globe Inn
Knowstone
Mason's Arms
Lydford
Castle Inn
Lynton
Blue Bell Inn
Moretonhampstead
Ring of Bells
Newton Abbot
Dartmoor Halfway
Okehampton
The Countryman
Sampford Peverell
Farm House Inn
Sidmouth
Bowd Inn
South Zeal
Oxenham Arms
Thorverton
Dolphin Inn
Dartington
Cott Inn
Totnes
See Trout Inn
Waterman's Arms
Wellington
Poachers Pocket

DORSET
Fiddleford
Fiddleford Inn
Nettlecombe
Marquis of Lorne
Piddletrenthide
Brace of Pheasants
Sherborne
Swans Inn
Wimborne
Horton Inn

DURHAM
Durham
Cock o' the North
Happy Wanderer

ESSEX
Brentwood
Eagle and Child
Saffron Walden
Eight Bells

GLOUCESTERSHIRE
Coleford
White Horse Inn
Clearwell
Wyndham Arms
Fossebridge
Fossebridge Inn
Whitminster
Old Forge

HAMPSHIRE
Hambledon
Bat & Ball Inn
Hook
White Hart
Romsey
White Horse Inn
Winchester
Cart & Horses Inn
Wykeham Arms

HEREFORD & WORCESTER
Tenbury Wells
Peacock Inn

HUMBERSIDE
Bridlington
The Friendly Forester
Hull
Hull Cheese

ISLE OF WIGHT
Arreton
Fighting Cocks

KENT
Appledore
Red Lion
Deal
Hare and Hounds
Faversham
Recreation Tavern
Selling
White Lion
Whitstable
Pearson's Crab & Oyster House

LANCASHIRE
Freckleton
Ship Inn

LEICESTERSHIRE
Uppingham
White Hart Inn

LINCOLNSHIRE
Bourne
Wishing Well Inn
Lincoln
Duke William
Skegness
Vine
Woolsthorpe-by-Belvoir
Chequers Inn

LONDON
N3
Moss Hall Tavern
N6
Flask Tavern
Barnet
Two Brewers
Harrow
Ploughman

ton in Northumberland where they serve the delicious Besom Broth, full of chunky vegetables, as well as pork and venison pie, and hare and beef casserole. Across the border, traditional pubs are not so plentiful as they are in England, but we felt it worth stopping at the *Horse Shoe Inn* at Eddlestone, just south of Edinburgh. Crossing the Firth of Forth it is not a great distance north to Perth, where the *Hunter's Lodge* at Bankfoot has already won awards for its pub food. The speciality pâté is very good and the curry is also popular. Best value for money, however, is traditional Scottish high tea. Finally, we visit a remote village on the West coast, Tayvallich on Loch Sween. The *New Tayvallich Inn*, where the beautiful views can be complemented by excellent food, including whole prawns in shells with homemade mayonnaise, mussels with garlic bread as well as some delicious sweets.

In the course of this tour from Kent through the length and breadth of Britain, many attractive traditional pubs have shown how successfully they can enliven their menus with enjoyable and unusual dishes which will undoubtedly encourage more people to eat out and enjoy all that British pubs have to offer.

Hampton Court
Cardinal Wolsey
Hounslow
Traveller's Friend

GREATER MANCHESTER
Bolton
Drop Inn
Manchester
Lancashire Fold

NORTHAMPTONSHIRE
Oundle
Falcon Inn
Thrapston
Court House

NORTHUMBERLAND
Hexham
Hadrian's Wall
Longframlington
Besom Byre

NOTTINGHAM
Clayworth
Blacksmith's Arms

OXFORDSHIRE
Abingdon
Queens Galley
Nettlebed
Dog and Duck
Steventon
Fox Inn

SHROPSHIRE
Church Stretton
The Studio
Ellesmere
Black Lion
Goldstone
Wharf Tavern
Nesscliffe
Old Three Pigeons
Shrewsbury
Dun Cow

SOMERSET
Ashcott
Ashcott Inn
Bleadney
The Stradlings
Cannington
Blue Anchor Inn
Martock
George Inn
North Petherton
Walnut Tree Inn
Ralegh's Cross
Ralegh's Cross Inn
Shepton Mallet
Kings Arms
Upton Noble
Lamb Inn

STAFFORDSHIRE
Enville
Cat Inn
Foxt
Fox and Goose

SUFFOLK
Ipswich
Great White Horse

EAST SUSSEX
Chailey
The Five Bells
Ewhurst Green
White Dog Inn

WEST SUSSEX
Billingshurst
King's Head
Petworth
Lickfold Inn

TYNE AND WEAR
Newcastle upon Tyne
Falcon

WARWICKSHIRE
Stratford-upon-Avon
Dirty Duck

WEST MIDLANDS
Birmingham
Old Mill Inn
White Swan

WILTSHIRE
Chippenham
Rowden Arms
White Hart Inn
Melksham
West End Inn
Pewsey
French Horn
Pewsham
Lysley Arms
Salisbury
Greyfisher
Wilton
Ship Inn

NORTH YORKSHIRE
Harrogate
Red Lion Inn
Wetherby
Alpine Inn

WEST YORKSHIRE
Leeds
New Inn

WALES

Clwyd
Abergele
Bull
Bridge Inn

Dyfed
Cardigan
Bell
Pembroke Dock
Hill House Inn

Gwynedd
Caergeiliog
Sportsman's Inn

Powys
Brecon
Red Lion
Hay-on-Wye
Old Barn Inn
Llowes
Radnor Arms
New Radnor
Red Lion Inn

SCOTLAND

Borders
Eddlestone
Horse Shoe Inn
Lander
Black Bull

Central
Killin
Old Mill

Dumfries and Galloway
Creetown
Creetown Arms

Grampian
Forres
Elizabeth Inn
Llanbryde
Tennant Arms
Stonehaven
Creel Inn

Strathclyde
Lanark
The Tavern
Tayvallich
New Tayvallich Inn

Tayside
Perth
Hunter's Lodge

Food in the Making

Most of us are guilty of taking food a little bit for granted most of the time – we take our weekly trip to the supermarket and there it all is. How often do we spare a thought for where it all came from (short of wondering why all the apples seem to be French these days)? Do we ever pause when we pick up that bag of flour and picture the millstones turning, or think of the cheeses maturing for month after month with not a little plastic package in sight? Can we imagine those kippers hanging amidst woodsmoke for days to acquire that wonderful flavour?

The truth of the matter is that we are all far too busy for such reverie amongst the groceries, but every now and then it is good to get back to basics a little and there are plenty of places in Britain where visitors are welcome to see food (and drink) in the making. In the following pages we tell you about some of them – and you can often buy their lovely fresh produce there too.

Corn Milling

There have been two major trends in recent years which go hand in hand when it comes to corn milling – a fascination with our past, the way things used to be done, and a desire for natural, wholesome food. The restoration of many of our old mills is fulfilling this need and all over the country it is possible to see the process of converting whole grain into fibre-rich stoneground flour. It is a fascinating process to watch, accompanied by the dull clicking of wooden cogs, the fast spinning of the grindstone and the mesmeric shuddering of the hoppers and shutes. Corn mills are always permeated with the distinctive aroma of fresh flour – and usually covered with a fine layer of it too.

More reliable than wind-power, the water wheel turns whatever the weather.

One of the most successful of our restored mills is the Felin Geri Mill at Cwmcoy near Newcastle Emlyn in Dyfed, which has received one of the coveted European Heritage Awards. Built in the 16th century, it is one of the last watermills in Britain using its original means of production on a regular commercial basis. Visitors will see all stages of production and can spend a pleasant day at the mill where there is also a water-powered sawmill, a bakery, a children's playground and a cafe selling flour and home-produced food. The mill is open from Easter to September from 10am to 5.30pm (11am to 5pm at weekends).

Windmills, rarely seen nowadays, were once prominent landmarks all over the country and the one which is now preserved at Skidby, Humberside, was no exception with its black tarred tower and white cap. It was built in 1821 and is now established as a milling museum, demonstrating both old and new methods. Outbuildings contain exhibits such as old milling machinery, horse-drawn vehicles and old farm tools, together with displays relating to corn and milling. The mill is actually in operation on alternate Sundays beginning on the first Sunday in May, until the end of September, but is open to visitors at other times too – Tuesday to Saturday 10am–4pm, Sundays 1–4.30pm (closed weekends and Bank Holidays from October to April).

The Lurgashall Watermill was in danger of being demolished when it was rescued and re-erected among a large number of similarly threatened buildings at the Weald and Downland Open Air Museum at Singleton, West Sussex. Now it operates daily producing flour for sale when the museum is open – that is every day from 11am–5pm between June and end of August; Tuesday to Sunday and Bank Holiday Mondays in April, May, September and October and Sundays only from November to March, when it closes at 4pm.

At the George Leatt Industrial and Folk Museum in Skipton, North Yorkshire, the huge mill building is used to exhibit all kinds of things from horse-drawn vehicles to old household items, photographs and magazines – an Aladdin's Cave of byegones. At the centre of all this, the machinery is still in working order and produces flour for sale – Mr Leatt himself can often be seen attending to the milling and is happy to talk about his work here. There are two waterwheels, a 1912 turbine and a winnower which took a prize in 1884. The mill is open on most days from 12 noon.

Farther north, another watermill is tucked away in the country lanes at Little Salkeld near Penrith, Cumbria. The long, low building houses the machinery on two storeys and an enthusiastic team are producing various kinds of flour on a commercial basis. Their tea room also provides some delicious and unusual cakes – made from their own flour of course. There is also a small pottery shop.

One of Dorset's few remaining watermills is at Sturminster Newton and it produces animal feed as well as flour. Although corn has been milled here since the Domesday survey, this particular one dates back to the 17th century. It was fully restored in 1981 and contains a 1907 water turbine – more efficient than the traditional wheel. This mill is open to visitors from 1 May to 30 September on Tuesdays, Thursdays and Saturdays from 11am–5pm and on Sundays from 2–5pm.

In a tranquil corner of Devon, near Budleigh Salterton, Otterton Mill harnesses the power of the River Otter to drive its machinery, some of which is 200 years old. The tour of the mill includes explanations and slides and, as well as the flour, home made bread and cakes can be bought. The mill buildings also include craft workshops and various craft items are for sale. The mill is open daily.

Wiltshire's only working windmill can be found near Great Bedwyn. It is 150 years old and has been fully restored to working order, operated and maintained by the voluntary Wilton Windmill Society. Its members show visitors around the mill on Sundays and Bank Holiday afternoons between Easter and September and, a fresh breeze permitting, flour is for sale.

Mapledurham Watermill, near Reading, is the last working corn and grist mill on the River Thames. It has been fully restored and is used for grinding wholemeal flour which can be purchased. A delightful way of reaching the mill is by taking the river launch from Reading's Caversham Bridge. The mill is open from Easter to September on Saturdays, Sundays and Bank Holidays from 2.30–5.30pm.

At Totton, near Southampton, the Eling Tide Mill is particularly interesting in that it uses the power of the tides to turn its wheels. This type of mill is totally dependent on the tides and the miller's life was consequently regulated to two or three hours in operation at a time. The Eling Mill is restored and flour is usually ground for demonstration purposes on alternate weekends when flour is available for sale. It is open from April to early October, Wednesday to Sunday 10am–4pm.

Farm Fare

It is a common misconception among many city dwellers that things in the country haven't changed for years. Thankfully, many things haven't, but farming has certainly moved with the times and farming is primarily 'food in the making'. In connection with this article it would be somewhat heartless to suggest you view that flock of sheep on the hillside as next week's Sunday lunch, but there are a number of processes associated with farming to which even the most sensitive amongst us wouldn't object at all.

Milk

The days have long gone since the milk-maid sat on her three-legged stool and if you want to see how it's done these days a visit to Dairyland at Tresillian Barton, Summercourt, Cornwall, will be most instructive. 160 cows are milked to music in one of Europe's most modern rotary parlours – described on their leaflet as 'space-age milking on a merry-go-round'. There are other farming exhibits with working models as well as animals and birds and a playground. Dairyland is open from Easter to early November daily and the milking can be seen between 3.15 and 4.30pm.

In contrast, the Acton Scott Working Farm Museum in Shropshire shows how things used to be done before the days of tractors and mechanisation. Visitors may participate in some of the farm work and craft demonstrations take place at weekends – these may include churning butter by hand. The museum is open from April to October daily from 10am to 5.30pm (6.30pm on Sundays and Bank Holidays).

If you happen to be visiting Chatsworth House in Derbyshire you can see milking demonstrations along with the animals, poultry and exhibitions in their Farmyard. The house and gardens and the Farmyard are open daily from April to October. The Farmyard opens one hour earlier than the rest at 10.30am and both close at 4.30pm.

Cheese and butter

The process of making cheese is a fascinating one and where better to see it than in the Cheddar area – a name synonymous with cheese all over the world. At Priory Farm, Chewton Mendip, the Cheese Dairy and Farm Shop are open to the public and demonstrations can be seen during the mornings (usually at 9.30am and 1.30pm, but check times beforehand to avoid disappointment – tel 076 121 560). Two or three times a week butter-making is also demonstrated. The farm shop is open daily, 8.30am–5pm on weekdays, 9am to 5pm on Saturdays and 9am–1pm on Sundays (closes at 4pm from January to March).

On the Isle of Wight, Curds and Whey is the appropriate name of another cheese farm at Dottens Farm, Cowes. Cheese, butter, buttermilk and yoghurt are all made by hand here and visitors can learn more about the processes at their talks and demonstrations. Another cheese farm is at Tyn Grug, near Pumpsaint, Dyfed which is open from Tuesday to Saturday 10am–5pm, and butter and cheese are also made by hand at Hamwood Farm, Trull, near Taunton in Somerset.

Honey

There are plenty of apiarists and honey farms in the country, but not many where visitors would willingly go to take a close look! The Quince Honey Farm at South Molton, however, would not deter anyone for the busy little creatures are safely confined behind glass partititions. This is England's largest honey farm with five or six large colonies of bees and their enclosures are a number of natural settings such as chimneys and hollow trees. There is also an observation hive and various extraction implements and a visual display explains their life cycle. The shop sells honey of course, but also a wide variety of by-products such as natural beeswax, candles, face cream and furniture polish. The farm is open all year from 9am–6pm and is open until 8pm on weekdays between Easter and October.

Tomatoes

Tomatoes may be a most unusual subject for a museum, but the fact that this one is situated on the Channel Isle of Guernsey is probably explanation enough. The Guernsey Tomato Centre near Castel consists of a group of glasshouses through which visitors can trace the development of tomato growing over the decades from 1890 to 1970. The museum shop sells tomatoes and other fruit and vegetables as well as tomato-growing equipment. The Centre is open daily from Easter to September 10am–5pm.

Fish

At one time the only way to get fish was to venture out onto the high seas or sit on a riverbank and catch them – that was until someone thought up the revolutionary idea of fish farming. So successful an idea was it that fish farms of one kind or another can now be found all over the country. Although some supply the wholesale trade, most can be visited by individuals, but they do not all cater for interested visitors – many just sell fish from the farm shop. Nevertheless, a number of fish farms are also developing as tourist attractions and visitors are encouraged to look round the various pools where fish are in different stages of their development. Often the grounds are nicely landscaped and there may be explanatory notes about the rearing of fish. Some even sell fish food so that you can throw some in and help them on their way.

The number of fish farms in Britain is far too great for us to be able to detail all of them, so if you happen to pass one, why not call in and see if you are able to take a look around.

The curing of fish is another fascinating process and there are a few Smokehouses which will show visitors how they work – east coast fishing ports such as Lowestoft and Craster are your best bet, as well as Arbroath in Scotland (where Arbroath Smokies come from).

Beer & Cider

To accompany all this natural, traditional food we are constantly being urged to eat, what could be better than a mug of our traditional brew. Here too the trend is back to the old methods and recipes and away from the mass-produced fizz. Many small, independent breweries are thriving now all over the country, but you will probably have to look out for an open day to get a chance to see how they operate.

It is actually one of the large breweries that provides the best opportunities to see how beer used to be made and that is at the Bass Museum in Burton-upon-Trent. This town has long been associated with brewing and several other large breweries have their homes here. A local custom, recently revived, is the annual Barrel Race down the High Street. The museum includes a model brewery which actually brews beer, along with its other exhibits and audio-visual presentations. There is also a restored steam locomotive and Director's Coach. The museum is open daily 10.30am–4.30pm on weekdays, 11am–5pm on Saturdays, Sundays and Bank Holidays and a visit can be combined with a tour of the Bass Brewery if it is booked in advance. Write to the Chief Brewery Guide at the museum or telephone Burton-upon-Trent 42031.

Down in the West Country it was not beer but cider which was the traditional brew and in the past most farms would produce their own particular brand. There are still a few farms which produce their own, but autumn is the time when it is made, to be stored through the year until the apples are ready again. Perry's Cider Mills at Dowlish Wake near Ilminster, Somerset make theirs in a 16th-century thatched barn, where it is fermented in traditional wooden barrels. The barn also contains an interesting collection of farm tools and wagons. Cider is on sale throughout the year 9am–1pm, 1.30–5.30pm on weekdays, 9am–1pm, 2–4.30pm on Saturdays.

Sheppey's Farmhouse Cider at Three Bridges, near Taunton, Somerset have 42 acres of apple orchards from which they produce cider which has won them over 200 awards. They too have a cider museum on the premises which is open from 8.30am to dusk on weekdays and from noon until 2pm on Sundays between Easter and Christmas.

The largest cider mill in the world belongs to the famous Bulmers company at Hereford. Not surprisingly, Hereford is the home of the Museum of Cider which includes a reconstructed farm ciderhouse, a working cooper's shop, original champagne cellars and a 1920's cider factory and vat house, with all its equipment in working order. It is open from April to October 10am–5.30pm (closed Tuesday in April, May and October), and its shop sells its own brand of cider and perry.

Distilleries

'Scotch' is famous the world over among whisky drinkers, but they, of course, will know that the drink known as Scotch is a blend of various malt whiskies with grain whisky. The liquor of which Scotland is so justifiably proud is the pure malt whisky which comes from no less than 110 distilleries north of the border.

Many of them are open to the public, but five of them have been particularly enterprising in getting together to form the world's only 'Whisky Trail'. This 70-miles route around Scotland's Grampian Region (where 60 of the country's distilleries can be found) takes in tours of some of the most famous names – Glenfiddich, Glenlivet,

Glenfarclas, Tamdhu and Strathisla. Allowing about one hour for each of the distillery tours and the driving between them, this could be one of the most alcoholic day trips of a lifetime – after all, who could resist sampling a 'wee dram' at each? Make sure you have a driver who can though! Details of the route are available from any of the distilleries concerned, or from the local Tourist Information Offices.

It is not absolutely necessary to take the Whisky Trail to visit those distilleries – each can be visited independently and there are others, too which open their doors to the public – Glendronach at Forgue, Glengarioch at Oldmeldrum and Glen Grant at Rothes to name but a few. At Inverdruie, near Aviemore, the Cairngorm Whisky Centre and Museum contains a number of displays and audio-visual presentations relating to the production of whisky as well as a tasting room with a staggering array of samples to choose from!

Whisky isn't the only liquor which is distilled in Britain – Plymouth Gin is very highly regarded too. Coates and Co. have been distilling gin since 1793 in Plymouth's picturesque old Barbican area. Its building is, in fact, the city's oldest – once a Black Friars monastery and reputed to be the place where the Pilgrim Fathers assembled before their momentous journey to the New World. The tour lasts approximately 15 minutes and shows the various stages of gin making from basic ingredients to the finished product. The distillery is open on summer weekdays, except Bank Holidays, from 10am–4.30pm.

In spite of our devious climate, production of English wine is on the increase.

English Wine

English wines and the vineyards which produce them have enjoyed increasing publicity and popularity in recent years. Even so, most people are still unaware of just how many commercal vineyards our climate has managed to support. There are over a hundred which welcome visitors, although some of these are limited to open days, visits by appointment or coach parties only. Those which do accept casual visitors are still too numerous to mention individually, but we list them below. Naturally, facilities and the extent and content of the tours will vary from place to place, but you can usually expect to tour the vineyard (where the grapes are grown) and see something of the winery (where they are converted into wine). You should also be able to sample some of the product and, without doubt you will be able to take home a bottle or two. Some vineyards have gone one step farther by providing special facilities for visitors, such as displays, slide presentations, museums and catering facilities.

The English Vineyards Association Ltd of 1 Vintners Place, Upper Thames Street, London EC4V 3BQ publish a complete list of English Vineyards which are open to the public. From their list we are giving below all those which are open to visitors without restriction:

Aldermoors (4½ acres)
M F Baerselman, Aldermoors, Picket Hill, Ringwood, Hants. Tel Ringwood 2912

Amery Farm (2 acres)
Mrs C Clifford, Amery Hill, Alton, Hants GU34 1HS

Astley (4½ acres)
R M Bache, The Crundells, Astley, Stourport-on-Severn, Worcs. Tel 02993 2907

Bardwell (½ acre)
J B Rowlands, Nethercote, Knox Lane, Bardwell, Bury St Edmunds, Suffolk.

Beaulieu (5½ acres)
Montagu Ventures Ltd., John Montague Building, Beaulieu, Hants

Biddenden (16 acres)
R A Barnes, Little Whatmans, Biddenden, Ashford, Kent. Tel Biddenden 291237

Braishfield Manor (½ acre)
D E Gibbs, Braishfield Manor, Romsey, Hants. Tel 0794 68331

Cavendish Manor (10 acres)
B T Ambrose, Nether Hall, Cavendish, Sudbury, Suffolk. Tel Glemsford 280221

Cherry Hill (2½ acres)
L T Bates, Cherry Hill, Nettlestead Green, Wateringbury, Kent. Tel Maidstone 812655

Chickering (2 acres)
P H Day, Chickering Hall, Hoxne, Diss, Norfolk. Tel Hoxne 227

Croffta (3 acres)
J L M Bevan, Croffta, Groes-Faen, Pontyclum, Glamorgan CF7 8NE. Tel Llantrisant 223876

Cuckmere (1 acre)
C M D Ann, Valley Wine Cellars, Drusilla's Corner, Alfriston, E. Sussex. Tel Alfriston 870532

Cufic (¾ acre)
A J Pinnington, Tuttors Hill, Cheddar, Somerset BS27 3JG. Tel 0934 742960

Dingledene (1 acre)
W/Cdr R. G Kellett, Trafford Farm, Benenden, Cranbrook, Kent. Tel Benenden 463

Ditchling (5½ acres)
D D Mills, Wick Farmhouse, Underhill Lane, Ditchling, E. Sussex. Tel Hassocks 2643

Frithsden (3 acres)
P G Latchford, Frithsden, Berkhamsted, Herts. Tel Hemel Hempstead 57902

Frogmore (3 acres)
P M Higgs, Frogmore Farm, Bradfield, Berks

Gamlingay (8½ acres)
G P Reece, The Vineyard, Drove Road, Gamlingay, Sandy, Beds. Tel 0767 50795

Garden House (½ acre)
N Harland, The Garden House, Saltwood, Kent. Tel Hythe 60163

Gypsy Glade (3½ acres)
R Matthews, Bow Hill Farm, East Marden, Chichester, West Sussex. Tel East Marden 255

Harefield (1¼ acres)
Dr I Williams, Harefield, Stream Lane, Hawkhurst Kent

Harling (6 acres)
J Miljkovic, Eastfield House, East Harling, Norfolk

Hascombe (5¾ acres)
Lt Cdr T P Baillie Grohman, RN, Lodge Farm, Hascombe, Godalming, Surrey. Tel Hascombe 343

Hill Grove (8 acres)
C J Hartley, Hill Gove Farm, Swanmore, Southampton, Hants. Tel Droxford 435

Holt (2 acres)
Lt Col W G R Turner, The Holt, Woolton Hill, Newbury, Berks

Horam (2 acres)
Merrydown Wine Company Ltd., Horam, Heathfield, E. Sussex. Tel Horam Road 2254

Kinver (1 acre)
Dr E I Garratt, Dunsley House, Kinver, Stourbridge, Worcs. Tel Kinver 2206

La Mare (6 acres)
R H Blayney, Elms Farm, St Mary, Jersey, Channel Islands. Tel Jersey 81491

Lamberhurst Priory (33 acres)
K McAlpine, Ridge Farm, Lamberhurst, Tunbridge Wells, Kent. Tel Lamberhurst 890286

Nevards (1 acre)
Dr R. E Barrett, Nevards, Boxted, Colchester, Essex. Tel Boxted 325

New Hall (18 acres)
S W Greenwood, New Hall, Purleigh, Chelmsford, Essex. Tel Purleigh 343

North Cotswold (½ acre)
M T Crabtree, Bank House, Weston sub Edge, Glos GL44 6QH. Tel 0386 840592

Penshurst (7 acres)
W A Westphal, The Grove, Penshurst, Kent. Tel Penshurst 870255

Pilton Manor (4½ acres)
N. de M. Godden, The Manor House, Pilton, Shepton Mallet, Somerset. Tel Pilton 325

Pine Ridge (1 acre)
W R Cook, Pine Ridge Vista, Staple Cross, E. Sussex

Polmassick (1½ acres)
P J Crowe, Mellyncoyse, Polmassick, St Ewe, St Austell, Cornwall. Tel Mevagissey 2239

St Andrews (1 acre)
R G Jenkins, Virgins, West Hatch, Taunton, Somerset. Tel Hatch Beauchamp 480614

Saxonhill (1 acre)
R H Fovargue, Kingsland, Battle, Sussex. Tel Battle 3187

Sherston Earl (4½ acres)
N W E Sellers, The Sherston Earl Vineyard, Sherston, Wilts. Tel Sherston (Wilts) 716

Snipe (2 acres)
R P Basham, Snipe Farm Road, Clopton, Woodbridge, Suffolk. Tel Charsfield 270

Tenterden (6½ acres)
S P Skelton, Spots Farm, Small Hythe, Tenterden, Kent. Tel Tenterden 3033

Woodfarm (2½ acres)
D Shepherd, Wood Farm, Fressingfield, Diss, Norfolk. Tel Fressingfield 223

Wootton (6 acres)
C L B Gillespie, North Town House, North Wootton, Shepton Mallet, Somerset. Tel Pilton 359

Wraxall (6 acres)
A S Holmes, Vine Lodge, Wraxall, Shepton Mallet, Somerset. Tel Ditcheat 331.

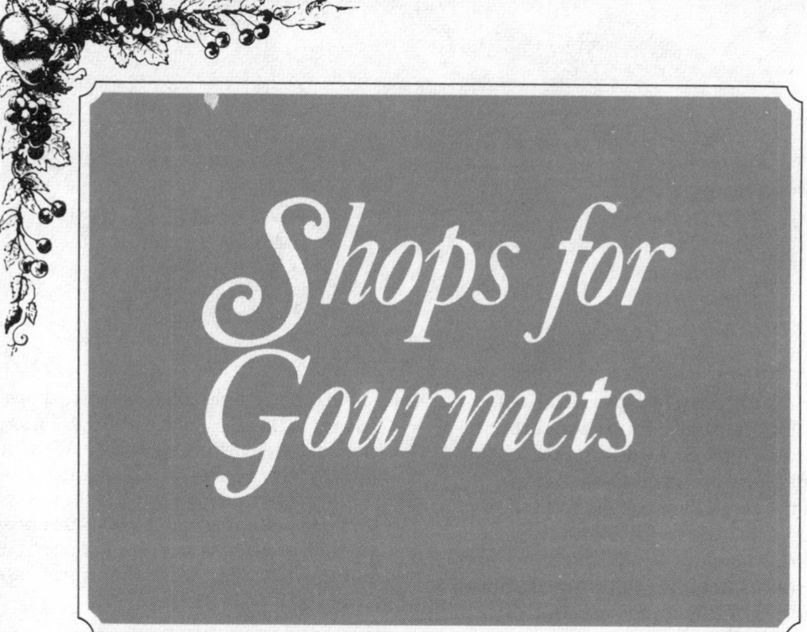

It is often said that 'all those nice little shops have disappeared now – there's no personal service any more', but this is not strictly true. Certainly a lot of small grocers have been unable to compete with the supermarkets, but many of the specialist food shops – where experts in their field deal in one particular kind of food – are going from strength to strength. In these shops you don't just go and buy – you pick up useful advice, recipe suggestions and maybe even a sample of something you haven't tried before. People who know food and enjoy cooking don't want to whiz around the supermarket (although there are some outstanding ones that can offer a little extra in the way of variety and expertise). More often they like to take time to seek out the best possible ingredients or something unusual to experiment with. All the best chefs will tell you that choosing the right raw materials is as important as knowing how to cook them.

In the following pages we give details of some of these specialist food shops around Britain. For a change, London takes a back seat here. There are so many that, if we listed all the capital's specialist food shops there would be little room left for the others. We do include some, and there is no shortage of further information available – any London guide includes a section on them and Tourist Information Offices will be able to help. Primarily we have looked for places out in the provinces, in all those old market towns and country villages. They haven't been easy to find, many are tucked away in back streets or amidst a maze of country lanes, available only to those 'in the know'. Undoubtedly we have missed many which would have been worthy of a mention, and we would be pleased to hear from anyone who could fill in the gaps. Don't forget to look at our article on 'Food in the Making' (p14) too, because most of the places listed sell their fresh produce to visitors.

Cheese Shops

There seems to be something about cheese which brings out a particular kind of enthusiasm in people – there are so many varieties, everyone has their own favourite, and there are so many ways in which it can be used. Those of us who have got into the rut of buying half a pound of the same cheese week after week would do well to venture into a real cheese shop and find out what we are missing. It is usually possible to have a taste before you decide and many shops will have a selection of 'nibbles' on the counter.

One of the country's most famous cheese shops is Wells Stores at Streatley in Berkshire. Proprietor Patrick Rance is eminently knowledgeable about his subject – he also gives talks and writes about cheese – and is particular about where he buys his cheeses from, preferring real farms where unpasteurised milk is used. As well as all of our traditional British cheeses, Wells Stores can offer more than 100 foreign varieties.

A comparable shop in the north is Robert Hill's 'The Cheesery' in Altrincham, Greater Manchester. Offering a variety of English and Continental cheeses, Mr Hill matures them in his own cellar and his research includes seeking out the prize-winners at all the agricultural shows. Another of Mr Hill's commodities is delicious Danish butter which he cuts from large blocks.

Although Farm Shops are far too numerous to list here, I can confidently make one exception which is my own favourite place for buying cheese. It is the Malt House Farm Shop at Ecchinswell near Newbury, Berkshire. Although the selection is not massive there are some more unusual kinds and they are all good 'real' cheeses. If you don't live too far away their meat for the freezer is very good too.

In Brighton's Kensington Gardens, the Cheese Shop specialises in English farmhouse cheeses while J H Matthews of Grainger Arcade, Newcastle upon Tyne has a selection which includes local Cheviot cheese.

Paxton and Whitfield of Jermyn Street is London's best known cheese shop – almost a tourist attraction in its own right with its 19th-century appearance and good old-fashioned service to match. The variety of cheeses is enormous and all are in excellent condition. Customers are encouraged to sample the cheese before they buy.

Meat & Mustard

The good old family butcher is one trade which, in general, has not suffered in the name of progress, and although most buy their meat wholesale there are still many who sell local (or even their own) animals. There is no need here to list butchers shops among the unusual specialists, but meat products is somewhat different. The curing of hams, making sausages to old recipes, making delicious pies etc., is something which has largely been taken over by factories and it is good to find the traditional methods being perpetuated.

Suffolk Hams are particularly famous, traditionally cured using black treacle, brown sugar and hot beer so that the outside is almost black. Cranmers of Holt still cure their own hams – they also smoke their own bacon using wood smoke – and Neaves of Debenham number Robert Carrier among their customers. Stiffs of Kersey, Ridleys and Barnwells both of Bury St Edmunds also sell the real Suffolk Hams.

For sausages, Greenstage Ltd of Newmarket can be congratulated for not allowing an old recipe to die – they bought the shop and the recipe for 'Musks', a delicious meaty variety. Curtis's of Lincoln specialise in making a variety of sausages from recipes handed down through six generations. More than twenty different kinds are sold in their shop in Lincolnshire and those in Lincoln, Newark and Scunthorpe also offer a tempting selection of recipe suggestions. If you happen to be passing a Curtis shop in Rawson Place, Bradford, stop and go in – it's another branch of the same family.

Melton Mowbray is famous for its pork pies and there is no shortage of shops in the area selling them. Pork Farms, prizewinners in this field, have a chain of shops and it is said that the first pork pies were made in the old building which houses Ye Olde Porke Pie Shoppe in Nottingham Street, now belonging to Dickinson & Morris Ltd.

Outside Leicestershire, one of the best pork pie shops can be found in Skipton on the bridge, almost opposite George Leatt's Corn Mill (see 'Food in the Making'), where they are often still warm when you buy them. In Basingstoke, Grigg's Pie Shops (one in the New Market Place, the other in London Street) make a delicious selection of meat pies, pasties and sweet pastries on the premises, usually available hot from the oven. Their sausages are very good too.

Game in season can usually be found in any good butchers shop, but a particularly noteworthy establishment is John Strange's in Lyndhurst, Hampshire. Right in the heart of the New Forest, his speciality is venison, although he does stock many unusual things in his grocery section, and he keeps unusually extended opening hours too.

For something really out of the ordinary you might like to try Northumberland Duck, which is not a duck at all, but lamb dressed to look like one! Go the W G Lough & Son in Holly Avenue, Jesmond, Newcastle upon Tyne.

Delicatessens are fairly common now and most are very good indeed – we can particularly recommend the one at 46 West Street, Alresford, Hampshire, Bon Viveur in Lymington, Hampshire and A T Welch & Co of Hospital Street, Nantwich, Cheshire.

To accompany your meat or pies what better than a little English mustard and nowhere better to buy it than in Norwich, acknowledged mustard capital of the world. The famous Coleman's company have been milling mustard here since 1804 and in the picturesque Bridewell Alley in the heart of this lovely old city is their equally picturesque Mustard Shop. Although it hasn't been open all that long, it is a carefully constructed piece of Victoriana with its small, brown-painted shop front and its dark interior where an ancient till rests on an old wooden counter. It serves as a Mustard Museum too but in spite of its obvious tourist attraction it offers a unique selection of mustards and a visit here is a must if you are in Norwich. (NOTE it closes all day on Thursdays).

Herbs

Herbs are enjoying something of a revival these days. Of course, we have always used the old favourites like mint, sage, thyme and bay leaves in our cooking, but we haven't really used them to full advantage that our country grandmothers once did. It isn't just in our cooking that we are becoming more adventurous with herbs – there are also herbal remedies and a vast range of toiletries and cosmetics to choose from. The sweet-smelling face creams and shampoos are lovely, but as for remedies, I think I might draw the line at rubbing the soles of my feet with garlic to relieve a cough!

If you want to cultivate your own herb garden we have found three Herb Farms – Forge Cottage Herbs of Tunstall, near Woodbridge, Suffolk, Dunsford Herb Farm near Exeter, Devon and Hollington Herbs at Woolton Hill near Newbury in Berkshire. The latter occupies the old walled garden of Hollington House and visitors can wander around the nursery, buy plants and get helpful advice on their various uses.

Of the Herb Shops, Culpeper's is probably the best known – they have a shop at 25 Lion Yard, Cambridge and another at 14 Bridewell Alley, Norwich. Hobbs of Garrick Street, London WC 2 have many unusual and even rare ingredients available along with their range of luxury goods.

Markets & Stalls

Always the best place to look for fresh fruit and vegetables and other foodstuffs too – you will often find excellent butchers' and fishmongers' stalls and good cheeses too. There are too many markets in Britain to mention, but they will be found to a greater or lesser degree in most of our towns and cities and those in the agricultural areas are more likely to have fresh local produce.

A London market with a difference, Chelsea Farmers' Market, which has been open since the beginning of 1983, is a gourmet's delight tucked away off Sydney Street, just opposite Chelsea Old Town Hall, and next door to an attractive garden centre, Jack Beanstalk. Small wooden Swiss chalets, grouped around an open courtyard, contain a wide range of speciality food shops, and here, in a compact area, the shopper can choose from a mouthwatering range of fresh foods and charcuterie and have a meal or a snack at Huff's Restaurant when the shopping is done. There is a greengrocer, selling out-of-season specialities and exotic fruit and vegetables, as well as good quality everyday produce. Next door, the butcher offers home-cooked ham, well-hung Scotch beef and high-quality sausages. Somewhat more exotic are the two delicatessens, one Italian and one French, the latter specialising in 'les delices de Gascogne' – pâtés, rillettes, foie gras, terrines, cassoulets etc. Other chalets house a health-food store, a fishmonger, whose trout can be selected live from a tank for perfect freshness, a cheese shop and a restaurant. Altogether this is a very attractive development, a far cry from the supermarket, but very nearly as convenient.

Roadside stalls are commonplace in the summer, particularly those selling strawberries (which may or may not be genuinely local-grown and can be very expensive). You are likely to get some lovely fresh fruit in season in the main orchard areas, though, and at the right time of year you will find asparagus stalls all around the Vale of Evesham. Michael Paske Farms Ltd of Hartford near Huntingdon are nationally renowned for their asparagus. Five grades are available from their farm shop – and they do mail order too. In Hampshire you can buy your watercress direct from the beds, particularly around Alresford where even the revived steam railway is known as 'The Watercress Line.'

Fish

Like good butchers shops, there is no shortage of fishmongers, but all around our coast there are places where you can buy fish direct from the quayside as soon as the catch is landed. Some admittedly sell to the wholesale trade, but you can either stock up your freezer here or find the ones that will also sell smaller quantities. At Aldeburgh in Suffolk fish can be bought direct from the boats where small huts are lined up along the beach. Sprats are a speciality here.

If quayside buying is not possible, the seaside fishmonger is the next best thing. For the famous Cromer crabs go to J Lee, Cox's or Bob Davies in that Norfolk resort.

Oysters can be bought direct from the oyster beds, particularly abundant on the Colne and Butley rivers at Colchester. The Butley Oysterage at Orford, the Colchester Oyster Fishery Ltd at North Farm, East Mersea or Mussetts of West Mersea and, of course, Wheelers Fish Bar, Whitstable are the places to go. Poole in Dorset also has an Oysterage, while 'Mariculture' at Brighton Marina sell a variety of shellfish.

Smoked fish is best bought from those establishments that smoke their own, using the old traditional methods (see also 'Food in the Making'). Brown's at High Street, Fordingbridge in Hampshire will even smoke your own catch for you. Springs Smoked Salmon of Edburton, East Sussex can supply you with smoked salmon of course, but also smoked trout, mackerel, eel and quail. They also sell shellfish, whole salmon and frogs legs. For fresh lobster try Leggetts of Beccles or 'Loaves and Fishes' of Woodbridge.

Sweet Things

In these days when sweets and chocolates are factory produced by the million it's nice to find a shop that makes its own. Rowland Confectionery in Folkestone's Old High Street is such a shop and their specialities are lettered rock and humbugs. Handmade chocolates are a real luxury and, not surprisingly, London has several outlets. Fortnum and Mason naturally have a good selection; Charbonnel et Walker of Old Bond Street number each chocolate on the bottom and even make their boxes by hand; Bendicks in Grosvenor Street specialise in Bittermints and Mint Crisps; Clares of Park Road, Baker Street, make superb liqueur chocolates and truffles as well as handmade after-dinner mints; Prestat make all their French-style chocolates on their premises at 24 South Molton Street.

Outside the capital, Audreys Chocolates of Regent Arcade, Brighton will make up on request selections of the chocolates they actually make in nearby Hove. In Salisbury, Michael Snell (listed in our gazetteer for their coffee shop) offer a mouthwatering selection of handmade chocolates. Their cakes and gâteaux are something special too.

If you are really looking for something special in the bakery line you needn't look much farther than the Mary Ford Cake Artistry Centre in the Bournemouth suburb of Southbourne. Not only are they specialists in decorated cakes they also make chocolates and confectionery and a range of breads and savouries – all baked on the premises. There is a school for cake decoration, confectionery etc., here too, both for serious students and holiday courses.

Among our regional specialities of baking there is the Old Original Bakewell Pudding Shop – in Bakewell, of course. This famous pastry dish is reputed to have been created quite accidentally when a local cook made a mistake with an entirely different recipe. The result was a resounding success (unlike most of us, whose mistakes really are disasters!) and they have been made to the same recipe in this same shop ever since.

Not too far away, is the Gingerbread Shop at Ashbourne – another local delicacy with a story. It is said to have been created by a French army cook brought to England amongst captured Napoleonic troops. No-one knows whether his incentive was to sweeten up his captors, but when he eventually went home he passed the recipe on to a local baker and it has been made here ever since. Another famous gingerbread shop is in Grasmere in the Lake District.

International

London is certainly the place to find all the different international speciality shops and once again there are too many to mention them all here. Shops representing not only the European countries but also Far Eastern, Asian and African can be found, particularly around the West End.

For European specialities go to the German Food Centre, 44 Knightsbridge where you will find all those lovely sausages and wines; The Swedish Table sells goods as well as food; The Danish Food Centre is in Conduit Street; for Swiss specialities go to Bartholdi of Charlotte Street or the Swiss Centre in Wardour Street whose Gourmet Corner has Swiss cheese, confectionery, cakes, bread and sausages etc. There are lots of good Italian food shops – try G Parmigiano Figlio of Frith Street or Fratelli Caniisa in Berwick Street.

Pimlico Road may be a little off the beaten track, but Pasta Pasta, a recently opened fresh pasta shop, is very well patronised. Not only can you buy delicious fresh pasta – some coloured green with spinach, some pink with tomato puree, some the ordinary creamy colour – you can also select a home-made sauce to accompany it. There is a large choice, ranging from *pesto*, a speciality of the Venice area, made with fresh basil, pine-nuts, garlic and parmesan, or a creamy paste of pounded walnuts and coriander to the more familiar tomato-based sauces, garnished with olives, anchovies, tuna fish etc. This small but lively shop also stocks a full range of other Italian delicatessen foods.

If you want a good selection of Chinese foods, the Hong Kong Supermarket in Shaftesbury Avenue is the place to go.

Closer to home, and perhaps an unexpected item under this heading, is a Scottish speciality shop – the Clifton Coffee House at Tyndrum in Scotland's Central Region. The selection of shortbread, confectionery, cheese, cakes and whisky are all Scottish specialities and the premises also contain a Restaurant and a Scottish Crafts Centre.

Gazetteer

The gazetteer gives locations and details of restaurants, pubs, wine bars, bistros, etc, listed in alphabetical order of placenames throughout Great Britain and the Channel Islands. Details for islands are shown under individual placenames. A useful first point of reference is to consult the location maps which show where establishments are situated.

ABERDEEN
Grampian *Aberdeenshire*
Map **15** NJ90

Kardomah 1 Union Bridge
☎ (0224) 50459
Open: Mon–Sat 9am–6.30pm

This modern eating house provides a quick service for shoppers and holidaymakers, with a ground-floor self-service coffee shop and upstairs restaurant. The restaurant menu is reasonably priced and offers dishes such as steak and kidney pie followed by deep apple flan. Two-and three-course set lunches are also available. There is a waist-preserver menu for the figure-conscious and a children's menu including an exciting variety of ice creams.

[C] [S] [🍷]

Stakis Steakhouse Holburn St
☎ (0224) 56442
Open: Mon–Sun 12noon–2.30pm, 5–11pm, 10pm–Sun

Stakis Steakhouses have a definite appeal for inveterate meat-eaters. Main courses include haddock, chicken and various steaks and the price covers a starter as well as vegetables and a roll and butter. Sweets are also on the menu.

[C] [P] [S] [🍷]

Victoria Restaurant 140 Union St
☎ (0224) 28639
Open: Mon–Sat 9am–7.30pm

Enjoy a nicely-presented yet inexpensive meal right here. The à la carte menu includes a selection of starters – soup or Florida cocktail; main dishes include omelettes, grills, salads and fish. Special two- and three-course lunches are served daily and there is a special children's menu. Morning coffee and afternoon tea are available.

ABERFOYLE
Central *Perthshire*
Map **11** NN50

Old Coach House Restaurant Main St
☎ (08772) 535
Open: Mon–Sun 10am–11pm

In this white-walled restaurant, decorated in Austrian style, wild flowers and candles on green-and-white tables, create a pretty effect. Meals are available throughout the day. Snacks include toasted sandwiches or enjoy a meal of grilled Glen Devon trout and fruit and ice-cream sundae, lavishly topped with cream. Children's portions are also available.

[♫] [P] [🍷] **VS**

ABERGAVENNY
Gwent
Map **3** SO21

The Llanwenarth Arms Hotel
Brecon Rd, Llanwenarth (2m W of Abergavenny on the A40)
☎ (0873) 810550
Open: Mon–Sat 11am–3pm, 6–11pm, Sun 12noon–2pm, 7–10pm

North American hospitality and local culinary expertise welcome the visitor to D'Arcy McGregor's inn and restaurant. Lunch and dinner are available and although the à la carte menu may be beyond the limit of this guide, the bar meals are excellent and prove good value for money. Among the wide range of dishes, try the house specialities, pineapple prawn indienne (half a fresh pineapple with curried prawns and salad) or steak and kidney pie. Other dishes on the menu include salads, grills and steaks. There is an extensive selection of home-made sweets.

[C] [P] [🍷] **VS**

ABERGELE
Clwyd
Map **6** SH97

Bull Hotel Chapel St ☎ (0745) 822115
Open: Mon–Sun 12noon–2.30pm, 7–8.30pm

Emphasis is on good home cooking in this traditionally furnished inn with a friendly, relaxed atmosphere. The dining room menu operates for lunch and dinner and offers basic English fare.

[♫] [P] [S]

ABERYSTWYTH
Dyfed
Map **6** SN58

Caprice 8–10 North Parade
☎ (0970) 612084
Open: Jun–Oct Mon–Sun 9am–8.30pm; the rest of the year Mon–Fri 9am–5.30pm, closed Winter Wed

Crabs straight from the harbour are a speciality at Jill and Alun Evans's cheerful restaurant. A three-course meal might be soup or fruit juice, a main course of roast, poultry or fish, and a sweet such as fruit tart and custard. The à la carte menu is also modestly priced, with starters of fruit juice or prawn cocktail and a selection of main courses.

[C] [♫] [S] [🍷]

Gannets St James Sq ☎ (0970) 617164
Open: Tue–Sat 12noon–2pm, 6.30–10pm

Previously a hairdresser's salon, now neatly converted into a popular, informal bistro, Gannets displays the work of local art graduates and students. Ann Jones and Gina Walpole, the proprietors, take turns in preparing the delicious home-made food. Typical dishes from the blackboard menu include carrot and mushroom bake, stuffed marrow, ratatouille, lasagne and chili con carne. Home-made soups and sweets supplement the menu.

[♫] [🍷]

Tapestry Restaurant Groves Hotel, 42–46 North Parade ☎ (0970) 617623
Open: Mon–Sat 12noon–2.30pm, 7–9pm (closed 8.30pm in winter) Closed

23 Dec–3 Jan

The Tapestry Restaurant in this small personal hotel offers an excellent value à la carte menu. Careful selection will keep you within our price range, and there are some imaginative dishes to choose from. Specialities include lamb chops 'Calon Lan' – a grilled double Welsh chop marinated in white wine, mint and garlic, and trout 'Owain Glyndwr' – trout filleted, stuffed with fish mousse and wrapped in pastry. A range of bar snacks is available and includes lasagne, fish dishes and vegetarian meals. It is advisable to book in advance if you wish to dine in the restaurant.

ABINGDON
Oxfordshire
Map **4** SU49

The Queens Galley Market Place
☎ (0235) 24961
Open: Mon–Sun 12noon–2pm, 7–10pm

A Georgian building in the centre of town houses the Queens Galley which has a spacious dining area on the first floor, decorated in a nautical style, and a bar on the ground floor. Proprietors John and Margaret Eveson offer good, English cooking at reasonable prices and dishes include home-made soup, pâté, salads, curry, pork chops in tomato and onion sauce and apple tart. Morning coffee with biscuits or gâteau is also available.

[P] [&]

ALCESTER
Warwickshire
Map **4** SP05

The Three Tuns Wine Bar 34 High St
☎ (0789) 764042
Open: Mon–Sat 11,30am– 2pm, 6–10.30pm, Sun 12noon–2pm, 7–10.30pm

You may have to look carefully for this small wine bar which is located, or rather dwarfed, by the two large pubs either side. But the search is worth the effort. In an 'olde worlde' setting you can enjoy home-made food, with a special dish of the day. Try seafood vol-au-vent with salad, or beef cobbler with vegetables. Lasagne and moussaka, both with salad, are also in the menu. There is a good range of wines.

[♫] [P] [&]

ALDERLEY EDGE
Cheshire
Map **7** SJ87

Alderley Rose Chinese Restaurant 34 London Rd ☎ (0625) 58557
Open: Mon–Fri 12noon–2pm, 5.30pm–mdnt, Sat 12noon–mdnt, Sun 12.30pm–mdnt

This old established and popular Chinese restaurant, conveniently situated in the main shopping street offers particularly good value lunches with a choice of English and Chinese dishes: The menu lists grills, omelettes and salads, served with chips and vegetables and curries, chow mein and chop suey dishes. The à la carte menu includes special Cantonese dinners for one to four people, as well as the usual large choice of Chinese dishes.

[P] [S] [&]

No. 15 Wine Bar 15 London Rd
☎ (0625) 585548
Open: Mon–Sat 12noon–2pm, 7–10.30pm, Fri–Sat 7–11pm

The blackboard menu offers mushroom and prawn mornay and seafood pancakes for starters and main courses include Boeuf Stroganoff and sweet and sour pork. Chocolate meringue is one of the delicious desserts. A good selection of wines is available by the glass. In summer you can eat in the walled and well-tended garden.

[♫] [P] [S]

ALEXANDRIA
Strathclyde *Dunbarton*
Map **10** NS37

Bees Nees 158–60 Main St
☎ (0389) 51427/52530
Open: Mon–Thu 10am–3pm, 5–11pm, Fri & Sat 10am–3pm, 5pm–1am

This modern Greek restaurant has a smart lounge bar and is furnished with banquette booths on a quarry-tiled floor, paintings of Greece are displayed on the walls. The day menu operates from 10am–3pm and includes haddock, chicken, hamburgers or a choice of the Greek dishes, such as moussaka, keftedes, pastitsio or dolmades. The dinner menu offers more variety and with care you can still keep within the budget. On Friday and Saturday evenings there is a disco dinner.

[♫] [P] [🍷]

ALFRISTON
East Sussex
Map **5** TQ50

Drusillas Thatched Barn Drusillas Zoo and Leisure Complex, Drusillas Corner
☎ (0323) 870234
Open: Apr–Oct Mon–Sun 10.30am–5pm

Part of the Drusillas Zoo and Leisure complex this barn restaurant offers morning coffee with home-made cakes, lunches and traditional teas. The 'Little Monkeys Menu' for the children includes Smugglers Sausage Platter – two Alfriston sausages, salad and crisps. There are both hot and cold dishes on the menu, all served with salad and home-made soda bread and butter. Sussex pie is made with local meat, mushrooms, onions and herbs in a rich shortcrust pastry and for pudding Tipsy Sussex Squire – a Victorian trifle with brandy, sherry, almonds and cream – sounds delicious. Traditional Sunday lunches are also available.

ALNWICK
Northumberland
Map **12** NU11

Billy Bones Buttery Hotspur Hotel ★★
☎ (0665) 602924
Open: Mon–Sun 12noon–2pm, 6–9pm

Billy Bones was piper to the Duchess of Northumberland in 1815, when the Duke leased Hotspur House to him. There he established a hostelry. In the Billy Bones Buttery you can get a super lunch of soup or fruit juice, a choice of four main dishes likely to include a roast, fish, and cold meat with salad, and an 'English' sweet – perhaps fruit crumble with custard or a sponge pudding. The à la carte menu is also within our budget and includes a range of basket meals. Starters include soup and fruit juice and sweets are ice cream-based.

[♫] [P] [S] [🍷]

Maxine's Kitchen 1 Dorothy Forster Court, Narrowgate ☎ (0665) 604465
Open: Mon–Sat 10am–5pm, Sun 2.30–6.30pm

Situated opposite the castle, Maxine's Kitchen is part of an 18th-century town house once owned by Dorothy Forster who was involved locally in the Jacobite Rebellion of 1715. The proprietors Joe and Maxine Hepple provide home-made dishes at very reasonable prices. A good range of snacks, salads and flans are served throughout the day. The separate lunchtime menu has plenty of hot and cold dishes, all home-made, including moussaka, steak and kidney pie and beef in beer. Wine is available by the glass.

[P] [🍷]

ALRESFORD
Hampshire
Map **4** SU53

The Bodega 32 Broad St
☎ (096273) 2468
Open: Mon–Sat 10.30am–2pm, 7–10.30pm, 11pm Fri & Sat

The Bodega is a smart and sophisticated wine bar in picturesque Alresford – a small town which with its quaint shops, steam engines and watercress beds, attracts tourists from all parts of the globe. Interior décor is unobtrusive, with cream-painted panels and dark wood tables and chairs, but on summer evenings many patrons prefer to sit in the pretty covered courtyard, hung with the works of local artists. Start your meal with a home-made soup of the day and move on to a selection from the extensive menu which features some interesting fish dishes. Sweets change daily, but could consist of chocolate mousse or ice cream with Grand Marnier. Specialities are chalked on a blackboard.

[♫] [P] [S]

ALTON
Hampshire
Map **4** SU73

Pilgrims Wine Bar 43 High St
☎ (0420) 84840
Open: Mon–Sat 10.30am–2.30pm, 6.30–10.30pm, (11pm Fri & Sat). Closed Sun

This recently-opened wine bar has been converted from an old butchers shop and has a simple but attractive décor and a warm atmosphere. There are two eating areas – the front half specialising in cold meats, salads and quiches, etc and at least one hot dish of the day. The more formal restaurant at the rear, has an à la carte menu serving such things as steaks and scampi and a daily special. An open courtyard in the centre of the building is used for eating out in the summer months. There is an extensive wine list.

[C] [♫] [P] [S]

ALTRINCHAM
Gt Manchester
Map **7** SJ78

The Cresta Court Hotel ☆☆☆ Church St
☎ 061-928 8017
Open: Lodge: Mon–Sat 12noon–2pm, 6–10.30pm, Sun 12noon–2pm
Quarterdeck: Mon–Sun 12noon–2.30pm, 6.30–110m, Sun 6.30–10.30pm

This bright, new hotel has two steak bar restaurants. The Tavern Lodge offers the usual combination of steak, chicken, scampi and fish all served with vegetables. The Quarterdeck is a little more sophisticated, with a good selection of vegetables in addition to those included in the price of the meal.

[C] [♫] [P] [🍷] **VS**

Ganders 2 Goose Green
☎ 061-941 3954
Open: Mon–Thu 12noon–3pm, 7–10.30pm, Fri 12noon–3pm, 7–11pm,

Sat 12noon–3pm, Sat–Sun 7–10.30pm, morning coffee: Mon–Sat 10–11.45am

Surprisingly, goose is not on the very varied menu of this pleasant wine bar and bistro, housed in a 300-year-old cottage in a quiet alley close to the town centre. A dozen appetisers range from soup to avocado with crab. Lancashire hot pot is a good, traditional main course but why not go overboard and try fondue bourguigon, a meal for at least two people with salad, baked potato, bread and various dips. Desserts include such delights as passioncake and 'real' sherry trifle.

[C] [S]

ALVESTON
Avon
Map **3** ST68

The Ship, Post House Hotel☆☆☆
Thornbury Rd ☎ (0454) 412521
Open: Mon–Sun 12noon–2pm

The Ship Inn at the Post House Hotel provides all the charm, character and history of an inn dating back to the 16th century. Available on the bar menu are home-baked hot and cold pies, salads, and French stick roles; gâteaux and fruit pie and cream are available for dessert.

[P]

ALYTH
Tayside *Perthshire*
Map **15** NO24

The Singing Kettle 12–14 Airlie St
☎ (08283) 2236
Open: Mon, Tue, Thu 10am–5pm, Fri & Sat 10am–4.30pm, Sun 12noon-5pm. Closed Wed

Situated on the main street into the village the Singing Kettle though small, is a real find. This restaurant/coffee shop is open throughout the day and everything on the menu is home-made from the tomato soup laced with sherry and cream to the delicious array of sweet and savoury pancakes. Apart from the set three course lunch, which is exceptional value, the menu also includes a casserole of the day served with baked potato and vegetables.

[P] [S]

AMBLESIDE
Cumbria
Map **7** NY30

De Quincey's Bistro and Wine Bar
Waterhead ½m from Ambleside (on the A593 on the north-east shore of Lake Windermere) ☎ (09663) 3440
Open: in season Mon–Sun 12noon–2.30pm, 7–11pm (last orders 10pm), out of season Thu–Sat 7–11pm

Definitely not a 'run-of-the-mill' bistro, De Quincey's specialises in offering provincial dishes from Italy, Spain and France, and great care is taken to provide wines to complement the food. Popular dishes include Lasagne Verdi, chicken Madras and herbie beef casserole. The attractive bistro overlooks Lake Windermere and is tastefully decorated in pastel shades and the patio provides open-air dining–Lakeland weather permitting.

Gemini Restaurant Lake Rd
☎ (09663) 2528
Open: Feb–Dec Mon–Sun 12noon–2pm, 5.30–approx 8.30pm

A friendly, informal family-run roadside restaurant with large rear car park. Two small open-plan areas and a bar area create a comfortable atmosphere and a good selection of wholesome hot dishes are provided. Starters include grapefruit and mandarin cocktail; the main courses are predominantly grills with specialities such as duckling à l'orange or sole in prawn and mushroom sauce. There is an excellent choice of desserts and a range of special children's dishes. There are a selection of wines available along with draught lager and beer.

[P] [S]

AMERSHAM
Buckinghamshire
Map **4** SU99

Bear Pit Bar and Bistro Whielden St
☎ (02403) 21958

Open: Mon–Sun 12noon–2.30pm, Sun–Thu 7–10.30pm, Fri–Sat 7–11pm.

A bear-baiting pit can still be seen inside this delightful, period bistro which is almost concealed in the courtyard of the 16th-century Saracen's Head pub. 'Beginnings' include 'Bloody Mary' soup (70° proof–B. marvellous!) or grilled smoked mackerel. Spicy chili con carne served with a crisp salad and hot pitta bread is a popular main course. The French dressing is outstanding. Alternatives include gammon, trout, crab salad Louis or Bear Pit Burgers. 'Endings' offer a good choice including chocolate gâteau. A traditional Sunday lunch is a little over our limit.

C ♫ ♧ **VS**

The Elephant and Castle High St
☎ (02403) 6410

Open: Summer Mon–Sun 12noon–2pm, 7–9.30pm

This historic pub, covered with climbing roses, offers good-value, well-prepared meals for the hungry public. Bolton Hotpot and steak pudding are popular choices. You can take lunch in any part of the low-beamed, olde-worlde pub that takes your fancy, and in addition, there's a small-budget à la carte menu offering mostly grills. Children are welcome in the pleasant beer garden.

C P ♧

The Hit or Miss Inn Penn Street Village
☎ (0494) 713109

Open: Mon–Sun 12noon–2pm, 6.30–10pm. Closed last week in Jul, first week in Aug

Within range of six from its own cricket ground across the road – any customer can join the club and play – this aptly-named wisteria-covered 17th-century inn is a big hit with the locals and visitors alike. In the Cricketers bar, they can also enjoy an excellent selection of home-cooked fare available every day for lunch or dinner. The menu includes mixed hors d'oeuvres, chicken à la king and cheesecake, or try a 'steak butty' – sirloin steak grilled with onion and garlic, sandwiched in French bread. The restaurant serves an excellent three-course budget menu at lunchtime but it is just over our limit.

P

Paupers 11 Market St ☎ (02403) 7221

Open: Mon–Sun 12noon–2pm, 7–10pm

Situated close to the parish church of St Marys, Paupers is housed in an attractive cottage with its black and white Tudor-style exterior gaily decorated with brass coach lamps and striped awnings. Inside is a warm 17th-century room which retains much of the period atmosphere with an inglenook fireplace, exposed beams, polished oak tables and pew seating. The lunch menu could include home-made pâté, roast chicken and apple crumble, whilst the more elaborate dinner menu could feature veal in lemon sauce. Sunday lunch is a speciality.

C P ♧

ANSTRUTHER
Fife *Fife*
Map **12** NO50

The Haven 1 Shore St, Cellardyke
☎ (0333) 310574

Open: Mon–Sun 12noon–10.30pm

Wander along the quaint narrow streets that connect the better-known Anstruther to the old fishing village of Cellardyke and you will find The Haven overlooking the harbour. Bar-lunches, lunches, afternoon and high teas are available, was well as à la carte dinners. Sea-food is naturally popular and there is also a good choice of grills and salads. A children's menu is available.

P ♧

APPLEDORE
Kent
Map **5** TQ92

The Red Lion 15 The Street
☎ (023383) 206

Open: Mon–Sat 10.30am–2.30pm, 6–10.30pm, Sun 12noon–2pm, 7–10.30pm

This comfortable inn boasts an open log fire during the winter months and has a patio where you can enjoy your meal on a sunny summer's day. David and Carole Waters are the proprietors and they personally supervise the preparation of the food. Locally causht fish are a feature of many of the dishes on the blackboard menu along with lamb cutlets or as an alternative try the home-made steak and kidney pie. Real also and mulled ale are served at the bar as well as a selection of wines and cocktails.

ARRETON
Isle of Wight
Map **4** SZ58

The Fighting Cocks
☎ (098377) 254/328

Open: Mon 12noon–2pm, Tue–Sun 12noon–2pm, 7–9.30pm

Built on the site of an inn that had stood for three centuries, and using much of the original stone. The Fighting Cocks boasts a smart restaurant specialising in grills and seafood. Salads and bar snacks are also available.

ASHBOURNE
Derbyshire
Map **7** SK14

The Ashburnian Compton
☎ (0335) 42798

Open: Mon–Sat 12noon–2pm, 6–10pm, Sun 12noon–6pm

The restaurant with its white rough-plaster walls and dark beams with reproduction brass lanterns, has a pleasantly olde worlde atmosphere. A comfortable cocktail bar adjoining has hessian-clad walls and copper-topped tables. The menu is very reasonably priced, with starters including prawn cocktail and a choice of 10 main courses (try half a roast chicken) all served with vegetables and including a sweet (such as apple tart with cream) in the listed price.

C S

Cary's Workhouse Yard, Dig St
☎ (0335) 42811

Open: Mon–Sat 10am–3pm, 7–11pm, Sun 12noon–2pm, 7–10.30pm

Named after John Cary, the famous 18th century cartographer, Cary's is a pleasant, rather trendy place, situated near the centre of this old market town in premises that date back some 300 years. It is run by the Blunstone family and some young female assistants in a friendly and informal manner. Décor is clean and fresh with exposed brickwork and ceiling beams and stripped pine furniture. Diners are entertained by piped music. A typical meal might include home-made pâté, two baby trout cooked with mushrooms, spring onions and lemon, and crêpes with butterscotch sauce and cream.

C ♫ ♧

The Shire Horse Inn Wyaston (3m S off A52) ☎ (0335) 42714

Open: Mon 6.45–10pm, Tue–Sat 11.30am–1.30pm, 6.45–10pm Sun 12noon–1.45pm, 7–9.30pm

In the mid 17th century the Shire Horse, then a cottage and blacksmiths forge, was built around the trunk of a large, living oak tree. The tree trunk is still a feature of the bar though now bound with brass. You can choose to eat in the carvery restaurant or the smaller à la carte dining room – both offer excellent value with generous portions. There is a good range of real ales to choose from.

C P ♧

ASHBURTON
Devon
Map **3** SX77

The Dartmoor Motel★★
☎ (0364) 52232

Open: Mon–Sun 12noon–2pm, 7–9.30pm

The three-course set lunch at this pleasant, family-run modern motel close to the A38 offers a good choice of main courses on the à la carte menu with an emphasis on fish and grills. Seafood special – scampi, prawns, mussels and cockles cooked in sherry and cream – is a delight, but you will have to choose a lower priced starter or sweet to keep within your budget when you sample it. Children are offered a half-portion lunch.

[C] [P]

Rising Sun Inn Woodland
☎ (0364) 52544 1½m off southbound A38 Exeter–Plymouth.

Open: Mon–Sun 11.30am–2pm, 7–10.30pm

Once used by sheep drovers as an overnight stop on the road to Dartmoor, this rustic old inn houses an interesting collection of prints dating from the early 1920s. Some of the people depicted still form a faithful band of locals who meet and drink here. A sumptuous cold buffet, which includes home-cooked cold meats, fresh salmon, salads and pies, is very reasonably priced, and there are grills and basket meals for those who like it hot, all freshly prepared on the premises. Children can enjoy a meal on the covered verandah or in the pleasant garden to the rear.

[C] [P]

ASHCOTT
Somerset
Map **3** ST43

Ashcott Inn ☎ (0458) 210282

Open: Mon–Sat 12noon–2pm, 6–10pm, Sun 12noon–1.30pm, 7–9.30pm

Peter, Allison and David Milne run this attractive roadside inn situated on the A39. Oil paintings enhance the cosy atmosphere of the inn and there is also a garden and patio area. The extensive daily bar menu is all home-made and local produce featured includes snails with herb butter. Moussaka, ratatouille, grills and roasts are also available. Puddings have exotic sounding names and mouthwatering ingredients – Black Goddess and Jamaican Sundae contain rum soaked into raisins and cream.

[P]

ASHTON-UNDER-LYNE
Gt Manchester
Map **7** SJ99

Corniche Grill Oldham Rd
☎ (061-339 5469)

Open: Mon–Sun 12noon–2.30pm, 6–10.30pm, Sun 7–10.30pm

Car dealers, Wm Monk claim that this gallery restaurant overlooking the car showroom is a new idea 'direct from Paris', and the first of its kind in this country. Grills are the main feature on the menu and all dishes include French fries or jacket potato and a roll and butter. Sweets or cheese and biscuits are also included in the price of lthe main course. Treat yourself to a connoisseur coffee such as a Monte Carlo (with Cointreau) or have a 'customised' coffee to suit your taste.

[C] [P] [S]

AVIEMORE
Highland *Inverness-shire*
Map **14** NH81

Chieftain Grill Colyumbridge Hotel
☎ (0479) 810661

Open: Mon–Sun 12.30–2pm, 5–10.15pm

The Colyumbridge Hotel occupies a heather-clad site on the road to the Cairngorm ski-slopes. The spacious grill-room, being part of one of the many hotels in the Reo Stakis chain, guarantees good food at competitive prices. Among the main courses (which include the price of a starter) are turkey cordon bleu and half a roast chicken, but the sirloin and fillet steaks are, alas, out of our league. Sweets include peach melba and lemon torte. During the summer various salads augment the menu, but a special children's three-course meal is available.

[C] [P]

Crawfords Restaurant Station Sq
☎ Aviemore (0479) 810678

Open: Jul–Sep & Etr Mon–Sun 9am–10.30pm, otherwise Mon–Sun 9am–7pm

Conveniently situated beside the station and opposite the AA Road Service Centre you can easily spot Crawfords with its attractive brown canopies. Serving mainly grills, burgers and salads, there is also a good selection of gateaux, cakes and scones which also makes this a popular place for coffee. There is a special menu for children and breakfast is served every morning.

[P] [S]

AYLESBURY
Buckinghamshire
Map **4** SP81

The Hen and Chickens at Aylesbury
Oxford Rd ☎ (0296) 82193

Open: Mon–Sat 12noon–2pm, Tue–Sat 7–10pm, Sun 12noon–2pm, 7–10pm

This popular pub with its attractive ship-boarding stands on the Oxford Road roundabout close to the original 'Aylesbury duck' pond. Manager Richard Stretton welcomes you to the pleasant buttery bar. A typical meal could be soup, followed by home-made pies with vegetables and potatoes. Meals are also available in the restaurant.

[C] [P] [S]

AYR
Strathclyde *Ayrshire*
Map **10** NS32

The Coffee Club 37 Beresford Ter
☎ (0292) 263239

Open: Mon–Sat 10am–10pm

This small and friendly establishment is situated near to Burns' Statue Square in the centre of Ayr. The clubby atmosphere extends to comfortable seating and low-level tables, making this a place to relax while you take your meal. An interesting variety of snacks, salads and light meals are served with a creative flair. Snacks range from pizza to substantial open sandwiches, clubhouse sandwiches, American beefburgers and savoury flan with salad.

[P] [S]

Elliots Bar and Restaurant 28–30 Newbridge St ☎ (0292) 286115

Open: Mon–Sat 11am–11pm (lunch served 12noon–2.30pm, dinner served 6.30–11pm). Closed Sun

Elliots has a comfortable cocktail bar on the ground floor and a restaurant on the first floor. Imaginative menus offer bar lunches, restaurant meals and a choice of 'Chefs Specialities', which change weekly, but could include braised beef bourguignonne followed by Swiss black cherries Cassis with lemon sorbet. The bar lunches include salads, quiche and pasta dishes. Our inspector voted Elliots a personal favourite because of the quality of the food.

C ♬ P S ☙

Stakis Steakhouse and Planters Bar 231 High St ☎ (0292) 262578

Open: summer Mon–Sun 11am–2.30pm, 5–11pm (Sun 10pm); winter Mon–Sat 12noon–2pm, 5–9pm (Sat 10pm)

Typical of the Stakis Steakhouses with rich red carpeting and olde worlde dark wood furnishings the restaurant offers the usual range of grills, with starters included in the price of the main course. Unfortunately the steaks are outside our budget. Upstairs you will find the Planters Lounge Bar with comfortable modern decor, offering a bar lunch menu which includes scampi and gammon steak – both served with chips. There is also a range of starters and desserts.

C ♬ P S ☙

The Tudor Restaurant 6–8 Beresford Ter ☎ (0292) 61404

Open: Mon–Sat 9am–8pm

The Tudor Restaurant may not be authentic 16th century, but for the family it offers a good wholesome meal at very reasonable prices. A table d'hôte lunch includes soup or fruit juice, a main course such as beefsteak pie, cold meat with salad, or haddock and chips, and a sweet or cheese. High tea, which comes with a pot of tea, bread, scone, jam and cake (all home-baked), gives a considerable choice, from eggs on toast to entrecôte steak. There are special children's menus. The restaurant is not licensed.

P S ☙

BAKEWELL

Derbyshire
Map **8** SK26

BALA

Gwynedd
Map **6** SH93

Fischer's Bath St ☎ (062981) 2687

Open: Mon–Sun 12noon–3pm, dinner 7.30pm onwards, closed Thu and Sun evenings

This olde-worlde restaurant, originally a barn, features white painted stone walls and cottage furniture. Set lunches consist of traditional, home-cooked dishes, with choices such as home-made soup followed by steak and kidney pie or a traditional roast and a home-made pudding. The evening meal is just beyond our limit.

P ☙

Neuadd Y Cyfnod High St ☎ (0678) 520262

Open: Summer Mon–Sun 9am–9pm, Winter Mon–Fri dinner only

In this imposing building, a long school hall, with its panelled walls and high ceilings, Gwyn and Ann Evans offer a taste or two of traditional Welsh cooking. The lunch and dinner menus offer excellent value and include Welsh farmhouse soup, local salmon and lamb. A particularly Welsh dinner includes a glass of mead. Children's portions are available. A speciality of the house is an authentic Welsh tea.

C P S ☙

BALDOCK

Hertfordshire
Map **4** TL23

The Vintage Wine Bar 31 Hitchin St ☎ (0462) 895400

Open: Mon–Sat 10.30am–2.30pm, 7–11pm

This old timber-frame house near the centre of Baldock has been converted into an attractive wine bar. Husband-and-wife team Barbara and Peter Clarke cook and wait at table. A choice of hot and cold dishes are available. You might start with mushroom fritters, followed by lamb and lemon casserole and chocolate mousse. The cellar bar serves draught real ale and ploughman's and toasted sandwiches.

C ♬ ☙

BALLATER

Grampian *Aberdeenshire*
Map **15** NO39

The Green Inn 9 Victoria Rd ☎ (0338) 55701

Open: Tue–Sun 12noon–2pm, 7–10pm. Closed Nov & Dec and Mon–Thu Jan–Mar

Built in 1840, this small pink granite house with colourful window canopies, has now been converted into a restaurant. Pine walls, tables and seating with wall prints and fresh flowers give it a cosy and restful atmosphere. A good three-course lunch includes soup, grilled lamb chops and lemon and meringue pie. On the dinner menu all main courses are served with potatoes, vegetables or salad. Sweets are home-made and the choice varies from day to day. Try the grilled venison with a port and redcurrant sauce if you feel like a change from ordinary restaurant fare.

♬ P ☙

BALLOCH

Strathclyde *Dunbartonshire*
Map **10** NS38

Spatz Lounge Bar 34 Balloch Rd ☎ (0389) 51385

Open: Mon–Thu 12noon–3pm, Fri–Sun 12noon–2.30pm, Mon–Sun 6–9.30pm

You'll have no trouble finding this lounge bar/diner in the main street of the village with its black painted brick frontage and black and white canopies. Inside the décor is modern with a black and red colour scheme. The menu offers many favourites at prices well within our budget and main courses include home-made curry, summer salad, fish and burgers and a daily 'Spatz Special'. Cheesecake and apple pie are among the desserts. Spatz offers value for money in a popular tourist area.

♬ P ☙

BARKING
Gt London

The Spotted Dog 15 Longbridge Rd
☎ 01-594 0288 London Plan4 **89**B6

Open: Mon–Sun normal licensing hours

Genuine East London atmosphere abounds in The Spotted Dog, one of Davy & Co's original enterprises (near Barking tube). The ground floor 'doghouse' offers good old steak and kidney pie with vegetables and potatoes. Bar snacks such as sandwiches, filled rolls and toasted fingers are also available. Downstairs, you find yourself in the 'clink' – a dungeon-like place complete with an ill-looking skeleton. No bread and water here, but plaice or scampi and chips is on the menu.

C S

BARMOUTH
Gwynedd
Map **6** SH61

The Angry Cheese Church St
☎ (0341) 280038

Open: Summer Mon–Sun 12noon–2pm, 6–10pm, Winter Fri–Sat 6–10.30pm

Inside this attractive restaurant pine tables give a cosy, rustic effect. The three-course set menu offers a choice of six items in each course, featuring main dishes such as pork schnitzel with beurre noisette or chicken chasseur. Vegetarians are tempted by such dishes as vegetarian cutlets. If you go à la carte, potatoes and fresh vegetables of the day are included in the price of the main course dish from that menu.

C P ♧

BARNET
Gt London
Map **4** TQ29

Franco and Gianni 45 High St
☎ 01-449 8300

Open: Mon–Fri 12noon–3pm. Closed Sat & Sun

This attractive little Italian restaurant is somewhat out of our league in the evenings but at lunchtimes a typically Italian table d'hôte menu prevails, offering such dishes as lasagne for starters, followed by veal escalope and cassata tutti frutti.

C S

The Two Brewers 64 Hadley Highstone
☎ 01-449 3558

Open: Mon–Thu 10.30am–2.30pm, Fri–Sat 10.30am–2.30pm, 5.30–11pm, Sun 12noon–2pm, 7–10.30pm

A one-time 'Pub of the Year', this superb Tudor-style building is well-known to the locals, and they take full advantage of the high standard of cooking. Meals are eaten in the restaurant which echoes the Tudor theme, with warm red curtains and carpet. A daily-changing menu offers traditional Old English dishes such as Lancashire hot-pot, home-made steak, kidney and mushroom pie and a choice of salads.

P

BARNSLEY
South Yorkshire
Map **8** SE30

Queen's Hotel★★ Regent St
☎ (0226) 84192

Open: Mon–Sat 12.30–2.30pm, 6.30–10pm, Sun 12.30–2.30pm, 7–9pm

An imposing Victorian three-storey building, conveniently close to the railway station and town centre, houses this cheerful split-level restaurant where décor is in the best tradition of Victorian design. The menu includes pork chop country-style and home-made steak and kidney pie. The recently modernised 'Old Vic' bar provides a delicious hot and cold buffet each lunch-time.

C S ♧ **VS**

BASINGSTOKE
Hampshire
Map **4** SU65

The Bistro 1 New St ☎ (0256) 57758

Open: Tue–Fri 12noon–2pm, 7–10pm, Sat 7–10pm

Doug and Suzy Palmer's homely little restaurant has deservedly acquired a very good local reputation since its conversion from a one-time doctor's surgery. Simple décor and furnishing create a typical bistro atmosphere. At lunchtime the à la carte menu is supplemented by a variety of salads and home-made hot dishes. A fully inclusive lunch menu offers excellent value with home-made soup followed by a hot dish of the day (or a salad) and a choice of sweet or a glass of wine. The full menu offers several choices within the budget including house specialities like Porc Dijon and marinated lamb kebabs.

C P S **VS**

Corks Food and Wine Bar 25 London St
☎ (0256) 52622

Open: Mon–Sat 10am–2.30pm, 6–10.30pm (11pm Fri & Sat)

Corks goes continental in the summer when customers can 'take a pew' on the paved area outside the restaurant. Inside, behind a screen of brown half-curtains, is a dark and mellow eating place with soft music playing. Church pews make unexpectedly comfortable and intimate seating, and fine engravings decorate walls which are either white-washed or cork covered. Starters include pâté and for your main course try one of the casserole-type meals with rice or jacket potato or a salad. There are at least six scrumptious puds to choose from. The special lunch of filled jacket potatoes, savoury crumble or meaty pasta with a glass of house wine is good value. There is a special three-course menu in the evenings, and live folk music two nights a week.

♫ S

The Light of Shahzalal 11 New St
Joice's Yard ☎ (0256) 3509

Open: Mon–Sun 12noon–2.30pm, 6–mdnt

Tucked away in an older part of the town, this Indian restaurant offers a wide range of food at surprisingly low prices. Service is the keynote here, with all staff genuinely anxious that you should enjoy your meal. The menu includes a plethora of curries (marked hot, medium and mild on the menu to avoid burnt palates!) and Tandoori chicken. Of the other specialities, chicken tikka, kabab or onion bhazia make delicious starters. For the less adventurous, English dishes, such as steak with mushrooms and chips, are excellent value.

C ♫ S ♧

Perrings Coffee Shop and Wine Bar
Seal House, Seal Rd ☎ (0256) 66266

Open: Tue–Sat 9.30am–4.30pm, lunch 11.30am–2.30pm

Nothing but the best is available at Perrings furniture store and lunch is no exception. A trellis-work ceiling with wicker-globed lighting and subtle exposed brickwork behind the serving counter complete a décor which is both relaxed and tasteful. Start with nourishing ham soup then choose from a wide selection of cold dishes, or a hot dish of the day such as chicken fricasée with peppers served on a bed of rice. The choice of salads is excellent and delicious desserts include feathery-light Black Forest gâteau and blackcurrent cheesecake.

♫ S ♧ VS

Tundoor Mahal Restaurant
4 Winchester St ☎ (0256) 3795

Open: Mon–Sun 12noon–3pm, 6pm–12mdnt

Once the Midland Bank, this listed building retains its original stately exterior while the inside is transformed into a smart restaurant with warm red décor, wood-effect walls, Indian-style arches and nicely-positioned alcoves with hanging lights. Fresh flowers, candle-lit tables and soft background music complete the pleasant atmosphere. Cuisine is basically Bangladesh and Indian specialities with some Malayan, Persian and English dishes. A special

For entry see Dodworth

three-course lunch has three choices for the main course including prawn, meat or chicken pillau. The à la carte menu includes a selection of original dishes – dhal soup with orange and beef Bangla curry served with fresh cream are worth sampling. Sweets are fairly standard Indian dishes.

[♫] [S]

BATH
Avon
Map **3** ST76

Clarets Wine Bar 6–7 Kingsmead Sq
☎ (0225) 66688

Open: Mon–Fri 10am–2.30pm, 6.30–11pm, Sat 11.30pm, Sun 7–10.30pm

Clarets is a beautifully converted white-walled cellar, with teak futniture. In fine summer weather, chairs and tables are set out under the large plane tree in the cobbled square outside. The owner Liza Tearle is a thoroughly experienced restaurateur and serves tasty dishes prepared from good fresh food. Choose from starters, casseroles (including a vegetarian vegetable and cheese version) with bread and butter and green salad and home-made sweets, with filter coffee to complete a very pleasant meal. Snacks are available at reasonable prices and wine is available by the glass.

[C] [♫] [P] [S]

Danish Food and Wine Bar Pierrepont Pl ☎ (0225) 61603

Open: Mon–Sat 11am–2.30pm

The Fernley's Danish Food and Wine Bar (behind the hotel), although small and simple, is both stylish and comfortable, and well worth a visit for the variety of its delicious open sandwiches of meat, fish and cheese. To these you can add salads (for a small extra charge), and finish with pastries and cream and good filter coffee. As an alternative try the cold table where you can help yourself to as much cold meat and salad as you can heap on your plate.

[♫] [P] [S] [♿]

Julius Geezer 31 Barton St
☎ (0225) 63861

Open: Mon–Sat 12noon–2.30pm, 6–11pm. Closed Sun

This newly-opened restaurant has a Roman theme to its menu. Brutus' Brew (soup of the day) and Boadiceas Breast (breast of chicken sautéd with mushroom cream sauce) are two of the dishes available. There is a cheaper lunch menu with two or three daily specials.

VS

KT's Restaurant 4–5 Grand Parade
☎ (0225) 61946

Open: Mon–Sun 12noon–3pm, Mon–Thu & Sun 5.30–10.30pm, Fri, Sat 5.30–11pm

Close to the city centre and adjacent to the market, this restaurant has a simple, bright décor and cheerful, efficient staff. Starters can be followed by one of the popular range of char-grilled burgers served with mixed salad and baked potato or chips. The delicious home-made waffles and profiteroles, are popular desserts with regular customers. A fascinating selection of cocktails is available and a number of New World wines.

[S] [P] [♿]

La Crêperie Janes Hotel, 7 Manvers St
☎ (0225) 65966

Open: Mon–Sun 7.30am–11pm

La Crèperie, in Janes Hotel just off the city centre and close to the railway station and bus station, is bright and freshly decorated, with a relaxed and informal atmosphere. Crêpes are the speciality of the house and there is a large range to chose from, both sweet and savory. Highly recommended are the cream chicken and mushroom in white wine sauce, or the apple sizzle (spiced apples topped with cinnamon sugar and nuts soaked in Calvados). Char-grilled burgers, steak and lamb cutlets complete the main-course menu, while soup makes an appetising starter. The Crêperie is licensed and has a selection of cocktails or try the Normandy cider.

C ♫ S P ♧ **VS**

The Laden Table 7 Edgar Buildings
☎ (0225) 64356

Open: Mon–Sat 12noon–3pm, Mon–Sun 6–11.30pm

A fully-licensed restaurant seating about 30 in a pleasant, relaxed atmosphere with soft background music. Proprietor Peter Slatter stays in the kitchen, concocting creations such as samosa (a crispy, deep-fried, filled Indian pastry), millet balls (millet mixed with fresh vegetables) and other dishes such as beef stroganoff and chicken à la Greque. His partner, Valerie Tranter, waits at table, and she will draw your attention to the constantly-changing blackboard menu. Sweets include fresh fruit cheesecake and honey baked apple.

♫ ♧ **VS**

Peaches 14 Pierrepont St
☎ (0225) 330201

Open: Mon–Sun 12noon–2pm, 6pm–11pm

This cheerful cellar restaurant, close to the city centre, is within a few minutes walk of the Roman baths and the Pump Room. There is a good choice of main courses including a variety of casserole dishes served with baked potato, crusty bread or chips. Salads, burgers and steaks are also included in the menu. Sweets include chocolate bombe and cheesecake. There is a 'special' for all three courses and a vegetarian dish is available. A jug of real ale or a glass of country wine go well with the food.

C S P ♧

Sportsman Steak House Rode Hill, Rode ☎ (0373) 830249

11m S of Bath on B3109 Rode–Bradford-on-Avon road

Open: Mon–Fri 12noon–2.30pm, 6.30–11pm

This converted stone barn has a copper-topped bar on the first floor, in an open-plan area where you can enjoy an aperitif while Philip, the resident chef, prepares your meal. Starters include fruit juices, prawn cocktail, and Strasbourg pâté with fingers of hot toast. Main dishes are unfussy but good, and include lamb and pork chops, gammon steak and steak and kidney pie. Ice cream is included in the price of the meal.

C P

BEAMINSTER
Dorset
Map **3** ST40

Nevitt's Eating House 57 Hogshill St
☎ (0308) 862600

Open: Mon–Sat 12noon–2pm Fri & Sat 7–10pm. Closed Sun.

This one-time ale house dating from the 16th century is situated near the town centre and owners Mr & Mrs Nevitt provide both snacks and substantial meals in warm attractive surroundings. Morning coffee and croissants are served between 10am and 12noon. Lunch could consist of a simple ploughmans or a three course meal, or choose from 'Todays Specials' which could feature roast quarter Corscombe duckling. There is an extensive dinner menu with starters listed under 'small eats' and main courses under 'big eats'. The Sunday Roast Lunch Menu offers excellent value for money.

P ♧

BEAULY
Highland *Inverness-shire*
Map **14** NH54

The Skillet The Square ☎ (0463) 2573

Open: Apr–Oct, Mon–Sat 9.30am–8pm, 7pm Apr, May, Oct, Sun 11am–8pm

The Skillet is an ideal place for the hungry tourist. The simple but wholesome fare is reasonably priced on the table d'hôte lunch and dinner menus. The à la carte menu offers a good selection of grills, fish and salads, with bread and butter or toast plus tea included.

P S ♧

BECKENHAM
Gt London

Dizzy's Diner 256–258 High St
☎ 01-650 6010 London Plan4 **90**D5

Open: Mon–Sat 6–11.30pm. Closed Sun.

Dizzy's is *the* place for American-style burgers. They come in two sizes 'standard' and 'hefty' and with a vareity of toppings. The French Burger is coated with a naughty French sauce of wine, mushrooms and tomatoes and the Hawaiian Burger is topped with fruity pineapple and cheese. Alternative dishes include lasagne and a salad platter with a selection of meats and fish. The desserts are guaranteed to ruin any diet and include chocolate fudge sundae and hot waffle served with syrup and cream. There is an extensive list of cocktails.

C

BERKHAMSTED
Hertfordshire
Map **4** SP90

Cooks Delight 360 High St
☎ (04427) 3584

Open: Tue & Wed 9.30am–6pm, Thu 9.30am–7.45pm, Fri 9.30am–8pm, Sat 10am–5pm, 7.30–10.30pm, Sun 12noon–7pm. Closed Mon.

Cooks Delights is a grocery shop and tea-rooms with seating on two floors and in the small garden. Special vegetarian dishes are on the menu and a hot lunch is served daily. There is a tempting display of cakes, cheesecakes, meringues, gateaux and superb quiches. Non-alcoholic beer is available and wine is sold by the glass.

P ♧

BERWICK-UPON-TWEED
Northumberland
Map **12** NT95

King's Arms Hotel★★ Hide Hill
☎ (0289) 307454

Open: summer: Mon–Sun 8–9.30am, 12noon–10pm, winter: Mon–Sun 12noon–2pm, 6.30–9pm

The King's Arms was once a coaching inn, a regular stop for the London to Edinburgh Highflyer – 18th-century equivalent of the Flying Scotsman. The oak-panelled Kings Room Restaurant offers a three-course table d'hôte lunch whilst the adjoining Brambles Bistro, open all day in summer provides a quick-service meal. Cold meat salads and sandwiches are available in the Hunting Lodge bar.

[C] [P] [S] [&]

Popinjays 30 Hide Hill ☎ (0289) 307237

Open: Mon–Sat 9.30am–5pm

Georgina Home-Robertson is the enthusiastic owner of this farmhouse-style coffee shop which boasts a walled patio at the rear with ruined stables providing a dramatic backcloth. Coffee shop Popinjays may be, but down market it definitely is not. Food here is simple but nicely prepared with salads and various hot dishes including basic grills and omelettes. All ingredients for a good meal are here except for a glass of wine – Popinjays is unlicensed.

[P] [S] [&]

Queen's Head Hotel★ Sandgate
☎ (0289) 307852

Open: Mon–Sun 7.30–9.30am, 12noon–2pm, 7–9.30pm

One of three Berwick hotels owned and run by Mr and Mrs Geoffrey Young and family, the Queen's Head lies at the bottom of Hide Hill, near the river. The pleasant restaurant with its dark oak furniture and flock wallpaper offers three-course table d'hôte lunch. There is also an à la carte menu with fish, entrées and roasts. A three-course dinner with a choice of steaks as the main course is available most evenings.

[P] [S] [&]

Ravensholme Hotel★★ Ravensdowne
☎ (0289) 307170

Open: Mon–Sun 7.30–10am, 12noon–2pm, 6.30–9.30pm

The Youngs own this hotel, too, as well as the Queen's Head. The Ravensholme has two restaurants, a downstairs Wallace Room with Wallace tartan carpet, and an upstairs Gold Room. The Wallace Room offers a good range of dishes including fried fillet of Eyemouth haddock or two lamb chops and various steaks on the à la carte menu. There is an excellent table d'hôte lunch. The Gold Room serves bar lunches and suppers in summer.

[C] [♫] [P] [S] [&]

The Rum Puncheon Restaurant Golden Sq ☎ (0289) 307431

Open: Mon–Sat 9.30am–9.30pm

You can't linger late over dinner here, but this oak-clad 18th-century restaurant is certainly worth a visit. The Stoddart family has been in business selling groceries, wines and spirits there since 1834. In the restaurant you can buy a full lunch as well as separate à la carte dishes such as scampi, steak or salmon. Substantial bar lunches are also available.

[C] [♫] [P] [S] [&]

BEVERLEY
Humberside
Map **8** TA03

Market Cross Restaurant Saturday Market ☎ (0482) 881603

Open: Mon–Sat 12noon–2pm, 6.30–10.15pm, Sun 12noon–2pm, 6–10.15pm

This restaurant is situated on the first floor of a converted town house overlooking the Market Cross in the centre of this historic market town. The three course lunch usually features a roast and home-made steak pie and is excellent value, but if you prefer you can order just a main course and coffee. Snacks are available in the mornings and afternoons and there is a High Tea menu. Most of the dishes on the dinner menu are within our budget and include steak, poultry and fish. Wine is available by the glass.

[C] [P] [&]

Upstairs Downstairs 47 North Bar Within ☎ (0482) 869145

Open: Mon–Thu 10.30am–3pm, 6.30–10.30pm, Fri 10.30am–3pm, 6.30–11pm, Sat 10.30am–4.30pm, 6.30–11pm, Sun 12noon-3pm, 7–10.30pm

Situated inside the medieval gates of the old town this wine bar is part of a row of smart shops housed in a building which dates from 1735. The cellar vaults have been restored and they now serve as a bar (wine only) offering inexpensive home-cooked meals. Lasagne, moussaka and avacado cream chicken are a few of the choices on the menu which is supplemented by a range of salads and vegetarian dishes. 'Weekend Specials' could include Turkey Morello and venison casserole and there are special menus using country farmhouse recipes. Children are catered for at lunchtime.

[♫] [P]

BEWDLEY
Hereford & Worcester
Map **7** SO77

Back of Beyond Coffee Shop 55 Load St ☎ (0299) 403114

Open: Mon–Sat 10am–4.45pm

You needn't go to the back of beyond to find a good meal or light snack – just visit this quaint historic town on the banks of the River Severn. Here, at the rear of a shop called 'Room Interiors' and across a covered courtyard, you will find the popular little restaurant run by Angela Collip. A variety of home-made goodies awaits your enjoyment, including the lunchtime special which changes daily and could be moussaka, cottage pie or beefburgers. Start with home-made soup with French bread and choose from a tempting array of cream cakes and gâteaux for dessert and you'll have a satisfying meal.

[S]

BICKLEIGH
Devon
Map **3** SS90

The Trout Inn ☎ (08845) 339

Open: Mon–Sat 11am–2.30pm, 6–10.30pm (11pm Fri & Sat), Sun 12noon–2pm, 7–10.30pm

Part of this delightful thatched and beamed inn, situated by a quaint river bridge on the outskirts of the village, date back to the 17th century. The bar area has been tastefully extended to incorporate a refrigerated cold buffet and salad display which is available lunchtimes and evenings. In addition hot dishes of the day are advertised on the backboard menu. There are separate rooms for parties and for children and the Inn's free car park is opposite.

[P] [&]

BIDEFORD
Devon
Map **2** SS42

Rose of Torridge The Quay
☎ (02372) 2709

Open: Mon–Sun 9am–10pm, Winter Mon–Sun 10am–10pm

This restaurant is named after the daughter of the first Mayor of Bideford. It is open for morning coffee, lunches, afternoon tea and dinner. At lunch-time, a range of light meals and salads is available. The steak-bar menu provides a choice of grilled and fried dishes.

[P] [&]

BILLINGSHURST
West Sussex
Map **4** TQ02

The King's Head High St
☎ (040381) 2921

Open: Mon–Wed, Sun 12noon–2pm, Thu–Sat 12noon–2pm, 7–10pm

This delightful 500-year-old coaching inn in the centre of the village boasts a restaurant extension with a separate entrance from the bar – though you can partake of the cold buffet or snacks there if you are in a hurry. Fresh, home-made fare is the hallmark of the restaurant, where you could start with soup or pâté. Main dishes include steak and kidney pie and delicious lasagne and form the basis of the set lunch. In winter good old treacle pudding helps you keep the cold weather at bay.

[C] [P] [S] [♣]

Old House Adversane ☎ (040381) 2186

Open: Mon–Thu & Sun 10am–6pm, Fri & Sat 10am–9.30pm

Manager Jeremy Steward supervises proceedings throughout the day in this quaint, 14th-century restaurant, its two rooms with low oak-beamed ceilings displaying an abundance of antiques – some for sale. Basic English fare includes a special lunch served at any time of the day. Soup of the day, home-made steak pie or home-made quiche and a sweet of the day – fruit pie, ice cream or fruit salad – is a typical menu. The à la carte menu includes grills and the special farmhouse meals include home-made pies and casseroles.

[C] [P] [♣] **VS**

BIRMINGHAM
West Midlands
Map **7** SP08

Black Horse Hotel Northfield
☎ 021-475 1005

Open: Mon–Fri 12noon–2pm, 7–10pm, Sat 7–10pm

The Barons' Bar Grill Room is upstairs in this impressive 'black and white' inn on the Bristol road. Overhead is the original raftered roof, but the barn-like aspect is counteracted by hessian-covered walls and the solidity of oak furniture. The menu is standard for Davenport inns, and the main dishes are those found in most grill rooms, the accent being on steaks, with other dishes including plaice and gammon.

C ♫ P S 🍷

Bobby Browns In Town Burlington Passage, New St ☎ 021-643 4464

Open: Mon–Sat 11am–3pm, 5.30–11pm, Sun 7–11pm

This large vaulted cellar, deep under New Street, was built at least 200 years ago and is known to have been a restaurant since around 1900. Exposed brickwork, oak beams and Victoriana help to make this a popular place with business people and shoppers alike. The salads are a riot of colour and texture, a bed of fresh crunchy salad may be topped with Ox tongue marinated in red wine and herbs, and an Italian-style salad consists of pasta, celery, ham, artichoke, chicken and mushroom served with tomato mayonnaise. Hot dishes of venison, veal, chicken and steaks are served with imaginative and well-made sauces.

C ♫ P S 🍷

The Conservatory, Holiday Inn☆☆☆☆ Holiday St ☎ 021-643 2766

Open: Mon–Sun 7am–10.30pm

Meals at the conservatory can be a little pricey, with an extravagant choice of starters. Main courses and desserts are reasonable. You can therefore eat a pleasant meal, but careful selection will be needed to keep within our limit. A novelty children's menu is available.

C ♫ P S 🍷

Dingos 6 Great Cornbow, Halesowen ☎ 021-503 0480

Open: Mon–Sat 10.30am–2.30pm, 7–10.30pm (11pm Fri & Sat) Sun 12noon–2pm, 7–10.30pm

If you think there is a holiday atmosphere in this wine bar and bistro, that's because the owners Brian Saxon and Brian Watson are ex 'Red-Coats'. The menu is chalked on the blackboard and at lunchtime home-made pizzas, lasagne and moussaka are available. Coffee is always available, but why not try one of the special wine cocktails.

C P S 🍷 **VS**

The Four Seasons Restaurants Lewis's, Bull St ☎ 021-236 8251

Open: Mon–Sat 11.45am–2.30pm

The decorative theme is, appropriately, the four seasons of the year depicted in relief in four attractive fibre-glass murals. The à la carte menu offers a traditional list of grills, omelettes, salads etc, at reasonable prices and the table d'hôte menu with two daily specialities is excellent value. A children's menu, cleverly designed in the form of a 'Wanted' posted entitled 'Big shots for small fry' offers a main course, ice cream and cold drink at prices to please any parent. There is even a bowl of assorted vegetables, potato and gravy plus a dish of custard for baby at half the children's price.

C S 🍷

La Galleria Paradise Pl ☎ 021-236 1006

Open: Mon–Sat 11am–2.30pm, 5.30–10.30pm, Closed Sun.

This modern wine bar and restaurant has small, old fashioned pub-style tables and deep red mahogany woodwork. The display counter houses a range of cold meat salads and a blackboard menu above lists ten different choices for 'dish of the day'. The emphasis is on Italian meals including pizzas and pasta dishes and there is a large selection of fresh fish dishes including King prawns and trout. Starters include minestrone soup, mussels or home-made pâté and there is a choice of desserts.

C ♫ P S 🍷

Ginger's Vegetarian Eating House 7 High St, Kings Heath ☎ 021-444 0906

Open: Mon–Sat 12noon–2pm, 7–10pm

You should have very little difficulty in locating this delightful little restaurant, as the restaurant name is emblazoned in large, colourful letters on the large window. The blackboard menu, which stands in one corner, offers such delights as carrot and rosemary soup, butterbean hotpot and creamed cottage cheese and parsnip bake. All main-course prices include a choice of two salads. Home-made sweets are also on the menu.

♫ P 🍷

Gino's Belvedere Restaurant East Mall Shopping Centre ☎ 021-643 1957

Open: Mon–Wed 12noon–11pm, Thu–Fri 12noon–11.15pm, Sat 12noon–11.30pm, Sun 12noon–10.30pm

Walls decorated with enlarged engravings of old Venice give an immediate Latin flavour to this popular, centrally-situated Italian restaurant. You can make do with just a pizza or omelette, or choose from the extensive à la carte menu. A three-course lunch is available and there is a speciality menu offering a selection of more sophisticated items which are a little more expensive.

C ♫ P S 🍷

Happy Gathering 54–56 Pershore St ☎ 021-622 2324/3092

Open: Mon–Sun 12noon–12mdnt

This successful Cantonese restaurant is situated on the outskirts of the main city centre. The interior is very clean and typically Chinese with red embossed wallpaper, wood panelling and brightly-painted oriental pictures. Food is authentic Cantonese and proprietor Mr Lai is particularly proud of the baked crab in black bean sauce and the duck in plum sauce. Because of the nature of Chinese eating, a choice from the à la carte menu can be as cheap or expensive as you like depending on the variety of dishes chosen. There is a more formal set dinner of four courses which comes just within our limit.

C ♫ P 🍷

Birmingham

Hawkins Cafe-Bar King Edward Buildings, 205–219 Corporation St ☎ 021-236 2001

Open: Mon–Fri 8.30am–10.30pm, Sat 10am–10.30pm, Sun 5–10.30pm

Situated close to the law courts and Aston University is this new concept in food and drink. The strong art nouveau décor proves an interesting blackcloth to the half-hour lighting extravaganzas on Friday and Saturday and occasional appearances of guests artists such as George Melly or Georgie Fame. On to the food – home-made soup and roast rib of beef with fresh salad would be a typical meal. A dish of the day, filled baked potatoes and pizzas are also available – all freshly-made on the premises.

[C] [♫] [P] [S] [🍷]

Heaven Bridge✕✕ 308 Bull Ring Centre, Smallbrook Ringway ☎ 021-643 0033

Open: Mon–Fri 12noon–11.30pm, Sat 12noon–12mdnt, Sun 12noon–11.30pm

The à la carte menu, in Cantonese and English, lists nearly 200 dishes. Hors d'oeuvres include rice rolls, dumplings, croquettes and water-chestnut pâté and in addition 24 choices of soup are offered. Main courses include an exciting array of dishes – seafoods such as cuttle-fish, crab, oysters and lobster and game and poultry in main guises.

[C] [♫] [P] [S] [🍷]

Horts Wine Bar and Bistro Harborne Rd, Edgbaston ☎ 021-454 4672

Open: Mon–Sat 12noon–2.30pm, Sun 12noon–2pm, Mon–Fri 5.30–10.30pm, Sat & Sun 7–10.30pm

Easily recognised in fine weather by the 'overspill' of tables and chairs onto the wide pavement outside and the distinct French flavour in the simple brown-and-beige décor, this is a popular haunt of local business people. An assortment of nourishing English and Continental food is available, including a dish of the day such as risotto, pâté and various salads. Desserts include gâteau and American cheesecake. There's a small raised area at the rear, for the more intimate and quiet meal.

[P] [S]

The Loft 8 Churchill Precinct, Dudley ☎ (0384) 57801

Open: Tue–Fri 11.30am–3pm, Sat 11.30am–4pm, Sun 12noon–2pm, Thu–Sat 7–10pm

This restaurant sits proudly over a butcher's shop, so take care not to miss the entrance which is a doorway between two shops. After climbing the stairs you will find yourself in a large, white-walled room with black-beamed ceiling and alcoves along one wall. There is a good range of dishes on the lunch menu including steak and kidney pie and a mixed grill. The evening menu has a range of three-course meals and one of the main features of the restaurant is the 'Recession Special' menu available Thursday to Saturday.

[P] [S] [🍷] **VS**

Madisons 40 Cannon St ☎ 021-643 3650

Open: Mon–Thu, Sun 12noon–12mdnt, Fri–Sat 12noon–1am

A quiet side street, close to one of the city's main shopping areas, is the setting for this American-style restaurant. Food is cooked in the open kitchen area and consists mainly of a variety of grills and more exotic Continental cuisine. Madison's cocktails are an experience in themselves, and during 'Happy Hour' they are even better value than usual. Tuesdays to Thursdays, diners can enjoy live blues and jazz.

[S]

Maxwell's Plum Wine Bar & Bistro 163 Broad St Fiveways ☎ 021-643 0274

Open: Mon–Sat 12noon–2.30pm, Mon–Fri 5.30–10.30pm, Sat–Sun 7–10.30pm

Plate glass windows and a gay striped awning distinguish this wine bar from its neighbours in the shopping area. A speciality worthy of note is the spicy

Welsh sausage, served with fried potato, tomato and onions, but a good selection of quiches, flans and home-made sweets are available on the buffet. Daily hot dishes include prawn provençale, lamb curry, pork chop Milanese and cod Mornay.

[♫] [P] [S]

Michelle✕ 182–184 High St, Harborne ☎ 021-426 4133
Open: Mon–Sat 12noon–2pm, 7–10pm

Step into Michelle's French restaurant and you move back in time – to the heyday of the small-time grocer's shop. Dark mahogany shelving, a tiled bacon area and large mirrors belonging to the original Co-op grocers shop it once was, form the basis of a most unsuaul décor. Of the typically French cuisine, the coq au vin and boeuf bourguignon are among the best French dishes to be had this side of the Channel. There is an à la carte dinner menu and the one-choice-only table d'hôte at lunchtime is excellent value.

[S] [🍷]

New Happy Gathering ✕✕ 43–45 Station St ☎ 021-643 5247
Open: Mon–Sun 12noon–12mdnt

Mr Eric Ming Fat Chan offers traditional Cantonese cuisine at this gracious and comfortable restaurant. A staggering menu boasts more than 100 dishes. Portions are generous and you can choose from a variety of not-so-familiar dishes such as a steamed duck with plum sauce, water-chestnut pudding or braised duck's web in oyster sauce. Sweets include various fritters in syrup and Chinese pastries. Set meals offer a good variety of savoury dishes.

[C]

Pinocchio's✕ Chad Sq, Hawthorne Rd, Harborne ☎ 021-454 8672

Open: Mon–Sat 12.15–2pm, 6.30–10.30pm

Tucked between a hairdresser's shop and a newsagent, in a tiny, modern shopping centre, close to the village of Harborne, this converted shop also acts as a sort of unofficial art gallery, for the restaurant exhibits and sells pictures by local artists. The menu is wide-ranging and tempts extravagance, but if you stick to the three-course table d'hôte lunch menu you'll be surprised how reasonable it is.

P S

Plaka Taverna 63 New St ☎ 021-643 6694

Open: Mon–Sat 12noon–12mdnt, Sun 5pm–12mdnt

Step out of busy New Street into the discreetly-illuminated interior of this restaurant and you can imagine yourself in Greece. Of the many Greek specialities served here, Kleftiko – lamb cooked in the oven, served with a Greek salad and pitta – is worth a special mention. For a starter one of the 'dips' may tempt you, or try the stuffed vine leaves. There are a number of main courses to choose from – kebab lamb or pork, two different sausage dishes, and fillet of sole served with chips and salad, are examples. There are also a range of vegetarian dishes.

C ♫ S

Rajdoot✕✕ 12–22 Albert Rd ☎ 021-643 8805

Open: Mon–Sat 12noon–2.30pm, 6.30pm–12mdnt, Sun 6.30pm–12mdnt

Ornate brass, red silk and hessian walls and burning joss sticks complete the transition from West to East, in this authentic Indian restaurant offering Punjab and Tandoori cuisine. Excellent set lunches are available from Monday to Saturday and dinners are à la carte, with an average meal coming just outside our budget. Tandoori specialities (charcoal clay oven barbecues) include delicious rashmi kebab – chicken minced with onion, chillies, fresh mint, coriander and herbs and spices.

C ♫ P S

Rock Candy Mountain High St, Harborne ☎ 021-427 2481

Open: Mon–Sat 12noon–2.30pm, 5.30–10.30pm, Sun 12noon–2pm, 7–11.30pm

Bright, gaudy, garish but immaculate is the only way to describe this 'latest concept in wine bars – music – restaurants – meeting places and astral food'. Set in the centre of Harborne, it hums with activity and welcomes everyone. 'Kiddies' have their own special spaghetti-hamburger-ice-cream menu. The comic-strip menu offers pizzas, salads, hamburgers, BBQ ribs, chicken Kiev, chili con carne and steaks. Kick off with corn on the cob and finish with chocolate fudge cake with ice cream – one of a selection of way-out desserts.

C ♫ S

The Salad Bowl, The Old Mill Inn Windmill St, Upper Gornal (just off the A459 Dudley – Wolverhampton Rd) ☎ (09073) 3000

Open: Wed–Sat 12noon–2pm, 7–10pm

It is worth leaving the main road to find this white-painted inn. The restaurant is above the inn and seats 40 people comfortably in traditional style. Old farming and riding equipment add to the cosy, rural atmosphere. In keeping with the name, the main meals are salads on a 'help yourself' basis. Scampi, rump and fillet steaks are also available. One of the original Black Country ales is served at the inn.

♫ P **VS**

Sandonia 509 Hagley Rd, Bearwood ☎ 021-429 2622

Open: Tue–Sat 11.45am–3pm, 6–11.30pm

Owner Mr Constantinou (known to his regulars as Mr Conn) comes from Cyprus and opened this restaurant over 18 years ago. 'Regulars' include a couple who have dined at the same table every Thursday night for 16 years – there's faithfulness for you! The table d'hôte lunch consists of soup or fruit juice, a choice of items such as roast or braised steak with vegetables, and ice cream or fruit pie with custard. An à la carte lunch and dinner menu is also available.

C S **VS**

Valentino's ✕ High St, Harborne ☎ 021-427 2560

Open: Mon–Sat 12.30–2pm, 7–10.30pm, Sun 12.30–2pm

A smart little Italian place, converted from one of the main street shops in which decoration is kept simple enough to have a relaxing effect. A typical table d'hôte lunch could be egg mayonnaise, grilled sirloin steak and a piece of gâteau, though the à la carte menu could tempt you over the limit if you have extravagant tastes.

C ♫ P S

Wild Oats 5 Raddlebarn Rd, Selly Oak ☎ 021-471 2459

Open: Tue–Sat 12noon–2pm, 6–9pm, closed Sun, Mon, Bank Hol wkend & two weeks Xmas and New Year

Not far from the Birmingham University complex, Roy Nutt's small vegetarian restaurant seats 32 at well-scrubbed kitchen tables; the brown and cream décor gives it a warm, earthy appearance. The daily menu consists of three or four starters and main courses which can be accompanied by salad or potato dishes. Our inspector had Maltese soup (a delicious blend of orange and tomato) followed by casserole of Chinese vegetables and pasta, with a fresh green salad. The restaurant is not licensed and there is a corkage charge if customers wish to bring their own wine. There is also an extensive menu of 'take-away' and 'freezer' dishes which is proving very popular.

P **VS**

BISHOP'S STORTFORD
Hertfordshire
Map **5** TL42

The Swan Restaurant 88 South St
☎ (0279) 52007/59439
Open: Mon–Sat 9am–9.30pm, Sun 12noon–2.30pm

A delightful Regency-style frontage with attractive half curtains on brass rails tempts you to explore further into this restaurant. On the à la carte menu, the home-made soups and selection of omelettes are to be recommended, although more exotic dishes such as melon liqueur and Porterhouse steak garni are offered at prices coming close to our limit. There is a daily lunch menu offering three courses plus coffee and a traditional Sunday lunch is available.

C ♫ P S ♧

BLACKBURN
Lancashire
Map **7** SD62

Kenyon's Studio Buttery 31 Penny St
☎ (0254) 60347
Open: Mon–Wed 9am–4.30pm, Thu 10am–1.30pm, Fri 9am–5pm, Sat 9am–4.30pm

This sparkling, modern coffee shop in the centre of town is a self-serve style operation offering good food at remarkably low prices. A three-course meal starting with soup of the day, followed by lasagne or steak and kidney and completed with Black Forest gâteau is excellent value.

P S

BLACKPOOL
Lancashire
Map **7** SD33

The Danish Kitchen Vernon Humpage, Church St ☎ (0253) 24291
Open: Mon–Sat 9am–5.30pm

Pine tables and pine beams with mock oil lamps adorn this bright, clean, split-level serve-yourself operation in the centre of town. The menu includes freshly-made soup, and there is a tempting array of Danish open sandwiches (crab, prawn, beef, smoked salmon etc). Salads, omelettes, pizzas and Danish pastries are also available.

P S

BLANDFORD FORUM
Dorset
Map **3** ST80

Anvil Hotel & Restaurant★★ Pimperne
☎ (0258) 53431
Open: Mon–Sun 12noon–2.30pm, 6–10.30pm, 11pm Fri–Sat

Real wood fires are a feature of the Anvil, and the only restaurant between Blandford and Salisbury is housed in a beautiful, thatched 16th-century building, reputed to have originated as an Elizabethan farmhouse. Satisfying snacks may be taken in the newly extended and cleverly restored bar. Home-made fare such as cottage pie, coquille St Jaques (made from fresh local scallops) or beef curry with rice are the order of the day. Salads, soup, pâté and basket meals are also available. The beamed restaurant, with its brick floor has an à la carte menu which could easily break the budget.

C ♫ P ♧

BLEADNEY
Somerset
Map **3** ST44

The Stradlings Bleadney
☎ (0749) 73576 On B3139 near Wells
Open: Mon–Sat 11am–2.30pm, 6.30–11pm, Sun 12noon–2pm, 7–10pm

This Somerset pub and restaurant has fine views over the moors and Mendip Hills. The blackboard menu lists about 30 dishes including steak and kidney pie, pizzas and pâté, all home-made. The more exotic snails in garlic butter and mushrooms Valencienne are also available. The separate restaurant is open in the evening but a two-course meal is outside our budget.

♫ P

BODELWYDDAN
Clwyd
Map **6** SJ07

Cromwell's Bistro, Faenol Fawr Manor✕✕ ☎ (0745) 590784
Open: Mon–Sun 12noon–2.30pm, 7.30–11pm (closed Sun in winter)

Faenol Fawr is a restaurant (a bit expensive for us) in a manor house built in 1597, but Cromwell's is *really* old, dating back to the early part of the 13th century. Here, you can take a pleasant yet inexpensive meal chosen from the Supper Bar menu. Starters include home-made soup and Arbroath smokies. There are casseroles – duck and blackberry and local pheasant in red wine, and meat platters with help-yourself salad and jacket potato.

C ♫ P

BODMIN
Cornwall
Map **2** SX06

Castle Hill House Hotel★★
☎ (0208) 3009
Open: Mon–Sat 7–8.30pm, Sun 12.30–2pm

Ken and Sylvia Flint's Castle Hill House Hotel is an elegant Georgian mansion set in two acres of lawns and gardens. Delicious home-produced food such as soup, pâté and steak and kidney pie proves popular with guests and locals alike, and it's as well to book in advance for dinner. There is a table d'hôte menu, and some items on the small à la carte menu are within our price range. A good selection of freshly-made sweets, including gâteaux and home-made fruit pies is served with clotted Cornish cream.

P ♧

BOGNOR REGIS
West Sussex
Map **4** SZ99

Tudor Rose 55 London Rd
☎ (0243) 23682
Open: Summer Mon–Sat 10.30am–10.30pm, Winter closed Mon

The restaurant is split into two sections and has olde-worlde wooden-beamed ceiling and walls. A daytime menu offers starters (such as chilled melon), followed by various fish, roasts and salads at sensible prices. The dinner menu includes specials such as chicken Maryland.

BOLTON
Gt Manchester
Map **7** SD70

The Drop Inn and Mr Bumbles, The Last Drop★★★ Bromley Cross
☎ (0204) 591131

Open: Inn: Mon–Sun 12noon–2pm, Mr Bumbles: Mon–Thu 7–10.30pm, Fri–Sat 7–11pm, Sun 3.30–9.30pm

A collection of derelict 18th-century farm buildings has been imaginatively converted to create a modern hotel complex with traditional village atmosphere. The Drop Inn pub even sports a honky-tonk piano to accompany evening sing-songs, as well as oak beams and a blazing log fire. Bar snacks are served in the evening, but it's at lunchtime that the food scene is best, with an excellent, self-service lunch. The stone-floored Mr Bumbles with its low-arched ceiling, wood and brick surfaces and candlelight, offers a menu which is changed monthly and includes fish, salad, burger and one or two more unusual dishes.

C ♬ P S **VS**

The Lamplighter 26 Knowsley St
☎ (0204) 35175
Open: Mon–Thu 12noon–2pm, 5.45–10.30pm, Fri 12noon–2pm, 5.45–11pm, Sat 12noon–11pm, Sun 3–6pm

Pictures, prints and posters of the Victorian era cover the walls, and gas lamps and stuffed animals' heads add to the overwhelming 19th-century atmosphere. Every dish is given the name of a Victorian cigarette card character; the Pawnbroker's Treat, for instance, is hot poached salmon dripping in best butter, and the Knocker's-Up Nosh – a juicy rump steak with garden peas and a garnish of cress, tomato and potatoes. Fresh fruit, ice cream or cheese is included in the main course price, so nothing tops our limit.

BOLTON-LE-SANDS
Lancashire
Map **7** SD56

Willow Tree By Pass Rd
☎ (0524) 823316
Open: Tue–Fri 9.30am–2pm, 4.30–8.30pm, Sat 4.30–9pm, Sun 11.30am–9pm

This single-storey building with its neatly tiled roof and white stucco walls is just the place to feed the family. Service is prompt and efficient in the two well-appointed, wood-panelled dining rooms, where a lunch menu includes soup or fruit juice, minute steak, lamb chops or grilled plaice, served with potatoes or chips and peas and a sweet and coffee. Light lunches are also available. The reasonably-priced evening menu offers more choice.

P ♿

BOROUGHBRIDGE
North Yorkshire
Map **8** SE36

Three Arrows★★★ Horsefair
☎ (09012) 2245
Open: Mon–Sun 12.30–2pm, 7.30–9.30pm

This restaurant has a long, tree-lined entrance through lawns and gardens. Elegant though it is, the place is not ruinously expensive. Table d'hôte lunch and dinner are both within our price range and they offer three courses of honest-to-goodness English fare, with a selection of vegetables; main courses include York Ham and roast meats. The à la carte menu may be out of our price range.

C ♬ P

BORROWDALE
Cumbria
Map **11** NY21

The Yew Tree Seatoller ☎ (059684) 634

Open: Tue–Fri & Sun 12noon–8pm, Sat 6–9.30pm

Nestling at the foot of the spectacular Honiston Pass, this whitewashed restaurant was originally built as two cottages in 1628. Massive oak beams and a slate floor emphasise the antiquity of the dining room, with its wheelback chairs and wooden tables. Food is simple and wholesome. Try home-made soup with a roll as a starter. Main courses offered are grills, omelettes and salads. Speciality of the house is Borrowdale trout with almonds and ham and eggs. A very tempting selection of sweets include pot of chocolate, brandy meringue or bilberries and cream. Starred items on the menu are available in smaller portions for children at two-thirds of the full price.

[P] [🍷]

BOSTON
Lincolnshire
Map **8** TF34

The Carving Room, New England Hotel★★ Wide Bargate ☎ (0205) 65255
Open: Mon–Thu 12noon–2pm, 7–10pm, Fri–Sun 12noon–2pm, 7–10.30pm

At the rear of the imposing New England Hotel is the elegant, Regency-style Carving Room, with white pillars, rich red-patterned carpet and green wallpaper, leather upholstery and tablecloths. Here you may eat a superb roast lunch or dinner. The carving table is bedecked with large roast joints, fresh vegetables and salads – you help yourself to as much as you want. This, together with the choice of a sweet from the trolley comes just within our price range. Appetisers are extra, but hardly necessary! Children can help themselves at the special reduced price.

[C] [P] [🍷]

BOURNE
Lincolnshire
Map **8** TF12

The Wishing Well Inn Main St, Dyke, 1½m N of Bourne off the A15
Open: Mon–Sun 12noon–2pm, Mon–Sat 7.30–10.30pm, Sun 7.30–10pm

This pleasant, old inn has a small restaurant with exposed beams and stonework. Grills are the speciality, but the menu also features poultry dishes and pork and lamb chops. Bar snacks are also available.

[P] [🍷] **VS**

BOURNEMOUTH
Dorset
Map **4** SZ09

Ann's Pantry 129 Belle Vue Rd, Southbourne ☎ (0202) 426178
Open: Summer Tue–Sat 10.30am–2pm, 6–10pm, Sun 10.30am–2pm, Winter Tue–Sun 10.30am–2pm

This corner-sited restaurant, only 100 yards from the seafront, has an exterior reminiscent of a superior Victorian pub. At lunchtime there is an extremely reasonable à la carte menu which includes pork chop and apple sauce and gammon with pineapple. Children's choices include the well-loved bangers, beans and chips. A three-course set lunch offers cottage pie and curry, and there is a traditional Sunday roast. In the evening choose from the table d'hôte or à la carte menus. Home cooking is a speciality of the restaurant.

[P] [S] [🍷] **VS**

La Fontaine 141 Belle Vue Rd, Southbourne ☎ (0202) 420537
Open: Tue–Sat 12noon–2pm, 6.30–9.30pm, Sun 12noon–2pm

Tucked away in a residential suburb of Bournemouth, this cosy restaurant has attractive pine-panelled walls and ceiling. Ivor Jones and his wife June assure you of a warm welcome. There is a regularly-changing chalked-up menu for both lunch and dinner at reasonable prices.

[S]

Fortes The Square ☎ (0202) 24916
Open: Florentine Restaurant Mon–Sun 12noon–10.30pm, Coffee Shop: Mon–Sun 8am–6pm. Self Service Restaurant: Mon–Sun 10am–10.30pm, Opening times may change in winter

This is a typical Trusthouse Forte operation, providing everything from takeaway snacks for the beach to three-course à la carte dinners in an elegant setting, at prices that represent very good value for money. The ground floor self-service restaurant serves an excellent lunch, high tea or supper as well as cakes and pastries, sandwiches, bowls of mixed salad, ice creams and beverages. The Coffee Shop serves hot snacks and grills throughout the day. The Florentine offers a choice of three-course lunches including various Italian dishes and a traditional weekend lunch. The à la carte menu is reasonably priced.

[C] [♫] [P] [S] [🍷]

The Old England 74 Poole Rd, Westbourne ☎ (0202) 766475
Open: Mon–Sun 9.30am–3pm, 6–10.30pm

A warm welcome awaits you at this delightful olde worlde restaurant. Cuisine, though, is 20th century and well-cooked with fresh vegetables. There is a set three-course meal (with reductions for children), alternatively the extensive à la carte menu offers a range of dishes including Dorset chicken which could be followed by fruit crumble. For light snacks try the Dickens Wine Cellar.

[C] [♫] [P] [S] [🍷]

Scruples 107 Poole Rd, Westbourne ☎ (0202) 767264
Open: Tue–Fri 12noon–2pm, Mon–Sun 7–10.30pm

Scruples is a modern attractive licensed restaurant in a pleasant shopping area, offering well-prepared food at reasonable prices. There are many varieties of pizza and pasta dishes which are also available on a 'take-away' basis. Salads, steak, duck and fish are also on the menu and wine is sold by the glass.

[♫] [P] [S] [🍷]

Trattoria Tosca 12 Richmond Hill ☎ (0202) 23034
Open: Mon–Sun 12noon–2.30pm, 6–11.30pm

The cuisine at Edward Cobelli's charmingly informal Trattoria Tosca in The Square is, not surprisingly, Italian but not expensively so. There is a good range of starters, spaghetti dishes and Italian specialities, including the romantically named filleto Casanova. Service is friendly, willing and speedy, but do book at the weekend if you want to be sure of a table.

C ♬ P S ♨ **VS**

BOVEY TRACEY
Devon
Map **3** SX87

Riverside Inn Fore St ☎ (0626) 832293
Open: Mon–Sat 11am–2.30pm, 6–11pm, Winter 10.30pm, Sun 12noon–2pm, 7–10.30pm

This large inn by a stream enjoys a picturesque situation. On display is the sword, broken in two, which is said to have been used by the knight, De Tracey in the murder of Thomas à Becket. There are two eating places to choose from; the Cavalier Restaurant offers a substantial à la carte menu of grills, while the King Charles Buttery has a more budget-priced selection, such as basket meals, pizzas, sandwiches or salads. A choice from the à la carte could be the Moorland grill (which includes kidney, egg, sausage, chop, gammon) with vegetables of the day and lemon sorbet. On Sundays there is a set three-course lunch with coffee.

♬ P ♨

The Rock Inn Haytor Vale, 4m W of Bovey Tracey off B3344
☎ (03646) 205/305
Open: Mon–Sun 11am–2pm, 6.30–10pm

This late Georgian inn nestles below Haytor, the best known of the Dartmoor Tors. The proprietors Mr and Mrs Deane spent 20 years in Nigeria before taking over the Rock Inn 5½ years ago, and they were joined by their son Adrian. There is a good choice of bar snacks, including crab mousse, Arabian lamb and steak and kidney pie. A three-course table d'hôte dinner (just over our limit) is served between 7.30 and 8.30pm, but is essential to book in advance. Try French onion soup, followed by pork chop cordon bleu, your choice of sweet and coffee.

P ♨

BOWES
Co Durham
Map **12** NY91

Ancient Unicorn Hotel★★
☎ (0833) 28321
Open: Mon–Sun 11.30am–2.30pm, 6–10pm

This attractive coaching inn, built around a cobbled courtyard, has been offering accommodation and refreshment to weary travellers since the 16th century. Prices in the restaurant of this two-star hotel are somewhat beyond our limit so we are concentrating on the very reasonable and extensive bar snack menu. A sample of dishes available are sardine and tomato salad for starter, chicken curry with rice and peas and a choice of sweet.

C P ♨

BOWNESS-ON-WINDERMERE
Cumbria
Map **7** SD49

The Quarterdeck The Glebe Centre, Glebe Rd ☎ (09662) 5001
Open: March–Oct, Mon–Sun 8.30am–10.30pm, Barbecue menu 7–10.30pm

This restaurant, with a coffee-shop and lounge is situated on the edge of Lake Windermere and has excellent views over the marina and surrounding hills. At lunch-time, roasts are a speciality and there is a barbecue menu in the evening. There is also a special menu for children. A typical evening meal would be gazpacho, spiced breast of chicken and a choice of dessert.

♬ P ♨

BRADFORD
West Yorkshire
Map **7** SE13

The Last Pizza Show 50 Great Horton Rd ☎ (0274) 28173
Open: Mon–Sat 12noon–2pm, 6–11.30pm (12mdnt Fri & Sat) Sun 6–11.30pm

A very Italian pizza-restaurant this – complete with marble-topped cast-iron tables, hanging baskets and helpful Italian waiters. If you stray away from the pizza and pasta main courses you could find the steak takes you above our limit, but with a choice of 12 pizzas, including the chef's special there should be no need. A set meal with a choice of dishes is just over our limit.

C P ♨

BRAMHALL
Gt Manchester
Map **7** SJ88

Ganders of Goose Green 9–11 Bramhall Lane South ☎ 061-439 2177
Open: Mon–Sat 12noon–3pm, 7–10.30pm (closes 11pm Fri & Sat), Sun 7–10.30pm

The speciality of this somewhat dignified wine bar is Fondue Bourgignonne – fillet steak cut into bite sized pieces, a baked potato, mixed salad, french break plus various dips and sauces and a pan of hot oil and fondue forks. Fondue is available for two or more people, so don't go alone. If you prefer to have your meal cooked for you there is a very good range of dishes on the menu to choose from, try honey baked spare-ribs followed by profiteroles. A selection of wines is available.

C ♬ P ♨

BRECHIN
Tayside *Angus*
Map **15** NO56

Northern Hotel★★ 2 Clerk St
☎ (03562) 2156
Open: Mon–Sun 12noon–2pm, 5–6.30pm, 7–8.30pm

For those who relish a proper 'sit down' meal within the realms of a tight budget, this hotel is the ideal place. A three-course dinner such as salami salad, farmhouse grill and vegetables of the day, followed by banana split comes within our price range. Snacks in the bar and satisfying high teas are also available.

C P ♨

BRENTWOOD
Essex
Map **5** TQ59

The Eagle and Child 13 Chelmsford Rd, Shenfield ☎ (0277) 210155
Open: bar snacks: Mon–Sat 11.30am–2pm
Carvery: Tue–Sat 7–10.30pm, Sun 12noon–2pm

This popular Tudor-style pub houses a carvery restaurant which has wood-panelled décor reminiscent of a private club. Fresh roast pork, topside of beef and whole turkeys are on display and James or Keith, the waiters, will only stop filling up your plate when you say so. All the roasts are served with generous portions of vegetables. Alternative main courses include home-made steak pie or salad selection. A choice of sweets is also included in the price. There is an attractive garden and if you're lucky you may see a display of Morris dancing.

♬ P

BRIDGE OF ALLAN
Central *Stirlingshire*
Map **11** NS79

Cranachan Restaurant 23 Henderson St
☎ (0786) 832918
Open: Tue–Thu 10am–7pm, Fri & Sat 10am–10pm, Sun 12.30–7pm. Closed Mon

This popular little restaurant is open all day serving fresh home-made cooking and baking. A typical lunch could be home-braised gammon followed by chocolate nut sundae. High Tea is another substantial meal served with French fries, bread and butter and tea. A dinner menu is available on Friday and Saturday and includes dishes such as escalope of pork dauphinoise and burgundy beef casserole.

♬ P ♨

BRIDGNORTH
Shropshire
Map **7** SO79

Baileys Wine Bar and Bistro 78 High St
☎ (07462) 3445
Open: Mon–Sat 11am–2.30pm, 6–10.30pm, 11pm Fri–Sat, Sun 12noon–2pm, 7–10.30pm

John Porter opened Baileys in September 1980, after he and his wife had completely gutted the original premises and removed a remarkable 300 tons of rubble. The exposed beams, stained wood floors and occasional rugs create a pleasing atmosphere, and diners should scan the walls for details of special offers of the day. Popular dishes such as beef provençale, Bailey's potato and meat pie, and turkey vol au vent take a lot of beating, but salads and open sandwiches are warm-weather winners. Sweets and starters are excellent value.

[S]

BRIDLINGTON
Humberside
Map **8** TA16

Barn Restaurant Prince St
☎ (0262) 75661
Open: Summer Mon–Sun 12noon–11pm, Winter Mon–Wed 12noon–3pm, Fri–Sat 12noon–11pm, Sun12noon–6pm

This bright and attractive restaurant, with a décor predominantly red, prides itself on being able to suit all tastes by serving a variety of home-made 'specials' such as lasagne, moussaka, and chili con carne alongside a more formal à la carte selection. Traditional dishes such as home-made steak and kidney pie are on hand for the less adventurous along with a variety of salads. Children are catered for with sausages, beefburgers or fish-fingers and chips, while other dishes are aimed modestly at the 'gourmet' (try the chef's own charcoal grilled steaks or gammon and roast duckling). A delicious selection of home-made sweets and ices is available, with liqueur coffee to follow.

[P] [S] **VS**

The Friendly Forester 1 Marton Gate
☎ (0262) 75515
Open: Mon–Sat 12noon–2pm, 7–10.30pm, Sun 7–10.30pm only

This smart, new 'Cavalier' pub and restaurant is situated in a residential area on the northern fringe of the town. The bargains at the restaurant are the Lunchtime Specials – mainly pies, quiches, fish and salad. The à la carte menu available for both lunch and dinner offers a range of char-grills, burgers and deep fried dishes all served with jacket potatoes, or chips, vegetables and salad. There is also a set price children's menu.

[P]

Mountbattens 22 The Promenade
☎ (0262) 72225
Open: Summer Mon–Sat 11.45–1am Sun 11.45am–2pm, 3–6pm, 7–10pm; winter Mon–Sat 11.45am–3pm, 6pm–1am, Sun 11.45am–3pm, 7–10pm

Situated in the main shopping street near the harbour Mountbattens is a pub with a restaurant and nightclub. The smart comfortable lounge-bar leads into the carvery area and the large ballroom sized restaurant. The lunchtime carvery offers a variety of freshly cooked roast meat, buffet-type meals and a casserole or curry. If you feel peckish in the afternoon try the afternoon grills and high teas which are available in the summer. The evening menu offers a good choice of dishes – casseroles, pies, omelettes, fish and steaks which, along with the other meals available here, are very reasonably priced.

[P]

The Old Forge Main St, Sewerby
☎ (0262) 74535
Open: Mon–Sat 10.30am–5.30pm, 7.30–10pm (Wed–Sat May–Oct only) Sun 10.30am–6.30pm

One of a double row of stone-built fishermen's cottages of some age and interest, modernised and converted from its more recent use as a blacksmith's forge, the Old Forge is a convenient eating place for visitors to Sewerby Hall with its gardens, museum and zoo. With children's portions at about half the price of the regular meal, this is a particularly attractive restaurant for the whole family. Service is efficient and a good selection of English fare is offered, locally-caught fish being a speciality.

[P]

BRIDPORT
Dorset
Map **3** SY49

Bistro Lautrec✕ 53 East St
☎ (0308) 56549/56716
Open: Mon–Fri 12noon–2pm, Mon–Sat 7–10pm

Food and environment go together in this typical French-style bistro. Candles in bottles, check tablecloths, Lautrec posters and chalked-up menus make just the right setting in which to enjoy a lunch of French onion soup, followed by lasagne. Evening meals, in a more sophisticated yet still informal atmosphere are also available but may be over our limit.

[P] [S]

Bull Hotel★ 34 East St ☎ (0308) 22878
Open: Mon–Sat 12noon–2pm, 7.15–9.15pm, Sun 7.15–9.15pm

The Terleski family have restored their 16th-century coaching inn. They are keen to offer good hospitality at a very reasonable price – and succeed. There's a wide range of bar meals, including a choice from the daily speciality menu and a range of hot or cold snacks. It can all be washed down with a glass of real ale. The daily speciality choice offers unfussy dishes such as fresh seafood, and the usual range of grills is available. For dessert try crème caramel or apple strudel.

The Marquis of Lorne Nettlecombe (5m NE of Bridport off the A3066)
☎ (030885) 236
Open: Mon–Sat 10.30am–2.30pm, 6–11pm, Sun 12noon–2pm, 7–10.30pm

This charming 16th-century inn situated in the heart of the picturesque Dorset countryside has exposed beams and stone walls. It also boasts its very own ghost story and you can learn all about it whilst enjoying one of the bar snacks or restaurant meals prepared and cooked by the proprietors Mr & Mrs Childs. Omelettes, basket meals, fish and steak are included on the bar menu and the 'Dish of the Day' is chalked on the blackboard. There are special meals for children. The 'Supper Menu' offers a choice of five starters and main courses and your choice of sweet from the trolley, there is also a traditional Sunday lunch.

[P]

BRIGHOUSE
West Yorkshire
Map **7** SE12

Black Bull Hotel Thornton Sq
☎ (0484) 714816
Open: Mon–Sat 12noon–2pm

The homely restaurant of the Black Bull Hotel with its rose-patterned wallpaper is an ideal place for shoppers and motorists who enjoy a traditional English lunch. The price of the main course includes a choice of starter and sweet; a roast, steak and kidney pie and salad are typical choices. Grills are more expensive but a two-course meal still comes just within our budget. Established in 1740, this hotel is the oldest in Brighouse and a faithful band of locals make up the best part of its clientele, although dinner is served to residents only.

[P] [S] **VS**

BRIGHTON
East Sussex
Map **4** TQ30

The Cypriana Steak House and Greek Restaurant 22 Preston St
☎ (0273) 202661
Open: Mon–Sun 12noon–3pm, 6pm–1am

This small, intimate restaurant specialises in Scotch beef and authentic Greek food. English dishes consist of about 11 appetisers, fish, poultry, grills, flambés and omelettes. Greek specialities include as appetisers houmous or taramasalata. Main courses include moussaka and stifado (beef cooked with shallots and served with rice and potatoes). For a real treat, try a Meze – 'a full two-course meal consisting of 14 delicious Greek dishes to satisfy the most discerning palate'. This is served for two or more people.

[C] [P] [S]

Meeting House Meeting House La
☎ (0273) 24817
Open: Summer Mon–Sun 8am–6pm, Winter Mon–Sat 8am–6pm

Tom and Sean Wall preside over their modern coffee shop-cum-snack bar with its wooden tables and bench seats, bright décor and counter service. Hot and cold dishes are available, including quiche lorraine and salad or steak and kidney pie and there is also a good selection of cold meats. Starters include minestrone or French onion soup and you can finish with a delicious Danish pastry or a slice of apfel-strudel.

[♫] [P] [S] [✿]

Richards' Restaurant 102 Western Rd, Hove ☎ (0273) 720058
Open: Mon–Thu 11am–10.30pm, Fri & Sat 11am–11.30pm Sun 12noon–10pm

This garden-style restaurant has wooden trellis with hanging plants and wicker chairs. Coffee and light snacks are served in the mornings and afternoon, lunches from 12noon and dinner from 6pm. Starters include Stilton and onion soup and home-made pâté, main courses range from various fish dishes to oyster and Guinness pie. There is a good selection of sweets on the trolley. Wine is available by the glass.

[C] [P] **VS**

Tureen Restaurant Upper North St
☎ (0273) 28939
Open: Tue–Sat 12noon–2pm, 7–9.30pm, Sun 12noon–2pm

This unpretentious bistro-style restaurant features a large Japanese tureen in the window and floral-patterned banquettes along the walls. Cuisine is English with French influence and the à la carte menu offers a host of delights. However, we suggest our readers stick with the set lunch, which offers three courses such as egg mayonnaise, sweet and sour pork, and summer pudding. On Sundays a traditional English roast may be just over our price limit.

[C] [♫] [✿]

BRISTOL

Avon
Map **3** ST57

Arnolfini Narrow Quay
☎ (0272) 299191
Open: Tues–Sat 11am–8pm

Presenting new developments in the visual arts, music, dance, theatre and cinema, the Arnolfini public arts complex boasts this airy and spacious bistro-style restaurant with its taped background music and blackboard menu, with salads, cold meats and cakes on display on long counters. There is always an exhibition of works of art on the walls. Once a docks warehouse, the restaurant overlooks St Augustine's Reach. Soups, pâtés and a hot dish of the day (try chicken in aubergine and corriander sauce) are all reasonably priced. Salads are particularly interesting, and there is a special mixed salad of new potatoes, beetroot onion and mackerel.

[♫]

Le Château Wine Bar 32 Park St
☎ (0272) 28654
Open: Mon–Sat 9.30am–2.30pm, 5.30–9pm

This informal, busy city centre wine bar brims over with business people at lunchtime – a tribute to good food and unpretentious but relaxing surroundings, with wooden furniture and lighting from candles in wax-encrusted bottles. Behind the Victorian bar a blackboard proclaims the range of hot lunchtime dishes including pork fillet kebabs in lemon garlic sauce and moussaka. Also at lunchtime and in the evening there is a selection of cold meats, pâté, cheeses, mackerel and attractively-prepared salads. Interesting desserts include peaches in brandy, and blueberry pie.

[♫] [S]

The Chequers Inn Hanham Mills, Hanham ☎ (0272) 674242
Open: Mon–Sat 12noon–2.30pm, 6.30–11pm, Sun 12noon–2.30pm, 7–11pm

This riverside haven, close to the city, offers an 'economy lunch' which is likely to include a casserole or joint of the day. No wonder The Chequers is a popular haunt, attracting not only local business people but family parties, particularly for Sunday lunch, and even yachtsmen taking a spot of shore-leave. Apart from the restaurant offering a comprehensive choice of grills or 'Fisherman's Choices', the self-service bar has a carvery specialising in 'Roasters' – succulent rare beef or roast pork with vegetables or cold ham off the bone. Lasagne, steak and kidney pie or turkey and ham in white sauce are also available along with snacks and pastries.

[C] [♫] [P] [✿]

Circles Restaurant Dingles, Queens Rd, Clifton ☎ (0272) 215301
Open: Mon–Sat 9am–5.30pm

This comfortable, modern, self-service restaurant displays cold meats, salads, pâtés and a variety of sandwiches, all at very reasonable prices. Staff are on hand to help you to the various permutations of interesting salads. Soup and cream gâteaux complete the menu making this a much sought-after filling station for shoppers.

[C] [♫] [S]

Dragonara Hotel☆☆☆☆ Redcliffe Way
☎ (0272) 20044
Open: La Galleria Mon–Sat 10am–10.30pm Closed Sun

La Galleria is a continental-style bar and coffee shop within the Ladbroke Dragonara Hotel offering a range of salads and snacks throughout the day. Snacks on the menu are listed under headings such as 'Light but filling' – here you'll find a tasty country pâté – and under 'Something more substantial' try the La Galleria – a triple decker, three layered toasted sandwich with delicious fillings. Also available are 'Great Sandwich Combinations' and a wide range of unusual salads.

[C] [♫] [P] [S] [✿]

Grand Hotel★★★★ Broad St
☎ (0272) 291645
Open: Brass Nails Restaurant 'Any Time Menu' Mon–Sun 7.30am–10.30pm

For the purpose of this guide we recommend the 'Any Time Menu' which is served by young and friendly staff in the bar area of the Brass Nails restaurant. This menu offers light meals all day and includes a 'Breakfast Platter', morning coffee with home-made cookies, and traditional afternoon tea. Other dishes include whitebait, vegetarian meals and omelettes, There is also the main restaurant adjacent but the prices come outside the limit for this guide.

[C] [P] [✿] **VS**

See advertisement on page 50

The Guild Restaurant Bristol Guild, 68–70 Park St ☎ (0272) 291874
Open: Mon–Fri 9.30am–5pm, Sat 9.30am–4.30pm (no hot meals on Sat)

The small Guild Restaurant, with its attractive extension on to a terrace, covered in winter, but opened in summer to allow patrons to eat in the sun, is a part of the smart Bristol Guild store in the city centre. Under the capable direction of Jean O'Malley and Julie Gregory, inexpensive lunchtime meals of good quality include a selection of home-made soup, quiches or pâtés chalked on a blackboard menu. A hot main dish of the day could be tarragon chicken or lasagne. Creamy desserts are delicious and modestly priced.

[S]

See advertisement on page 50

Llandoger Trow 5 King St
☎ (0272) 20783
Open: Mon–Fri 12noon–2.30pm, 6–11pm, Sat 11.30, Sun 12noon–2pm, 7–10.30pm

King Street boasts a number of impressive 17th- and 18th-century buildings, including the long-running Theatre Royal, first opened to the public in 1766. But none is more interesting, or has attracted more legends, than Llandoger Trow, built in 1664, one of the oldest inns in the city and now run by Berni. Duckling and T-bone steaks are specialities of the house here and the steak and duck restaurant does an extremely good local trade. There is a smaller steak and sole restaurant.

[C] [♫] [P] [S] [✿]

Marco's Trattoria Queen Rd
☎ (0272) 28508
Open: Mon–Sat 12noon–3pm, 6–10.30pm, Fri & Sat 11pm

Down a short flight of steps, below the busy shopping street of Queens Road, you will find the quiet haven of Marco's Trattoria. This intimate little restaurant is simply-furnished with comfortable chairs and polished-wood tables in a cellar-type décor, complete with the original flagstone flooring. Your needs will be attended to by one of the charming waitresses. A satisfying meal can be based on the traditional English steak or one of the Italian specialities such as bistecca al pizzaiola or scaloppine milanese. All meals are served with French fries or jacket potato (or spaghetti with the Italian dishes), garden peas, roll and butter, and include in their price ice cream for dessert, a selection of Italian cheeses with biscuits.

[S]

Parks 51 Park St ☎ (0272) 28016
Open: Mon–Sun 12noon–11pm

Although the restaurant itself is only five years old Parks, situated in Bristol's busy Park Street and close to the city's lovely university and museum is housed in a Georgian listed building. It is fresh and bright, bedecked with attractive plants, grand mirrors and fans from the once-far flung Empire. Specialities here are savoury pancakes made with buckwheat and filled with such things as chicken in mushroom and white wine sauce, or smoked haddock in cream sauce and served with salad. Main-course dishes, served with vegetables or salad, and jacket potato with butter or sour cream, include 8oz sirloin steak. In addition there is a Chef's Special. Wine is available by the glass.

[♫] [P] [♧]

Trattoria Sorrento 239 Cheltenham Rd
☎ (0272) 45879
Open: Mon–Thu, Sun 6pm–2am, Fri–Sat 6pm–3am

This spacious, modern trattoria, bedecked with Chianti flasks, is noted for its home-made pastas and pizzas. Freshly made for each customer, the pizzas are rated by gourmets as 'the finest this side of Mount Vesuvius', and the Chef's Special is a particularly praiseworthy specimen – brimming over with Italian cheeses, tomatoes, bacon, salami, corn, peppers, mushrooms and anchovies! Steak and chicken dishes, English or Italian style, are also on the menu. So generous are the main courses that the luscious sweets (including speciality ice cream), Italian cheeses and speciality coffees prove to be quite a challenge. Whatever your choice, dishes will be served to you in true Italian style by cheerful (and sometimes singing) Italian waiters who look as though they have just been plucked from the sunshine of Italy.

[P]

BRIXHAM
Devon
Map **3** SX95

The Elizabethan 8 Middle St
☎ (08045) 3722
Open: Summer Tue–Sun 12.15–2pm, Wed–Sat 7–9.30pm, Winter Tue–Sun 12.15–2pm

Small-paned windows, stuccoed walls and ceiling beams lend an air of cosy antiquity to this small restaurant in the town centre. Fresh flowers are a complement to the fresh, home-made fare. The lunch menu offers a choice of main courses and desserts at very reasonable prices. Roast chicken, pork or fillet of plaice could be followed with apricot crumble or Devonshire junket with clotted cream. Appetisers include home-made soup of the day, pâté and scampi. Dinners are served during the season and strips of beef in wine sauce with peppers and mushrooms is a typical main course. The restaurant is conveniently situated opposite Brixham bus station and near to the multi-storey car park in the town centre.

[C] [P] [S] [🍷]

BROADSTAIRS
Kent
Map **5** TR36

The Mad Chef's Bistro The Harbour
☎ (0843) 69304
Open: Mon–Sun 10am–3pm, 6–11pm, (closed Tue in Winter)

Paul Ward is the Mad Chef at this little bistro on the harbour at Broadstairs. The emphasis here is on freshly caught fish and seafood. Lobster and turbot can be expensive but sample the lunch-time Quickies menu which includes crab or cockle and mussel omelettes. The à la carte menu offers other specialities such as fish pie or chilli con carne, and there is also a vegetarian and wholefood menu. Lovers of Dickensian memorabilia will be interested to note that the Mad Chef's is situated between Dickens' House Museum and Bleak House. Booking is essential on summer evenings.

[C] [P] [🍷]

BROADWAY
Hereford & Worcester
Map **4** SP03

The Coffee Pot 76 High St
☎ (0386) 858323
Open: Mar–Oct Mon–Sat 10am–5.30pm, Sun 11am–5.30pm, Nov–Feb Fri–Sat 10am–5.30pm, Sun 11am–5.30pm

This charming converted house lies on the edge of the village. In winter log fires blaze in the huge, open, stone fireplace in the restaurant, where an impressive embroidered silk hanging decorates the wall. Tea, coffee and home-made soup and cakes are available throughout the day. The lunch menu has a choice of three main dishes, including chicken and mushroom pie, and is very reasonably priced. There is a small but selective wine list.

[P] [🍷] **VS**

Cotswold Café and Restaurant The Green ☎ (0386) 853395
Open: Summer Mon–Fri 10am–6pm, Sat–Sun 10am–8pm, Winter Mon–Sat 10am–5.30pm, Sun 10am–6pm

The Cotswold Café and Restaurant has counted amongst its customers John Wayne and the pop group Genesis. Delicious home-made ice creams are for sale, a speciality of Mrs Susan Webb's family since 1945. The restaurant serves snacks and three-course à la carte meals throughout the day, including roast beef with fresh vegetables and sirloin steak. There is a range of home-made sweets.

[🍷]

Goblets Wine Bar High St
☎ (0386) 852255
Open: Mon–Sun 12noon–5pm, 6–9.30pm

Dating back to 1532, this stone-built one-time inn is now a thriving wine bar. A stone-flagged floor with scatter rugs, and black and white half-timbered walls adorned by tapestry panels make an ideal setting for the numerous antiques. Imaginative home cooking and a warm welcome have made Goblets very popular with the locals. Bourride of Beef (cooked in beer with a cheese topping) and chicken Marengo with rice are two of the delicious meals on the menu.

[C] [♫] [P] [S]

Quills
North St ☎ (0386) 853555
Open: Tue–Sun 12noon–2.30pm, Tue–Fri 7–9pm Sat 7–9.30pm. Closed Mon & Jan

A former 16th-century coach house, this restaurant's white-painted interior has a wealth of black timbers supporting the barn-type ceiling and a minstrel's gallery at the far end. At lunchtime a hot and cold buffet is available with a hot dish of the day which could be steak and kidney pie. The dinner menu is outside our price range.

[P] [🍷]

BROMLEY
Gt London

Hollywood Bowl 5 Market Parade, East St ☎ 01-460 2346 London Plan4 **91**D6
Open: Mon–Thu 11.30am–2.45pm,

6–11.15pm, Fri–Sat 6–11.45pm, Sun 6–11pm

Old enamelled bill posters and hanging plants decorate this popular hamburger restaurant. There are nine burgers to choose from, all with interesting names; for example, the 'hen house' has a fried egg topping and the 'Bronx boiger' is 'overflowing with spicy baked beans'. The star of this show is 'Hollywood Bowl's de-luxe cheeseburger' – a hunky half-pounder with a generous topping of melted cheese, lettuce, tomato and pickles smothered in thick mayonnaise. All of them are served in a toasted sesame bun with French fries. Lasagne and barbeque ribs are alternative main courses.

[♫] [P] [S]

BROMYARD
Hereford & Worcester
Map **3** SO65

The Old Penny ✕ 48 High St
☎ (0885) 83227

Open: Wed–Sun 12.30–2pm, Wed–Sat 7–9.15pm

This simple, 17th-century restaurant has exposed beams and white walls. The dining room is divided by an attractive archway. Proprietors Norman and June Williams are known locally for using only best-quality meat and fresh vegetables in their wholesome English meals. Speciality of the house is roast duckling with orange sauce. The budget conscious are advised to stick to the table d'hôte lunch as the dinner menu is over our limit. A typical meal would consist of home-made soup, followed by roast sirloin of beef and apple pie and cream. It is advisable to book in advance.

[C] [S]

BROUGHTON
Lancashire
Map **7** SD53

The Orchard Whittingham La
☎ (0772) 862208

Open: Tue–Sat 12noon–2pm, 7.30–9.30pm, Sun 12noon–2pm

The cluster of buildings which forms 'The Orchard' includes a barn now used for functions. Natural stone walls and beams are a foil for brass, copper, china and pictures, the general effect being neat, bright and cheerful. The set lunches are excellent value, the main course giving several choices including traditional roasts. The à la carte menu offers a wide range of speciality dishes, but may take you over our limit.

[C] [♫] [P]

BUCKFASTLEIGH
Devon
Map **3** SX76

Dart Bridge Inn Totnes Rd
☎ (03644) 2214

Open: Mon–Sun 12noon–2pm, 7–10pm

Just across the road from the River Dart, this mock Tudor inn has pleasant gardens, a sun terrace and a family room. It is less than 100 yards away from the A38 Exeter–Plymouth road. The interior is furnished in pub lounge-bar style. Hot and cold meals are served, the former consisting mainly of grills with chips and peas.

[♫] [P] **VS**

BUDE
Cornwall
Map **2** SS20

Red Post Restaurant Launcells ($3\frac{1}{2}$m E of Bude on A3072) ☎ (028881) 305

Open: Summer Mon–Fri & Sun 9am–10pm, Sat 6.45am–10pm, Winter Mon–Wed 9am–5pm, Fri–Sun 9am–10pm

The restaurant is housed in a converted stable attached to a former coaching inn where there is also an authorised Tourist Information Bureau. A substantial breakfast, a large range of snacks, and cream teas are served. With the exception of some of the steak dishes you can enjoy a full meal within our budget. Children are very welcome here.

[P] **VS**

BUDLEIGH SALTERTON
Devon
Map **3** SY08

The Lobster Pot 16 High St
☎ (03954) 2731

Open: Mon–Sat 10.15am–2pm, 7–10pm, Sun 10.15am–2pm (7–10pm summer only)

Near the sea front you will find this bright, white-painted restaurant with its small-paned windows and gay red canopy. Renowned for its fresh seafood specialities, you can enjoy an array of other dishes too in the comfortable, Georgian-style interior. There is a three-course set lunch and an à la carte menu. Particularly recommended are the pâté with salad garni and mixed seafood and salad. Dinner offers specialities such as scallops à la crème (scallops cooked in white wine sauce), and vegetables are included in the price of the main course.

[C] [♫] [S]

BURFORD
Oxfordshire
Map **4** SP21

Windmill Restaurant Asthall, 3m E of Burford off the A40 ☎ (099382) 2594

Open: Mon–Sun 12noon–2pm, Mon–Sat 7–10pm

This recently-opened restaurant, situated in a six-acre site overlooking the Windrush Valley, is a useful stopping place for travellers. The park offers picnic facilities, and packed meals are available from the restaurant and can either be eaten in the park or taken away. If you prefer to eat in the lovely 18th-century, Cotswold-stone building, the restaurant offers a cold buffet in the summer and a reasonably priced à la carte menu featuring simple dishes such as grilled fish or omelettes. Morning coffee (10am–noon) is available as well as afternoon tea. In the evening the menu is more expensive but represents good value for money.

[C] [P] **VS**

BURLEY
Hampshire
Map **4** SU20

Charcoal's Grill and Bar Burley Manor Hotel ☎ (04253) 3564

Open: Mon–Sun 12noon–2pm, 6.30–10pm

Charcoals is situated in the grounds of the Burley Manor Hotel deep in the heart of the New Forest. A black and white Tudor-style timbered building houses this popular restaurant where you can watch your meal being cooked to perfection on the open char-grill. Aptly named dishes include Eastern Promise (pork kebabs with apricots, mushrooms and tomatoes served with barbecue sauce and rice) and the Midshipman (rainbow trout wrapped in foil and char-grilled). Lamb steaks are also on the menu, unfortunately the sirloin and T-bone steaks are over our limit. There is a good selection of wines and cocktails and real ale is served.

C ♫ P

BURNHAM-ON-CROUCH
Essex
Map **5** TQ99

Boozles 4 Station Rd ☎ (0621) 783167

Open: Tue–Sat 10am–2.30pm, 7.30–10pm, Sun 12.30–2.30pm. Closed Mon

This warm and friendly bistro-style restaurant is recommended for the excellent cold buffet lunch, available Tuesday to Saturday, offering three courses and coffee at a set price within our limit. For the 'not so hungry' the courses are available priced separately. A hot dish is also on the menu. Fresh, local produce is used wherever possible and the service is by friendly young staff supervised by the proprietor Tony Clodd. The excellent à la carte dinner menu is a little over our limit.

C P

BURNLEY
Lancashire
Map **7** SD83

Smackwater Jacks Ormerod St ☎ (0282) 21290

Open: Mon–Sun 11.30am–3pm, 7–11pm

A town centre steak and hamburger joint set in a stone and brick-built cellar. The lighthearted menu is written in brash Americanese – start with fruit juice ('we got orange an' we got tomato') and move on to stuffed baked potatoes or a 'hillbilly chili' – ('the way Pa likes it'). For dessert there's cheesecake 'frigate', fruit salad and various sundaes.

♫ P S

BURNTISLAND
Fife *Fife*
Map **11** NT28

Copper Kettle 144A High St ☎ (0592) 874080

Open: Apr–Sep Mon–Sun 9.30am–10pm, Oct–Mar Tue & Wed only 9.30am–2.30pm

Open throughout the day during the summer the Copper Kettle offers simple but wholesome fare at very reasonable prices. The limited lunch menu includes soup, lamb cutlet with chips and peach Melba, whilst the dinner menu offers more variety with roast lamb and chicken Maryland among the main courses. Morning snacks and High Teas are also available.

♫ P

BURY ST EDMUNDS
Suffolk
Map **5** TL86

The Beefeater Restaurant 27 Angel Hill ☎ (0284) 4224

Open: Tue–Sat 12noon–2pm, 6–12mdnt, Sun 12noon–3pm, 6–11pm

Don't let the name mislead you, this is a Greek restaurant typical of any to be found on the Greek islands – the weather being the only difference! However, you'll hardly miss the sun as you sit amidst the fishing nets and Greek bric-à-brac enjoying the traditional moussaka, kleftiko or dolmadakia. Go for a Greek dish such as fresh squid with rice and salad, rounding off with traditional Greek coffee. The less adventurous may have to pay more for the conventional English dishes; the charcoal-grilled steaks are a credit to proprietor Andreas Paraskeva and his family.

C ♫ P S

Peggotty's Carving Room 30 Guildhall St ☎ (0284) 5444

Open: Tue–Fri 12noon–2pm, 6.45–10pm, Sat 12noon–2pm, 6.30–10.30pm, Sun 12noon–2.30pm

Notice the Dickensian-type exterior with eye-catching red canopies over the windows. Inside, the heavy wooden tables, tapestry-upholstered chairs, brick pillars and sand-coloured walls lined with prints create a cottage-like atmosphere. Starters are served to your table, then, in the carvery style, you take your pick from an array of hot or cold roasts, carved for you by the chef, or proprietor Luigi, and add to this your own selection of vegetables or salad. Roll and butter and sweet are included in the price of the main course with starters and coffee additional. After a good lunch at Peggotty's why not take time to explore Bury Cathedral or the Athenaeum, where Dickens gave two readings.

C ♫ S

BUXTON
Derbyshire
Map **7** SK07

Barbecue 25 Spring Gardens ☎ (0298) 4312

Open: Mon, Tue, Thu–Sun 10am–8pm

This busy restaurant, situated in the centre of town, provides meals all day long. It is pleasantly furnished with local prints on the part-wood-panelled walls. Morning coffee and afternoon tea with cakes and pastries are available and there is a special late breakfast. The set three-course lunch offers a choice of three main dishes. There is a separate à la carte menu and a children's menu.

[C] [🍷]

CAERGEILIOG
Gwynedd
Map **6** SH37

Sportsman's Inn ☎ (0407) 540512

Open: Mon–Sat 12noon–2.30pm, 7–9.30pm, Sun 12noon–2pm, 7.30–9.30pm

This village inn has an open fireplace along with collections of sporting guns and stuffed game. A range of basket and plate meals are available in both bars and most meals are served with either chips or salad. The menu includes home-made steak and kidney pie, scampi and a choice of cold meats.

[P]

CAERNARFON
Gwynedd
Map **6** SH37

Y Felin Wen Pont-rug (2m E of Caernarfon on A4086) ☎ (0286) 3070

Open: Mon–Sun 12noon–3pm, 7–10pm. Closed Mon in winter

Val and Alan Ashcroft are the proprietors of this licensed restaurant which was converted from a 17th-century cottage. Dishes such as mixed grill are available for lunch, whilst the dinner menu includes coq au vin. On Sundays a traditional roast lunch is excellent value.

[♫] [P] [🍷]

The Stables Restaurant and Hotel☆☆☆ ☎ (0286) 830711/830413

Open: Mon–Sun 12noon–1.45pm, 7–9.45pm

Some of the best food that Caernarfon has to offer is to be found at Mrs Jenny Howarth's Stables Restaurant, some three miles outside the town, on the A497 road to Pwllheli. Formerly the stables to Plas Fynnon, the building was very cleverly and tastefully converted for its present use in 1972. The menu is a long and impressive one but the locals, who ought to know, swear by the barbecued spare ribs starter, ham and asparagus mornay, grilled trout with almonds, local lamb chops in wine sauce and pineapple flambé. A table d'hôte menu is also available. Live entertainment is frequently provided in the evenings.

[C] [♫] [P] [🍷]

CALLANDER
Central *Perthshire*
Map **11** NN60

Dalgair House 113–115 Main St ☎ (0877) 30283

Open: Summer Mon–Sun 8am–10pm, winter Mon–Sun 12noon–9pm

This family-run hotel restaurant and cocktail lounge is at the southern end of Callander's busy Main Street. Tasty snacks are available throughout the day in the cocktail lounge, but if you want a more substantial meal then try the three-course lunch or high-tea served in the restaurant. The lunch menu includes cold roast Scotch lamb with salad and home-made rhubarb pie whilst the high-tea menu has a choice of main course served with scones, shortbread, toast and a pot of tea. Both the à la carte and table d'hôte dinner menus are outside our price range.

[P] [S] [🍷]

Pips 23 Ancaster Sq ☎ (0877) 30470

Open: Summer Mon–Sat 9am–9pm, Sun 11am–6pm, Winter Mon–Tue 10am–5pm, Thu–Sun 10am–5pm

This eye-catching little restaurant snuggles in a corner of the square. From the outside, attractive brasswork, tinted windows and a sophisticated striped canopy invite further inspection. The interior is equally striking with white laminated tables and chairs and a bold décor; there is also a picture gallery. Salads and home-baking are the specialities of the house, and desserts are served with lashings of cream. During the summer a fixed-priced menu is available Mon–Sat 6–9pm featuring three or four hot dishes.

[C] [P] [S] [🍷] **VS**

CAMBRIDGE
Cambridgeshire
Map **5** TL45

Eros 25 Petty Cury ☎ (0223) 63420

Open: Mon–Fri 12noon–3pm, 5.30–11pm, Sat–Sun 12noon–11pm

Eros has the atmosphere of a taverna, complete with Greek music, despite very English décor with college arms on panelled walls. The menu is enormous, with fish, omelettes, roasts, grills, salads and a formidable variety of steaks, not to mention Greek, Cypriot and Italian dishes by the dozen. For a satisfying Greek meal, start with taramasalata, followed by sousoukakia and round it off with Grecian-style gâteau.

[C] [♫] [S] [🍷]

The Roof Garden and **The Pentagon** The Arts Theatre, 6 St Edwards Passage ☎ (0223) 355246

Open: Roof Garden: Mon–Sat 9.30am–8pm Pentagon: Mon–Sat 12noon–2pm, 6pm–11.30pm

These self-service restaurants over the Arts Theatre comprise one of the busiest rendezvous in the city. The main dining area of the Roof Garden is light and airy but in fine weather many customers prefer to sit outside on the roof. You can eat here from early morning when a full English breakfast is served, through to the 'theatre supper' of hefty ploughman's, cottage pie, fried chicken in a basket and the like. At the Pentagon a selection of cold buffet dishes are available, with at least three hot dishes. A special item is a two-course lunch.

[C] [S]

University Arms Hotel★★★★ Regent St ☎ (0223) 351241

Open: Mon–Sun 12.30–2pm, 7–9pm

The large ground-floor restaurant of this imposing hotel overlooks the park through windows which depict the arms of the colleges in stained glass. Only by sticking to the table d'hôte menu will you be safe on the budget as an á la carte meal may take you over our limit. You can choose from a menu of traditional dishes such as fried lemon sole, roast leg of pork with apple sauce, or cold ham salad plus a sweet. A simpler lunch may be chosen from the buffet set up in Parker's Lounge, where sandwiches and simple salads, and a selection of cold meats and savouries are available.

C ♬ P S ☘

Varsity Restaurant 35 St Andrew's St ☎ (0223) 56060

Open: Mon–Sun 12noon–3pm, 5.30–11pm

This two-storey Greek restaurant is housed in one of Cambridge's many listed buildings in one of the city centre's not-so-busy streets. The atmosphere is very authentic, with Greek pictures scattered on white-washed walls, an effect which is emphasised by black wooden beams and doors. Food is basically Greek with some French and English dishes. Kebab of the house – two skewers of tenderloin, served with Greek salad and fetta cheese, is one of four speciality dishes. Service is quick and friendly despite the fact that the restaurant seats 105.

S

Wilson's Restaurants 14 Trinity St ☎ (0223) 356845

Open: The Restaurants: Mon–Thu 12noon–3pm, 6–11pm, Fri–Sat 12noon–3pm, 6pm–12mdnt The Granary: Mon–Sat 10.30am–10.30pm, Sun 10.30am–6pm

Wilson's is a fine black and white, 16th century building housing three restaurants. The two restaurants, on the top floors, retain the Tudor style. There is a good choice of starters, desserts and main courses served by waitresses. Light snacks are also available. There is a carvery where the chef will carve beef and pork for Sunday lunch. For a quicker, less expensive meal, try The Granary. A separate entrance takes you into the original cellars and here up to 10 hot dishes are on display. Beef casserole, sweet and sour pork and hot quiches are on offer.

P S

CAMELFORD

Cornwall
Map **2** SX18

Lanteglos Farmhouse Hotel Lanteglos, 1½m SW off the A39 ☎ (0840) 213551

Open: Easter–end Oct, Mon–Sun 11am–2pm, 7–10.30pm

Set in its own grounds, this attractive small hotel offers delicious snacks. They are available in the elegant hotel bar, or in the garden in good weather, at lunchtimes and in the large cellar bar at night. There is a good range of dishes available including pizza and cottage pie. A table d'hôte and an à la carte menu are available in the evening but are generally outside the limits of this guide.

C P ☘

CANNOCK

Staffordshire
Map **7** SJ91

Roman Way Hotel Watling St, Hatherton, 1m SW of Cannock on the A5 ☎ (05435) 72121

Open: Restaurant: Mon–Fri 12.30–2pm, 7.30–10pm, Sat 7.30–10pm, Sun 12.30–2pm, 7.30–9.30pm
Lounge carvery: Mon–Fri 12.15–2.15pm, 6–8.30pm, Sat 12.15–2.15pm

This modern hotel complex offers diners a choice of menus in the restaurant and the lounge carvery. In the restaurant a three-course table d'hôte menu could offer melon and orange cocktail, veal Milanaise and gâteau. If you prefer a simpler meal, then try the lounge carvery, which offers a range of home-made dishes including curry and steak and kidney pie. There is also a comprehensive buffet.

C ♬ P ☘ **VS**

CANTERBURY

Kent
Map **5** TR15

Alberry's Wine and Food Bar 38 St Margarets St ☎ (0227) 52378

Open: Mon–Sat 12noon–2.30pm, 6.30–12mdnt (11pm Tue). Closed Sun

A genuine Roman flint wall in the basement bar is the talking point of this establishment, where for the price of a simple meal you buy a whole evening of entertainment. Jazz and rock musicians often play beneath the arched ceilings. A good selection of wholesome food includes kidneys in sherry sauce with rice, or chunky steak and kidney pie. There is a good choice of sweets.

C ♬ P S

CARDIFF

South Glamorgan
Map **3** ST17

The Himalaya Restaurant 24 Wellfield Rd ☎ (0222) 491722

Open: Mon–Sun 12noon–3pm, 6pm–2am

'The best Indian food in Cardiff' is the local verdict on Bakshi Suleman's restaurant. The Himalaya has a vaguely Oriental décor. Biriani dishes, chicken curries and meat or prawn curries are included on the menu. Be warned: the helpings are enormous.

C ♬ S ☘ **VS**

See advertisement on page 56

Savastano's 302 North Rd ☎ (0222) 30270

Open: Mon–Sat 12noon–2.30pm, 7–11.30pm, Thu–Sat 12mdnt

Giacomo Savastano's restaurant doesn't strike one as particularly Italian, for the décor is plain and the furniture pine. But his food is very Italian, very good and – as Italian restaurants go – extremely reasonably priced. The menu is extensive and includes pasta, fish, chicken and steak dishes, or try veal Nizzarda – escalope of veal dipped in egg and cheese and cooked in butter. Service is very efficient at this restaurant.

Ye Olde Wine Shoppe Wyndham Arcade, St Mary St ☎ (0222) 29876

Open: Mon–Sat 12noon–2.30pm, 7–11pm

Don't be put off by the name. This must be the best-stocked wine bar in Cardiff and well worth a visit, for its friendly bars and bright little bistro. The downstairs bar and bistro serve the same food at the same prices – the menu features three course meals from 10 different countries. The Hungarian meal consists of mixed salamis and pickles, lamb goulash, and cream cheese and nut pancake. The Italian meal includes minestrone soup, lasagne, and cassata ice-cream. Whilst the above full meals are served in the restaurant any single dish can be served as a snack in the bar.

♬ P S

Yr Ystafell Gymraeg 74 Whitchurch Rd ☎ (0222) 42317

Open: Mon–Fri 12noon–2pm, 7–11.30pm, Sat 7–11.30pm

Yr Ystafell Gymraeg (The Welsh Room to you) is just that, with its Welsh-weave drapes, Welsh tapestry curtains, Welsh Tourist Board posters, the Welsh dresser and a Welsh menu (with English subtitles). A new bar was added in 1983 to give diners more room. The owners sound Italian and, indeed, proprietor Umberto Palladino is, but his wife is just about as Welsh as it is possible to be. Starters include Penclawdd Cockles and there are a range of poultry dishes, including chicken Snowdonia. Home-made fruit pies, gâteaux and trifle are also available.

C ☘

See advertisement on page 57

CARDIGAN

Dyfed
Map **2** SN14

The Bell Hotel Pendre ☎ (0239) 612629

Open: Mon–Sat 12noon–2pm, 7–9pm

Malcolm and Jenny Wood have a good lunchtime trade at The Bell. They offer a wide range of basket and plate meals, and the evening menu gives a considerable choice of main courses.

P S ☘

The Black Lion Hotel High St ☎ (0239) 612532

Open: Mon–Sat 12noon–2.30pm, 8–10pm

Inglenook fireplaces, exposed beams and stone walls set the scene at the Black Lion. You can have a satisfying meal in the Linenfold Bar (rounded off by a speciality ice-cream) and perhaps even try a cocktail or two. Drivers are catered for with non-alcoholic wine and lager, and tea, coffee or hot chocolate served at the bar. Try the meals in baskets which are served in the lounge.

[♬] [S] [🍷]

Cliff Hotel★★★ Gwbert-on-Sea
☎ (0239) 613241/613242/612517

Open: Mon–Sun 12.45–2pm, 7–9pm

This restaurant offers an interesting choice of menu but unfortunately they are priced over our limit. The Buttery menu includes locally-caught sewin (a type of salmon) and there is a good choice of starters and sweets.

[C] [♬] [P] [🍷]

CARLISLE
Cumbria
Map **11** NY35

The Central Hotel★★ Victoria Viaduct
☎ (0228) 20256

Open: Mon–Sun 12noon–2pm, 7–9pm

A comfortable and popular Greenall Whitley hotel managed with great style by Stanley Cohen. Bar lunch here is excellent with a good ploughman's, a wide range of cold and hot dishes and specials including scampi. The table d'hôte dinner is outside our range.

[C] [♬] [P] [S] [🍷] **VS**

The Citadel Restaurant 77–79 English St ☎ (0228) 21298

Open: Mon–Sat 11.30am–10.30pm, Sun normal licensing hours

Is this the ideal haunt? Certainly the friendly ghosts keep coming back for more. So, it seems, do the patrons who claim to have seen several unearthly apparitions in this 100-year-old citadel, including a wizened old lady and a chap in 18th-century garb. The restaurant is situated above a tangle of ancient passageways which once led to the cathedral and old jail. Now it's handy for the station and shops. Warm and bright, it serves straightforward no-nonsense meals at fairly reasonable prices. Particularly good value are a three-course shopper's lunch including coffee, and the à la carte seafood dishes.

[C] [♬] [P] [S] [🍷]

The Crown and Mitre★★★ English St
☎ (0228) 25491

Open: Restaurant Mon–Fri 12.30–2.30pm, Mon–Sat 6.30–10pm

The Restaurant, within the Crown and Mitre Hotel, offers table d'hôte and a full à la carte menu with main courses including lamb cutlets, pork chops and a selection of Cumberland specialities. A typical sweet would be gâteau or ice cream. There are two bars; the Peace and Plenty has a substantial lunch bar menu.

[C] [♬] [P] [S] [🍷] **VS**

Cumbrian Hotel Court Sq
☎ (0228) 31951

Open during normal licensing hours. Cumbrian Carver Restaurant: Mon–Sun 12noon–2pm, 7–10pm; Cumbrian Kitchen: summer Mon–Sun 9.30am–9.30pm; winter Mon–Sun 10am–8pm.

The Cumbrian Carver offers a two-course lunch in very elegant surroundings. Choose one of the succulent roasts at the Carving Table and either a starter or sweet from the menu. There is a hot dish of the day as an alternative. The three-course dinner menu is over our limit. The Cumbrian Kitchen is a different matter altogether offering snacks and substantial meals. Bar snacks are available at lunchtime.

[C] [P] [S] [🍷]

The Malt Shovel Rickergate
☎ (0228) 34095

Open: during normal licensing hours, Brew House Restaurant Mon–Sat 12noon–2pm, 7.30–9.30pm

The Brew House Restaurant has a most appropriate décor of malt sacks and malt shovels and is very bright and clean, with comfortable chairs and a relaxed, intimate atmosphere. Dishes on the lunch menu range from a ploughman's to steak. But the Malt Shovel is at its best in the evening, with 19 starters and a superb selection of fish dishes, poultry, roasts, grills and entrées. Incidentally, Scottish bard Robert Burns slept at the Malt Shovel, we are told. It's a pity he missed the food.

[C] [P] [S]

CARMARTHEN
Dyfed
Map **2** SN42

The Old Curiosity 20A King St
☎ (0267) 232384

Open: Mon–Sat 9.30am–5pm

The Old Curiosity is much, much more than a convenient place for a coffee, a snack, or a meal. The Indian salad contains brown rice, not white, and vegetarians may choose from a number of appetising dishes. The seafood salad is excellent, and omelettes include mushroom, ham or chicken. 'Gap fillers' include curry butter prawns and quiches.

[S]

Queensway Restaurant Queen St
☎ (0267) 5631

Open: Mon–Sat 10am–2.30pm, 6.30–11pm

This ground-floor restaurant serves traditional roast lunches and grills, with a selection of help-yourself salads and, on certain days, a carvery. The first-floor wine bar serves a selection of bistro-type meals such as Lasagne, home-made pies and a wide selection of salads and sweets.

[C]

CARNOUSTIE
Tayside *Angus*
Map **12** NO53

Glencoe Hotel★★ Links Parade
☎ (0241) 53273

Open: Mon–Sun 12noon–2pm, 7.30–9pm

The name Carnoustie is synonymous with golf, and this neat, family hotel has the distinction of overlooking the famous championship golf-course. Table lamps and soft music create a soothing atmosphere in the dining room, and the patio extension provides an ideal eating place with views of the golf-course. A table d'hôte dinner of five courses with coffee incorporates the best local produce available though it is priced a little over our limit. Bar lunches are served and as well as soup and sandwiches there is also a 'hot dish of day' which could be a casserole or curry.

[C] [P] **VS**

CARTMEL
Cumbria
Map **7** SD37

Priory Hotel★ The Square
☎ (044854) 267

Open: Mar–Nov: bar lunch: Tue–Sat 12noon–2pm

This delightful stone-built hotel, close to the Priory, offers a good variety of snacks and more substantial meals on the bar lunch menu. The owners, Mr and Mrs Dawson, ably assisted by Mum and Dad, aim to provide good home-cooking, using the best ingredients. The menu includes excellent home-made soup, Cumberland sausages and omelettes. The dinner menu, though tempting, is too expensive for us.

[C] [P]

CASTLE DONINGTON
Derbyshire
Map **8** SK42

Barbeque Bar, Priest House Hotel
Kings Mills ☎ Derby (0332) 810649 (2m W of Castle Donington)

Open: Mon–Sun 12noon–2pm, 7–10pm (Barbeque Bar closed Mon evening and Sun lunchtime)

The Barbeque Bar forms part of the Priest House Hotel, at the historic beauty spot of Kings Mills on the River Trent. Starters are not served in the bar, and main courses consist of quiche, ribs with barbecue sauce, grilled trout, chicken or steak all served with jacket potato or chips, peas and salad. There is a limited choice of sweets. Meals for children – sausages and burgers, both served with chips – are on the menu. Bar snacks are always available and the Riverside Restaurant offers three-course meals.

[C] [P]

CASTLETON
Derbyshire
Map **7** SE18

The Castle Hotel and Restaurant
☎ (0433) 20578

Open: Mon–Thu, Sun 12noon–2pm, 7–10pm, Fri–Sat 12noon–2pm, 7–10.30pm

Within the Peak District National Park and in the village centre, is this stone-built 17th-century coaching inn, its interior a wealth of exposed stonework and beams. Excellent table d'hôte menus operate for lunch and dinner, though the dinner menu is priced a little over our limit. The lunch menu lists over 25 starters including pâté-filled mushrooms in batter. Four roasts head the long line of main dishes along with loin of pork in spiced apricot and wine sauce. A selection of sweets on the trolley are all served with fresh cream.

[C] [P]

CASTLETOWN
Isle of Man
Map **6** SC26

Chabus Cellar 21 Bank St
☎ (0624) 823527

Open: Tue–Sat 12noon–2.30pm, 7–10pm, Sun 12noon–2.30pm. Closed Mon.

This popular bistro/wine bar, which is situated near the harbour, has pictures, brasses, pot plants and posters to add to the 'olde worlde' atmosphere. The menu is chalked on a blackboard and there are five main courses to choose from – all home-made and brought to your table. A typical three-course meal would be French onion soup, lasagne and lemon cheesecake. There is a 10 per cent service charge.

[♫] [P] [⌂]

CHAILEY
East Sussex
Map **5** TQ31

The Five Bells on A275 6m N of Lewes
☎ (082572) 2259

Open: Mon–Sat 12noon–2.30pm, 7–10.30pm, Sun 12noon–2pm.

This attractive 15th-century pub stands within its own gardens. The restaurant offers an impressive cold buffet of succulent cold meats, pies, pâtés and quiches. Hot dishes are also on the menu – mainly chicken, fish and gammon all served with french fries and salad garnish, the steaks are priced over our limit. There is a good range of wines to choose from and wine is also available by the glass.

[♫] [P] [⌂]

CHELMSFORD
Essex
Map **5** TL70

Corks 34a Moulsham St ☎ (0245) 58733

Open: Mon–Sat 12noon–2.30pm, 6–11pm, Sun 7–10.30pm

Situated opposite the AA office, this trendy wine bar is a popular place for a good meal or informal drink and chat. A brown-painted window front and the Tudor beams beyond entice you over the threshold, where a tempting menu chalked on the ubiquitous plât du jour blackboard announces dishes such as moussake and salad, or turkey pie and pâté. The competent staff is led by Michael Dunbar who is always on hand to extend a friendly welcome to his guests.

[C] [♫] [P] [S]

Pizza Pasta Rendevous 44 Moulsham Rd ☎ (0245) 352245

Open: Mon–Sat 12noon–2.30pm, 6–10.30pm

A decorative brown awning and Venetian blinds adorn this highly original-looking Italian restaurant and garden terrace. The simple but appetising menu specialises in the pizzas and pastas anticipated. An imaginative pizza is napoletana, with mozzarella cheese, tomatoes, capers, anchovies and olives. Pastas include delicious fetuccine mastriciana (noodles with tomato, onion and bacon). Selection of sweets is good with home-made cheesecake and strudel. A 'Happy Family Menu' is available Mon–Fri for lunch, and dinner with reductions for children under 10.

[C] [P] [S] [⌂] **VS**

CHELTENHAM
Gloucestershire
Map **3** SO92

Forrest's Wine Bar Imperial La
☎ (0242) 38001

Open: Mon–Sat 10.30am–2.30pm, 6–10.30pm

Forrest's is tucked away in Imperial Lane just behind Habitat. The large, high-ceilinged ground-floor premises were formerly a bakery but have been cleverly adapted, with low-slung pendant lights and intimate eating areas cordoned off by waist-high walls. There are over 20 wines sold by the glass here at reasonable prices. The menu changes daily but a typical one might well include a choice of soups, a continental ploughman's (with sausages) and a choice of three enticing plats du jour such as lamb kebabs with spiced rice and salad.

[♫] [P] [S]

Mister Tsang✕ 63 Winchcombe St
☎ (0242) 38727

Open: Mon 5–11.30pm, Tue–Fri 12noon–2pm, 5–11.30pm, Sat 12noon–12mdnt

Food 'to indulge the palate and encourage good health' is what Mister Tsang and his family aim to provide. We were impressed by the nutritious and tasty house hors d'oeuvres: beef in black bean sauce and king prawns with ginger and spring onions. To keep within the budget and do justice to the extensive menu, go with a friend or three! The hot spiced fillet steak is very tasty and Mister Tsang's 'Introduction to True Cantonese Cuisine' for two or more people offers a good variety at a reasonable price.

[C] [S] [⌂]

Montpellier Wine Bar and Bistro
Bayshill Lodge, Montpellier St
☎ (0242) 27774

Open: Mon–Sat 12noon–2.30pm, 6–10.30pm, 11pm Fri–Sat, Sun 7–10.30pm

This imposing Regency building behind the Montpellier Rotunda has been converted from a long-established grocer's shop into a ground-floor wine bar and cellar bistro. There is a choice of 10 or so wines which are sold by the glass. Notice boards display the daily menu, which includes hot soup among the dozen or so starters, a hot speciality dish of the day, a variety of pies, smoked meats and fish, interesting salads, and tempting sweets.

[C] [♫] [P] [S] [⌂]

CHEPSTOW
Gwent
Map **3** ST59

Castle View Hotel★★ Bridge St
☎ (02912) 70349

Open: Mon–Sat 12.15–2pm, 6.30–9pm, Sun 12.15–1.45pm, 6.30–8.30pm and normal licensing hours

As its name suggests this charming, ivy-clad hotel is oppostie Chepstow Castle. Meals in the bar include imaginative home-made soup such as salmon and cucumber. Prawns au gratin is a popular main course choice so is fresh Wye salmon with salad. Vegetarians are also catered for. The restaurant menu is out of our price range.

[C] [P] [S] **VS**

The First Hurdle 9 Upper Church St
☎ (02912) 2189

Open: Mon–Sat 12noon–9pm

Just off Chepstow's town centre is this small hotel, immediately attractive because of its Edwardian furniture and pretty, soft furnishings. At lunchtime, roast joints carved hot from the oven represent good value, as well as Welsh lamb chops and daily specials such as home-made steak and kidney pie or curry. In the evening diners can choose from the French menu, where a good choice would be French onion soup, followed by trout with almonds and fresh vegetables, and a sweet from the trolley, or the grill menu which includes prawn cocktail, gammon with pineapple, salad, peas and chips.

[C] [P] [S]

The Grape Escape 24 St Mary St
☎ (02912) 70959

Open: Mon–Sat 10am–3pm, 5.30–11pm, Sun 12noon–2pm, 7–10.30pm

This small and friendly wine bar and bistro is situated in the heart of this historic town. The bar is on the ground floor and the informal first-floor dining room offers inexpensive home-made dishes served by local waitresses. Home-made sausages and kebabs in barbecue sauce are on the menu along with home-made soups and roasts. The set two-course lunch with coffee offers exceptional value. An extensive and well balanced wine list includes wines from New Zealand, Lebanon and Greece.

[C] [♫] [P] [S]

CHESTER

Cheshire
Map **7** SJ46

The Carriage Restaurant Mercia Sq, Frodsham St ☎ (0244) 23469

Open: Mon–Sat 12noon–2.30pm, 5.30–10.30pm, Sat 5–11pm, Sun 5–9pm. Summer only

This modern glass-fronted restaurant, with its separate wine bar, is to be found in a shopping precinct close to the city walls. The interior is of unusual design with iron and wood arches forming banquettes at one end of the room and an open-plan area with mock-Gothic ceiling at the other. The restaurant also boasts two refurbished carriages. An extensive menu offers a three-course meal, with coffee within our price range. To be on the safe side however, choose from the excellent selection on the more modestly priced set menu: chicken provençale and Cumberland grill are among the main dishes. There is a delicious range of puddings all freshly-made on the premises.

[C] [P] [S] **VS**

Claverton's Wine Bar Lower Bridge St
☎ (0244) 319760

Open: Mon–Sat 12noon–2.30pm, 5.30–10.30pm, Sun 12noon–1.45pm, 7–10.30pm

Come early to this popular basement wine bar, as it's sure to be busy, especially in the evenings. The white rough-cast walls, stone floors and polished tables with white cloths give a bright, clean appearance, enhanced by the tempting array of food. You could choose your meal from the cold table or you might try the pork goulash. There is a good range of home-made starters and desserts. On a fine day you can sip your wine on the patio and watch the world go by.

The Courtyard✕✕ 13 St Werburgh St
☎ (0244) 21447

Open: Mon–Sat 10.30am–2.30pm, 7–10pm

This popular gourmet restaurant is set round a pretty courtyard, within the city walls and the sound of the Cathedral bells. Upstairs at lunchtime a 'help yourself' smørgasbrød operates and there are also an à la carte menu and a set three-course menu to choose from, with roast chicken and grilled trout as typical main courses. Dinner offers more adventurous dishes on the à la carte menu but the hot and cold buffet in the evening Bistro is out of our price range.

[C] [♫]

The Farmhouse 9–13 Northgate St
☎ (0244) 311332

Open: Mon–Sat 9am–6pm

This friendly mid-city eaterie, situated above Millet's camping stores, has a pine-equipped interior interspersed with oodles of pot plants. The daily-changing choice of dishes is chalked up on a blackboard, but there's always a very good salad selection and hot dishes such as steak and kidney pie, all reasonably priced. You should find this farmhouse-style kitchen an economical haven.

[P]

The Gallery 24 Paddock Row
☎ (0244) 47202

Open: Mon–Sat 12noon–2.15pm, Tue–Sat 6.30–9.30pm

Owner Edward Jones has created a refreshingly-different eating place along the lines of a conservatory with earthy brown carpets and tree-green walls. A beautiful array of pot plants adds to the atmosphere. Meals too are a little out of the ordinary. Soup of the day is laced with sherry and cream and main dishes include asparagus and cheese-filled crêpes and rainbow trout – pan fried with almonds and cream. Situated at one end of one of Chester's Rows in the centre of town it is also the ideal rendezvous for shoppers.

[♫] [P] [S]

Maison Romano 51 Lower Bridge St
☎ (0244) 20841

Open: Mon–Sat 11.30am–2.30pm, 5.30–11.30pm, Sun 12noon–2pm, 7–11pm

The lower-ground-floor restaurant is part of a city-centre hotel and caters for English, French, Italian and Spanish tastes. The three-course lunch represents excellent value for money. Our inspector had the lasagne and was suitably impressed. The à la carte menu has an extensive list of dishes, but many will take you over our limit.

[C] [♫] [P] **VS**

Pierre Griffe Wine Bar 4–6 Mercia Sq
☎ (0244) 312635

Open: Mon–Fri 11.30am–3pm, 5.30–11pm, Sat 11am–3pm, 5.30–11pm, Sun 12noon–2pm, 7–11pm, Sun in summer only

Close to the Cathedral, this very popular wine bar has brown walls and carpeting which give emphasis to the attractive pine furniture. A long bar counter has a good display of salads and meats. The menu is displayed on a blackboard and three courses can easily be savoured well within our price limit. Start with French onion soup, then try pork goulash with rice, Malayan chicken salad or minced beef curry. Cheesecake and gâteau are popular desserts.

[P] [S]

Sir Edward's Wine Bar 30 Bridge St
☎ (0244) 24921

Open: Mon–Sat 12noon–2.30pm, 6.30–10.30pm, 11pm Fri & Sat

This cosy little wine bar enjoys an attractive situation on street level beneath one of Chester's famous 'Rows'. Inside, walls of open brick-work, 200-year-old wood panelling and dark paintwork are adorned with old books, posters and pots. Green gingham tablecloths and flickering candles contribute to the intimate atmosphere and enhance the simple décor. A good selection of starters includes avocado, pâté and home-made soup (with fresh ingredients). A typical meal would be corn-on-the-cob (hors d'oeuvres), gammon steak with peaches and side salad, gâteau and coffee. Service is at the customer's discretion. As one would expect from a wine bar, there is a comprehensive range of wines available with red, white or rosé house wine.

[C] [♫] [P] [S]

CHICHESTER
West Sussex
Map **4** SU80

The Coffee House 4 West St
☎ (0243) 784799

Open: Mon–Sat 10am–5.30pm, (half day Thu during Winter months)

Emphasis here is upon simple, no-nonsense food made from fresh ingredients and cooked on the premises. Plats du jour include reasonably priced shrimp or chicken salads. Three-egg plain omelettes are also available, as is Welsh rarebit. The licensed restaurant menu is restricted but is excellent value, particularly the cold buffet dishes.

[S]

Jason's Bistro Cooper St, off South St
☎ (0243) 783158

Open: Mon–Sun 12noon–2pm, 7–10.30pm

Tucked away in Chichester's Cooper Street is Jason's Bistro, where a team of staff headed by Gerhard and Enid Boesser serve bistro-style lunches and dinners in this spacious and imaginatively-modernised old outhouse building. Starters include home-made soup with hot garlic bread, or try the 'Chef's Dish of the Day' which is very reasonably priced.

[♫] [S]

Micawber's Kitchen 13 South St
☎ (0243) 786989

Open: Mon–Sat 11.30am–3pm, 6–10.30pm, Sun 11.30–3pm, closed Sun in Winter

Named after the character in Charles Dickens' novel, *David Copperfield*, this restaurant has a warm and friendly atmosphere. The dinner menu differs very slightly from the luncheon nenu and fish dishes are a feature on both, as starters and as main courses. Try Jamaican grapefruit, baked trout with fresh rosemary and apple pie.

[P] [🍷]

CHIDDINGFOLD
Surrey
Map **4** SU93

The Crown Inn Bistro The Village Green
☎ (042879) 2255/6

Open: Mon–Sun 8am–10pm

One of the oldest inns in England's history, The Crown was built circa 1285. It is listed here mainly for the Bistro Family Restaurant which has an inglenook fireplace, genuine oak beams and linenfold panelling. The bistro is open for breakfast, luncheon, afternoon tea and dinner. The menu includes snacks, a cold buffet, a monthly set menu comprising three courses, and a range of dishes which could include stilton and walnut pâté, braised pigeon and home-made apple strudel. On summer weekends, weather permitting, there is a barbecue in the courtyard.

[P] [🍷] **VS**

CHIPPENHAM
Wiltshire
Map **3** ST97

The Lysley Arms Pewsham
☎ (0249) 652864 (on A4 2m SW of Chippenham)

Open: Mon–Sun 12noon–2pm, 7–10.30pm (10pm Sun)

This pleasant whitewashed inn, dating from 1750, is run by Peter and Joy Reeves who offer a good range of bar meals. Boiled beef and carrots, braised oxtail and shepherd's pie are on the menu along with fish, curries, basket meals, grills and salads. Starters and sweets are also available if you want a three-course meal. The à la carte meals in the restaurant are a little expensive for this guide, but the three-course Sunday lunch is within our limit and represents excellent value for money.

[C] [♫] [P] [🍷] **VS**

The Rowden Arms Bath Rd
☎ (0249) 3870

Open: Mon–Thu 12noon–2pm, 7–10pm, Fri–Sat 12noon–2pm, 7–10.30pm, Sun 12noon–1.30pm, Summer only Sun 7–10pm

On the main Bath Road out of Chippenham is this attractive, modern pub with a colourful painted farmhouse wagon in the forecourt. You can sip cocktails in the comfortable lounge bar while surveying the very extensive menu offering freshly-prepared food. A selection of 14 starters ranges from soup of the day to more substantial hors-d'oeuvres. Fish dishes, grills, salads and specialities, such as loin of pork Marsala are available for the main course and there is an impressive choice of sweets at a variety of prices.

[C] [P] [🍷]

White Hart Inn Ford ☎ (0249) 782213
Off A420 Bristol/Chippenham on slip road to Colerne

Open: Mon–Sun 12noon–2pm, 7.30–9.30pm

Idylically situated beside a trout stream and overlooking the lush Weavern valley, this 16th-century stone-built pub is the epitome of Olde Englande. Low, beamed ceilings, log fires and suits of armour set the scene, while Ken Gardner, Fleet Street journalist and writer, personally attends to the food preparation. Home-cooked ham-on-the-bone and steak and kidney pie are served in the Buttery or you can savour locally caught trout. Some dishes from the à la carte menu could be sampled within the budget.

[P]

CHIPPING SODBURY
Avon
Map **3** ST78

The Lawns Inn Church Rd, Yate
☎ (0454) 314367

Open: Bar snacks: Mon–Fri 12noon–1.45pm, 7.30–9.30pm (10pm on Fri, 10.30pm on Sat). Sun 12noon–1.45pm

Part of the Lawns is Jacobean – built in 1625. It is a popular eating place in lovely surroundings. The restaurant boasts authentic period plasterwork which complements the comfortable modern furniture; the accent here is mainly on grills. A bright little buttery offers a wide range of hot or cold snacks including cottage pie and lasagne.

[P]

CHUDLEIGH
Devon
Map **3** SX87

The Wheel Craft Centre Restaurant
Clifford St ☎ (0626) 853255

Open: Mon–Sun 10am–5.30pm (please ring for evening bookings)

Created on the site of the original Town Mills which were used to grind corn, the Wheel Craft Centre has a restored watermill complete with working wheel. Visitors can watch the group of craftsmen and women at work and browse around the wholefood and craft shops which form part of the centre. The restaurant offers a wide variety of home-made snacks and meals using fresh local produce. Quiches, pasta dishes, omelettes, salads and a tempting range of vegetarian dishes are available along with afternoon cream teas. During the summer you can enjoy your meal outside. The restaurant is licensed.

[P] [🍷]

CHURCH STRETTON
Shropshire
Map **7** SO49

The Studio 59 High St ☎ (0694) 722672

Open: Summer Mon–Sat 12noon–2pm, 7.30–10pm, Winter Mon 7.30–10pm, Tue–Sat 12noon–2pm, 7.30–10pm

After housing a potter's studio earlier this century, part of this row of 300-year-old white-painted cottages has reverted to its former business of hospitality. For in the days when there were reputedly more pubs than houses in Church Stretton, the 'studio' was an inn. Inside is a small, cosy bar and a dining room with an atmosphere of clean simplicity. The standard lunch menu is excellent value, and features home-made steak and kidney pie. The more exciting dinner à la carte has tempting specialities together with more conventional dishes, but is likely to break the budget.

[C] [♫] [P] [S] [🍷]

CINDERFORD
Gloucestershire
Map **3** SO61

The White Hart Hotel Restaurant and Bistro St White's Rd, Ruspidge
☎ (0594) 23139

Open: Mon–Sun 12.15–2pm, 7.30–9.45pm

Meals can be taken in the restaurant or bistro. An extensive à la carte menu features the popular Forester's Grill. The cold table in the bistro has meats and interesting salads which you serve yourself. A snack menu includes Californian salad (chicken, sweetcorn and home-cooked ham with lightly curried mayonnaise) and hot dishes such as chili con carne. Traditional Sunday lunch is available.

[P]

CIRENCESTER
Gloucestershire
Map **4** SP00

Shepherd's Wine Bar and Coffee House Market Pl ☎ (0285) 2680

Open: Mon–Sat 10.30am–3pm, 7.30–11pm, Sun 12noon–2pm, 7–11pm

This Dickensian-style wine bar in this popular market town serves fresh food in a relaxed atmosphere. Main courses include a plate of finest Alderton ham off the bone and game pie. Raspberry, hazelnut and Jersey cream meringue is a delicious dessert. A special feature in the evenings are the cheese and meat fondue meals.

[P]

CLAYWORTH
Nottinghamshire
Map **8** SK78

Blacksmith's Arms Town St (off A631 Gainsborough/Bawtry road)
☎ (0777) 817348

Open: Bar snacks Tue–Sat 12noon–2pm, 7–9.30pm, restaurant Mon–Sun 12noon–2pm, 7pm–closes at proprietor's discretion.

This traditional country village inn is 150 years old, and as the name suggests it was once a blacksmith's forge. The proprietors, Paul and Janet Langhorne, offer a good selection of bar snacks including pizzas, grilled gammon and a ploughman's lunch which are served in the bar and lounge areas. The restaurant has its own cocktail bar but the wide range of plain dishes are mainly outside the scope of this guide.

[P]

CLEARWELL
Gloucestershire
Map **3** SO50

The Wyndham Arms✕ Clearwell
☎ (0594) 33666

Open: Tue–Sat 12noon–2pm, 7–10pm, Sun 12noon–2pm, 7–9.30pm

Built in 1340, in the centre of the ancient Dean Forest village of Clearwell, this picturesque inn has long been renowned for the excellence of food served in the à la carte restaurant. The Wyndham Arms has also gained an enviable reputation for satisfying bar snacks and for appetising meals in the Grill Room. Bar snacks include whitebait and mushrooms tartare, whilst fresh local trout and pork chop are available in the Grill Room. A three-course lunch of the day is good value and the main courses are offered separately.

[C] [P]

CLEETHORPES
Humberside
Map **8** TA30

Commodore Restaurant, The Lifeboat Hotel★★ Promenade Kingsway
☎ (0472) 697272

Open: Mon–Fri 12noon–2pm, 6.30–10.15pm, Sat–Sun 6.30–10.15pm

The Lifeboat Hotel overlooks the North Sea, so the lounge bar, where you can sip an aperitif and have a quick meal, such as lamb cutlets and vegetables or just a snack, has a nautical theme. The restaurant, with contrasting white chipboard décor and dark wooden cubicles under a beamed ceiling, also has nautical pictures and fittings. A special table d'hôte menu operates from Mondays to Fridays – you can enjoy soup, pork casserole or gammon steak, for example, followed by a sweet from the trolley. There is also an à la carte menu, but it is beyond our price range.

C P S ☕

CLENT
Hereford & Worcester
Map **7** SO97
Four Stones Adams Hill
☎ (0562) 883260

Open: Tue–Sat 12.30–2.30pm, 7–11.30pm, Sun 12.30–2.30pm

In the heart of the scenic Clent Hills, just south of the A456 between Kidderminster and Halesowen, is this quaint little bow-window-fronted cottage which has been converted into a country-style restaurant. Dark wooden beams, posts and horsebrasses complete the rural atmosphere. Here you may enjoy a set thrre-course lunch which could include soup of the day, a choice of roasts and a home-made dessert at a very reasonable price. The à la carte menu is much more extensive, and provided you avoid the Chef's Specials, you should be able to have a feast within our budget.

♫ P ☕

CLEVEDON
Avon
Map **3** ST47
Mon Plaisir Restaurant 32–34 Hill Rd
☎ (0272) 872307

Open: Mon–Sat 12noon–2pm, 7–10pm

For Mr Luis Moran and his staff 'Mon Plaisir' is certainly the operative phrase, for here nothing is too much trouble and with their warm, friendly welcome they hope to make eating here 'your pleasure' too. You will dine in comfort at this Victorian house, set just off the sea front, where well-prepared food is served in generous portions. The three-course set lunch (with a choice of five main courses) is excellent value. In the evening a three-course dinner with a choice of sweets and starters, and a main course such as steak chasseur, gammon or sirloin steak and all the trimmings will still come within our limit.

P

CLEVELEYS
Lancashire
Map **7** SD34
Savoy Grill 6 Bispham Rd
☎ (0253) 853864

Open: Summer Sun–Mon 11.30am–7pm, Tue 11.30am–8.30pm, Wed–Sat 11.30am–10pm, Winter Tue–Fri 11.30am–7pm, Sat–Sun 11.30am–9pm

A popular, corner-house restaurant near the seafront, the Savoy Grill is well-known for its friendly atmosphere and unpretentious food. Soups and pies are all home-made by proprietor Mrs Dorothy Richardson, and a set three-course meal could include steak and mushroom pie or a roast as the main course. From 6pm each evening a three-course 8oz steak meal is available. A special children's menu lists old favourites such as fish fingers, beefburgers or roast beef though apart from these budget meals, a full à la carte also operates.

P S ☕

COLCHESTER
Essex
Map **5** TM02
Bistro 9 9 North Hill ☎ (0206) 76466

Open: Tue–Sat 12noon–1.45pm, 7–10.45pm

This small bistro has a short menu of home-made dishes served with fresh vegetables and home-made bread. It will be easier to keep within budget in the basement, where substantial 'snacks' are served. Home-made soup and bread, the hot dish of the day (such as moussaka or chili con carne), and a pudding from the à la carte menu – try the brown bread ice cream – will make a satisfying meal. The bistro always offers a vegetarian dish of the day and on Saturdays there is a set lunch of two courses and coffee. The service by friendly waitresses is guaranteed to please, as is the pleasantly informal atmosphere, the large refectory tables (you may have to share), and pretty country décor.

C S [wine] **VS**

Pippins 82A East Hill ☎ (0206) 866860

Open: Mon 12noon-1.45pm Tue–Fri 12noon-1.45pm, 7.15–9.30pm, Sat 7.15–9.30pm. Closed Sun

The young staff in this elegant and comfortable restaurant are ably supervised by 'Morph' the manager. Pippins provides excellent fresh food at very reasonable prices. All the first courses (try stuffed mushrooms or whole prawns) are served, in larger portions, as main courses. The regular main courses offer a range of imaginative dishes including cushion of crab – delicious puff pastry filled with crab and served with a cucumber dressing.

P [wine]

Wm Scragg'sXX 2 North Hill
☎ (0206) 41111
Open: Mon–Sat 12noon–2.15pm, 7–10.30pm

This elegant seafood restaurant bears the name of the journeyman bricklayer who bought the premises in 1832, and lived there peacefully until the ripe old age of 78. Many of the appetising dishes come dangerously near to our limit, a couple of the cheaper ones being fried scampi and poached skate. However, a fine selection of bar snacks is available; try the crab mousse with salad or smoked mackerel, and there is a good choice of inexpensive sandwiches such as prawn and lettuce.

C

COLEFORD
Devon
Map **3** SS70

The New Inn 4m NW of Crediton on A377
☎ (03634) 242
Open: Mon–Sat 11am–2pm, 6–11pm, Sun 12noon–2pm, 6–10.30pm closes ½hr earlier winter evenings Mon–Thu

This 13th-century residential free-house with a thatched roof and old beams offers the unique charm of a country inn. It is set in an unspoilt Devonshire village. Lunchtime bar snacks are very reasonably priced and a meal chosen from this menu could include soup followed by sirloin steak and cheesecake. But if you want something more simple try the ploughman's lunch or ham salad with chips. In fine weather the food can be eaten outside while watching the ducks on the stream, which runs through the gardens.

[music] P [wine]

COLEFORD
Gloucestershire
Map **3** SO51

White Horse Inn Staunton
☎ (0594) 33387
Open: Mon–Sat 12noon–2pm, 7–9pm, Sun 12noon–1.15pm, 7–9pm

This early Victorian pub, strategically sited between Coleford and Monmouth on the A4136 in the beautiful Forest of Dean, was built on top of a much older hostelry which now forms the inn's Cellar Restaurant. Prices are a little above our limit here, but the Saddle Room Grill, complete with beams and stable paraphernalia, offers well-prepared food which is both economical and interesting. Dishes on the menu include home-made liver pâté and local trout. Dish of the day could be coq au vin or home-made chicken and mushroom pie.

P

COLWYN BAY
Clwyd
Map **6** SH87

Penrhos Restaurant LLandudno Rd (on A546 between Colwyn Bay and Llandudno) ☎ (0492) 49547
Open: Summer Mon–Sun 12noon–2.30pm, 5.30–10pm. Winter Mon 12noon–2.30pm, Tue–Sun 12noon–2.30, 5.30–8.30pm

This licensed restaurant has an old-world atmosphere and offers excellent value for money. The set three-course lunch has a choice of roasts for the main course but if you want a lighter meal then try an omelette or salad. The à la carte high tea and dinner menu lists mainly grills, fish dishes and salads or try the speciality of the house – chicken cooked in red wine with mushrooms, tomatoes, herbs and onions. Coffee and home-make pastries are served in the morning and afternoon.

[music] P S [wine]

CONGLETON
Cheshire
Map **7** SJ86

The Gingerbread Coffee Shop 3 Duke St ☎ (02602) 71627
Open: Mon–Tue 9.30am–4.30pm, Wed 9.30am–1.30pm, Thu–Sat 9.30am–4.30pm

This is a quaint cream-and-brown painted restaurant where many of the dishes, such as chicken casserole, savoury flan, or pizza are available at very modest prices and all are served with vegetables or salad. Starters include grapefruit segments and soup of the day whilst home-made fruit pie with fresh cream is a typical sweet.

P S [wine]

CONGRESBURY
Avon
Map **4** ST46

The White Hart – The Inwood Wrington Rd (½m S of Congresbury off A370)
☎ (0934) 833303
Open: Mon–Sat 12noon–2pm, 7–10pm, Sun 12noon–1.30pm, 7–9.30pm.

The White Hart is an original and attractive 17th-century beamed inn and the Inwood an equally attractive modern (1981) buttery and bar facing the odd inn. The meals are good, hot and excellent value for money. Many of the dishes are home-made and menus change daily. Our inspector enjoyed cream of smoked trout soup with fresh bread followed by chicken cooked with mushrooms and white wine served with rice and vegetables. Tasty home-made sweets are also available. Real ale is served and there is a moderately-priced wine list.

P [wine]

COOKHAM
Berkshire
Map **4** SU88

The Two Roses High St
☎ (06285) 20875
Open: Wed–Mon 12.15–2.15pm, (closed 2 weeks mid-Feb and 1 week mid-Nov

A delightful 400-year-old cottage restaurant where Marian Smith excels with her home cooking, using only fresh ingredients. Home-made pâté, steak and kidney pie and bread and butter pudding are popular dishes. There are always five 'specials' on offer daily as well as traditional grills. Cosy wooden pew seating and period décor complete the scene. The restaurant is licensed and open in the evenings. but the menu is more expensive and elaborate.

S P [wine]

CORRIS
Gwynedd
Map **6** SH70

Corris Craft Centre Restaurant
☎ (065473) 343
Open: Jun–Sep Mon–Sun 9am–8pm, Oct–Mar Mon–Sun 10am–4pm, Apr–May Mon–Sun 10am–6pm

The restaurant is situated on the A487 and is part of the Corris Craft Centre, a group of modern grey brick buildings. This is an ideal stopping place for the hungry tourist who wants well-prepared food in spotlessly clean surroundings. An excellent selection of salads includes cider-baked ham and quiche, and there is a choice of at least three hot meals on the menu which could include lasagne or beef hot pot. If you just want a snack then try the Danish pastries or home-made scones.

[P] [♿]

CORSHAM
Wiltshire
Map **3** ST86

Methuen Arms Hotel★★
☎ (0249) 714867
Open: Mon–Sat 10am–2.30pm, Mon–Thu 6–10.30pm, Fri 12noon–2.30pm, Fri & Sat 6–11pm, Sun 12noon–2pm, 7–10.30pm

Situated midway between Chippenham and Bath on the A4, the hotel is in close proximity to Corsham Court, the country seat of Lord Methuen, whose heraldic arms are displayed above the entrance portico. In fact, the building is steeped in history and Winter's Court, where lunch and dinner are served, retains the oak beams and Cotswold stone of a grandiose bygone age. The midday three-course businessperson's meal is popular (especially as minute steak is on the menu), but unfortunately the candlelit dinners are just beyond our range. However, there are further options in the Long Bar such as sandwiches, basket meals, and a cold table, all reasonably priced.

[C] [P] [♿]

COSHESTON
Dyfed
Map **2** SN00

Hill House Inn ☎ (0646) 64352
Open: Mon–Sun 12noon–2pm, 7–10.30pm, 11pm in Summer

There's a touch of Welsh patriotism at this early Georgian inn, which offers a comfortable, welcoming atmosphere along with several real ales. The bar meals are good value and charcoal-grilled steaks and kebabs are the speciality of the house.

[C] [P] [♿]

COVENTRY
West Midlands
Map **4** SP37

Corks Wine Bar Whitefriars St
☎ (0203) 23628
Open: Mon–Fri 11am–2.30pm, 6–10.30pm, Sat 6–11pm, Sun 7–10.30pm

Dark green walls, a raftered ceiling, tiled floor and old tulip-shaded wall lights create a yester-year effect enhanced by cast-iron and refectory tables, old French street name plates, prints and mirrors. Two plat du jour blackboards list the range of daily 'specials' such as chicken marengo or a savoury pie and jacket potato. Lasagne and pizza are also on the menu and if you are feeling adventurous then escargots are an interesting alternative.

[♫] [P] [♿] **VS**

Nello Pizzeria 8 City Arcade
☎ (0203) 23551
Open: Mon–Thu 9.30am–11.30pm, Fri–Sat 9.30am–1am

An informal atmosphere and freshly-baked food have established the Nello as a popular eating place – ideal for weary shoppers and tourists alike. Pastas are listed as starters on the menu, though a plate of home-made lasagne or cannelloni is a tasty meal in itself. Pizzas include the Special Pizza Nello – a banquet of cheese, tomato, tuna, prawns, mushrooms, anchovies, egg, ham and olives. Grills and roasts are also available.

[C] [P] [S]

CRAIL
Fife *Fife*
Map **11** NO60

The Tolbooth 37 High St ☎ (03335) 709
Open: Summer Mon–Sun 9am–9pm; winter Tue–Sun 10am–6pm. Closed Mon

The Tolbooth is a pleasant little restaurant in the centre of the fishing village. Prices are low and you can enjoy a three-course meal of soup followed by local scampi and apple pie and cream and still stay within our budget. The children's menu offers the popular sausage and fish-finger type meals. Refreshments and snacks are available in the mornings and afternoons.

[♫] [P] [🍷]

CRAWLEY
West Sussex
Map **4** TQ23

Solomons Ancient Priors Restaurant and Wine Bar High St ☎ (0293) 36223
Open: Mon–Sat 12noon–2pm, 6pm–10.30pm. Closed Sun

Ancient it certainly is, for this lovely beamed building dates from the 14th century, with some parts even earlier. You should certainly enquire about its eventful and colourful history over your glass of wine. The table d'hôte menu in the restaurant is over our limit, but the wine bar offers excellent value for money. The food is all cooked fresh to order and specialities are added each day. These might be lamb kebabs and rice, or roast beef, supplementing the usual grills, pasta and pizza dishes.

[♫] [S] [P]

CREETOWN
Dumfries & Galloway *Kirkcudbrightshire*
Map **11** NX45

Creetown Arms Hotel St John St
☎ (067182) 282
Open: Summer Mon–Sun 12.30–2pm, 7–9pm, Winter Mon–Sun 12.30–2pm, 7–8pm

This small granite inn with its blue shutters dates from 1780 and is situated on the main road (A75), in this attractive village overlooking Wigtown Bay. A good range of Scottish fare is offered here with specialities including venison, Galloway beef and fresh local salmon. Meals are served in the bar or restaurant and prices vary accordingly. A typical bar meal might be egg mayonnaise followed by braised steak with vegetables and croquette potatoes and fresh cream trifle for dessert. In the restaurant you could have pâté maison followed by gammon steak and pineapple with meringue glacé. A more adventurous á la carte menu is also available.

[P] [🍷] **VS**

CREWE
Cheshire
Map **7** SJ75

Cheshire Casserole Earle St
☎ (0270) 585479
Open: Tue–Fri 12noon–2pm, 8–10.15pm, Sat 8–10.15pm

As the name implies, this bistro is famed for its excellent casseroles. Owned and run by Brian and Joan Shannon for the past six years it is well worth a visit. The lunch menu offers the best value, the casserole of the day is very modestly priced, and a three-course meal comes well within our budget. The evening menu is more extensive but it is still possible to stay within our limit.

[P] [🍷]

CREWKERNE
Somerset
Map **3** ST40

The Old Parsonage★★ Barn St
☎ (0460) 73516
Open: Mon–Sat 12noon–2pm, 7–8.30pm, Sun 12noon–2pm

On the corner of a quiet lane you will find this charming old rectory, personally run by Kenneth Mullins. Home cooking is the big attraction here. Interesting dishes such as cockles in cheese sauce and grilled rainbow trout with almonds and Pernod, are scattered liberally throughout the à la carte menu (most of which are unfortunately outside our price limit). The table d'hôte menus for lunch and dinner are reasonably priced. A traditional Sunday lunch of three courses plus coffee and cream is available, with a special children's version at a reduced price.

[C] [P] [🍷]

CRICCIETH
Gwynedd
Map **6** SH43

Bron Eifion Country Hotel★★★
☎ (076671) 2385
Open: Mon–Sun 8.30–9.30am, 1–2pm, 7.30–9pm

Bron Eifion was built in the 1870s as the summer residence of slate master John Greaves. Its main hall boasts superb wall panelling and a magnificent central gallery of pitch pine. The hotel's three-course lunch gives a tempting choice of starters and desserts.

[P] [🍷]

The Moelwyn Restaurant Mona Terr
☎ (076671) 2500
Open: Mon–Sun 12.30–2pm, 7–9.30pm, closed Mon all day and Sun pm in winter

Mr and Mrs Peter Booth worked for the previous owners for four years before purchasing the Moelwyn Restaurant, a creeper-clad Victorian house with panoramic views over Cardigan Bay and the Cambrian Range, six years ago. Tasty lunch offerings include a good quality home-made soup, lasagne verde, fresh crab salad (when available) and a choice of sweet or cheeseboard. A children's menu is available and on Sundays you can enjoy a traditional roast lunch. A special four-course dinner is outside the scope of this guide.

[C] [P] [🍷]

CRIEFF
Tayside *Perthshire*
Map **11** NN82

Chatterbox 43 King St ☎ (0764) 4495
Open: Summer: Mon & Tue, Thu–Sat 10am–7.30pm, Wed 10am–12noon, Sun 12noon–7.30; Winter: Mon & Tue, Thu–Sat 10am–6pm, Wed 10am–12noon, Sun 12noon–6pm

This cosy and popular restaurant, just off the town square, is run by Mr and Mrs Brewer and their cheerful local staff. The Chatterbox is busy for both morning coffee and afternoon tea as well as for High Tea and lunch when a selection of freshly prepared hot dishes and salads are served. Typical main courses are gammon steak with peaches, and fried haddock.

[S] [P] [🍷]

The Highlandman East High St
☎ (0764) 4866
Open: Mon–Sat 10am–7pm, Sun 12noon–7pm

The premises of The Highlandman, once a garage showroom and filling station, have been converted into a pleasant restaurant-cum-tearoom, where one can get anything from a cup of tea and a piece of home-made shortbread to a full three-course meal, any time from morning to evening. Main dishes include sirloin steak, scampi and various grills. Toasted sandwiches, hamburgers and salads exist for those who like a light lunch, and children's meals include sausage and chips. Incidentally, disabled persons will find access easy.

[P] [🍷]

Star Hotel★ East High St ☎ (0764) 2632
Open: Mon–Sun 12noon–2pm, 4.30–6pm (High Tea), 7–9pm

The pleasant surroundings of the panelled dining room which overlooks the main street of this attractive Perthshire town provides an ideal venue for shoppers and tourists alike. Lunchtime specials such as fried fillet of haddock with lemon, grilled liver and onions or pizza – all served with French fried potatoes and two vegetables of the day – are very reasonably priced. The à la carte menu is more extensive but still reasonable and includes grilled Tay salmon and chicken Suedoise (sautéed in a delicious sauce of mushrooms, cream and white wine). A high tea menu served from 4.30–6pm offers a selection of grills or cold meat salad with French fries and vegetables, tea, bread and butter, scones and cakes.

[C] [P] [S] [🍷] **VS**

CROYDE
Devon
Map **2** SS43

The Thatched Barn Inn
☎ (0271) 890349
Open: Mon–Sat 12noon–2pm, 6–10pm, Sun 12noon–2pm, 7–10pm

Situated in this relatively unspoiled North Devon coastal village the Thatched Barn Inn, dating back to the 14th century, was originally used by the monks of nearby St Helen's Priory as a storage barn and shelter for farm animals. The inn is run by Pat and Bruce Jefford who offer a good range of freshly prepared food ranging from bar snacks to four-course meals. Many dishes are home-made including pâté, quiche, and pasties and there is a good selection of home-cooked meats and fresh steaks. A traditional roast lunch is available on Sunday.

[P] [♧]

CROYDON
Gt London

Fusto D'Oro Pizzeria Leon House, 237–239 High St ☎ 01-688 4869 London Plan4 **91a**E4
Open: Mon–Sat 11am–3pm, 6pm–12mdnt

If pizza's your dish you'll be quite spoiled for choice at this popular Italian pizzeria There are 22 varieties. For the quickie meal, eat your pizza in the busier section of the restaurant where the décor is simple. When you want to linger and enjoy a more romantic atmosphere, dine by candlelight in the other section. Wherever you eat, the food is the same, with pizzas from the basic Margherita to an elaborate Mediterraneo with seafood and tomatoes, pasta dishes, salads and steaks. For dessert there's a choice including such tempters as rum baba, zabaglione or cheesecake.

[C] [♫] [P] [S]

The Wine Vaults 122–126 North End ☎ 01-6802419 London Plan4 **91b**E4
Open: Mon–Sat 11am–2.30pm, Mon–Thu 5.30–10.30pm, Fri 5.30–11pm, Sat 7–11pm

One of Davy & Co's many outlets, the Wine Vaults have a solidly Victorian décor and sawdust on the floor. Their basement premises are on Croydon's busy High Street, next door to Marks & Spencer. Savoury fingers of toast with anchovy paste, make an interesting snack and are sold individually as well as by the plate of six. Otherwise, menu and prices are fairly typical of Davy & Co's wine bars. A popular meal is charcoal-grilled ribs of prime beef with a tossed mixed salad.

[C] [P] [S]

CUCKFIELD
West Sussex
Map **4** TQ32

The Cuckoo's Nest High St
☎ (0444) 459000
Open: Tue–Sat 12.30–2.30pm, 7–10pm. Closed Mon & Sun

Lyn Stevens runs this cottage-style restaurant which is furnished with pine tables and chairs. All the food is freshly prepared and portions are generous. Starters include home-made pâté and soup which can be followed by dishes such as braised beef and onions, chicken kiev and prawn salad. Finish the meal with a home-made dessert – try apple pie, fruit salad or pancakes.

[C] [♫] [S] [P]

CULLIPOOL, ISLE OF LUING
Strathclyde *Argyll*
Map **10** NM70

Longhouse Buttery ☎ (08524) 209
Open: Mon–Sun 11am–5pm, Thu–Sat 7.30–11pm

It's well worth the journey from the Scottish mainland across the Island of Seil to the Cuan ferry for the 90-second trip to the beautiful little island of Luing. (**NB** Passenger ferry only on Sundays – Buttery is 3 miles from the ferry.) The high spot of a visit must be this converted, whitewashed croft which incorporates a white and pine-clad restaurant with dispense bar and small gallery where partner Edna Whyte displays and sells gifts bearing her 'Old Rectory' designs. The other half of the partnership, Audrey Stone, is to be seen serving the delicious meals including such delicacies as buttery venison pâté, and fresh Luing prawns, served on wholemeal bread with crispy salad. Home-made sweets include the mouthwatering triple meringue with cream. A three-course lunch is excellent value but unfortunately the special dinner, including fresh lobster or salmon, would over-stretch our pocket.

[P]

CUMBERNAULD
Strathclyde *Dunbartonshire*
Map **11** NS77

Neelans Dalshannon Farm, Condorrat (SW of Cumbernauld off A80)
Open: Mon–Thu 12noon–2pm, 5–11.30pm, Fri & Sat 12noon–12mdnt, Sun 5–11.30pm

This former farmhouse has been converted into two restaurants and here we are concerned with Neelans – an Indian restaurant. The menu lists the usual favourites, Bhuna lamb as well as a selection of kebabs and tandoori chicken, but the standard of cuisine is certainly above 'the usual'. For the less adventurous, alternative dishes include omelettes and scampi, both served with chips. There is a take-away service.

[C] [♫] [P] [♧]

Old World Inn Allanfauld Rd
☎ (02367) 27509
Open: Mon–Sat 12noon–2.30pm, 5–11pm, Sun 12noon–2.30pm, 6.30–11pm

Situated on the west side of Cumbernauld, on a hill overlooking the main Glasgow/Stirling road, this restaurant is typical of the Stakis Steakhouse chain to which it belongs. Decorated in mock-Tudor style with beams and dark-wood furnishings, the room exudes a restful, relaxing atmosphere. Each main course on the menu incorporates in its price a choice of starters. Haddock, gammon steak and roast half chicken are all served with suitable accompaniments or try a ½lb prime Angus steak. Children get a good deal here with three courses, plus roll and butter and a choice of cola or orange drink for a reasonable charge.

[C] [P] [♧]

CUMNOCK
Strathclyde *Ayrshire*
Map **11** NS51

The Royal Hotel★★ 1 Glaisnock St
☎ (0290) 20822
Open: Mon–Sat 12noon–2pm, 5–6.30pm, 7–9pm, Sun 12.30–2.30pm, 5–6.30pm, 7–9pm

It is a well-deserved compliment to this traditional and comfortable hotel that local business people are regular customers. In the attractively lit dining room, a conventional choice of dishes is very well presented, and very well priced. Three lunch courses focusing on roast sirloin (with perhaps banana fritters or green figs with cream to follow) is excellent value, or treat yourself to the fresh salmon. The very substantial high tea might include a mixed grill, tea, scones, and cakes. Dinner will be just over our price limit.

[P] [S] [♧]

CUPAR
Fife *Fife*
Map **11** NO31

Findlay's 43 Bonnygate ☎ (0334) 52830
Open: Mon–Sat 12noon–2pm, 6.30–10.30pm. Closed Sun

Here in a pleasant little shop-fronted bar restaurant situated in the main thoroughfare of the town, Mr and Mrs Findlay and their small staff offer a relaxing atmosphere and friendly service. Soups and sweets are home-made and main courses for lunch include beef in red wine and baked haddock in white-wine sauce. Careful selection from the dinner menu with dishes such as sole with prawns and cold chicken salad will keep you within our limits. Wine is available by the glass and real ale is served.

[♫] [P]

Gatsby's 76A Grossgate
☎ (0334) 52750
Open: Mon–Sat 12noon–2pm, 8–10pm. Closed Sun

This small and intimate bar restaurant is situated on the first floor of a listed Victorian building with shops at street level. Popular for lunches and bar suppers the restaurant offers a choice of main courses ranging from lamb casserole to sauté kidneys Turbigo with several fresh-fish dishes. A three-course lunch with pâté as a starter and Scottish cheddar for dessert comes well within our limit. Grills and deep fried dishes feature on the supper menu. Children are welcome for lunch.

[♫] [P] [🍷]

DALBEATTIE
Dumfries and Galloway
Kirkcudbrightshire
Map **11** NX86

Auchensheen Cottage Colvend
☎ (055662) 634
Open: Etr to October 12noon–2pm, 6–9pm. Closed Tue

This attractive little restaurant, built in the garden of the owner's house, is cosily fitted out with raftered ceiling, log fire, antiques and brasses. David and Ann Oldham ensure that where at all possible all items are home made using fresh produce. The emphasis at lunchtime is on cold platters, but there is always one hot dish available – perhaps a game pie or braised steak. Dinner, for which booking is advisable, could include paprika beef goulash or roast duckling, but save room for one of the delicious home made sweets.

[P]

DALKEITH
Lothian *Midlothian*
Map **11** NT36

Giorgio Pizza & Spaghetti House and Cavaliere Steak House 128 High St
☎ 031-663 4492
Open: Mon–Sun 12noon–2.30pm, 5pm–1am

Grapes, hanging bottles, wrought-ironwork and lighting by lanterns convey the atmosphere of an Italian bistro, and indeed owner Giorgio Crolla does come from Rome. Pasta dishes are prevalent as may be expected, and substantial main courses include lasagne al forno or spaghetti marenara. A three-course business lunch offers exceptionally good value, and high teas are served from 5pm to 7pm. If you want a special meal, you may prefer to choose escalope Garibaldi or bistecca pizziola, or you can enjoy a starter and a choice of steaks in the Steak House.

[C] [♫] [P] [S] [🍷] **VS**

DARLINGTON
Co Durham
Map **8** NZ21

Taj Mahal Tandoori 192 Northgate
☎ (0325) 68920
Open: Mon–Sun 12noon-2.30pm, 7pm–12mdnt

A small, intimate restaurant situated very close to the town centre, the Taj Mahal offers unbelievable value with its three-course lunch. The lunch menu includes 12 Indian dishes such as chicken and prawn curry and four English dishes including rump or sirloin steak with soup or fruit juice to start and a sweet to follow. A prominent feature of the dining area is a large Eastern-style mural covering one wall, the other three walls are hung with soft drapes, and the Indian atmosphere is enhanced by traditional background music. The à la carte menu offers a large variety of dishes with many tandoori specialities.

[C] [♫] [P]

DARTINGTON
Devon
Map **3** SX76

The Cott Inn ☎ (0803) 863777
Open: Mon–Sun normal licensing hours

A charming 14th-century building – long, low and warmly lit. The split-level, stone floor and timbered ceiling create a fine, olde-worlde atmosphere. Meals here nowadays are all home-made and presented buffet-style. Examples from the excellent daily spread are pork escalop and apricot meringue. So successful has the operation become, that owner Mr Shortman has recently added an extension to accommodate the growing number of diners.

[C] [P] [🍷] **VS**

DARTMEET
Devon
Map **3** SX67

Badger's Holt ☎ (03643) 213
Open: Mon–Sat 9.30am–6pm, Sun 10.30am–6pm. Closed Nov–Apr

The tumbling waters of the boulder-strewn river flow past this white-painted timber restaurant nestling in the shadow of Dartmoor. Rare birds such as the strange silver pheasant from the Far East are on view in the garden. The food is not exotic, but is very good for all that. Table d'hôte lunch is oustandingly good value. A choice of starters includes home-made chicken and tomato soup served with fresh home-made bread, and smoked mackerel salad. Hot main course dishes such as roast turkey, loin of pork with pineapple or fried scallops with tartare sauce are served with ample portions of well-prepared vegetables. Home-cooked gammon or roast lamb with a mixed salad are two of the cold alternatives. Desserts include a delicious almond-flavoured trifle, apple pie or junket.

[C] [♫] [🍷]

DARTMOUTH
Devon
Map **3** SX85

The Steam Packet 3 Duke St
☎ (08043) 3886
Open: Mon–Sun 12noon–2pm, 6.30–10.30pm (Sun 7–10.30pm)

Everything is ship-shape in this neat little glass-fronted wine bar situated just 300yds from the river front, and as one might expect from such a nautical name, seafood is a speciality. As seating is limited to 25 people you may have to wait for a place or book in advance – either way you'll be well justified in paying the Steam Packet a visit. Young owner David Hawke has a background of hotels and catering in this country where he did his training, and in the West Indies, Brazil and Switzerland where he worked. So you can be sure that when you taste his home-made quiches, pizzas or steak and kidney pie you're tasting some of the best around – and the price is right too!

[♫] [S]

DATCHET
Berkshire
Map **4** SU97

Chez Petit Laurent Country Life House, Slough Rd ☎ (0753) 49314
Open: Mon–Thu 11am–2.30pm, 6–10.30pm Fri–Sat 11am–2.30pm, 6–11pm

Formerly The Upper Crust, Chez Petit Laurent is run by Steven Winter. Good food at moderate prices is offered in typically French surroundings. A typical meal could be home-made soup, seafood and mushroom pancake with parsley sauce followed by mandarin gâteau.

DEAL
Kent
Map **5** TR45

The Hare and Hounds Northbourne
☎ (03045) 65429
Open: Mon–Sun 12noon–2.30pm, 6–11pm

Here's a charming country pub where everyone is catered for; you can have a quick nibble at a bar snack or enjoy a leisurely restaurant meal at a modest price. There are three or four 'specials' which are changed daily, one of which could be mussels in garlic butter, cod steak in prawn and scallop sauce and lemon cheesecake. Alternatively you can sample one of a wide variety of home-made quiches or a succulent steak and kidney pie with vegetables. Finish with a slice of home-made cheesecake or Black Forest gâteau.

[C] [♫] [P]

DENBIGH
Clwyd
Map **6** SJ06

Brook House Mill Tavern 2m E of Denbigh on the A525 ☎ (074571) 3377
Open: Mon–Fri 12noon–3pm, Sun 12noon–2pm, Mon–Sun 7–11pm

The mill is run by David Hall whose family also runs the Faenol Fawr Manor (Cromwell's Bistro) at Bodelwyddan (see p. 44). The mill has been well restored and retains the old watermill workings. Much of the produce used in the kitchen is bought at local markets and there are many fresh and seasonal dishes listed on the blackboard menu. Prawn cocktail, chicken curry and fresh fish are popular dishes and cooked snack meals are also available. Sunday lunch is followed by a children's disco from 2–3pm.

[P]

DERBY
Derbyshire
Map **8** SK33

Ben Bowers 13–15 Chapel St
☎ (0332) 367688/365988
Open: Mon–Fri 12noon–2pm, 7–11pm, Sat 7–11pm, Sun 12noon–2pm

Located above the Blessington Carriage public house is this charming 'olde worlde' restaurant with seating for about 60. A three-course lunch of (for instance) home-made soup of the day, chicken chasseur, new potatoes, salad and a sweet is very reasonably priced, children's portions are half price. Downstairs in Betty's Buffet Bar, excellent pub meals are served.

[C] [P] [S] **VS**

The Lettuce Leaf 21 Friar Gate
☎ (0332) 40307
Open: Mon–Sat 10am–7.30pm

Beyond the little craft shop selling handthrown pottery, woodcrafts and books on yoga and health food is this white-walled restaurant with its bright curtains, basket-work lamp shades, wooden tables and tasty vegetarian menu. Vegetable soup or fruit juice are inexpensive starters. Omelettes, salads, savouries and snacks supplement a daily speciality such as marrow provençale, gratin Dauphinois, pizza or celery hotpot. Sweets such as fresh fruit salad, yoghurt with honey or lettuce leaf muesli are popular. Finish with a dandelion coffee – full of flavour.

[P] [S]

The Rheinlander Darley Abbey Mills, Darley Abbey ☎ (0332) 364987
Open: Tue to Fri 12noon–1.45pm, 7.30–10pm; Sat 7.30–10pm. Closed Sun and Mon

Margaret and Gerald Hanel have created an uncompromisingly German restaurant in what was once the works canteen of this famous cotton mill on the River Derwent. It may sound rather unromantic, but the interior has been transformed with pictures, memorabilia and the music of Germany and there is a dramatic view over one of the finest weirs in Derbyshire. Although evening prices are a little over our budget, a very good lunch can be enjoyed here for under £5. Choose from a variety of pork fillet 'schnitzels', minced lamb with sage and onions or a number of traditional German sausage dishes. Wines, of course, are German – both red and white.

[C] [P]

Swiss Cottage 23–4 Audley Centre
☎ (0332) 32593
Open: Mon–Sat 9.30am–7pm

One of a chain of similar establishments in Nottingham and Leicester, the Swiss Cottage is situated in modern premises in a shopping precinct in the city centre. It is very popular with shoppers who enjoy morning coffee and afternoon tea as well as satisfying three-course meals. There is a good range of starters, omelettes, fish dishes, salads, snack meals, grills and desserts. The Forge Salad and Wine Bar is situated on the first floor.

[P] [S]

DISLEY
Cheshire
Map **7** SJ98

The Ginnel 3 Buxton Old Rd
☎ (06632) 4494
Open: Tue–Sat 7–10.30pm, Sun 12.30–2.15pm

Entry to this cosy bistro is by means of a narrow passageway, hence the name Ginnel – a local word for passage. Old silk embroideries and open brickwork add character to the delightfully furnished interior, where a tempting menu (using fresh produce) awaits your attention.

Tasty starters include home-made terrine and seafood pancake which could be followed by chicken Kiev or noisette of lamb and blackcurrant and chesnut flan. Traditional Sunday lunch with special children's portions is also available.

[C] [♫] [P] [🍷]

DODDISCOMBSLEIGH
Devon
Map **3** SX88

The Nobody Inn✕ ☎ (0647) 52394
S of Exeter, 2m E of Christow
Open: restaurant: Tue–Sat 7.30–9.30pm
Bar snacks: normal licensing hours

At one time weary travellers would stop at this inn in vain. An unknown purchaser had refused hospitality by locking the door, causing them to continue on their journeys in the belief there was 'nobody in'. Now, in the heavily-beamed bar with its imposing stone fireplace, a varied range of bar meals awaits you, and more substantial fare in the charming 'character' restaurant. The menu here includes some comparative rarities – 'Nobody' soup, lamb sweetbreads and duck à l'orange, but they will prepare your favourite dish on request.

[P]

DODWORTH
South Yorkshire
Map **8** SE30

Brooklands Restaurant Barnsley Rd
☎ (0226) 84238/6364
Open: Mon–Sun 12noon–2.30pm, (2pm Sat & Sun) 6–9.30pm

Within 500 yards of the M1 is this single storey building housing three dining rooms, each featuring splendid displays of fresh fruit and wines. The choice of dishes on the lunch menu is excellent and imaginative – try the chicken on a bed of poached spinach, covered with a cream sauce. Careful selection from the dinner menu (booking is necessary) will give a two-course meal within our price range. You are also invited to ask for more – 'and it shall be freely given'!

[C] [P] **VS**

See advertisement on page 35

DONCASTER
South Yorkshire
Map **8** SE50

Bacchus 44 Hallgate ☎ (0302) 20232
Open: Mon–Sat 12noon–3pm, 6pm–12mdnt, Sun 7.30–12mdnt

It's tempting to believe that Bacchus, the god of wine, also knew a thing or two about the importance of good quality food – his disciples certainly believed they inherited the powers inherent in what they ate. If you're feeling adventurous you might like to try some stuffed shrimps for a starter and spicy kebabs with pitta bread, yoghurt and fresh green salad sounds like a mouth-watering main course. Evenings are table service only, when the bill can nudge the £5 limit if you're not careful, but you queue at a self-service counter for lunch, choosing from a menu chalked on a blackboard offering a stew of the day and other English dishes. The wine list is extensive and reasonably priced – and there's even live music for good measure. From Monday to Saturday, drinks are cheaper during 'Happy Hour' – 6–7pm.

[C] [♫] [S] [🍷]

Pizzeria San Remo 8 Netherhall Rd
☎ (0302) 60501
Open: Mon–Sat 12noon–2.30pm, Mon–Thu 5.30–11.30pm, Fri & Sat 5.30–12pm

This small Italian restaurant is situated in a modern terrace of shops close to the town-centre market. It serves entirely Italian food. Choose from the tempting variety of pasta and pizza dishes, or try the fish, chicken, veal or steak meals which are also on the menu. Finish your meal with a traditional Italian ice cream or one of the sweet pancakes.

[♫] [P] [🍷]

Regent Hotel Restaurant★★ Regent Sq
☎ (0302) 64336
Open: Mon–Sat 12noon–2pm, 6–10pm, Sun 12noon–2.30pm, 7–9.30pm

At the edge of Doncaster's main

shopping area, this restaurant serves, in the words of our inspector, 'good substantial, no-nonsense' meals matched by low prices. Sunday lunch (roasts or trout) table d'hôte is available, and the weekday three-course business lunch offers various home-made pies, chicken or plaice as the main course. In the evenings, an à la carte menu only is available, with three courses priced by the main dish but some of the choices may be outside our budget.

P S ♨ **VS**

Ristorante Il Fiore in Legards 50–51 High St ☎ (0302) 23287
Open: Mon–Sat 9.30am–5pm

Situated above a smart ladies' boutique, this elaborately-named ristorante has a fresh green décor and overlooks the busy shopping street below from original Georgian bow windows. The menu offers a wide selection of sandwiches, gâteaux and toasted snacks, served all day. There is a three-course lunch with a choice of dishes. A typical meal could be soup, home-made steak and kidney pie and apple pie and cream.

C S **VS**

Maigret's Wine Bar High St, Bawtry ☎ (0302) 711057
Open: Mon–Sat 12noon–3pm, 6–11pm, Sun 7–10.30pm

This two-storey wine bar overlooks the old market place, and has murals of racing and showjumping scenes on its walls. On the ground floor the main room serves bar meals for lunch-time and evening, Home-made minestrone soup is hot favourite here and, along with lasagne, spaghetti or quiche appears chalked on a blackboard menu behind the bar. The first-floor restaurant is open evenings only with waitress service, offering a more varied menu, also with an Italian bias. A typical meal might be melon, spaghetti bolognese and a scrumptious gâteau from the trolley. House wine is Italian too, and is sold by the glass.

♫ P S ♨

Vintage Steak Bar Cleveland St ☎ (0302) 64786
Open: Mon–Sun 11.30am–2.30pm, 5.30–11.30pm

A Victorian flavour here, with red furnishings and mellow wooden chairs and tables. The varied menu offers 14 starters, including smoked trout, iced melon and fried scampi, with a selection of fish, omelettes, grills and salads to follow. Each main course dish, such as steak, duck, chicken, lamb and pork, is served with French fried potatoes, tomato and garden peas. A sweet or cheese and biscuits may be chased down by a potent liqueur coffee in the restaurant or bar-lounge, and there's a separate room available for private parties and receptions. The central position of the Vintage Steak Bar is another plus.

C ♫ P S ♨ **VS**

DORCHESTER
Dorset
Map **3** SY69

Judge Jeffrey's Restaurant High West St ☎ (0305) 64369
Open: Summer Mon–Sat 10am–5.30pm, 7–9.45pm, Sun 12noon–2pm, Winter Mon–Sat 10am–5.30pm, Thu–Sat 7–9.45pm, Sun 12noon–2pm

Viewed as a building, Ann and Anthony Coletta's Judge Jeffrey's restaurant is of great historical and architectural interest. It was sympathetically restored and put to its present use in 1928, but had been first monastery property and then a private house for something like five centuries before. Judge Jeffreys lodged here in 1685 while making his mark in the town with orders for 74 executions. Today, the restaurant which bears his name is a friendly place, full of atmosphere, providing morning coffees, bar snacks, lunches, afternoon teas and dinners at prices which could hardly be accounted a trial to anyone. The evening à la carte menu is very English, listing scampi, veal, gammon steak and Dorset pork fillet all reasonably priced.

♫ S ♨

DOVER
Kent
Map **5** TR34

Le Rendezvous Restaurant and Bar Cliffe Court Hotel, 25–26 Marine Parade ☎ (0304) 211001
Open: daily 12noon–2.30, 7–10pm

Situated adjacent to the Eastern Docks complex, the restaurant offers good views of the sea. Efficient service is provided by Mr Gonzalez and his young team of staff who offer a table d'hôte menu for lunch and dinner. There is a selection of six starters and six main courses, a typical meal could be smoked mackerel, Veal Viennoise and a sweet from the trolley. Breakfast is also available.

C P ♨ **VS**

DOWNHAM MARKET
Norfolk
Map **5** TF60

Crown Stables, Crown Hotel ☎ (0366) 382322
Open: Mon–Sun 10am–10pm

This 300-year-old coaching inn has always been a popular haunt of locals in the quiet town of Downham Market. However, since the spring of 1980, the old stables have been converted into a slick grill room and buttery with natural wood tables, tiled floor, brick walls and horsey bric-à-brac creating a clean and simple atmosphere. Here, a very reasonably-priced cold buffet comprises home-cooked cold meats and hand-raised pies, quiches, pâtés and flans with a selection of salads. Charcoal grill steaks or kebabs are more pricey, but ploughman's platter, pizza or a steak sandwich are tasty (and cheaper) alternatives.

C P ♨

DROITWICH
Hereford & Worcester
Map **3** SO86

The Spinning Wheel Restaurant 13 St Andrews St ☎ (0905) 770031
Open: Mon–Sat 10am–5.30pm, Tue–Sat 7.30–10pm, Sun 12noon–2.30pm

Popular with shoppers, tourists and local business people, the Spinning Wheel enjoys a prime position in Droitwich's new shopping centre. Access to this attractive cottage-style restaurant is across a paved patio area complete with fish pond and garden furniture. Friendly waitresses will serve you from a comprehensive menu ranging from light snacks to more substantial grills, omelettes etc. A table d'hôte three-course meal could consist of soup of the day, roast pork and apple sauce with vegetables, plus a sweet. Main dishes from the à la carte are reasonably priced with pizza, steak and kidney pie, and grilled gammon with pineapple as a few of the choices.

♫ P S ♨

DUMFRIES
Dumfries & Galloway *Dumfriesshire*
Map **11** NX97

Monokel 9 George St Mews ☎ (0387) 67450
Open: daily 11.30am–2.30pm, 6pm–mdnt

Tucked away behind St George's Church, this Bistro has a simple but effective décor of natural stone and *objets d'art*. Owner David Shields was formerly a catering lecturer at Dumfries Technical College and he has naturally brought all his skills to bear to ensure that his customers get a good blend of quality and extremely reasonable prices. Home-made soup or pâté could start the meal followed by moussaka, sweet and sour pork or trout. Desserts include cheesecake, Black Forest gâteau and banana split. Wine is available by the glass.

♫ S ♨

Opus 95 Queensberry St ☎ (0387) 55752
Open: Mon–Wed, Fri–Sat 9am–5pm, Thu 9am–2.30pm

A bright, cosy restaurant decked out with red tables and much wood panelling, but tricky to locate. You'll find it up two flights of stairs above a fabric shop. Snacks are served throughout the day, but at lunchtimes a blackboard menu offers a bewildering variety of goodies. Take your pick from several salad bowls and cold meats. Or how about the hot dishes? Try the spicy vegetable pie, aubergine casserole or lasagne. Desserts, calculated to test a weightwatcher's resolve, include cheesecake and fresh cream gâteau. The restaurant is unlicensed, but try the excellent coffee.

[P] [S] [&]

Pancake Place 20 English St
☎ (0387) 68523
Open: Apr–Sept Mon–Wed 9.30am–5.30pm; Thu–Sat 9.30am–5.30pm, 8pm–12.30am; Sun 11.30am–5.30pm

This is one of a growing number of Pancake Places to open in Scotland. As the name suggests the menu is devoted to pancake dishes, except for soup as a starter. Take your pick from savoury or sweet, large or small. The main dishes have a variety of savoury fillings and the evening menu includes some rather special French-style crêpes containing such delights as Supreme of Turkey Divan or Smoked Haddock and Herbs. These are served with a baked potato and green salad. Sweet pancakes for dessert are delicious and if you are too full to manage a regular portion, spoon-sized portions are available at about half the size and price.

[S] [&] **VS**

DUNBLANE
Central *Perthshire*
Map **11** NN70

Fourways Restaurant Main North Rd
☎ (0786) 822098
Open: Mon–Sat 9.15am–6pm, Sun 10am–6pm

This small restaurnat and gift shop enjoys a prime position within walking distance of the magnificent 15th-century cathedral and the Bishop's Palace and is consequently very popular with tourists. A friendly and caring staff serve mainly grills and home-made soups or pies. A typical meal could be soup, home-made steak pie and apple tart. Fourways is unlicensed.

[P] [&] **VS**

DUNDEE
Tayside *Angus*
Map **11** NO33

Gunga Din 99c–101 Perth Rd
☎ (0382) 65672
Open: Mon–Sat 12noon–2.15pm, 6–11.30pm

For the lover of classical Indian dishes Gunga Din is the place to eat. Situated on the main road west of the city centre this attractive little Indian restaurant sits in the heart of the University area. All dishes are freshly-prepared and only the finest basmati rice, best cuts of meat, proper herbs and spices for each dish, and fresh seasonal vegetables are used. Patrons are asked to appreciate the time involved in preparing and cooking dishes, which are made as closely as possible to the original recipes, and not to expect the chef to sacrifice quality for speed. Mullagatawny soup provides a suitable starter and the main dishes should be mixed and blended in the Indian tradition (ideally friends should order dishes and share). Kofta (meatballs in curry sauce) or chicken curry are typical dishes along with sag gosh (meat with spinach) and a seafood muchi curry. There is also a speciality chicken tandoori masala and thaiti (a tray consisting of several Indian vegetarian dishes). Friendly staff will assist in the choosing and blending of dishes with their correct accompaniments. For dessert you should try kulfi, an Indian ice cream.

[C] **VS**

Olde Worlde Inn 124 Seagate
☎ (0382) 21179
Open: Mon–Sat 12noon–2.15pm, 5–10pm, Sun 6.30–9.30pm

Handy for the new Wellgate shopping centre and opposite the main bus station, this is a typical Reo Stakis steakhouse, serving items from the organisation's standard menu. Main course items range from fillet of haddock to prime Angus steak and include a choice of starters. A choice of sweets to finish with are all reasonably priced. Bar lunches are served between 12noon and 2.15pm, and there is a special children's menu.

[C] [♫] [S] [&]

Pizza Gallery 3–7 Peter St
☎ (0382) 21422
Open: Mon–Sat 10am–11pm

A bright and modern eaterie situated in a quiet lane off a pedestrianised precinct in the city centre. The Gallery is on two levels and its walls are adorned by the works of local artists, which are for sale. Starters (they call them primers) are soup, spaghetti and fruit juice. The main-course pizzas are named after famous artists (the Goya is topped with anchovies, green pepper and olives). There are a range of sweets to complete your meal.

[S] [&]

DUNLOP
Strathclyde *Ayrshire*
Map **10** NS44

Burnhouse Manor Farm Hotel
Burnhouse ☎ (05604) 406
Open: Tue–Sat 12noon–2pm, 5–9pm, Sun 5–9pm

Just off the A736 Paisley/Irvine Road, this large restaurant has tartan carpeting and modern furnishings. The menu offers many familiar items ranging from chicken, lamb cutlets, and salads to duck in orange sauce. A three-course evening meal can come within our budget, but the steak dishes are over our limit. A three-course lunch of soup, lasagne, apple pie and ice-cream and coffee is very reasonably priced. High Teas range rom beef burgers to sirloin steak and include chips, vegetables, tea, toast and cakes. There is also a children's menu.

[P] [&] **VS**

DUNOON
Strathclyde *Argyllshire*
Map **10** NS17

The Haven Bar Hafton House Leisure Complex and Country Club (on A815 1m NW of Hunters' Quay) ☎ (036985) 205
Open: Mon–Sat 12noon–10pm, Sun 12.30–2pm, 6.30–11pm

Part of a new leisure complex, the Haven is an attractive bar housed in the basement of a Georgian house. The menu offers the usual bar favourites – scampi, beefburgers, home-made lasagne and a daily 'special'. A three-course meal will come well within our budget.

[♫] [P] [&]

Woosters Clyde St, West Bay
☎ (0369) 2761
Open: Summer: daily 10.30am–10.30pm; winter: Tue to Sat 7–10.30pm. Closed Sun and Mon

Although part of the Shelbourne Hotel, this coffee parlour and steak house has a separate entrance. Tastefully decorated in shades of green, the L-shaped room has a small cocktail bar area and some windows overlook the river. At lunchtime the emphasis is on salads, baked potatoes and quiches. At dinner the main course price includes a starter of home made soup and a speciality ice cream dessert. Choose from sirloin steak, roast chicken, mixed grill or scampi and you will still be within our budget. A supplement will get you a wider choice of starters and desserts. At half price for children, Woosters offers exceptionally good value.

[C] [♫] [P] [&]

DUNSFORD
Devon
Map **3** SX88

Royal Oak Inn ☎ (0647) 52256 6m SW of Exeter, just off B3212 to Moretonhampstead
Open: Mon–Sat 11am–2.30pm, 6–10.30pm, (11pm Fri & Sat), Sun 12noon–2.30pm

A charming village inn in a rural setting, the Royal Oak offers sustenance either in the comfortable bar or in the dining room. A wide range of salads is available in the summer, and in the winter there is a hot carvery with fresh vegetables. Home-made bar specialities include steak and kidney cooked in Guinness and chilli con carne. A selection of grills is always available along with delicious home-made desserts.

[C] [P] [&]

DURHAM
Co Durham
Map **12** NZ24

Dennhöfers 4 Framwellgate Bridge, Milburngate Centre ☎ (0385) 46777
Open: Mon–Sat 12noon–3pm, 7–10.30pm

Situated in the shadow of the Gothic cathedral and castle is this olde worlde eating place. The lower of the two wine bars has a limited and inexpensive menu, and the upstairs bar offers a greater variety of dishes, both at lunch-time and in the evening. A typical meal could be ham and paté cones, beef in burgundy followed by home-made cheesecake.

[C] [P] [S] [🍷]

The Happy Wanderer Finchale Rd, Framwellgate Moor, 1m N of Durham ☎ (0385) 64580

Open: Mon–Sat 12noon–2pm, 7–9.30pm, Sun 12noon–1.30pm

Midway between Durham City and the ancient monument of Finchale Priory stands this popular pub with its comfortable restaurant. Bar meals represent excellent value, but for a little extra, diners can enjoy the comfort of the restaurant and its very friendly service. Chef's pâté and 'Wanderer' mixed grill would satisfy a large appetite and for those with a sweet tooth why not complete your meal with banana fritters. Real ale is served at the bar.

[P] [🍷]

Mr Toby's Carving Room Cock o' the North, Farewell Hall ☎ (0385) 43789

Open: Mon–Sun 12noon–2pm, 7–10pm

The excellent carvery in the dining room of this large pub offers a choice of three roasts (pork, beef and chicken when our inspector visited) and salads; a sweet from the trolley is included in the set price. There is also a small range of starters. Snacks available in the comfortable lounge bar include steak and kidney pie, scampi and chicken, all served with a choice of potatoes and vegetables of the day. The bar menu also includes starters and sweets so it is possible to enjoy a three-course meal here.

[P] [🍷] **VS**

Rajpooth Tandoori Restaurant 4 North Rd ☎ (0385) 61496

Open: Mon–Sat 12noon–2.30pm, 6pm–12mdnt, Sun 6–11.30pm

Tandoori dishes are the speciality of this Indian restaurant run by Mr B. Noor. Situated on the first floor the large dining room, with red walls and carpet, is divided by a low central trellis displaying a range of pot plants. Apart from tandoori the menu also includes biriani dishes and a large selection of curries. Chicken tikka, sheek kabab and Dall soup are among the starters. The special 'Businessmans lunch' served daily offers particular value.

[C] [P] [🍷]

Royal County Hotel★★★★ Bowes Coffee House Old Elvet ☎ (0385) 66821

Open: Mon–Sat 10am–8pm, Sun 10am–5.30pm

Youngsters enjoy their meals in this attractive buttery as there is a menu of children's favourites such as bangers and mash and sweets which include Thunder and Lightning' – ice cream, golden syrup and whipped cream! À la carte dishes are reasonably priced and you can choose an appetising meal such as soup with roll and butter, fried fillet of lemon sole and chocolate and kirsch mousse.

[C] [♫] [P] [S] [🍷]

EAST KILBRIDE
Strathclyde *Lanarkshire*
Map **11** NS65

Hong Kong 46–48 Kirkton Park ☎ (03552) 20112

Open: Mon–Sat 12noon–12mdnt, Sun 2pm–12mdnt

A patio garden allows al fresco eating in summer, a touch which gives this Chinese restaurant a certain individuality. Inside, décor is unmistakably oriental with golden dragons set against black walls, and the à la carte is extensive and fairly typical, but it's the speciality teas, desserts and the extensive wine list which makes this restaurant stand out from the rest. Excellent value are the three-course business lunch and the tasty salads and ploughman's. One of the special sweets is the Hong Kong Special – a delicate concoction of peaches, sparkling wine, soda water and angostura bitters which is available for two persons. Otherwise try one of the 16 unusual teas such as 'gunpowder green tea' described as an 'attractive clear fragrant liquor' and a cocktail from the imaginative list of 29.

[C] [♫] [P]

See advertisement on page 75

EASTLEIGH
Hampshire
Map **4** SU41

Piccolo Mondo 2 1 High St ☎ (0703) 613180

Open: Mon–Sat 10am–10pm

Decorated in the Italian national colours Piccolo Mondo 2 (sister restaurant to Piccolo Mondo 1 in Southampton) offers dishes such as home-made sausages cooked in tomato sauce and veal escalope which supplements the usual range of pasta dishes and freshly-made pizzas. Elaborate ices and pastries are available for dessert and there is a range of Italian wines to accompany your meal.

[♫] [S] [P] [🍷]

EDDLESTON
Borders *Peebles-shire*
Map **11** NT24

Horse Shoe Inn ☎ (07213) 225

Open: Mon–Sat 11.30am–2pm, 5–10pm; Sun 12.30–2.15pm, 6.30–10pm.

The emphasis is on the food at this Inn, formerly the village smiddy, although drinks on offer do include a range of real ales. The menu is extensive with an international air – Stilton soup, hors d'oeuvres or lasagne are among the starters while main courses include Chicken Suedoise, Beef Bourgignon, Hungarian goulash, curries and pizzas – and good old fish and chips too. A mouthwatering selection of sweets includes Raspberry and Drambuie Creams, Green figs in Brandy and Chocolate and Rum mousse. All three courses can be sampled well within our budget.

C ♫ P

EDINBURGH
Lothian *Midlothian*
Map **11** NT27

Bar Italia 100–104 Lothian Rd
☎ 031-228 6379
Open: Mon–Sun 12noon–4am

Pizza delle Stagioni, with tomatoes, mozzarella, ham, salami, clams, mushrooms, artichokes and green peppers, is just one of the many varieties of pizza on the menu. There is also a good choice of pasta dishes and some more straight forward dishes such as roast chicken and chips.

P S

Bar Roma 39a Queensferry St
☎ 031-226 2977
Open: Mon–Sun 11am–2.30am

This bright, spacious restaurant-cum-pizzeria is a sister to the Bar Italia in another part of the city. A very good selection of Italian dishes appear on the menu at fairly keen prices. Risotto con funghi (rice with mushrooms) and penne piccanti (hot chili and tomato sauce) are examples of the pasta range. There are over a dozen different pizzas to choose from. Desserts include offocato al cognac and various ices.

S

Mr Boni's 4–6 Lochrin Buildings
☎ 031-229 5319
Open: Restaurant Mon–Sat 5.30–10pm Ice-Cream Parlour Mon–Sat 10.30am–10.30pm, Sun 12noon–9.30pm

Juicy steaks and American burgers feature at Mr Boni's, a restaurant and ice cream parlour famous hereabouts for its ice cream and extremely popular – particularly with King's Theatre folk, both audiences and performers – for its good, but inexpensive, home-cooked food. Italian dishes include various spaghettis and juicy steak is also on the menu. McBoni Burgers and ordinary burgers are popular.

C ♫ P S

Café Cappuccino 15 Salisbury Pl
☎ 031-667 4265
Open: Mon–Sat 9am–8.30pm

The menu includes a wide variety of omelettes, salads, toasted sandwiches and filled rolls, all very reasonably priced, and if you are looking for a real meal there is an equally wide choice of fish or meat dishes. There is also a good selection of ice-cream confections. The Café Cappuccino is not licensed but you can take your pick from a range of 20 non-alcoholic beverages of which frothy cappuccino coffee is one choice.

P S

Le Château Castle Ter ☎ 031-229 1181
Open: Mon–Thu 12noon–2.30pm, 5pm–12mdnt, Fri, Sat open all day

From its impressive frontage you might expect Le Château prices to be well above our limit, but Bill Morgan's restaurant is recommended for good food at reasonable prices, for its bright and comfortable interior, and friendly atmosphere. Starters include a house pâté, prawn cocktail and piping-hot soup. There is a choice of four or five dishes and of the usual grills at reasonable prices. Among the house specialities are lasagne and chicken chasseur.

C P ♫

Crawford's 31 Frederick St
☎ 031-225 4579
Open: Summer Mon–Sat 8am–11pm, 7pm Winter

This is one of the very handy Crawford's chain of restaurants, catering for families and shoppers. The ground-floor restaurant's décor has a country theme with pine wood and terra-cotta ceramic tiles. As with most Crawford's you can get a quick and reasonably-priced meal from the attractively laid out cold counter, or if you prefer, there is a tempting range of flans, pies and casseroles. To finish with, the range of gâteaux befits one of Scotland's best known bakeries. Wine and beer is available to accompany your meal.

S

The Doric Tavern✕ 15–16 Market St
☎ 031-225 1084
Open: Mon–Sat 12noon–2.30pm, 6–9.30pm

If local lawyers and journalists gather in a restaurant, it's a sure sign that you'll get value for money. The set three-course lunch and four-course dinner both represent excellent value for money. Filling British dishes such as boiled silverside and dumplings or haggis and turnips are featured. The extensive à la carte, which includes an excellent mixed grill, is also very good value. Mr McGuffie, proprietor for the last quarter-century, believes in traditional service.

S

Es Danes 45 Thistle St ☎ 031-225 9830
Open: Mon–Sat 10am–2.15pm, 5.30–10.15pm

If you like smørrebrød – Danish open sandwiches – then this is the place for you. It is a small, compact restaurant and the all-white décor includes the tablecloths, crockery, flowers and ornaments. All the sandwiches come on a base of rye bread and two or three should be sufficient for the average appetite. For a full meal, start with soup and finish with gâteau. Because of the size of the restaurant, it is advisable to book in advance.

C P S

Fortrose Grill 71 Rose St
☎ 031-225 8012
Open: Summer Mon–Sat 11am–10pm, Sun 12.30–10pm, Winter closed Sun

Rose Street, with its boutiques and upmarket restaurants is the 'in' shopping and eating area of Edinburgh. The Fortrose Grill is small and simple, the welcome and service friendly and informal. There is a good-value business lunch and the à la carte menu is quite reasonable. Main courses include salads, pastas, omelettes and a mixed grill. Sweets are variations on the theme of ice cream. The menu finishes with the words 'Servis non compris' which doesn't mean 'I don't understand how the washing machine works' but suggests discretion when tipping.

S

Nimmo's 101 Shandwick Pl
☎ 031-229 6119
Open: Mon–Sat 11am–2.30pm, 5–10.15pm. Closed Sun

This is a complex comprising restaurant, lounge bar and wine bar and although a lunch in the restaurant could come within our limits (dinner would go over the top) it is for the wine bar that we list it here. This cheerful and friendly meeting place offers an attractive display of cold foods – pâtés, meats, pies and salads – which customers serve themselves from the counter. Almost everything is fresh and home made and there is a daily 'dish of the day' which could be Pork Wellington. Desserts include brandied raspberries and cream, gâteau and cheesecake.

C ♫

See advertisement on page 76

The Pancake Place 130 High St
☎ 031-225 1972
Open: Mon–Sat 10am–6pm, 9pm Summer, Sun 11am–9pm

Occupying a prime position in the city's historic Royal Mile, this restaurant, as its name suggests, specialises in pancakes large and small, sweet or savoury. The limited range of starters offers soup of the day or fruit juice. You then launch into the mind-blowing array of savoury pancakes; hot ones with such fillings as haddock Mornay, bacon and maple syrup (an American favourite), and a selection of 'cool crisp salads', try ham served with two thin pancakes, mayonnaise or pickle on a bed of lettuce, tomato or cucumber. If you have enough room to spare (the menu does warn that all sweet pancakes can ruin your diet) try an 'American' – three sweet pancakes layered with butter and served with a jug of maple syrup.

♫ S

See advertisement on page 76

Savour Eastern Flavour

Savour delights suited to the taste of a mandarin in the Hong Kong restaurant.
Although a little off the main thoroughfare, the Hong Kong is heading in the direction for the connoisseur. It is a Chinese restaurant that is aiming for individuality.

The Hong Kong have concocted a menu that is easily on par with others and includes a few dishes special to themselves for European and Chinese tastes. What really distinguishes the Hong Kong from others is its astounding wine list, and inventive cocktails. You could be about to spoil yourself if you dine at the Hong Kong.

Lafites Restaurant

formerly Hong Kong Restaurant

46-48 KIRKTON PARK
EAST KILBRIDE
Telephone 20112

Post House Hotel☆☆☆ Corstorphine Rd ☎ 031-334 8221
Open: Coffee Shop Mon–Sun 12.30–10pm

Very handy for the zoo, this bright and modern coffee shop serves anything from large and colourful double-decker sandwiches to a three-course meal. Try soup, followed by an omelette, burger or salad, and finish with cheesecake or sherry trifle. Babies are well-catered for here with 'strained dinner' or boiled egg and buttered fingers – and everything consumed within earshot of the animals!

C P S

Sorrento 15 Albert Pl ☎ 031-554 7282
Open: Mon–Sat 12noon–2.30pm, Mon–Thu & Sun 5.30pm–12.30am, Fri & Sat 5.30pm–1am

The infectious, cheery attitude of the owners in looking after their guests is alone worth a visit to this friendly Italian restaurant. The varied menu has all the popular dishes including a good selection of pastas and pizzas and is priced to satisfy all pockets. Minestrone soup followed by a pasta or pizza dish leaves sufficient to indulge in a tasty sweet – try zabaglione (beaten egg, sugar and marsala). Veal and steak dishes are also available. All main dishes (except pastas and pizzas) come suitably garnished and are served with chips; vegetables are priced separately The table d'hôte menu is particularly good value.

C P S

St John's Restaurant 259 St John's Rd, Corstophine ☎ 031-334 2857
Open: Mon–Sat 11am–10pm, Sun 3pm–10pm

This compact restaurant with Mexican-style décor is next door to a modern fish and chip shop which is part of the same operation. The à la carte menu offers a choice of dishes to suit even the tightest budget, with main courses such as haddock and chips and beefburger and chips. Omelettes, steaks, pastas and pizzas are also available and there is a three-course business lunch.

P S

Stakis Steakhouse 26 Frederick St
☎ 031-225 2103
Open: Mon–Sat 12noon–2.30pm, 5–10.30pm, 11pm Fri, Sun 12.30–2pm, 6–10pm

This is one of the Stakis Organisation steakhouses, and typical of its kind, offering a starter of soup, pâté or prawn cocktail, and sweets of peach melba, gâteau or apple pie inclusive in the cost of the main course. Haddock, gammon, chicken, or beefburger are all served with jacket or chipped potatoes and peas. The steaks may come over our limit. It is in the heart of Edinburgh, just off Princes Street and is spacious, and ideal for the family, as there is a three-course children's menu.

C

EGGESFORD
Devon
Map **3** SS61

Fox and Hounds Hotel★★
☎ (0769) 80345
Open: Bar: Mon–Thu 11.30am–1.45pm, 6–9.30pm, Fri–Sat 11.30am–1.45pm, 6–10pm, Sun 7–9.30pm
Restaurant: Mon–Sun, 7.30–9pm

The Fox and Hounds Hotel, close to the River Taw, halfway between Exeter and Barnstaple, is a rambling country hotel, the mecca of fishermen. The Eggesford Bar offers a wide range of snacks at a reasonable price. A salad bar in summer offers an impressive choice. A Fox's lunch, consisting of French bread, ham and cheese, garnished with tomato and pickle is served. In the tourist season, a four-course dinner is served in the hotel dining room though it is outside our limit.

P

EGHAM
Surrey
Map **4** TQ07

Maggie's Wine Bar 2 St Judes Rd, Englefield Green ☎ (0784) 37397
Open: Mon–Thu 11am–2.30pm, 7–10.30pm, Fri–Sat 11am–2.30pm, 7–11pm, Sun 12noon–2pm, 7–10.30pm

If you are energetic enough you can 'do' the Runnymede Memorial, the Kennedy Memorial, the RAF Memorial before dropping in at Maggies Wine Bar. Here John Barnikel creates daily menus which include unusual soups such as egg and prawn, home-made pâtés, moussaka and lasagne and for the trencherman, an English sirloin steak platter.

C P S

ELLESMERE
Shropshire
Map **7** SJ33

The Black Lion Scotland St
☎ (069171) 2418
Open: Restaurant Mon–Fri 6.30–9.30pm
Bar: Mon–Sat 11.30am–2pm, 6.30–9.30pm, Sun 12noon–1.30pm, 6.30–9.30pm

This early 16th-century inn stands in the centre of Ellesmere. In the dining room, with its exposed beams and simple décor, steak, chicken and scampi are supplemented by sole in prawn and mushroom sauce (one of the most expensive dishes), and lasagne. There's a wide range of standard bar meals. The special Black Lion Ploughman's is guaranteed to satisfy the most ravenous ploughman, with its red and white Cheshire and Stilton cheeses, bread and salad.

C P S

ENFIELD
Gt London
Map **4** TQ39

Divers Wine and Cocktail Bar 29 Silver St ☎ 01-367 2549
Open: Tue–Fri 12noon–2.30pm, Mon–Sun 7.30–10.30pm, 11pm Fri & Sat

This rather smart little wine bar is a distinctive feature of the tree-lined street. The backboard menu offers daily specialities such as chili con carne, goulash or roast chicken. Pizzas, quiches and ploughman's are always available and desserts include a delicious chocolate cherry gâteau. A dazzling selection of wines and good background music make this a popular mealtime haunt. Summer visitors may like to eat in the sheltered, paved garden to the rear of the restaurant.

♫ P S

ENVILLE
Staffordshire
Map **7** SO88

Granary Wine Bar, The Cat Inn
☎ (038483) 2209
Open: Mon–Sat 12noon–2pm, 7.30–10.30pm

The wine bar is located on the first floor of this original coaching inn. It is furnished with country-style tables and chairs and the countryside theme is completed with a display of farming implements. Salads are served during the summer, except for Friday evenings when a large roast is available and hot dishes including casseroles are served during the winter. Fresh salmon is on the menu, as is lobster (when in season).

P

EPPING
Essex
Map **5** TL40

Beaton's Wine Bar 319 High St
☎ (0378) 72096
Open: Mon–Sun 12noon–3pm, 6–11pm (opens 7pm–Sun evening)

This small wine bar is very popular with the locals. Have a look at the blackboard menu and choose from lasagne verdi, trout riesling or try one of the Beatons 'specials' such as carbonnade of beef. There is simple wooden pew seating and a pleasant candle-lit atmosphere. A small selection of wines is available.

♫ P

ESHER
Surrey
Map **4** TQ16

Julie's Bistro 10 High St
☎ (0372) 66697
Open: Mon–Sun 10am–4.30pm, Tue–Sat 6–10.30pm

This tastefully-decorated bistro is situated in the centre of Esher, near the race course and on the main A3. Burgers with salad or jacket potato or chips, boeuf bourguignon, chicken supreme and sauté turbigo are just a few of the main dishes. There is a good range of starters and sweets.

[♫] [P] [♧]

ETON
Berkshire
Map **4** SU97

The Eton Buttery 73 High St
☎ (07535) 54479
Open: Mon–Sun 9.30am–10.30pm

Alongside the Thames and next to the bridge joining Windsor to Eton is this bright, modern buttery with its smart French cane chairs and elegant pot plants. Take a tray and make your choice from the cool and colourful salads, cold meats and poultry on display, or try a hot dish such as home-made steak and kidney pie. Find a window seat and watch the boats on the river below, with Windsor Castle in the background. There is an à la carte menu in the evening.

[C] [♫] [S] [♧] **VS**

Eton Wine Bar 82–83 High St
☎ (07535) 55182/54921
Open: Mon–Thu 11.30am–2.30pm, 6–10.30pm, Fri–Sat 11.30am–2.30pm, 6–11pm, Sun 12noon–2pm, 7–10.30pm

Within earshot of the famous College, this attractive wine bar is the place to go for good wholesome food and a folksy atmosphere. Décor is simple, with scrubbed wooden floors, church-pew seating and stripped-pine furniture. Alternatively you can sit out in the small garden. Mike and Bill Gilbey and their wives do the cooking, producing such delights as smoked haddock soup and old English beef and mussel pie.

[S]

EVANTON
Highland *Ross & Cromarty*
Map **14** NH66

Foulis Ferry 1½m S of Evanton on A9
☎ (0349) 830535
Open: Mon–Sat 10am–11pm, Sun 12noon–6pm

Who pays the Ferryman? It's not important in this white-painted converted cottage restaurant where the ferryman once lived and where reasonably-priced meals are now served. Salads, quiches and simple, home-baked meals are available daily. The evening à la carte menu is too expensive for us.

[P]

EVESHAM
Hereford & Worcester
Map **4** SP04

The Vine Wine Bar 16 Vine St
☎ (0386) 6799
Open: Mon–Sat 11.30am–2.30pm, Mon–Thu 6.30–10.30pm, Fri & Sat 6.30–11pm

This small, intimate wine bar is situated opposite the old stocks in Evesham. Inside the tables are decorated with fresh posies, and church pews are used for seating. Meals are ordered at the servery and the main courses are accompanied by fresh vegetables or by one of the 20 salads which are available. There is a good range of dishes available at lunchtime and the evening menu could include pear in curry cream sauce and supreme of chicken wrapped in smoked bacon with stilton sauce. There is also a delicious range of home-made desserts. The extensive wine list includes wines from America and Australia as well as Europe.

[P] [♧]

EWELL
Surrey
Map **4** TQ26

The Loose Box 2 Cheam Rd
☎ 01-393 8522
Open: Mon–Sat 11am–2.30pm, Mon–Thu 5.30–10.30pm, Fri, Sat 5.30–11pm

This stylish wine bar is a hub of activity in this suburban Surrey village. One attraction is the dazzling array of bargain-priced food – the menu includes game pie and salad, a selection of home-made quiches, with salad and lasagne. Cheesecakes, gâteaux and home-made applie pie are also available.

[♫] [P] [S] **VS**

EWHURST GREEN
East Sussex
Map **5** TQ72

The White Dog Inn Ewhurst Green
☎ (058083) 264
Open: Mon–Sat 12noon–2pm, 6–10pm, Sun 12noon–1.30pm, 7.15–10pm

This part 17th-century village inn, with recent additions, is set in 11 acres of gardens and woodlands in a peaceful Sussex village. Mine hosts are Tim and Pat Knowland. While Pat prepares the meals Tim looks after the bar and restaurant. The menu is chalked on the wall and features mainly English dishes. You could try home-made soup, home-made steak and kidney pie with fresh vegetables, and tipsy cake.

[P] [♧] **VS**

EXETER
Devon
Map **3** SX99

Clare's 13 Princesshay ☎ (0392) 55155
Open: Mon–Sat 9.30am–5.30pm

There are some classy shops in Princesshay, a pedestrian area just off the High Street and not far from the Cathedral, and Clare Dowell and Simon Shattock's brightly modern counter-service restaurant is just the place for a snack or lunch when you tire of looking in the gift shops and boutiques. It's justly popular with office workers, too, who have to find the quickest and cheapest good food around. Clare's goes 'Continental' in the summer with tables and chairs shaded by umbrellas on the pavement outside the restaurant. 'Country style' hot dishes such as lasagne with rice and salad garnish, steak and kidney pie and gammon and courgettes in a cheese sauce are on the menu along with salads served with quiche, pizza and meats. Clare's is licensed to sell wines, beer and cider.

[P] [S] [♧]

Coolings Wine Bar 11 Gandy St
☎ (0392) 34183
Open: Mon–Sat 12noon–2.15pm, 5.30–11.30pm

Tucked away in one of the older, interesting streets behind the main shopping area is this stylish, family-run wine and food bar where all the food is freshly-prepared on the premises. Beams and checked tablecloths create a welcoming interior and you can also dine in the converted cellars. An excellent range of meats, pies and salads is displayed on the long self-service bar, including such delights as chicken Waldorf and salad and sugar-baked ham and salad. Hot dishes such as lasagne and cottage pie are chalked up on the blackboard. There is a choice of about six sweets.

[P] [S]

Great Western Hotel St David's Station Approach ☎ (0392) 74039
Open: Mon–Sun 12noon–2pm, 6–9.30pm

Situated close to St David's Station this hotel with obvious railway connections is popular with both road and rail travellers and local residents. The 'Loco' bar displays prints and sketches of steam engines and has a menu ranging from sandwiches to a more substantial pot of beef bourguignonne served with sauté potatoes and vegetables. Alternatively the Pullman Restaurant offers a set three-course lunch or dinner with a good choice of dishes at a very reasonable price.

[P] [♧]

The Red House Hotel★ 2 Whipton Village Rd, Whipton ☎ (0392) 56104
Open: Mon–Thu 12noon–2.30pm, 7–10pm, Fri–Sat 12noon–2.30pm, 7–10.30pm, Sun 12noon–1.30pm, 7–9.30pm

This imposing red brick building about a mile from the city centre has a warm comfortable décor with oak refectory tables and settles. There is an excellent bar menu from which one may select a snack or a satisfying three-course meal. A crock of delicious home-made soup served with French bread may be followed by a cold platter (a variety of cold meats, pâtés, pies and fish with self-service salad), or a bar grill such as minute steak, chicken or scampi. Large steak platters are also available. There is always a good selection of sweets including gâteaux.

[C] [P] [♧]

The Ship Inn Martin's La
☎ (0392) 72040
Open: Mon–Sat 12noon–2pm, 6.30–10.30pm

Sir Francis Drake wrote in a letter dated 1587 'Next to mine own shippe I do most love that old 'Shippe' in Exon'. Today, good wine and victuals are still there to be enjoyed, and at quite reasonable prices. The upstairs restaurant is perhaps a little dark and cramped, with deep red wallpaper and upholstery, high-backed settles, and windows within a few feet of the building across the lane, but the atmosphere is right and service is very quick and cheerful. All food is à la carte – the same menu for lunch and dinner. Starters include Scott's pâté and – a speciality of the house – whitebait. Fresh Torbay sole is the most popular fish dish. Roasts and grills are also available. All dishes include peas or tossed salad, fried or croquette potatoes, roll and butter. Sweets include vanilla ice with cream and meringue Chantilly.

[C] [♫] [S] [♧]

The Swan's Nest Exminster
☎ (0392) 832371 4m S of Exeter on the A379 to Dawlish
Open: Mon–Sat 12noon–2pm, 6–10pm, Sun 12noon–1.30pm, 7–10pm

Melvyn and Joan Ash have run the Swan's Nest for 16 years, and in that time they have managed to create a delightful and popular inn. Lots of rich, dark oak – and a fresh flower for every table – make for a warm welcome. The menu is simple but very good value – help yourself to crisp, green salads, cold meats, pâtés, sandwiches and fresh filled rolls; plus a superb selection of gâteaux, cheesecakes and fruit flans.

P

EXMOUTH
Devon
Map **3** SY08

Nutwell Lodge Lympstone
☎ (039287) 3279 3m N of Exmouth on the A376
Open: Mon–Sat 12noon–2.30pm, 6–11pm, Sun 12noon–1.30pm, 7–10pm

The vast lounge of this rambling Georgian hotel with its massive, dark wooden bar, glowing pink-shaded lamps, antiques, oil-paintings and intimate sunken area with soft upholstered settees serves a selection of snacks to tempt anyone's palate. Pork and red wine pâté with salad, chutney and toast is a meal in itself. The menu offers a wide selection of hot dishes both at lunchtime and in the evening including grilled lemon sole and roast chicken. Platters of cold meats, crab and prawn are also available. Sweets such as apple strüdel with cream, gâteaux and cheesecake are popular.

P

Ye Olde Saddler's Arms Lympstone
☎ (03952) 72798 2m N of Exmouth on the A376
Open: Mon–Sat 12noon–2pm, 7–10pm, Sun 12noon–2pm

Nestling in the picturesque village of Lympstone is this charming cream-painted inn, with tables and gay umbrellas in the pleasant garden when the sun shines. The food bar offers a range of home-made daily specials which are chalked on the blackboard, dishes include steak and onion pie and ham, egg and chips. A choice of salad platters, grills and fish dishes are available on the à la carte menu and there are special children's meals.

C P ♧

FAKENHAM
Norfolk
Map **9** TF93

The Crown Hotel Market Pl
☎ (0328) 2010
Open: bars: Mon–Wed, Fri–Sun, licensing hours, Thu 10.30am–4.30pm, 5.30–11pm
Restaurant: Mon–Sat 12.15–2pm, 7.15–9.15pm, Sun 12.15–2pm

In the restaurant, dark oak beams and panelling are offset by gold tablecloths and napkins, a red carpet and red-globed oil table lamps. A three course table d'hôte lunch offers a good choice for all courses. Sardine and tomato salad, Florida cocktail or ravioli are examples of starters, a selection of roasts make up the main course and sweets from the trolley include cheesecake, fruit and cream or éclairs. A slightly extended menu operates for a three-course dinner. A three-course Sunday lunch is good value. The à la carte menu offers more exotic dishes but they are outside the range of this guide.

C ♫ P S

The Limes Hotel Bridge St
☎ (0328) 2726
Open: Mon–Sat 10.30am–2.30pm, 6.30–11pm, Sun 12noon–2pm, 7–10.30pm

This friendly free house was created in 1975 and has an excellent reputation for fresh, home-cooked food. The 'Summer Special' three-course lunch offers a good choice of dishes for each course. The 'Winter Specials' offers warming starters and sweets. A cold lunch buffet is on offer in the conservatory – and all the meats are home-cooked. À la carte dinner by candlelight offers a very wide selection.

P S

FALKIRK
Central *Stirlingshire*
Map **11** NS87

Hotel Cladhan Kemper Ave
☎ (0324) 27421
Open: Mon–Sat 12noon–2pm, 7–9.15pm, Sun 12noon–2pm

This large, modern hotel is built on the site of a Roman wall, and the personal touch is provided by the owners Mr and Mrs Reid, who serve modestly priced bar meals in the spacious lounge bars (children's portions are available). The dining room offers a good à la carte menu, but many of the selections will take you over our budget.

C ♫ P ♧

FALMOUTH
Cornwall
Map **2** SW83

Crill House Hotel Golden Bank
☎ (0326) 312994
Open: Mar–Oct Mon–Sun 11.30am–3pm, 7–8pm

This attractive, peaceful, small country hotel lies just west of Budock Water Village and personal service is provided by the owners, the Fenton family. Morning coffee, cream teas and snack lunches ranging from sandwiches to scampi and chips are all available. There are three dinner menus two of which are within our price range. Snacks can also be served in the evening.

C P **VS**

Greenbank Hotel★★★ Harbourside
☎ (0326) 312440
Open: Mon–Sun 12.30–2pm, 7–10pm

Officers and passengers would leave their full-rigged packet ships and tea clippers at anchorage just off the pier of this attractive harbourisde hotel before unwinding with a good meal. The names of ships and their captains and other nautical memorabilia adorn the walls of the Greenbank. Today this traditional hotel offers good honest food to a different clientele. The lunch is especially good value and offers a fair choice. And how could one better complement a main course of fresh grilled fillet of mackerel meunière than to sit before spectacular views of the mouth of the River Fal?

C P

FAREHAM
Hampshire
Map **4** SU50

Gabbies 30–32 West St
☎ (0329)284853
Open: Mon–Sat from 10am until late

This smart hamburger restaurant in the older pedestrian shopping area boasts far more than weighty burgers on its menu. You can enjoy a good three-course meal here or just catch a snack – filled jacket potatoes, French bread sandwiches, pancakes, pizzas, etc. Sweets include gâteaux, cheesecakes, and ice cream sundaes. If you have a taste and appetite for burgers, Gabbies special is excellent – a ¼lb or ½lb lean beefburger topped with mushrooms, peppers, tomato and melted cheese and served in a toasted roll.

C ♫ P S

FARNHAM
Surrey
Map **4** SU84

Lion and Lamb Tea Room The Courtyard, West St ☎ (0252) 715434
Open: Mon–Sat 9.30–11.30am, 12.15–1.30pm, 3–4.45pm, Fri & Sat 7.30–9.30pm. Closed Sun and Bank Hols

This attractive café, in a quaint cobbled courtyard, is run by Mr Manzoli who personally supervises the cooking and service. All the dishes are home-made and the menus are changed daily. Morning coffee, lunch, afternoon tea and dinner (Fri and Sat only) are available. Especially recommended are the almond slices, sausage rolls, and Danish pastries, or at lunchtime try steak and kidney pie served with fresh vegetables and potatoes. There are two Italian dinner menus for Friday and Saturday with a choice of dishes.

P S ♧

Sevens 7 The Borough ☎ (0252)715345
Open: Mon–Sat 12noon–2.30pm, 6.30–10.30pm, Fri–Sat 11pm

Sevens has an intimate atmosphere – from the crowded wine bar at the front to the low-ceilinged bistro at the rear and on the first floor. Starters include a delicious mushroom pâté and lasagne and veal escalope in cream and mushroom sauce are typical of main course dishes. There is a good range of delicious desserts. Very popular with business people and shoppers, it is wise to get to Sevens early!

C ♫ P S ♧

FAVERSHAM
Kent
Map **5** TR06

The Recreation Tavern Restaurant 16 East St ☎ (0795) 6033
Open: Mon–Sun 12noon–2pm, 7–10pm

Once a 17th-century, square oast house this small tavern has been tastefully restored by the present owner. You can choose from a hot or cold buffet including over a dozen salads, meats cut from the bone and a variety of dishes accompanied by salad. You may also be tempted by one of Chef Nita Evans' delectable sweets. Interesting hot dishes are always available.

C ♫ P S ♧

The White Lion Coach House Restaurant, The Street, Selling
☎ (022785) 211
Open: Mon–Sat 12noon–2.30pm, 7–10.30pm, Sun 12noon–1.30pm, bar snacks only 7–9.30pm

This former coaching house is more than 300 years old and has no less than three inglenook fireplaces which add to its character and warmth. Good, traditional hospitality can be found here and there is a good range of bar snacks, including Stilton ploughman's, Goujons of Plaice or home-made beefburgers. A table d'hôte menu offers three courses within our price limit and is available at lunch or dinner.

P ♧

See advertisement on page 000

FELIXSTOWE
Suffolk
Map **5** TM33

Buttery Bar, Orwell Moat House★★★★ Hamilton Rd
☎ (03942) 5511
Open: Mon–Sat 12noon–2pm, 6–9.15pm, Sun 12noon–2pm

This elegant buttery with its dark oak panels and richly-ornamented ceiling offers you all the comfort and luxury of a four-star hotel without the prices. Home-made soup of the day could be followed by smoked Scotch salmon, Norfolk turkey, ox tongue or other cold meats all served with salads, pickles, and a roll and butter. Finish with home-made fruit pie and you'll still be within the budget. The restaurant offers a table d'hôte lunch.

C P ♧ **VS**

FENNY BRIDGES
Devon
Map **3** SY19

The Palomino Pony 3m W of Honiton on the A30 ☎ (0404) 850380
Open: Mon–Sat 10.30am–2.30pm, 5.30–11pm, Sun 12noon–2pm, 5.30–10pm, closes 10.30pm in Winter

This 17th-century thatched inn, originally an old coaching house, oozes with charm and character. The food bar offers a good range of home-made meals and snacks using fresh local produce wherever possible. Salads, pies, quiches and grills are just a few options. Real ale is served at the bar and there is a large selection of knock-out cocktails. There is a children's room and families are always welcome. The Palomino Pony also provides accommodation.

C P ♧

FIDDLEFORD
Dorset
Map **3** ST83

Fiddleford Inn ☎ (0258) 72489
Open: Summer: Mon–Sat 12noon–2.30pm, 6–11pm; Winter: 6.30–10.30pm (11pm Fri and Sat); Sun 12noon–2pm, 7–10.30pm

This creeper-clad inn makes a welcome stopping-place on the beautiful, but remote A357 – the Sturminster Newton/Blandford road. Informality is the keynote and your hosts Philip, Valerie and Joyce Wilson ensure that there's a warm and cosy atmosphere. The emphasis is on home-made foods using fresh ingredients. The bar menu offers jumbo sausage and wholemeal pizza (both served with chips) and other dishes such as chicken Kiev and Dorset cured ham, all competitively priced.

P ♧ **VS**

FOLKESTONE
Kent
Map **5** TR23

Pullman Wine Bar 7 Church St
☎ (0303) 52524
Open: Mon–Sat 12noon–2pm, 7–9.30pm

The Tudor-style building housing Michael and Janet Barnwell's wine bar is thought by some to be the most beuutiful in Folkestone. Hot and cold dishes are presented buffet-style. Oven-fresh pizzas, home-made casseroles and pies feature on the menu along with gâteau and home-made fruit pies. In fine weather, meals may be enjoyed in the attractive garden.

♫ P S ♧ **VS**

FOLKINGHAM
Lincolnshire
Map **8** TF03

Quaintways 17 Market Pl ☎ (05297) 496
Open: Mon–Sun 11.30am–2.30pm, Thu–Sat 7–10.30pm

The Dutch-barn-style brick building with a bow window stands in the centre of this lovely village. Andrew and Robert Scott opened the restaurant and tea room in June 1982, and hospitality combined with value for money is the simple secret of their success. Robert entertains the diners in the evening by playing the organ. The lunch menu is excellent value though there is a rather limited choice, this also applies to 'Tonight's Supper Menu'. The 'Chef's Specialities' menu offers some very tempting meals but they are beyond the price range of this guide.

♫ P ♧

FORFAR
Tayside *Angus*
Map **15** NO45

August Moon 114 Castle St
☎ (0307) 64105
Open: Mon–Sat 11.30am–2pm, 5–11.30pm, Sun 4–11.30pm

For those who think that all Chinese restaurants have a stereotyped appearance with very little individuality, a visit to August Moon will prove a pleasant experience. No embossed wallpaper or Chinese lanterns here. This little eating place has a charm and character all of its own, with white roughcast walls and cosy Tudor-style banquettes. A comprehensive à la carte menu offers the usual complement of Oriental dishes plus a selection of European ones. The price of all main courses includes boiled rice, and a heated stand is laid on your table to keep the whole thing hot. A set meal for two of fried spring roll, sweet and sour pork, chicken with cashew nuts and vegetables, mixed vegetables, egg fried rice plus coffee or tea offers excellent value.

FORRES
Grampian *Moray*
Map **14** NJ05

The Elizabethan Inn✕✕ Mondale
☎ (0309) 72526
Open: Mon, Tue, Thu–Sun 10.30am–3pm, 7.30–8.30pm, Wed 12.30–1.30pm

An authentic cottage atmosphere and honest-to-goodness home-cooked fare can be found about two miles west of Forres. Built of stone and close to the River Findhorn, the interior has brick and stone walls, Victorian and antique tables and chairs and a rare air of relaxation. Table d'hôte lunches of two or three courses come well within our limits, but dinner would be more expensive.

FORT WILLIAM
Highland *Inverness-shire*
Map **14** NN17

The Angus Restaurant 66 High St
☎ (0397) 2654
Open: Summer Mon–Sat 10.30am–10pm, Sun 6–10pm

The Angus first-floor restaurant and ground-floor lounge bar has been strikingly created from former shop premises. Red is the colour theme of the well-appointed restaurant which offers an 'Angus' lunch – two courses plus tea or coffee at a very reasonable price. Particularly recommended on the à la carte menu are the salmon steak (available in season) and the grilled 'Lochy' trout.

S ♧

McTavish's Kitchen High St
☎ (0397) 2406
Open: Restaurant Easter and mid-May to end Sep Mon–Sun 12noon–2.30pm 6–10.30pm
Self-service Mon–Sun Summer 9am–7.30pm or later

Excellent food, Scottish cabaret acts (summer evenings) and obliging staff are features here. Although prices in the main restaurant are rather near the limit, there is a popular three-course 'budget special' lunch. Fish, steak and omelettes are also available. The ground-floor and self-service restaurant offer a less pricey selection of meals.

♫ P S

FOSSEBRIDGE
Gloucestershire
Map **4** SP01

Fossebridge Inn★★ ☎ (028572) 310
Open: Mon–Sun 12noon–2pm, Sun 1.30pm, 7–9.30pm

Ideally-placed in a wooded valley and beside a small river is this part-Georgian, part-Tudor inn, with its roaring log fires, stone walls and beautiful antiques. Most of the dishes on offer are home-made including soup, pâté, pies, and sweets. There is also a cold buffet with a choice of eight salads. Daily 'specials' are chalked on the blackboard.

P

FOVANT
Wiltshire
Map **4** SU02

The Cross Keys Hotel Shaftesbury Rd
☎ (072270) 284
Open: Buttery Bar: summer: Mon–Sat 10am–2.30pm, 6–11pm, Sun 12noon–2.30pm, 7–10.30pm winter: Mon–Sat 10.30am–2.30pm, 6–10.30pm Sun 12noon–2.30pm, 7–10.30pm

The famous highwayman Jack Rattenbury enjoyed the victuals prepared at the Cross Keys. This charming stone-built hostelry was built around 1485, and can be found in the heart of beautiful countryside. Meals from the extensive menu available in the Buttery Bar include curry, cottage pie and salads; ploughmans and toasted sandwiches are popular snacks. Pauline Story prepares more elaborate dishes for the evening meal.

C P ♧ **VS**

FOWLMERE
Cambridgeshire
Map **5** TL44

Chequers Inn ☎ (076382) 369
Open: Mon–Sun 12noon–2pm, 7–10pm.

This historic and interesting inn, built in 1675, has a Minstrel Gallery and a Priest Hole and is said to have been a chapel of rest at one time. It was frequented by Samuel Pepys and extracts of his writings are displayed on the walls. It was also a popular place with the British and American pilots who were stationed nearby during the war and pictures of the planes and their crews are also displayed. The varied menu has some unusual items such as Hot Duck's Liver on a bed of Sorrel or Battons of Bacon and Prawns tossed together on a bed of lettuce. Meals can be enjoyed either in the lounge bar or in the attractive gardens to the rear of the inn. Half portions can be ordered for children.

[C] [P]

FOXT
Staffordshire
Map **7** SK04

The Fox and Goose Foxt, off the A52
☎ (053871) 415
Open: Mon 7–10pm, Tue–Sat 12noon–2pm, 7–10pm, Sun 12noon–1.30pm, 7–10pm

This charming 17th-century inn is situated in the rather remote village of Foxt on the Staffordshire moors. It is popular with both locals and tourists and the proprietors, Ken and Eve Tudor, extend a warm and friendly welcome to all. A three-course meal in the extended dining room could be grapefruit Florida, mixed grill and lemon and meringue pie. If you prefer something lighter then try one of the bar snacks.

[P]

FRAMLINGHAM
Suffolk
Map **5** TM26

Market Place Restaurant 18 Market Hill
☎ (0728) 723866
Open: Tue–Sat 12noon–2pm, 7–9.30pm

This tiny cottage restaurant on the corner of the market place has shuttered windows and a light, modern interior. A range of light snacks and elaborate meals is available suitable for both families and the discerning diner. Paul Stracey, the manager and head chef, also offers a series of light-hearted but interesting cookery lessons at the restaurant. Main courses at lunch time include open sandwiches, burgers, omelettes, beef salad and tagliatelle. Vegetables are extra. There is a range of sweets to choose from. Take care with your choice as some of the dishes will take you over the limit. The extensive dinner menu is, alas, too expensive for this guide.

[P]

FRECKLETON
Lancashire
Map **7** SD42

The Ship Inn ☎ (0772) 32393
Open: Quarter Deck Restaurant: Mon–Sun 12noon–2.30pm, 7–9.45pm
The Gallery: Mon–Sun 12noon–2.30pm, Sat 7.30–10.15pm

The Ship was built about 10 years ago on the site of a hostelry of the same name which dated back to 1630. The interior is designed along the lines of a ship, with a 'Sharp End' bar and another called the Galley. In the latter you can get a help-yourself repast called 'Scandhovee' which is very popular locally. You can take an à la carte meal in the Quarter Deck Restaurant but it would be all too easy to top our limit. The speciality is fish with even the salads weighted on the side of seafoods. The table d'hôte lunch is well within limits, melon, grilled pork chop and apple sauce with vegetables, followed by sherry trifle, is an example of what to expect.

[C] [P] [S]

FROME
Somerset
Map **3** ST74

The Settle Cheap St
Open: Mon–Sat 9am–5.30pm (closes 2.30pm Thu), May to Oct Sun 2.30–6.30pm

The Settle Restaurant, a scheduled building dating back to the 17th century, is situated in Cheap Street, a picturesque walkway in the centre of this Somerset market town. Here you can enjoy breakfast, morning coffee, lunch and afternoon tea and, during the summer, Sunday teas. The emphasis is on home-cooking and specialities include cheese muffins, shepherds purse (a variety of treacle cake) and the Frome Bobbin created by proprietor Margaret Vaughan – apricots and figs soaked in Somerset cider and baked in pastry. Three course lunches feature traditional dishes using fresh local produce, try the West country chicken casserole or local trout and mackerel. The Settle is licensed.

[S]

GARTHMYL
Powys
Map **7** SO19

The Nag's Head Hotel ☎ (068685) 287
Open: Mon–Sat 11am–2.30pm, 6–10.30pm (11pm Fri & Sat), Sun 12noon–2pm, 7–10.30pm

The atmosphere is cosy and intimate at the Nag's Head, where tasty home-cooked meals are served in the restaurant. Locally grown fresh produce is used where possible and the home-made dishes include steak and kidney pie and beouf bourguignon. There is also a daily 'Chef's Special'. When it comes to choosing the wine to accompany your meal why not try the house wine which carries the Nag's Head own label?

[C] [P]

See advertisement on page 84

GATESHEAD
Tyne & Wear
Map **12** NZ26

The Griddle 409 Durham Rd, Low Fell
☎ (0632) 874530
Open: Mon–Sat 9am–5.30pm, 7.30–10pm

Morning coffee and afternoon tea are served with a range of snacks in this first-floor restaurant. At lunch-time salads and a choice of hot dishes are available. The delicious pastries and pies are home-made. Tempting three-course meals (just within our budget) are on the menu in the evenings.

[P]

GISBURN
Lancashire
Map **7** SD84

Cottage Restaurant Main St
☎ (02005) 441
Open: Mon 12noon–2pm, Tue–Sun 11.30am–6pm, closed Wed

With its low-beamed ceilings and warmth of welcome from proprietors Mr and Mrs Farnworth, the Cottage Restaurant lives up to the traditional charm suggested by its name. Home cooking – the steak and kidney pie and home-cooked ham are particularly good – is accompanied by chips and peas, salad or jacket potato. A three-course meal will come well within our budget.

♫ P ♧

GLASBURY
Powys
Map **3** SO13

Llwynaubach Lodge★★
☎ (04974) 473
Open: Mon–Sun 12noon–2.30pm, 7.30–10.30pm

Llwynaubach Lodge enjoys a peaceful situation in the Wye Valley with 10 acres of grounds including its own trout-filled lake and an outdoor swimming pool. At lunchtime during the week, hot and cold bar snacks, sandwiches and salads are available. Chef's carving table offers hot roast joints in the evenings and for Sunday lunch.

C ♫ P ♧

GLASGOW
Strathclyde *Lanarkshire*
Map **11** NS56

Ad-Lib (Mid Atlantic) 111 Hope St
☎ 041-248 7102
Open: Mon–Sat 12noon–2am, Sun 6pm–1am

With stainless steel floor (yes floor), painted brick and hessian-hung walls covered with original movie posters of yesteryear, checked tablecloths and excellent service from friendly staff, this American diner, opposite Glasgow Central Station, is a good place for a quick lunch or a leisurely evening meal. A selection of American hamburgers, served with chips, salad and a choice of pickles, is available. Main courses include kebabs, vegetarian pancakes, and Texas-style chilli. Sweets include pancakes with hot fudge and cream, and American cheesecake with fruit and cream, which explains perhaps, the diner's popularity with children. A business lunch of ¼lb hamburger with potatoes and salad, pancake, and coffee is available at a very reasonable price.

C ♫ S ♧ **VS**

The Belfry 652 Argyll St
☎ 041-221 0630
Open: Mon–Fri 12noon–3pm, 6–10pm, Sat 6–10pm. Closed Sun

There can't be many restaurants which include a stuffed alligator in their ornamentation! This is just one of the unusual items in this atmospheric wine bar in the basement of one of Glasgow's oldest and most popular restaurants. The décor is interesting with polished wooden floorboards, stone and wood-panelled walls, bookshelves and bric-à-brac. The menu is equally imaginative, including such items as Avocado and Strawberry Vinaigrette or Potato skins with melted cheese and soured cream as starters. The main course could be trout, chilli or a variety of char-grilled burgers, followed by such mouthwatering delights as American Nut Cake or Butterscotch Pie.

C ♫ P ♧

La Buca 191 Hope St ☎ 041-332 7120
Open: Mon–Sat 12noon–11pm

There is a definite Italian air to this pleasant pizzeria in the heart of Glasgow, accentuated by the Italian background music and the red-shirted Italian waiters. Pizzas are freshly prepared and the range includes pizza Quattro Stagioni, a delicious concoction of ham, olives, anchovies and mozzarella cheese. With a starter of insalata di mare (seafood salad) and figs with fresh cream for dessert you have a satisfying three course meal. If you don't like pizza there are many other grills or pasta dishes to choose from such as sirloin steak with salad or lasagne all forno.

♧ **VS**

Cul de Sac 44 Ashton La, Hillhead
☎ 041-334 4749
Open: Mon–Sat 10am–12mdnt, Sun 12noon–12mdnt

This continental-style crêperie has an informal atmosphere and is popular with businessmen, shoppers and students alike. Crêpes form the basis of the menu, try the savoury seafood and avocado or the sweet bananas and rum. Other dishes include omelettes and steaks. Cul de Sac is licensed so you can enjoy a glass of wine with your meal.

[♫] [P]

Delta Restaurant 283 Sauchiehall St
☎ 041-332 3661
Open: Mon–Sat 10am–7.30pm

Situated at the western end of Sauchiehall Street, this tartan-floored basement restaurant with pine-clad walls welcomes you with soft music for a three-course meal which includes such wholesome dishes as Loch Fyne herrings in oatmeal or sizzling roast pork with apple sauce. Smart waitresses serve morning coffee, lunch and, after three o'clock, high tea consists of a main dish such as fried fillet of haddock with French fried potatoes plus a pot of tea and buttered toast.

[♫] [S]

Epicures Bistro 46 West Nile St
☎ 041-221 7488
Open: Mon–Sat 8.30am–6pm

A first-floor restaurant usefully sited in the heart of the shopping centre, Epicures has an attractive tiled floor and director's chair seating. If you're lucky you can enjoy your meal in a window seat overlooking West Nile Street. Food is reasonably priced and the menu offers some interesting dishes. Try smoked haddock mousse, a delicately flavoured mousse made with fresh cream, eggs and smoked haddock, followed by crépe poulet forestière, savoury pancakes filled with chicken, peppers, tomatoes, onions, bacon and other vegetables, and finish with Martian Moondust, chocolate ice-cream, banana, pineapples, fresh whipped cream, chocolate suace, ground almonds, sprinkled cocoa and cherries, all within our budget. Attentive and fast service.

[S]

Hansom Bar, The Fountain Restaurant
2 Woodside Cres ☎ 041-332 6396
Open: Mon–Fri 12noon–2.15pm, 5–9pm, Sat 5–9pm

Not so much a bar, more a sort of bistro is the Hansom, downstairs in the elegant Georgian building which houses the upmarket Fountain Restaurant. There is always a good choice of cooked dishes available, such as mussel and onion stew and Hansom Pie. If you are hungry after 9pm then pâté and toast and cheese and biscuits are available. The Hansom is very popular and inclined to be crowded at lunchtime, but the atmosphere is friendly and relaxed nevertheless.

[C] [♫] [S]

Massimo's 465 Clarkston Rd, Muirend
☎ 041-637 8568
Open: Mon–Sun 10am–8pm

This simple eating house on the south side of the city puts the emphasis on quality and value for money. All food is freshly prepared daily and this is a place where the proprietor always finds time to chat with his guests and thank them for their custom. The almost obligatory chianti-bottle lights stand on clean pine tables with benches which seat around 30 people. Minestrone soup followed by roast beef salad and rum baba is an inexpensive meal.

Moussaka House 36 Kelvingrove St
☎ 041-332 2510
Open: Mon–Sat 12noon–2pm, 6pm–12mdnt, Sun 6.30–11pm

'The best value in town' is the claim made for this restaurant's lunchtime menu – and they could be right. As the name suggests, a variety of moussaka dishes are the main feature, but kebab, stuffed pepper, or plainer dishes are also available. Soup and sweet are kept simple. It should be easy to choose an appetising meal of Greek specialities from the à la carte and still keep within our budget. Try houmous (chick pea 'pâté'), moussaka special (mince, aubergines, courgettes, potatoes, cheese and tomatoes) and a sweet from the trolley. A red and brown colour scheme, a plastic vine draped over a wooden archway and Greek music contribute to the Mediterranean atmosphere.

[C] [♫] [P]

The Pancake Place 8–12 Stockwell St
☎ 041-552 4528
Open: Mon–Sat 9.30am–6.30pm, Sun 12noon–5pm

Just around the corner from one of the city's busiest shopping streets is this attractive restaurant serving pancakes 'just like your mother's'. Full-size and snack-size savoury pancakes are available. Try the Rocky Mountain burger two pancakes, layered with two beefburgers and topped with a cheese sauce. Sweet pancakes, for those not watching their waistlines are also on the menu or try a 'spoon sized' portion.

[♫] [P] [S]

Pizza Park 515 Sauchiehall St
☎ 041-221 5967
Open: Mon–Sun 10am–11.30pm

At the western end of Sauchiehall Street this bright, airy restaurant attracts office workers and shoppers alike. There is a good selection of pizzas, and also burgers, chilli, barbecue spare ribs and spaghetti bolognese all at reasonable prices. For starters and desserts, try corn on the cob and strawberry cheesecake. There is a small selection of wines and beers.

[C] [♫] [P] **VS**

Ramana 427 Sauchiehall St
☎ 041-332 2528/2590
Open: Mon–Sun 12noon–12mdnt

Never tried Indian food? Try Ramana then, for the well-designed menu explains what each dish contains and how it is cooked. The lounge bar, too, is well-designed with lush Kashmir furniture. Tandoori dishes (cooked in a charcoal-fired clay oven) are the house speciality – there's chicken tandoori with salad or sheesh kebab Turkish (made with fillet steak) served with rice, salad and sauce. And especially recommended for the 'beginner' are birianies and pillaus. If you're still not convinced that Indian food is for you, there's a list of Western dishes too, so you can choose fish and chips or grilled steak if you must. The business person's lunch is very popular – doubtless for the oriental atmosphere which wafts the diner away from Glasgow for a little while, as well as for the good, low-priced food.

C ♫ P S ✿ VS

Secrets 1487 Gt Western Rd
☎ 041-334 9491
Open: Mon–Thu 12noon–11pm, Fri & Sat 12noon–12mdnt, Sun 6.30–10pm

This ultra-modern restaurant diner is part of the Esquire House complex. The daytime menu offers soup, burgers, pizzas and chicken and pork goujons along with a daily 'Chefs Special'. The extended evening menu offers a good variety of dishes – but take care or you will exceed the budget.

C ♫ P ✿

Silver Moon 5 New Kirk La, Bearsden
☎ 041-942 4592

This nicely-appointed Cantonese restaurant is tucked away in the middle of Bearsden's town centre. However, once you have found it you will not forget it. It is furnished with comfortably padded chairs and the walls are hung with Chinese paintings and embroidery. The staff are friendly and attentive and the food is interesting and good value for money. The business lunch offers exceptional value and in the evening an extensive à la carte menu includes grilled chicken Peking style.

♫ P ✿ VS

Stakis Steakhouse Great Western Rd
☎ 041-339 8811
Open: Mon–Sat 12noon–2.30pm, Sun 12.30–2.30pm, Mon–Sun 5–11pm

This steakhouse (part of a popular chain) is situated on the ground floor of the recently rebuilt Grosvenor Hotel which was destroyed in a fire in 1978. The steakhouse is decorated in the Victorian style, and the service is fast, friendly and attentive. The normal steakhouse menu is available, offering a wide choice of main courses, but take care when choosing your meal as you might exceed the budget.

C ♫ P S ✿ VS

GLASTONBURY

Somerset
Map **3** ST53

Rainbow's End Café 17A High St
☎ (0458) 33896
Open: Mon, Thu and Fri 10am–4.30pm; Tue and Sat 9.30am–4.30pm. Closed Wed and Sun. (Lunch served 12.15–2pm).

Shelagh Spear runs this delightful café which spills out into a sunny courtyard when the weather is nice enough. Inside stripped wood and Laura Ashley prints set the scene and one wall provides a 'gallery' for art exhibitions. The menu, chalked on a blackboard, changes daily and includes wholefood and vegetarian dishes.

S P ✿

GLOSSOP

Derbyshire
Map **7** SK09

Collier's 14 High St East
☎ (04574) 63409
Open: Tue–Sat 12noon–2pm, 7–9pm

If Victoriana is your scene you'll love this restaurant. For behind its brown and cream exterior lies an eating place furnished in the style of great-grandmama's front room – complete with black lead grate! The food however is right up to date with soup, a ploughman's, fish and ice cream on the lunch menu. For dinner scampi and gammon with pineapple are typical main courses. Finish your meal with a tempting sweet and coffee and mints. The restaurant is also open for morning coffee and afternoon tea.

P S ✿ VS

GLOUCESTER

Gloucestershire
Map **3** SO81

The Comfy Pew & the College Green Restaurant College St ☎ (0452) 20739
Open: Comfy Pew Mon–Sat 9am–5.30pm
College Green Restaurant: Mon–Sun 12.15–2pm, Wed–Sat 6.30–9.30pm
Salad Room: Tue–Sat 11.30–2pm

On the main approach to the cathedral, The Comfy Pew lives up to its name with some entirely appropriate seating. David Spencer's food is home-cooked and wholesome. A variety of meat or fish salad platters, and snacks on toast are available along with hot home-made dishes at lunchtime. Upstairs you'll find the College Green Restaurant (also owned by David and Frances Spencer) which offers a very reasonable lunch menu with main courses such as escalope of veal and grilled plaice. The dinner menu is, alas, too expensive for us. The Salad Room offers an excellent choice at lunchtime.

C S

Moran's Eating House 23 Worcester St
☎ (0452) 422024
Open: Tue–Sat 11.30am–2.30pm, Mon–Sat 6.30–11pm. Closed Sun

This small, attractive wine bar and bistro, close to the centre of this cathedral city, is personally managed by Lyn and Brian Moran. In the kitchen Lyn creates interesting and imaginative home-made dishes which complement the intimate and informal atmosphere. Tomato and orange soup, followed by curried beef pancake and salad and enormous home-made sweets such as fresh strawberry meringue should satisfy the largest appetite. Also on the menu are pies, burgers and pasta dishes and Lyn also provides daily specials which are chalked on the blackboard.

P S ✿

GODSHILL

Isle of Wight
Map **4** SZ58

Essex Cottage Restaurant High St
☎ (098389) 232
Open: Etr–Oct Tue–Sat (out of season Sat and Sun only) 12.30–5.30pm, 7–9pm

Godshill is cream tea country with more tea gardens to the square inch, probably, than any other part of the British Isles. The Essex Cottage does a very good cream tea, as well as an excellent table d'hôte lunch. Dinner from the table d'hôte will just exceed our price limit but you will have four courses. The lunch menu is basic English fare including roast beef or chicken and cherry pie and cream.

[C] [P] [S]

GOLDSTONE
Shropshire
Map **7** SJ63

The Wharf Tavern Goldstone Wharf (off A529 S of Market Drayton)
☎ (063086) 226
Open: Mon–Sun 12noon–2pm, Mon–Fri 7–9pm, Sat & Sun 7–9.30pm

This small canal-side inn was once a bargees' alehouse and stables, looking after the needs of up to 100 bargees, their families and horses. It now caters for the new generation of Shropshire canal users who can tie up at the moorings. The chef has been here for over 20 years and is so organised he can be found serving and clearing the tables as well as cooking the huge succulent steaks. The evening menu, offers a variety of grills and most of the dishes are prices just over our limit, but if you want to splash out a bit you will have a thoroughly enjoyable meal. Lunch-time bar snacks and basket meals are also available.

[P]

GOREY
Jersey Channel Islands
Map **16**

The Jersey Pottery Restaurant
☎ (0534) 511119
Open: Mon–Fri 9am–5.30pm. Closed Sat and Sun

We do not usually list cafeterias, but this is one with a difference. It is situated at the famous Jersey Pottery – a popular tourist attraction – and, as well as its modern interior, includes most attractive outdoor seating beneath vines. Meals are served all day in usual cafeteria fashion, but the counter displays are appetising and fresh. Crab or lobster with a crisp salad are particularly recommended and all the pastry dishes are made on the premises. Lovely strawberries-and-cream teas are available too and the cafeteria is licensed.

[C] [P]

GRANTHAM
Lincolnshire
Map **8** SK93

Catlin's 11 High St ☎ (0476) 5428/9
Open: Mon–Tue 9am–6pm, Wed 9am–2pm, Thu–Sat 9am–6pm

Steeped in history, the olde worlde grocery and confectionery shop of Catlin Bros Ltd, boasts a restaurant with wood-panelled walls, oak beams, pottery and bric-à-brac on the first floor. The property dates back to 1560 and its claims to fame include the 'discovery' of Grantham gingerbread and the ghost of one Captain Hamilton, a Royalist officer during the Civil War. Snacks are served throughout the day and a typical meal from the à la carte menu might be home-made soup, pepper and salami pizza with salad and fresh fruit pancake with cream, and the bill will be well within budget. French house wine is very reasonable and, in fact for the buff there is an interesting range of wines from non-fashionable countries. Service is efficient and courteous.

[P] [S]

GRANTOWN-ON-SPEY
Highland *Moray*
Map **14** NJ02

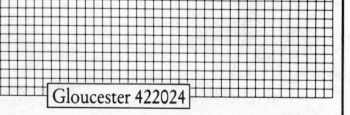

Craggan Mill Restaurant
☎ (0479) 2288
Open: Summer Mon–Sun 12.30–2pm, 6–10pm, Winter Mon–Sun 7–10pm

A plain and rustic style is favoured by proprietors Bruno and Ann Bellini. Cuisine is a winning mixture of Italian and British, as the stylish menu reflects. A starter, such as mussels in wine or mushrooms and Stilton soup, should be followed by scampi provençale or chicken in cream. Interesting sweets are available.

[P] [wine]

GRANTSHOUSE
Borders *Berwickshire*
Map **12** NT86

Cedar Cafeteria ¼ S off A1
☎ (03615) 270
Open: Mon 9am–6pm, Tue–Fri 8am–6pm, Sat 8am–closes at discretion of proprietor, Sun 11am–6pm

A small, family-run roadside café which impressed our inspector with its spotlessness, and the fact that all food is freshly prepared on the premises. Main courses always available are roast beef, mixed grill, gammon steak and sirloin steak all well within our budget. The hot and cold sweets are well above the usual cafeteria standard, with fresh strawberries and ice cream or banana split firm favourites with the many regular customers.

[P] [wine]

GRASMERE
Cumbria
Map **11** NY30

The Singing Birds Restaurant Town End ☎ (09665) 268
Open: Mar–Nov Mon–Sun 10.30am–3pm, 3.30–6pm, 7–9.30pm

Close to Dove Cottage and the Wordsworth Museum is a quaint white cottage housing an antique shop and restaurant. Inside, rough-cast walls, dark beams and brass and copper bric-à-brac emphasise the rustic atmosphere. All the lunch menus include a host of home-made dishes. 'Light' lunches include soup of the day with granary bread, savoury flan or quiche served with an interesting salad and open sandwiches such as 'shrimps in a crowd'. Three-course lunches vary in price and include pâté maison, home-made chicken and mushroom pie or spaghetti bolognese. A three-course Sunday table d'hôte lunch offers excellent choices – try egg and prawn surprise followed by chicken chasseur or lamb's kidneys turbigo.

[C] [P] **VS**

GREENOCK
Strathclyde *Renfrewshire*
Map **10** NS27

Bangalore Indian Restaurant 119 West Blackhall St ☎ (0475) 84355/6
Open: Mon–Thu 12noon–2pm, 5pm–12mdnt, Fri–Sat 12noon–12.30am, Sun 5–12mdnt

Just off the main Glasgow–Gourock road is this modern Indian restaurant. Decorated in traditional style, the interior is dimly lit and the walls have dark flock wallpaper decorated with Asian paintings. There is seating for about 100 at white-clothes tables; some in cosy alcoves offer a more intimate dining place. An extensive menu of Indian dishes is offered at reasonable prices; beef roghan josh, a spicy dish in tomato and onion sauce, is recommended. Tandoori specialities include shaslik or tandoori chicken. The three-course business persons's lunch is excellent value. There is a free disco every night.

[C] [music] [P] [S] [wine]

Rico's Pizza Parlour 1–3 Tobago St
☎ (0475) 21327
Open: 12noon–2.30pm, 6–11pm

White walls, green carpeting, hanging pot plants, bentwood chairs and marble-topped tables create a spacious and airy atmosphere here and the Italian proprietors and staff are friendly and efficient. A special business lunch of 2 courses – soup, pasta or pizza and coffee – is very good value and there is also a good range of Italian dishes on the menu. Starters include the traditional Minestrone soup and the main courses promise something a little more unusual like spaghetti with clams in a tomato and wine sauce. Mouthwatering desserts include Black Forest Gateau and oranges in brandy sauce.

[♣]

GRETNA GREEN
Dumfries & Galloway *Dumfriesshire*
Map **11** NY36

The Auld Smiddy Restaurant Headless Cross ☎ (04613) 365
Open: Summer 8am–7pm

Although you can no longer elope here with your sweetheart, you can enjoy a pleasant snack or full meal at very reasonable prices. Tucked just behind the world-famous blacksmith's shop, this low-ceilinged restaurant is festooned with brass bric-à-brac. A three-course lunch (which might consists of soup, roast beef with Yorkshire pudding followed by apple tart) with coffee and a glass of wine comes well within the budget. In the early evening a high tea menu offers a variety of grills and cold meats.

[P] [S] [♣]

GUILDFORD
Surrey
Map **4** SU94

The Castle Restaurant 2 South Hill
☎ (0483) 63729
Open: Tue–Sat 12noon–2pm, 5.30–11.30pm (last orders 9.30pm), Sun 12noon–2pm

The older part of this restaurant blends well with the garden effect of the extension, with its stone floor and brick walls. The two- and three-course table d'hôte lunches are within our price range. Seafood pancake is one of eight interesting starters on offer, and of 11 main courses, kidneys with mushrooms in red wine sauce is recommended. The list of sweets is impressive, chestnut ice cream sundae being one of the more unusual examples. Dinner is outside our limit.

[C] [P]

Pews Wine Bar 21 Chapel St
☎ (0483) 35012
Open: Mon–Sat 12noon–2.30pm, 6.30–11pm

David Allen runs Pews with flair and a friendly smile. Formerly an old ale house, the building's split-level rooms have dark beams and wood panelling, but are bright with log fires in their proper season and fresh flowers all the year round. The blackboard menu has a choice of hot dishes, for example chicken Portugaise and chili con carne and a variety of curries. There is a large selection of wines.

[♫] [S] [♣]

Yvonne Arnaud Restaurant Millbrook
☎ (0483) 69334
Open: Mon–Sat 12.30–2pm, 6.15–11pm

You won't go far in Guildford without seeing mention of the Yvonne Arnaud Theatre. The curved Theatre Restaurant offers two and three course set lunches. The menu is constantly changing, as a high percentage of patrons are regular playgoers. Evening meals are excellent, but alas, out of our league.

[C] [♫] [P] [S] [♣]

GUISELEY
West Yorkshire
Map **7** SE14

Harry Ramsden's White Cross
☎ (0943) 74641
Open: Mon–Sun 11.30am–11.30pm

Claiming to be 'the most famous fish and chip restaurant in the world', this biggish restaurant has changed hands since Harry Ramsden first opened up over 60 years ago. Outside the mainly brick building, several benches are interspersed along a verandah for 'eating out'. Inside, the smartly-dressed waitresses scurry between the many pot plants with high efficiency. After a soup or fruit juice starter, you can choose from any one of the nine main fish dishes which include chips, bread and butter and a drink in the price, (children's portions are available). If you're not already full up, a strawberry sundae or choc 'n 'nut dessert will soon put that right!

[P] [♣]

See advertisement on page 90

HALE
Gt Manchester
Map **7** SJ78

Hale Wine Bar 106–108 Ashley Rd
☎ 061-928 2343
Open: Mon–Thu 12noon–2pm, 7–10pm, Fri–Sat 12noon–2pm, 7–11pm

Two dress shops were transformed into this fashionable wine bar by enterprising owners, Nick Elliot and Tim Eaton. Victoriana is the theme of the two rooms which are on different levels. An excellent menu offers starters such as cheese and tuna pâté or quiche Lorraine, main courses include lasagne, and a cold table buffet. Jamaican fudge cake, lemon soufflé cake or chocolate mousse are some of the choices for dessert. Lunch here is a treat for the weary shopper or jaded office woworker.

[P] [S]

Village Green Ashley Rd
☎ 061-928 3794
Open: Mon–Sat 10am–6pm (closes 2pm on Wed). Closed Sun

The Village Green is situated at the entrance to the Ashley Hotel, and the young waitresses serve both light snacks and full meals. At lunchtime the cold larder offers such dishes as meat platter served with a variety of saldas. Apart from the regular hot meals on the menu, which include steak and kidney pie, there is also a hot dish of the day. Waffles are a speciality and are served with a variety of toppings.

[C] [P] [S] [♣]

HALSTEAD
Essex
Map **5** TL83

Halstead Wine Bar (Pendle's) 70a High St ☎ (0787) 477736
Open: Tue–Sat 10.30am–2.30pm, Sun 12noon–3pm, Wed–Sat 8–11pm. Closed Mon

Home cooking at its best is provided by the proprietors Hazel and Ray Boyle along with cordial and efficient attention. The simple wooden tables and seating are complemented by the authentic exposed old beams in this 16th-century wine bar. The many home-made dishes are listed on the 'blackboard' menu and you might choose lasagne, chicken with almonds or coq au vin. The dinner menu also provides a wide variety of dishes. There is a good selection of fine wines to enjoy with your meal.

[S] [P] [♣]

HALWELL
Devon
Map **3** SX75

The Old Inn ☎ (080421) 329 On A381 6m from Totnes
Open: Mon–Sat 12noon–2pm, 7–10pm, Sun 12noon–1.30pm, 7–9.45pm

There's an emphasis on home-cooked meats, soups and sweets at this old country inn. Choose from a wide range of grills and salads (the cold meat platter is partiularly good value) and eat from a refectory table in the wood-panelled bar or, weather permitting, in the well-kept beer garden. A 1-lb T-bone steak with chips, peas etc, is over our limit, but you'll be well within the budget with the popular honey-roast gammon steak, fish, or basket meals. Sweets with clotted cream are available.

[C] [P] **VS**

HAMBLEDON
Hampshire
Map **4** SU61

The Bat and Ball Inn Broadhalfpenny Down, Hambledon Rd, Clanfield
☎ (070132) 692
Open: Mon–Sat 12noon–2.15pm, 7–10.30pm, 10pm Winter, Sun 12noon–1.45pm, 7.30–10pm

Even in the mid-18th century, when the cricket club at Hambledon became the strongest team in England and turned a rustic pastime into a national sport, the

WELCOME TO

Harry Ramsden's

The worlds largest fish and chip shop.

Enjoy traditional Yorkshire fish and chips in this famous restaurant with its chandeliers, plush decor and waitress service. A choice of prime fish, chips, bread and butter, with tea, coffee or mineral all for around £2.40 per head.

Restaurant and take-away open every day
11.30 am-11.30pm

Situated at Guiseley on the A65 between
Leeds and Ilkley Moor.

White Cross, Guiseley, nr Leeds, West Yorkshire
Telephone: (0943) 74641.

Bat and Ball was a hit with the locals, and the players who (wise chaps) would repair to it after, and sometimes even during, a match. Today the inn is even more popular so it's always advisable to book a table. Hosts Frank and Katherine Rendle (Katherine does the cooking) have retained a cricketing atmosphere in the front bar, while the other bar is decorated in the more traditional beams-and-brass style. Order food at the bar and eat here if you like, or have your meal waitress-served in the cosy restaurant which overlooks an attractive garden. Starters range from soup to a generous prawn cocktail and main courses include mouth-watering meat pie and sirloin steak served with all the trimmings. Salads and ploughman's are also available. If you're not stumped when it comes to the sweet course, try an apple pie or gâteau or finish off with cheese and biscuits. No children or dogs allowed except on the front patio.

[C] [♫] [P]

HAMILTON
Strathclyde *Lanarkshire*
Map **11** NS75

Pir Mahal 78 Brandon St
☎ (0698) 284090
Open: Mon–Sat 12 noon–12mdnt, Sun 3pm–12mdnt

This first-floor restaurant really sets the scene for a good Indian meal with Indian paintings, brass platters and light shades and specially imported furniture. On each table there is a dish of Bombay mix and spiced gaam peas to nibble on while making your choice from the extensive menu of both Indian and Western dishes. The 3-course Business Lunch is very good value, but if you visit in the evening you will be treated to being served by waiters in traditional dress.

[♫] [P] [🍷]

HAMPTON COURT
Gt London

Cardinal Wolsey The Green
☎ 01-979 1458. London Plan4 **92**D2
Open: Mon–Sun 12.30–3pm, 7–10.30pm

This charming inn, pleasantly sited close to Hampton Court, offers sound home-made English fare for the footsore and famished foreign tourist's enjoyment – and British visitors are equally welcome. A three-course table d'hôte meal, changed daily, but always providing interesting choices, is just over our limit. Portions are very generous and old favourites frequently featured include Chef's stock pot soup, home-made pâté, roast beef and Yorkshire pud, steak and kidney pud, apple pie and peach Melba – a taste of old England at its best.

[C] [P] [🍷]

HARLECH
Gwynedd
Map **6** SH53

Castle Cottage ☎ (0766) 780479
Open: Summer Mon–Sun 10.30am–2pm, 6.30–9pm, Winter Fri–Sun 10.30am–2pm, 6.30–8.30pm (closed Sun eve)

Castle Cottage had a variety of uses before it became a restaurant and guest house some 25 years ago; it was once a farm, a smithy, a butcher's shop and originally, a gin shop. Jim and Betty Yuill cater for up to 35 people in their 16th-century beamed cottage which can be found adjacent to Harlech Castle. Simple lunch dishes include cottage pie, smoked haddock kedgeree and tagliatelle alla bolognese (all home-made). A special three-course table d'hôte menu is excellent value. At dinner time the à la carte menu is more adventurous and includes starters such as New Orleans prawn with main course of haddock in cream, and coffee granita for dessert, you have a substantial meal, or if you prefer you can have one of the light meals which are available at lunchtime. There is an extensive and modestly priced wine list.

[C] [🍷] **VS**

HARLESTON
Norfolk
Map **5** TM28

The Dove Wortwell ☎ (098686) 315
Open: Tue–Sat 11am–2.30pm, 7–9.30pm, Sun 12noon–3pm

Freshly-prepared food and friendly service are the watchwords at John and Pat Oberhoffer's tiny restaurant. Once a pub and smithy, it is conveniently placed at the junction of the A143 and B1062 for travellers in need of refreshment on their way to and from the coast. The limited lunch menu offers a three-course meal which could be home-made pâté, followed by mixed grill and cream meringue. The more extensive dinner menu costs considerably more and is outside the scope of this guide. Cream teas and light grills are available between 3.30 and 6pm.

[C] [P] [⊛] **VS**

HARROGATE
North Yorkshire
Map **8** SE35

Betty's 1 Parliament St ☎ (0423) 64659
Open: Mon–Sat 9am–5.30pm

This popular tea-room offers tea and cakes, snacks and salads all day long. Daily specials such as home-made soups, pâtés, pies and cauliflower cheese are available at lunch-time. An excellent three-course lunch could be home-made celery soup, chicken pie and chocolate supreme. Tasty home-made cakes and pastries are also sold in the confectionery department at the entrance. Betty's enjoys a fine view across the Montpelier Gardens.

[♫] [P] [S] [⊛]

Drum and Monkey 5 Montpellior Gdns
☎ (0423) 502650
Open: Mon–Sat 12noon–2.30pm, 7–10.15pm

Although this sounds like a pub, it is, in fact, a restaurant specialising in fish dishes, housed in a late Victorian building in the town centre. An extensive lunch menu includes some tempting variations of seafood, including salmon and watercress mousse, monk fish Dijonnaise, prawn, crab or lobster salads as well as a fine array of hot dishes such as grilled mackerel, stuffed with cream cheese and garlic or poached seatrout with asparagus hollandaise. Desserts to complement these fish dishes include fresh pineapple with kirsch, brandy chocolate fudge and a selection of ice creams and sorbets.

[C] [P] [⊛]

The Empress Church Sq
☎ (0423) 67629
Open: Mon–Fri 12noon–2pm, 7–10pm, Sat 7–10.30pm, Sun 12noon–1.45pm

In a stone building on the edge of town, with rich gold, turquoise and purple Regency décor and tasteful fittings, the restaurant is on the first floor, above the ground-floor lounge bar. A three-course business person's lunch including a choice of varying hot dishes or cold meat salad, served with potatoes and two veg is particularly good value, and even an extensive à la carte comes easily within our limit except in the case of a few speciality dishes. An extensive buffet table laden with flans, cold meats and salads is available at lunch-time. Children are also well catered for with a specially-designed menu complete with children's puzzles which they can take away as a souvenir.

[C] [P] [⊛]

Mae's Dining Car Station Rd, Pannal
☎ (0423) 870982
Open: Tue–Sun 12noon–2pm, Tue–Thu 7–11pm, Fri & Sat 7–11.30pm

This smart Pullman railway coach is drawn up outside the village railway halt and offers a daily fixed-price menu, which may include roasts, casseroles, or steak and kidney pie, with a choice of first course and sweet. Wine is available by the glass. There is also an à la carte menu, but it is beyond our budget.

[C] [P]

Mr Pickwick 6 Royal Pde
☎ (0423) 504766
Open: daily 9am–6pm

Right in the town centre, opposite the pump room, this Georgian town house contains a cosy café on the ground floor and a small, intimate bar upstairs. A full English breakfast is served between 9 and 11am. Lunch (from 12noon to 2pm) might consist of home-made soup, a roast or home-made pie and a sweet of apple pie or fresh fruit. To round it off try a cup of their own blend of fresh-ground coffee.

[♫] [P] [⊛]

Open Arms 3 Royal Parade
☎ (0423) 503034
Open: Tue–Sun 12noon–2pm, Tue–Sat 6–10pm

Now with the extra title of 'Taste of Yorkshire' this town-centre licensed restaurant offers a warm welcome with a glowing red décor, oak-clad walls and a menu designed to tempt the family. The famous Yorkshire pudding is available for lunch or dinner as a starter, main course (served with a stewed meat and veg filling) or even as a sweet. Traditional English roasts, home-baked pies, grilled meats and fried fish dishes are always on the menu. Children's portions of Yorkshire pork sausages or fish are available.

[C] [S] [⊛] **VS**

Pinocchio's Cheltenham Parade
☎ (0423) 60611
Open: Mon–Sat 11.30am–2.30pm, 5.30–12mdnt, Sun 5.30–11.30pm

Immediately you walk inside this pizzeria, with its gay posters and pictures of the Italian homeland, unashamedly deep pink and brown walls plus foot-tapping Latin music, you could easily imagine yourself on an Adriatic holiday. Once seated at one of the marble-topped tables, you'll find that the menu continues the dominant theme with a mouth-watering variety of pastas and pizzas. Calamari Fritti (deep-fried squid with oodles of lemon) is specially recommended. Apart from Italian dishes there's chicken Kiev, chili con carne or barbecue spare ribs. Starters and desserts (including Black Forest gâteau and profiteroles) are reasonably priced.

[C] [♫] [⊛]

HARROW
Gt London

Harvesters The Ploughman Station Rd
☎ 01-427 1071. London Plan4 **93**A2
Open: Mon–Fri 12noon–2pm, 5.30–7.30pm, Sat 12noon–2pm. Closed Sun

A friendly atmosphere awaits you in this town centre pub where meals can be taken in the bar, buffet style, or with waitress service in the upstairs restaurant at lunchtime. The menu is similar in both locations with lots of home-made pies, quiches and curries followed by a selection of home-made sweets.

[♫] [S] [P] [⊛]

Plato's 294 Preston Rd ☎ 01-904 8326. London Plan4 **94**B2
Open: Mon–Sat 12noon–3pm, 6–11pm

CLOSED

This Greek restaurant is furnished in the modern style and specialises in French and English as well as Greek cuisine. The manager is always on hand to ensure your enjoyment of his food. The à la carte menu offers a dazzling choice of over 20 starters, more than 30 main courses and about 20 sweets. You could break the bank by going for all the most expensive items, but there is still a wide choice awaiting you. An all-Greek meal could include tzatsiki as an appetiser with dolmades or kleftiko as your main dish and baklava or kateifi as delicious desserts. Vegetables are extra and there is a cover charge for bread and butter.

[C] [P] [S]

HARTINGTON
Derbyshire
Map **7** SK16

Ye Olde Spinning Wheel Sheen (3m NW of Hartington off B5054) ☎ (029884) 329
Open: Mon–Thu 7.30–9pm, Fri & Sat 7.30–10.30pm, Sun 12noon–2pm, 7.30–9pm

The bright and pleasant restaurant situated on the first floor of this stone-built inn boasts exposed stone walls and ceiling beams. There is a good selection of simple but wholesome dishes on the menu, including a traditional Sunday lunch. Specialities include chicken chasseur followed by apple pie and ice cream. A range of bar snacks (mainly basket meals) are available at lunchtime.

[P] [⊛]

HARTLEY WINTNEY
Hampshire
Map **4** SU75

Whyte Lyon ☎ (025126) 2037
Open: Mon–Sat 12noon–2.30pm, 6–10.30pm, Sun 12noon–2pm, 7–10.30pm

East of the picturesque village of Hartley Wintney, nestling in a hollow beside the A30, is the rambling, historic one-time coaching inn now owned by Berni Inns. The manager, claims that part of the building dates back to the 14th century. At present two grill bars, heavily beamed and partioned in the usual Berni manner, offer a range of old favourites at competitive prices. The Portcullis Restaurant has a salad counter from which you can serve-yourself to as much side salad as you want. Ice creams or cheeses are included in the price of most of the main courses which could be half a roast chicken in barbeque sauce, fillet of place or sirloin steak. A starter will add a little extra to your bill. Apart from a bigger selection of starters, Dover sole and duckling, the Cromwell Bar boasts the ghost of a girl who hanged herself in that very room. So popular is the Whyte Lyon with the locals that a third restaurant – the Hartford Grill has been opened upstairs.

[C] [P]

HASLEMERE
Surrey
Map **4** SU93

Darnleys Wine Bar High St
☎ (0428) 3048
Open: Mon 9.30am–5pm, Tue–Sat 9.30am–5pm, 7.30–10.30pm

This well-established, popular eating place in the centre of the town is open for morning coffee, luncheons and afternoon tea, while evening opening is as a wine bar. The décor is cheerful and comfortable with checked tablecloths and candlelight. Lunchtime dishes include leg of lamb and gammon steak with bread-and-butter pudding for dessert. The evening menu offers a choice of barbecued spare ribs, steak and Guinness pie, spaghetti bolognese, followed, perhaps, by creme brulée or creme caramel. Specially recommended are Chicken Darnley and feuiletage of lemon sole and prawns. All the dishes are home made.

[P]

HASTINGS
East Sussex
Map **5** TQ80

Crossways Lower Pett Rd, Fairlight
☎ (042486) 2356
Open: Tue–Sun 12.30–2.30pm, 7.30–9.30pm (last orders)

Well-prepared, good-value English cooking is the keynote of this small restaurant, looking very like a modern village home at the corssroads in Fairlight. A three-course lunch offers such old favourites as home-made steak and kidney or chicken and mushroom pie, roast beef with Yorkshire pud or roast chicken. Sweets, also home-made, include blackcurrant and apple pie or rhubarb crumble. The dinner menu is à la carte and more exotic fare such as rainbow trout with almonds is available. Starters include soup of the day and prawn cocktail and there is a choice of desserts.

[P] **VS**

Fagin's 73 George St ☎ (0424) 439319
Open: 12noon–12mdnt

Facing the seafront, this modern Italian-style restaurant has an attractive décor of pine walls, hanging plants and wooden cane seating. The restaurant specialises in a wide variety of pizzas, freshly made and baked in a brick oven. Try deep dish pizzas with prawns, tuna, sardines, anchovies and mussels. Other traditional Italian dishes on offer include lasagne verdi. Cheesecake, gâteau or apple pie are among the desserts to round off your meal.

[P]

HATFIELD
Hertfordshire
Map **4** TL20

Corks and Crumbs 23 Park St, Old Hatfield ☎ (07072) 63399
Open: Mon–Sat 10am–11pm, Sun 11am–9pm

This wine bar and coffee house, with pretty patio and terrace, in the old part of Hatfield, is run by a husband-and-wife team. Small, attractive and imaginative, with a menu to match, Corks and Crumbs wins points for offering a vegetarian pie, hot cheesy pepper, or courgette and tomato gratin at very reasonable prices. For meat eaters, the daily special main courses may feature Mexican lamb with savoury rice and vegetables, or kidneys in red wine sauce. Wines are imaginatively chosen too, the restaurant is not afraid to offer lesser known varieties from Chile or Bulgaria.

[C] [P]

HATHERSAGE
Derbyshire
Map **8** SK28

Bradgate Buttery Main Rd
☎ (0433) 50665
Open: Tue–Sun 10am–9pm

English cuisine is the order of the day at this attractive Tudor-style restaurant with its Ministrel's Gallery where 50 evening diners can enjoy a meal with a view. Entrées include lamb chops with mint sauce, mixed grill and chicken, and there is also a range of starters and desserts. A snack menu is available during the day and there is a special children's menu.

[P] [S]

HAWICK
Borders *Roxburghshire*
Map **12** NT51

Kirkland Hotel West Stewart Pl
☎ (0450) 72263
Open: Mon–Thu 12noon–2pm, 7–9.30pm, Fri 12noon–2pm

This small, tastefully decorated Victorian house has a cosy lounge bar and an immaculate dining room. You can eat in either and at lunchtime you will find a wide choice of cold platters, smoked salmon with salad or omelettes. The evening menu includes chicken provencale, farmhouse grill and a choice of desserts from the sweet trolley.

[P]

HAY-ON-WYE
Powys
Map **3** SO24

The Old Barn Inn Three Cocks, on A438
☎ (04974) 500
Open: Mon–Sat 12noon–2.30pm, 6.30–9.30pm, Sun 12noon–1.30pm, 7–9.30pm

This old barn was converted about three years ago and still retains the original high ceilings and beams. The dining area is suitable for children and is furnished with old oak tables and wheelback chairs. There is a small cold counter display and the dish of the day is chalked on the blackboard. The standard menu lists typical pub fare, soup, cottage pie topped with cheese and scampi and chips are examples. The children's menu contains the ever popular fish fingers, chips, sausages, etc and when they have finished eating there is a play area with swings and climbing frames. Sunday lunch is also available (with children's portions).

[C] [P] [🌳]

HAYWARD'S HEATH
West Sussex
Map **4** TQ32

Country and Wine 124 South Rd
☎ (0444) 458040
Open: Mon–Sat 10am–10pm

This modern bistro specialises in home-cooked fresh food and choice wines and real ale. Décor is rather exotic, with plush wall-to-wall seating, bamboo cane divides, and fresh flowers on every table. Salads and other dishes are on show in a large display cabinet. The menu includes various cold meat salads and a hot dish such as chicken casserole. Home-made soup and pâté are tasty starters and sweets include huge fresh cream meringues. A thriving take away service also operates.

[C] [♫] [P] [S] [🌳]

HELENSBURGH
Strathclyde *Dumbartonshire*
Map **10** NS28

Le Jardin Ardencaple Garden Centre Rhu Rd Higher ☎ (0436) 2245
Open: Summer: Mon–Sat 10am–5pm, Sun 2–5pm; winter: Mon–Thu 10am–4pm, Fri–Sat 10am–4pm, 7–9.30pm

In the Ardencaple Garden Centre this attractive stone and white-painted timber building houses a coffee shop restaurant and a small red-brick bar. Drinks are available all day in the restaurant which has white washed walls and pine seating. At lunchtime start with home-made soup or pâté followed by such tasty main courses as haddock au gratin or steak. The dinner menu has some more exotic dishes – try Crevettes Méditeraneanne with diced peppers, onions and prawns in mayonnaise and garlic sauce or truite de riviere tyrolienne – trout coated in breadcrumbs with a spiced tomato sauce. There is a full selection of desserts from the trolley which varies from day to day.

[P] [🌳]

Sangam Indian Restaurant 45 Sinclair St ☎ (0436) 71650/4817
Open: Sun–Thu 5pm–12.30am, Fri & Sat 12noon–1am

You'll find this spacious, well-appointed restaurant on the first-floor of a corner site in Helensburgh's main shopping area. Maroon wallpaper and curtaining, plus imitation oil lamps, create a cosy, intimate atmosphere. A variety of typical Asian food (for instance, beef byriani or shami kebab with salad) is agumented by 'western dishes' such as steak and chips or prawn omelette. A midday feature is the special three-course lunch, which is very good value for money.

[C] [P] [S] [🌳]

HEMEL HEMPSTEAD
Hertfordshire
Map **4** TL00

The Old Bell Hotel High St
☎ (0442) 52867
Open: Mon 12noon–2pm, Tue–Thu 12noon–2pm, 7–9pm, Fri–Sat 12noon–2pm, 7–10pm

Built in 1580, and an inn since 1603, the Old Bell is a fine example of a 17th-century hostelry. Here you can dine by candlelight in the original Tudor dining room with its intriguing 19th-century French wallpaper. Appetisers include melon with orange segments and curaçao. Main courses include lamb kebab or supreme of chicken. A special three-course menu available for both lunch and dinner is just a little over our price limit.

[C] [P] [S]

HENLEY-IN-ARDEN
Warwickshire
Map **7** SP16

The Little French Café 28 High St
☎ (05642) 4322
Open: Tue–Sat 10am–6pm, Sun 2.30–6pm

Stop at this pretty creeper-clad cottage with its heart-shaped sign in picturesque Henley-in-Arden for a snack or a well-prepared, home-cooked light lunch. Mike and Linda Parker have recently re-opened the café which is now convincingly Olde Worlde in style – whitewashed walls, exposed beams, stone-flagged floor, chintzy curtains and all. Start with home-made pâté, then decide between a selection of cold savoury flans with salad or Hot Dish of the Day – such as kedgeree served with a selection of side salads. A delicious home-made dessert could be apricot sponge.

[🌳]

HEREFORD
Hereford & Worcester
Map **3** SO54

Cathedral Restaurant Church St
☎ (0432) 265233
Open: Tue–Sat 10.30am–2.30pm, 7–10.30pm, Sun 11.30am–2.30pm. Closed Mon

As its name would suggest, this small restaurant is set close to the cathedral. John Browne, who for eight years worked in Florida and Burmuda, owns the restaurant with his Spanish wife Maria who is in charge of the cooking. Special meals of the day are listed on a blackboard, and usually include fresh local produce. Main courses include Pork Cathedral-style, pork steak cooked in cream and apple sauce with Hereford cider. A three-course traditional lunch is available on Sunday.

[C] [♫] [S] [🌳]

The City Walls 67 St Owen St
☎ (0432) 67720/69134
Open: Wed–Fri 12noon–2pm, Tue–Sun 7–11pm

This restaurant is built on part of the original city wall – at a point where taxes were collected in bygone days. Included in the price of the main dish (half roast duckling or chicken, for instance) is the vegetable of the day, French fries, home-made apple pie with cream or ice cream.

[♫] [P] [S] [🌳]

Tudor Restaurant 48 Broad St
☎ (0432) 277374
Open: Mon–Sat 9.30am–5.30pm, Sun (Jun–Oct) 10.30am–4.30pm

This 17th-century building in one of the busiest streets of Hereford is situated near the cathedral. A variety of appetising salads such as continental salad with salami and olives, the Tudor Danwich (brown bread with lettuce, cheese, egg and tomato) and many others, supplement the usual list of grills and pies. Children are given a particularly warm welcome in this homely restaurant.

[S] [🌳]

HERTFORD
Hertfordshire
Map **4** TL31

Bottles 11 Old Cross ☎ (0992) 50405
Open: Mon–Sat 12noon–2.30pm, 6.30–10.30pm

A pretty, conservatory-style restaurant with lots of trellis work and unusual fabric-covered walls opens off the wine bar with its blackboard menu, pink pews and scrubbed floor boards. Cold dishes include quiche and lobster; hot dishes include boeuf bourgignon and trout. All main courses are served either with fresh vegetables or brown rice and salad. Sweets include lemon posset or apple and walnut cake and a variety of wines are available by the glass.

[P] [wine]

HEXHAM
Northumberland
Map **12** NY96

Hadrian's Wall ☎ (0434) 81232
Open: Mon–Sun 12noon–2pm, 7–9pm

Overshadowed by the Roman wall, this smart ivy-clad inn dating back over 250 years enjoys a well-deserved local reputation for its good and efficient service. A typical meal could be home-made soup, a main course of steak and kidney pudding, lemon sole, curry or trout plus a sweet. Cold meats and salads are also available.

HONITON
Devon
Map **3** ST10

Knights, Black Lion Court, High St
☎ (0404) 3777
Open: Mon–Sat 12noon–2pm, Tue–Sat from 7.30pm. Closed Sun and Bank Hol

Good, wholesome, home-made dishes are the order of the day at Knights. Try the home-made soup with cream and a slice or two of fresh cracked wheat bread for starters, followed by cider-baked ham, salad and foil-wrapped jacket potato with yoghurt and mint dressing – and, if you feel there's room under your belt for more, you can top the meal off with home-made sherry trifle or spicy rhubarb crumble with cream for a mouth-watering finale.

[C] [P] [S]

Monkton Court Inn Monkton
☎ (0404) 2309 On A30 2m N of Honiton
Open: Mon–Fri 10.30am–2.15pm, 5.30–10.15pm, Sat 10.30am–2.15pm, 5.30–10.45pm, Sun 12noon–2pm, 7–10.30pm

This imposing stone-built 17th-century inn with distinctive mullioned windows has a comfortable, welcoming interior – all dark polished wood and soft seating. American hamburgers with chips and salad, a range of meat salads and sirloin steak are all on the menu. Appetisers include soup and pâté, and 'afters' (you're in Devon now!) such as Dutch apple pie are served with clotted cream.

[P] [wine] **VS**

HOOK
Hampshire
Map **4** SU75

White Hart London Rd ☎ (025672) 2462
Open: Mon–Sat 12noon–2pm, 7.15–10pm, Sun 12noon–1.30pm, 7.15–10pm

On the old coach road from London to Exeter stands the White Hart, one of the oldest pubs in the country. Entrance from the car park is through an out-of-the-past courtyard, by a row of old cottages which were once the stable boys' quarters. The dining room, with its dark-wood fittings and a lattice work of beams, has one wall etched with the ghostly outline of a coachman and his horses. Fruit juice, pâté or soup can be followed by a mixed grill served with chips or new potatoes and the vegetable of the day. A sweat such as apple pie and cream or cheese and biscuits complete the meal. Bar snacks are of a high standard, and a three-course meal of cream of chicken soup, a veal or pork dish or sausage and mash and strawberry gâteau is reasonably priced.

[music] [P] [wine]

HORSHAM
West Sussex
Map **4** TQ13

Pilgrim's Halt 24 West St
☎ (0403) 63281
Open: Mon–Sat 12noon–2.30pm, 6–9.30pm, 10pm Sat

A sister restaurant to 1982s' 'thousandth entry' winner in Maidstone, this first-floor premises in a 13th-century building is run along the same lines as its now-famous twin by Ruth and Dennis Treadaway. Home-made soup or pâté are typical starters, main dishes include Southdown lamb chops and there is a choice of sweets from the trolley.

[P] [S] [wine]

HORTON
Dorset
Map **4** SU00

Horton Inn ☎ (0258) 840252
Open: Mon–Sat 12noon–2pm, 7–9.45pm, Sun 12noon–1.30pm, 7–9.45pm

Good bar snacks are a feature of this attractive 18th-century free house. There's a paved patio where you can savour your food when the sun shines. Dorset pâté or smoked mackerel pâté are tasty snacks, and there is a range of attractive salads. The restaurant has an à la carte menu, avocado and prawns, beef carbonade, and Dorset Apple Cake is a typical meal, though some meals may go over our budget.

[P]

HOUNSLOW
Gt London

The Travellers Friend 480 Bath Rd
☎ 01-897 8847. London Plan4 **95**C1
Open: Mon–Fri 12noon–2.30pm, Fri–Sat 7–9.30pm

Tudor architecture is reflected in the oak beams, pillars, plain brick and stone walls and olde worlde furnishings of the charming restaurant in this hostelry. Cuisine is basically English with the odd French dish to vary the pace. Starters include soup, pâté maison and prawn cocktail. Main courses include fish, grills and entrées such as escalope of veal cordon bleu. Vegetables are extra and there is a choice of sweet.

[C] [P]

HUDDERSFIELD
West Yorkshire
Map **7** SE11

Pizzeria Sole Mio Units 3 and 4, Imperial Arcade, Market St ☎ (0484) 42828
Open: Mon–Fri 12noon–2.30pm, 5–11.30pm, Sat 12noon–11.30pm, Sun 5.30–11pm

Here you will discover Italy in the heart of Huddersfield, in a shopping arcade. Outside it has a terrazza and canopy blinds, inside roughcast walls, open brickwork, ceramic tile-topped tables and high-backed ladder chairs emphasise the Italian atmosphere. There is an extensive menu of home-made pastas including lasagne and cannelloni, and a formidable list of pizzas. Imaginative starters, including snails, are available.

[S] **VS**

HULL
Humberside
Map **8** TA01

Pecan Pizzeria 32 Silver St
☎ (0482) 20835
Open: Mon–Sat 12noon–2.30pm, Mon–Sun 6–11.30pm

As part of an imposing stone Victorian building in the heart of Hull's commercial district, the Pecan could be taken for another finance house. Even inside, there are strong overtones of the Stock Exchange, with lofty ceilings, classical pillars and arches and Victorian décor. But enthusiastic Italian waiters in red-check shirts, contemporary music and an extensive, mainly Italian menu dispel any stodgy banking atmosphere. The menu is almost a meal in itself with its mouthwatering descriptions, but tread carefully as far as the specialities are concerned. If you stick to the interesting starters, pizza or pasta dish and a sweet you should keep within our budget.

VS

The Hull Cheese Paragon St
☎ (0482) 225314
Open: Mon–Sat 11.30am–2pm. Closed Sun

This town centre pub is in a corner position in the main shopping area. Lunch in the first-floor restaurant offers straightforward English dishes at modest prices, Granny's Steak and Kidney Pie, pork sausages and freshly made salads are examples. The 'special' changes daily and includes home-made soup, a main course and sweet at an unbelievably low price.

HUNGERFORD
Berkshire
Map **4** SU36

The Tutti Pole 3 High St ☎ (04886) 2515
Open: Mon–Fri 10am–5.30pm, Sat & Sun 10am–5.45pm

Open for morning coffee, luncheons and home-made afternoon teas this cosy cottage tea-shoppe is very popular especially on the 2nd Tuesday after Easter when the 'Tutti-Men' come to collect their dues. Ask the manageress, Val, about this fascinating local tradition. Good home-cooking is the order of the day and the lunch menu includes omelettes, sandwiches, quiche and salads. There is a special hot dish of the day and a range of sweets.

[S] [P]

HUNTINGDON
Cambridgeshire
Map **4** TL27

Old Bridge Hotel ★★★ ☎ (0480) 52681
Open: Mon–Sun 12noon–3pm, 6.30–10.30pm

An ivy-clad building situated by the river Ouse, where the garden and car park extend to the river and a small private jetty. You can enjoy your meal in one of the lounge areas or, weather permitting, outside on the large patio. The extensive menu offers a good choice of soups and for your main course our inspector recommends the turkey and mushroom pir or the deep fried lambs sweetbreads. Sword fish is also available. Service by smart young staff is friendly and swift.

[C] [P]

HYTHE
Kent
Map **5** TR13

The Butt of Sherry Theatre St
☎ (0303) 66112
Open: Mon–Sun 10.30am–2.30pm, Tue–Sat 6–10.30pm

This cosy wine bar is housed in a part 17th century building and an intriguing feature is the millstone which is set into an internal wall. You can be sure of a warm welcome from Mary Freeman – try her home-made steak and kidney pie or a plate of ham off the bone, roast beef or ham and tongue. Starters and sweets are also available. The Butt of Sherry is well-known for its good wine. French beer is also available.

[S] [P]

ILCHESTER
Somerset
Map **3** ST52

Ivelchester Hotel The Square
☎ (0935) 220
Open: Mon–Sun 12noon–2pm, 7–9.15pm

Bang in the centre of this sleepy Somerset town, which is a through-route to the West Country, you'll find this unpretentious hotel-restaurant where orders are taken at the bar for the excellent table d'hôte meals both at lunchtime and in the evening. A three-course lunch can come within our price range. Appetisers include home-made soup or fruit juice and there is a choice of five main courses, including roast duckling and apple sauce. A home-made sweet or ice cream completes the meal. Dinner offers four choices of starters, including rollmop herring, five main courses and a wide selection of sweets.

[P] **VS**

ILFORD
Gt London

Harts 545 Cranbrook Rd, Gants Hill
☎ 01-554 5000. London Plan4 **96**A6
Open: Mon–Thu 12noon–3pm, 6–10.30pm, Fri–Sat 12noon–3pm, 6–11pm, Sun 7–10.30pm

Leonard and Alan Hart's wine bar specialises in good home-made cooking ideal for business people and travellers alike. Start with home-made cabbage soup or crab cocktail then sample lasagne. Freshly caught trout from Hanningford or Australian Pacific prawns cooked with garlic may stretch the budget but are good value. Hard-to-resist desserts include hot black cherries with port and ice cream. In fine weather you can enjoy your meal on tree-lined terrace to the rear.

[C]

ILKLEY
West Yorkshire
Map **7** SE14

Betty's Café Tea Rooms 32–34 The Grove ☎ (0943) 608029
Open: Mon–Sat 9am–5.30pm, Sun 2–5.30pm

In Ilkley's main shopping street, Betty's modern restaurant serves snacks all day with a limited selection of hot dishes and a mouth-watering variety of cakes, sandwiches and savouries. A satisfying meal could consist of home-made soup, Welsh rarebit (made with farmhouse cheddar and Yorkshire ale) served with apple or tomato chutney or ham and pineapple salad, followed by Yorkshire curd tart and coffee. A wide selection of speciality coffees and teas can be chosen from separate descriptive menus. Alsatian wine is available by the glass.

[P] [S]

Café Konditorei Spa Flats, The Grove
☎ (0943) 601578
Open: Mon–Sat 10am–5.30pm, Sun 12noon–5.30pm

Converted from one of the old spa hotels, all the produce served in this café is home-made. Lunches start at noon and high teas after 4pm, when children's portions are available. Cork walls and classical pillars create an elegant, restful atmosphere. Soups are home-made and are delicious eaten with hot herb or garlic bread. Special dishes of the day include seafood vol-au-vents with chips and salad. Danish open sandwiches – try chicken with peach and Waldorf salad, omelettes and salads are also served. Desserts include fruit-filled pancake, and continental gâteaux.

[P] [S] **VS**

INGLETON
North Yorkshire
Map **7** SD67

Linden House Main St ☎ (0468) 41020
Open: Easter–end Sep Tue–Sun 12noon–2pm, Tue–Sat 7.30–9.30pm, closed Mon; out of season Thu–Sat 7.30–9.30pm

Situated in the centre of the village, this small, spotlessly clean restaurant is listed here mainly for the summer lunch menu. Soup and steak and kidney pie (both home-made) represent excellent value along with sirloin steak and Wensleydale cheese salad. There is a selection of fresh home-made sweets. The dinner menu is mainly beyond our price range.

C P

INSCH
Grampian *Aberdeenshire*
Map **15** NJ62

The Rothney 2 Commercial Rd
☎ (04642) 604
Open: Summer: Mon–Sun 10am–10pm; Winter: Mon–Thu 11am–7pm, Fri & Sat 11am–10pm, Sun 2–8pm

A simple little country restaurant with a menu to satisfy most tastes. Pleasant service is provided by Mrs Christine Cooper and her staff who make good use of local produce (including venison from the family owned deer farm) when preparing the meals. A full three-course lunch with home-made soup, a main course of fish, beef or venison and a sweet offers excellent value. High tea is also available. The dinner menu offers a good choice of dishes, but it is priced over our limit.

C P

INVERNESS
Highland *Inverness-shire*
Map **14** NH64

Crawfords Restaurant 19 Queensgate
☎ (0463) 233198
Open: Mon–Sat (also Sun Jul & Aug)
Self-service 8am–5.30pm
Restaurant 10am–7pm

Crawfords in Queensgate is a restaurant for all the family offering good food and friendly service both in the self-service and the restaurant. The self-service offers snacks including filled rolls and gammon steak. A wide range of pure beef hamburgers and of course steak is available in the basement restaurant.

S

The Pancake Place 25 Church St
☎ (0463) 226156
Open: May–Sep Mon–Sat 9.30am–8pm, Sun 12noon–6pm; Oct–Apr. Closes 6pm, and Sun

It has not taken long for this 'old world' style pancake restaurant to become a firm favourite with the locals. After soup of the day try a savoury pancake (haddock mornay and ham and chicken are examples) or choose a 'cool crisp salad' of chicken served with two pancakes and salad. There is an extensive range of sweet pancakes for dessert including 'Canadian' with maple syrup and fresh cream. Local wine from Moniack Castle, Inverness is available.

♫ S P

Pizzaland Lombard St ☎ (0463) 234328
Open: Mon–Sat 10am–11pm, Sun 12noon–6pm, Summer 8pm

This bright, modern pizzeria is conveniently situated in a pedestrianised shopping precinct. Inside, tiled floors and stucco walls with mirrors are in pleasant contrast to the city atmosphere outside. There are 19 varieties of pizza to choose from, as well as open sandwiches, spaghetti bolognese and cannelloni. There is also a 'help-yourself' salad bar.

S

Stakis Steakhouse Bank St
☎ (0463) 236577
Open: Mon–Sat 12noon–2.30pm, 5–10.30pm, Sun 4–10.30pm

All the usual friendly, efficient service you'd expect from an establishment in the Reo Stakis chain makes this a popular Inverness eating-house. Main courses include the price of a starter and, apart from some steak options, are quite within the budget. Gammon steak with peach is an appealing choice, and why not spoil yourself with hot apple pie and cream? Children are well catered for as well – their whole meal (that's three courses and a drink) is very reasonably priced in this charming restaurant.

C S

INVERSHIN
Highland *Sutherland*
Map **14** NH59

Invershin Hotel★ ☎ (054982) 202
Open: Mon–Fri 8am–9pm, Sat 8am–10pm, Sun 9am–9.30pm

You'll be encouraged to eat Scots at this traditional Highland hotel. Successful consumption of 'freshly-killed Highland haggis with tatties', roast ribs of Angus beef, and sweet little Cloutie dumplings, should leave you with a sense of achievement. And the old Scottish trait of getting good value for money holds true, too – both lunch and dinner come within our price range. Local fish features on all menus.

C P

IPSWICH
Suffolk
Map **5** TM14

Great White Horse★★ Tavern St
☎ (0473) 56558
Open: Coffee Shop: Mon–Sun 11am–9.30pm
Courtyard Lounge for snacks: 12noon–2pm

A leading inn in Ipswich since the 16th century, the Great White Horse was once the haunt of Charles Dickens when the author was employed as a reporter on the *Ipswich Chronicle* and it was to receive a mention in his *Pickwick Papers*. The newly-decorated Coffee Shop offers a wide range of food from cream teas to omelettes and grills served all day. There is a special menu for the under 14's, and a good selection of fine wines. Lunches served from the Courtyard Table Buffet include hot and cold dishes, from a bowl of soup with granary bread to ploughman's lunches and home-made sweets.

C S

Henekey's Hotel ★★ Westgate St
☎ (0473) 58506
Open: Mon–Sun 12noon–2.30pm, 6–10.30pm, Fri–Sat 11pm

Behind an ornate gothic, stone façade, this Trusthouse Forte concern has been completely modernised and refurbished. There are two comfortable restaurants, the Grill and the Sherry Restaurant. Although described as 'Henekey's Steak Bars', plaice, Barnsley chop and chicken cordon bleu are also available and the price of the main course includes a sweet or cheese. Appetisers are also available, and include whitebait and smoked mackerel.

C ♫ P S

Marno's 14 St Nicholas St
☎ (0473) 53106
Open: Summer Mon–Wed 10am–2pm, Thu–Sat 10am–2pm, 7.30–10pm, Winter closed Wed pm

A vegetarian restaurant with dishes imaginative enough to tempt the most confirmed meat-eater. The lunch menu includes tagliatelle, nut roasts and salad with a choice of sweets – fresh fruit salads and flans – all at rock bottom prices. A meal from the evening menu (which is more extensive) could be home-made soup, followed by rice, mushroom and cheese pie and a sweet pancake and herbal tea. Live music is provided by local folk musicians at weekends.

♫

Noble Romans 9 Buttermarket
☎ (0473) 219376
Open: Mon–Sat 12noon–11pm, Sun 5.30–10.30pm

Claudius and Tiberius are among the 13 noble Romans whose names are taken in vain for the pizzas in this trendy Italian restaurant. A 'Claudius' has mozzarella cheese with tomato while a 'Tiberius', at the top of the range, has tuna, sardine, anchovy, onion, lemon, olives, capers, mozzarella and tomato. A full three-course meal here is very reasonably priced, with appetisers suchas melon and chocolate fudge cake or morello cherry and fresh cream waffle for dessert. All this and décor in oatmeal, fawn and brown with basket-weave chairs has attracted a regular clientèle.

♫ S

IRONBRIDGE
Shropshire
Map **7** SJ60

Old Vaults 29 High St ☎ (095245) 2295
Open: Mon–Sat 11.30am–3pm, Sun 12noon–2pm, Mon–Thu 6.30–10.30pm, Fri & Sat 6.30–11pm

Situated in the centre of Ironbridge, close to Thomas Telford's famous 18th-century bridge, this compact wine bar offers visitors and locals alike good, basic dishes, with wine, well within our financial limits. Pâté, home-made quiches, beef in red wine and Shropshire fidget pie all feature on the menu, along with a range of sweets. The interior has been imaginatively renovated on two levels. There is a dining area at street level, and the wine bar, also with dining area at cellar level has a glass roof leading out to the terrace which gives it an airy spacious feel. The terrace overlooks the river Severn and accommodates 24 diners. Real ale is served in the wine bar and the selection is changed regularly.

[♫] [P] [🍷]

IRVINE
Strathclyde *Ayrshire*
Map **10** NS33

The Coffee Club 140 High St
☎ (0294) 71313
Open: Mon–Sat 10am–10pm

As in the other Ayrshire Coffee Clubs, this neat, modern restaurant with friendly waitress service offers an exciting selection of snacks, light meals and desserts at prices well within our budget. Choose from the wide range of fish, grills, salads and omelettes and dishes such as moussaka or chili con carne. For a meal on bread try one of the 14 'Danwiches' – open sandwiches with a mouthwatering variety of toppings. In the 'children's corner', there is Paddington's Plateful (gammon, pineapple and chips) or Snoopy's Surprise (hamburger, beans and chips).

[S] [🍷]

Gulab Bank St ☎ (0294) 79141
Open: Mon–Fri 11am–2pm, 5–11.30pm (12mdnt Fri), Sat 11am–12mdnt, Sun 4.45–11.30pm

This first-floor Indian restaurant offers a large range of traditional Indian dishes from an à la carte menu all at reasonable prices. The three-course business lunch, available Mon–Fri, provides excellent value with a good choice of Indian and Western main courses. Tandoori is a speciality.

[♫] [P] [🍷]

JEDBURGH
Borders *Roxburghshire*
Map **12** NT62

The Carter's Rest ✕ Abbey Pl
☎ (08356) 3414
Open: Mon–Sun 12noon–2pm, 6–9pm, closed Sun in Winter

This restaurant is built on stone plundered from the nearby Abbey, whose ruins dominate the outlook, and was the local 'Penny' School for a hundred years or so from 1779, then a real Carter's Rest for patrons of Jedburgh's horse fair. Today it offers excellent grills, bar lunches and dinners. There is a special menu in the evening consisting of a main course, coffee and a glass of wine, or make do with bar snacks. Hot buffet lunch specials include beef olives with trimmings, a ham omelette, American-style burgers made with Scotch beef or a fresh Eyemouth haddock fish platter.

[♫] [P] [🍷]

KEENTHORNE
Somerset
Map **3** ST23

Apple Tree Cottage Hotel Keenthorne, Nether Stowey ☎ (027867) 238
Open: Mon–Sun 10.30am–2.30pm, Mon–Sat 6.30–10pm

This restaurant has a 1930s style dining room and a contrasting, olde-worlde beamed bar with a stone inglenook. Menus and meals are planned and produced by owner Manfred Krombas, who served his cooking apprenticeship both here and on the continent. Chili con carne, cottage pie, steak and kidney pie or speciality boeuf bourguignon are typical hot dishes, while meat salads, sandwiches and assorted ploughmans supplement the cold collation. A three-course table d'hôte lunch, with the choice of five starters and five main courses, a selection of fresh vegetables and a sweet from the trolley comes within our limit in the restaurant.

[C] [P] [🍷]

KEIGHLEY
West Yorkshire
Map **7** SE04

The Vaults 61 North St ☎ (0535) 681550
Open: Mon–Sat 12noon–2pm, 6.30–10.30pm Sun 12noon–2pm

This pleasantly decorated wine bar was once a branch of Barclays Bank, and is now furnished with circular tables and barber's-shop chairs. There is a regular menu with weekly specials. Our inspector chose a lasagne that would have graced the best of Italian restaurants. Also available were sandwiches made with wholemeal bread, a variety of crêpes, grilled gammon and a choice of sweets. The dinner menu is more extensive but with careful selection you can still enjoy a meal within our budget.

[C] [♫] [P] [🍷]

KENDAL
Cumbria
Map **7** SD59

Cherry Tree Restaurant 24 Finkle St
☎ (0539) 20547
Open: Mon–Sun 10am–9.30pm, closed early Thu in winter

The entrance to the Cherry Tree lies up an alleyway. The main first-floor restaurant is very bright and clean, with good dark furniture and excellent quality crockery. The décor has white rough-cast walls and beams. You can buy hot and cold snacks here and Danish open sandwiches, as well as a four-course lunch which will come well within our price range. Dinner costs very little more and offers an excellent choice with salmon, veal, chicken and turkey.

[S]

Gateway Hotel Crook Rd, Plumgarths (2m NW on B5284) ☎ (0539) 20605
Open: Mon–Sat 12noon–2.30pm, 6–10pm, Sun 12noon–1.45pm, 7–9.30pm

There is a varied menu and you can choose to dine either in the bar, lounge or the restaurant. Starters or snacks are excellent value and the popular main meals, including traditional Cumberland sausage, are served with baked potato, French fries or salad. Grills, game and fish dishes are also available. There is a good choice of desserts and a range of children's meals.

C P

The Brewery Restaurant The Brewery Arts Centre ☎ (0539) 25133
Open: Mon–Sat 10am–3pm, lunch 12noon–2pm

The restaurant is housed in a converted stone-built brewery in its own delightful grounds. The food is under the personal supervision of Annette Tarver. Popular with local business folk and visitors the restaurant offers a choice of pies, quiches and seafood all with chips or salad, as well as a great variety of fish or cold meat salads. There is a choice of three sweets.

P

The Woolpack Hotel ★★★
Stricklandgate ☎ (0539) 23852
Open: normal licensing hours, Ca Steean Restaurant Mon–Sat 12noon–2pm, 7–10pm
Shepherd's Pie Buttery, Summer Mon–Sat 10am–9.30pm, Winter Mon–Sat 10am–6.30pm

The Ca Steean Restaurant offers fine food in elegant surroundings. A satisfying meal can be had from the à la carte menu (stick to the lower price range to keep within the budget) or there is the table d'hôte lunch with hot grill-style main courses or cold buffet. The Shepherd's Pie Buttery is a more casual eating place with pine-clad walls and lantern-style lighting. Bar snacks include a good ploughman's lunch.

C P S

KENILWORTH
Warwickshire
Map **4** SP27

Ana's Bistro, 121 Warwick Rd
☎ (0926) 53763
Open: Tue–Sat 7–10.30pm, Diments: 12noon–2pm, 7–10pm

This cosy cellar bistro is part of Diments restaurant in the small town of Kenilworth. The bill of fayre is recorded each day on a blackboard and includes a choice of four or five hot dishes of the day with such exotic items as chicken in courgette and mint sauce or dressed crab. Although the main menu in the upstairs restaurant is above our limit there is a good table d'hôte menu which offers a set lunch at a very reasonable price. With a stock of over 80 wines you'll be spoilt for choice for an accompaniment to your meal.

P

George Rafters 42 Castle Hill
☎ (0926) 52074
Open: Mon–Sat 12noon–2pm, 7–10.30pm, Sun 12noon–2.30pm, 7–10pm

This little terraced cottage, almost in the shadow of Kenilworth Castle, now houses a cheerful restaurant with a 'country' atmosphere. Well-made soups are served with chunks of hot garlic bread and Tsaziki, a dip of cream cheese, cucumber and garlic, is also popular. Main courses include moussaka and supreme of chicken. Vegetables are priced separately and with careful selection you can enhoy a delicious two-course meal without breaking the bank.

C P

KENNFORD
Devon
Map **3** SX98

Haldon Thatch Bottom of Telegraph Hill, on A38 4m S of Exeter ☎ (0392) 832273

Open: Mon–Sun 10am–3pm, 6–11pm

As you'd expect from the name, the restaurant is housed in an attractive thatched property, perched high above the road commanding fine views of the surrounding countryside. Décor is predominantly red with well-spaced tables and Ercol chairs. There are over a dozen starters to choose from. Of the main courses, you can sample a medium sirloin steak or deep-fried scampi at very reasonable prices and the Haldon mixed grill (8oz hamburger, sausage, fried egg and bacon) is excellent value. Traditional Devon teas are served during late afternoon and there is an à la carte evening menu which is mainly outside our price limit.

[C] [P] [♧]

KENTALLEN
Highland *Argyllshire*
Map **14** NN05

Holly Tree Restaurant on A828, 3m SW of Ballachulish Bridge ☎ (063174) 292
Open: restaurant 10am–2.30pm Coffee Shop 10am–5.30pm

This restaurant is delightfully situated at the water's edge by Kentallen pier, allowing diners to gaze across the lovely Loch Linnhe to the misty mountains beyond. The eatery is housed in a converted extension of the old Kentallen railway station and faithfully reproduces much of the original Edwardian-style décor. The coffee shop is open all day until 5.30pm and serves home baking, teas and light lunches. The menu is changed daily and might include venison pie, lasagne or fresh salmon crêpes. In the evening a large à la carte menu is offered but it is beyond our limit.

[P] [♧]

KESWICK
Cumbria
Map **11** NY22

Bay Tree 1 Wordsworth St
☎ (0596) 73313
Open: Mon–Sat 10am–4.30pm, 7–9pm, Winter evenings only

This attractive terrace restaurant and guesthouse is easy to spot by its brown canopy and corner position. Victorian is the style for interior décor, with old prints, china, porcelain and highly-polished tables and chairs. The three-course dinner menu (changing daily) is just in our range.

[P] [S] [♧] **VS**

Derwentwater Hotel ★★★
Portinscale ☎ (0596) 72538
Open: Mon–Sun 8.30–9.30am, 12noon–2pm, 7.30–9pm

A friendly, informal hotel this, in a superb position close to the shores of Derwentwater. An excellent bar lunch menu (available Mon–Sat) includes a variety of salad platters and a range of snacks. Lunches are also available in the Deer Leep Restaurant where lamb and trout are on the menu.

[C] [P] [♧]

KEW
Gt London

Le Provence 14 Station Parade, Kew Gardens ☎ 01-940 6777 Plan4 **97**C2
Open: Tue–Sat 6–9.15pm, Sat 12noon–3pm

This traditional French restaurant, tucked away under the oak tree-lined parade at Kew Gardens, offers honest French cooking at no-nonsense prices. Daily specials are excellent value – fresh artichoke vinaigrette, risotto du chef and foie saute à la Venitienne (sliced liver cooked in butter with sherry and sliced onions, served with a selection of vegetables) are typical examples. The desserts are a delight – real fruit sorbet (usually raspberry) or meringue glacé Chantilly are both superb. Booking is essential.

[P]

Maids of Honour 288 Kew Rd
☎ 01-940 2752 Plan4 **98**C2
Open: Monday for coffee only, no lunches. Tue–Fri 10am–5.30pm, Sat 9am–5.30pm

The Maids of Honour has a pretty, double bow window frontage and the tiny cottage restaurant, decorated with Staffordshire pottery, is very popular, so you will probably have to queue and share a table, but it is well worth it. The restaurant is open for morning coffee, lunch and afternoon tea. For lunch, traditional English food is served, usually a choice of two roasts and steak pie, plus delicious pastries and cakes. Home-made soup to start your meal is also available. Children's portions of main course and sweet are very reasonably priced. Maids of Honour offers excellent value for money and presents English food at its very best.

[P] [♧]

KEYNSHAM
Avon
Map **3** ST66

The Grange Hotel ★★ 42 Bath Rd
☎ (02756) 2130
Open: Bar snacks: Mon–Sun 11.30am–2.30pm Restaurant: Mon–Fri 6.30–9pm, Sat–Sun 7–9pm

Once the main farmhouse in the area, this Georgian building in the centre of Keynsham has a comfortable air. A collection of Cries of London prints and medallioned cartoon prints adorn the restaurant walls. Lunchtime bar snacks include pâté, chicken drumsticks and traditional pasties. Dinner in the restaurant may be selected from an à la carte menu, where you will have to restrict your choice, but at lunchtime a meal of tasty soup, plaice dippers, followed by wholesome apple pie and cream should leave change from a fiver. There is an additional menu featuring home-made dishes.

[P]

KEYSTON
Cambridgeshire
Map **4** TL07

Pheasant Inn (signposted off the A604 between Huntingdon and Thrapston)
☎ (08014) 241
Open: Mon–Sun 12noon–2.30pm, 7–9.30pm

This attractive thatched black and white inn is situated on the edge of the quiet village green. Although the set price restaurant menu is too expensive for us there is a varied bar snack menu. Dishes include fried squid with garlic rolls and seafood shell and salad which can be washed down with a glass of real ale.

[C] [P]

KILKHAMPTON
Cornwall
Map **2** SS21

The Coffee House ☎ (028882) 484
Open: Etr to Oct Mon–Sun 10am–10pm. Out of season by prior arrangement only

Set in a small square in the centre of Kilkhampton these 300-year-old cottages were recently converted into a small complex which includes the restaurant. The menu covers snacks, cream teas, grills, fried food and roasts, many of the dishes are home-made using locally grown produce. A three-course meal of melon cocktail, fried chicken, fruit pie and cream, with coffee and a glass of wine comes within our price limit. In warm weather meals can be taken in the courtyard garden.

[P] [S] **VS**

Penstowe Manor Penstowe Rd
☎ (028882) 354
Open: Mid May–mid Sep, bar menu Mon–Sat 12noon–2.15pm, 7–9.30pm, Sun 12noon–1.45pm, 7–9.30pm
Restaurant Mon–Sun 7–9.30pm

A pleasant granite building, in a secluded spot, yet just a short distance from the A39. The large bar overlooking the gardens serves a variety of normal bar meals from soup to rump steak. The attractive dining room, with cheerful friendly staff, offers good cooking and most three-course meals are within the limit of this guide. There is a good choice of fish, meat and poultry dishes and a 'Sunday Special' of roast beef.

[C] [♫] [P]

KILLIECRANKIE
Tayside *Perthshire*
Map **14** NN96

Killiecrankie Hotel on the A9, 3m NW of Pitlochry ☎ (0796) 3220
Open: early Apr–mid Oct
12noon–2.30pm, 7–10pm (last orders)

This white-painted building with its well-tended gardens is set in woodland close to a National Trust beauty spot. Bar lunches are very popular here and there's a good range of food for you to sample. After soup with roll and butter, two of the options on offer are fried haddock with chips and peas and smoked trout. A similar bar supper service operates during the evenings and includes Angus steak. 'Taste of Scotland Dishes' are always available.

[P] **VS**

KILLIN
Central *Perthshire*
Map **11** NN53

The Old Mill Restaurant and Lounge Bar Glendochart, 4m W of Killin on A85
☎ (05672) 434
Open: May–Oct Mon–Sun 9am–10pm

An attractively modernised 17th-century inn sits at the side of the A85. The wooden beamed restaurant has recently been extended and now has a lounge bar offering a wide range of bar snacks. Good home cooking is the speciality of the restaurant, where the standard menu for lunch and dinner offers a reasonably priced selection of hot dishes and salads. Try soup, steak pie, and fruit pie and cream, all home-made. Morning coffee and afternoon tea are also available.

[P]

KILMARNOCK
Strathclyde *Ayrshire*
Map **10** NS43

Bistro Jacquadonna 19–21 Nelson St
☎ (0563) 20660
Open: Mon–Sat 12noon–2.30pm, 6–10pm. Closed Sun and first two weeks in July

This newly-opened bistro stands in a small lane in the old part of the town centre just off John Finne Street. The lunch menu offers a good choice of pastas available in full and generous half portions. Main course scampi and steak can be followed by apple pie and fresh cream. The dinner menu is more extensive but only a few dishes are out of our range.

[C] [♫]

The Coffee Club✕ 30 Bank St
☎ (0563) 22048
Open: Mon–Sat 9.30am–10pm, Sun 12noon–5.30pm

Friendly, speedy service and a pleasant décor, with roughcast walls, alcoves and tiffany lamps make this a popular meeting and eating place. 'Fast food' such as baked potatoes, American-style hamburgers and home-made pizzas are available in the self-service on the ground floor. Coffee, snacks and full meals, with waitress service can be enjoyed in the basement. A galaxy of grills offers a Scotsman's grill (haggis, peas, carrots and chips) or Italian grills (meat balls, onion, tomato sauce and spaghetti) to name a few. Fish dishes and 'a few foreign foods' are also available. A three-course shopper's lunch is excellent value. A delicious selection of desserts is certain to tempt you – lemon meringue pie is hard to resist.

[♫] [P] [S]

KILMARTIN
Strathclyde *Argyll*
Map **10** NR89

Kilmartin Hotel ☎ (05465) 244/250
Open: Mon–Sat 11.30am–2pm, 6–9pm, Sun 12.30–2pm, 6.30–9pm

Situated some 30 miles south of Oban on the A816, this traditional roadside inn has built up a local reputation for its good food and friendly atmosphere. All items from the extensive light meal menu are served in a simple six-tabled dining area, after you've ordered at the lounge bar. Starters include home-made soup whilst fried, breaded scampi and sirloin steak with onion rings are two of the more popular main dishes. Pavlova is a recommended dessert. If you book in advance, a more formal meal can be had in an intimate, candlelit dining room, but the price is over our limit.

[P] **VS**

KINGSBRIDGE
Devon
Map **3** SX74

Globe Inn Frogmore ☎ (054853) 351
Open: Mon–Sat 11am–2.30pm, 6–11pm, Winter 10.30pm, Sun 12noon–2pm, 7–10.30pm

This 17th-century free house is personally supervised by the proprietor. The substantial bar menu includes Cantonese prawns, Devon lamb, cottage pie and steak and kidney pie. There is a choice of starters and desserts.

C P

Woosters The Quay ☎ (0548) 3434
Open: Mon–Sun 12noon–2pm, 7–10pm, Winter open only Tue–Sat

Woosters – housed in a two-storey cottage – specialises in fish, which is not surprising since it is situated right on the quay. If you choose one of the superb main course dishes prepared from locally-caught fish you may exceed our limit. Nevertheless, the blackboard menu lists inexpensive dishes such as prawn and pork chop suey and steak and kidney pie, with starters such as avocado prawns and grilled sardines. There is a selection of home-made sweets. Portions are generous and Woosters definitely offers value for money.

C P S

KINGSCOTE
Gloucestershire
Map **3** ST89

Hunters Hall ☎ (0453) 860393
Open: Mon 12noon–2pm; Tue to Sat 12noon–2pm, 7.30–10pm, Sun 12noon–1.45pm

This former coaching inn is reputed to have been licensed for 500 years and is full of character with oak panelling, stone walls and log fires. A lunchtime buffet, served in the Berkeley dining room offers a selection of salads or hot dishes such as trout, chicken or steak and kidney pie. Bar meals are displayed on a blackboard and are equally good value.

P

KINGSTON-UPON-THAMES
Gt London

Blueys 2 Station Buildings, Fife Rd
☎ 01-546 6614 Plan4 **99**D2
Open: Mon–Thu 12noon–11.15pm, Fri & Sat 12noon–11.30pm

This small, two-storey restaurant has polished table tops and simple dècor. A three-course meal of soup, chilli con carne, cheesecake and coffee offers excellent value for money. There is also a good range of snacks, including baked potatoes served with salad, and burgers served with chips or baked potato, and salad.

C P

Clouds 6–8 Kingston Hill
☎ 01-546 0559 Plan4 **100**D2
Open: Mon–Sun 11am–11pm

This busy, friendly restaurant operates on two floors, the first floor is a cocktail bar. The ground floor menu offers stuffed mushrooms among other appetisers; and main courses include hamburgers, salads and home-made steak and kidney pie. Ice cream and cheesecake are popular desserts. Children's meals are available, and a three-course Sunday lunch with coffee comes within our price limit.

P S

The Farmhouse Kitchen 3/5 Thames St (rear of Millets) Plan4 **101**D2
Open: Mon–Sat 9am–5.30pm

This self-service style cafeteria, with padded bench seating, offers a range of good, hot, tasty dishes. Cheese and potato savoury, chicken in wine sauce, with mushrooms, tomatoes and parsley and apple pie and cream are popular dishes. There is also a special area for non-smokers. If you just want a snack try one of the cakes or pastries from the wide selection on display.

P

Flames 14 Kingston Hill ☎ 01-549 5984 Plan4 **102**D2
Open: Mon–Sun 12.30–2.30pm, 7–11pm

There is a continental air about the rustic wood-and-house-plant dècor of this restaurant. Its windows overlook the wide tree-lined pavement of Kingston Hill, on the outskirts of an old market town which is now almost part of London. Food is imaginative and not overpriced though one could exceed the limit when choosing from the à la carte menu. Chicken farci and Grand Marnier pancakes make a delicious meal, there is a small cover charge. A traditional three-course Sunday roast is also available.

C P

KINGSWINFORD
West Midlands
Map **7** SO88

Bickley's Bistro 11 Townsend Pl
☎ (0384) 287148
Open: Tue–Fri 12noon–2.15pm, Tue–Sat 7–10pm

Tucked away in a small shopping area off the busy A491 is this charming little bistro. Originally the local post office, it has been transformed into a cosy eating place of mainly black-and-white brickwork decorated with antique cooking utensils and pot plants. The tempting menu offers excellent variety but it is, unfortunately over our limit, so try the plat du jour which changes daily and represents excellent value.

C P S

KINGUSSIE
Highland *Inverness-shire*
Map **14** NH70

Wood'n Spoon Restaurant 3–7 High St
☎ (05402) 488
Open: Mon–Sat 10am–9.30pm, Sun 12.30–9.30pm

The recently renovated restaurant has exposed stonework, a log fire, natural pine partitions and a self-service counter where home-made cakes, pies, quiches and other goodies are arrayed. Starters include smoked fish pâté. Chef's specials include game casserole and poached salmon, both served with baked potato and vegetables. Home-baked pies, fresh salads, cold roasts and venison burgers are always available.

Sweets from the trolley are home-made and served with cream or ice-cream.

C P S VS

KINLOCH RANNOCH
Tayside *Perthshire*
Map **14** NN65

Gitana Grill Loch Rannoch Hotel
☎ (08822) 201
Open: Mon–Sun 8am–10pm

The Grill is named after the steam yacht *Gitana* which sank in Loch Rannoch in 1906. She was raised in 1980 and will hopefully be back in service again soon. The menu here offers breakfast, snacks and a range of children's meals. The main courses (mainly grills) include gammon steak, a variety of burgers and the chef's dish of the day. There is a good choice of starters and sweets.

C P

KIRBY MISPERTON
North Yorkshire
Map **8** SE77

Bean Sheaf Restaurant✕✕
☎ (065386) 614
Open: Tue–Sun 12noon–2pm

This single-storey wayside cottage, converted and extended, offers a comfortable respite to the motorist, and to visitors to Flamingo Land Zoo. On entry, a comfortable lounge bar decorated in quiet fawns and browns leads through to a large, colourful dining room divided in two by an arch with classical pillars. Evening meals are rather above our limit but three-course lunches, weekdays and Sundays are very good value. All dishes are prepared personally by the proprietor and include such main meals as steak and kidney pie, whole grilled sole and jugged hare. An extensive wine list offers a choice of over 100 reasonably-priced wines.

P

KIRKCALDY
Fife *Fife*
Map **11** NT29

Green Cockatoo Restaurant 275–277 High St ☎ (0592) 263310
Open: Mon–Sat 9am–5pm, closed Wed

At the north end of the High Street, you'll find a bakery and confectioner's shop. Go through the shop and up some stairs and on the first floor you will find the Green Cockatoo, a traditional Scottish tearoom with polished wood panelling, fresh white linen on the tables, and friendly service. Tea is obviously *the* meal here, with all those delicious scones and cakes downstairs, but the lunch menu is good value too with the most expensive dish – fresh salmon and salad – priced within our budget. Sweets include Bakewell tart and custard, fresh cream gâteau and ice creams. On the second floor is a grill room, the 'Drouthy Crony' with a more limited menu at similarly moderate prices.

C P S VS

The Pancake Place 28 Kirk Wynd
☎ (0592) 264982
Open: Mon–Sat 10am–5.30pm

Housed in a converted stone building dating from 1779, this is a comfortable restaurant specialising in pancakes-with-everything. You can start with soup, but there is a choice of 12 snack-sized pancakes with intriguing fillings such as ham and peach. For your main course, large savoury pancakes such as chicken and pineapple or Rocky Mountain Burger are recommended. Alternatively you can try one of seven crisp salads, served with two thin pancakes. There are a dozen varieties of sweet pancakes available for dessert. 'Pippin', a large spicy pancake with a delicious hot apple and cinnamon filling topped with cream is a gourmet's delight.

P S

KIRKCUDBRIGHT
Dumfries & Galloway *Kirkcudbrightshire*
Map **11** NX65

The Coffee Pot 5 Castle St
☎ (0557) 30569
Open: Summer only Mon–Sat 10am–5pm, 6.45–8.30pm

The Coffee Pot with its bow-windowed frontage is a snug little restaurant just across from the old castle in the centre of historic Kirkcudbright. George and Rona Bower have devised an interesting à la carte menu to tempt the tourist and shopper alike. Starters include mushrooms provençale and seven main courses include fried local trout, seafood crêpes and chicken Kiev. Raspberries St Moritz and crêpes Suzette are desserts.

C S

KIRK LANGLEY
Derbyshire
Map **8** SK23

Meynell Arms Hotel★★ Ashbourne Rd
☎ (033124) 515/6
Open: Bar meals Mon–Sat 12noon–2.30pm, 6.30–9.30pm, Sat 8.15pm, Sun 12noon–2pm, 7–8.30pm
Restaurant: Mon–Sat 12noon–2pm, 6.30–9pm

An excellent stopping place en route for the Peak District, the lounge bar serves a range of wholesome dishes at lunchtime and in the evening. Three courses can come well within the budget – soup of the day, followed by farmhouse grill or home-made steak and kidney pie and a sweet from the trolley is a typical example. A three-course table d'hôte lunch offers a good choice but the dinner menu is a little expensive for us. Main courses include roasts, lemon sole and Meynell mixed grill.

C P

KIRKMICHAEL
Strathclyde *Ayrshire*
Map **10** NS30

Jock's Coffee Shop 24 Patna Rd
☎ (06555) 499
Open: Summer Mon–Sun 10am–5pm, Fri & Sat 7.30–9.30pm, Winter Tue–Sun 10am–5pm, Fri & Sat 7.30–9.30pm. Closed Mon

This is a popular and busy coffee shop despite its rather remote location. Home-baking is a speciality and there is an extensive range of fruit pies, cakes, scones and shortbreads – the doughnuts and meringues are a must. Special hot lunches are good value and a traditional lunch is available on Sundays. With careful selection you can enjoy a meal from the dinner menu, but most of the main course dishes are too expensive for us.

P

KNOTTINGLEY
West Yorkshire
Map **8** SE52

The Bay Horse Fairburn, 4m N of Knottingley just off the A1
☎ (0977) 85126, 82371
Open: Mon–Fri 12noon–2pm, 7–10pm, Sat 7–10pm Sun 12noon–2pm

This attractive restaurant boasts a large tabled'hôte menu and you can enjoy two courses (a main course and starter or sweet) within our budget. This certainly represents good value for money as it includes 'silver service' by uniformed staff – something the Roman 9th Legion never had as they trudged up the Great North Road to York. The modern traveller could choose chicken Kiev or fillets of sole bonne femme. There is also a tabled'hôte Sunday Lunch Menu.

C P

KNOWLE
West Midlands
Map **7** SP17

Ye Olde Bakehouse Warwick Rd, Chadwick End ☎ (05643) 2928 On the main A41 Birmingham/Warwick road
Open: Tue–Sun 12.30–1.30pm, Mon–Sat 7.30–9.45pm

Inside this black-and-white shuttered cottage with its bright flower tubs, diners receive a warm welcome from mother-and-son team Nick and Iris Worrall. Bits and bobs of bric-à-brac and open fires add to the homely atmosphere. A table d'hôte lunch, with the choice of four starters and five main courses, comprises fresh vegetables such as new potatoes, French beans, peas, broad beans, carrots and stuffed marrow and the price includes a home-made sweet and coffee. In the evening the à la carte menu lists specialities such as Bakehouse breast of chicken.

C P

KNOWSTONE
Devon
Map **3** SS82

The Mason Arms Knowstone, near South Molton ☎ (03984) 231
Open: Mon–Sat 11am–2.30pm, 5.30–11pm, Sun 12noon–2pm, 7–11pm

Beside the foothills of Exmoor a truly rural 13th-century picture postcard inn is the delightful location of this warm and intimate restaurant. Here in the evenings the menu offers a tempting range of dishes including steak and pigeon pie and veal Elizabeth (veal in a mild curry sauce with pineapple). If you want a more simple meal then try the bar menu (available lunchtime and evenings) which offers a range of pies, salads and a ploughman's, with soup and pâté as starters.

P

KNUTSFORD
Cheshire
Map **7** SJ77

Sir Frederick's Wine Bar 44 King St
☎ (0565) 53209
Open: Mon–Sat 12noon–2.15pm, 7–10.15pm

You'll enjoy the relaxed and friendly atmosphere at this pleasant town centre wine bar. Décor is simple with rough cast walls and arches decorated with posters and block board prints. A limited à la carte menu is accompanied by an ample wine list. Two and sometimes three courses will come within our budget (depending on the choice of dishes). Salmon steak garni and gammon steak are two of the main courses. There is also a choice of cold table and continental salads.

C ♫ P S **VS**

KYLEAKIN, Isle of Skye
Highland *Inverness-shire*
Map **13** NG72

Crofters Kitchen Allt Anavig
☎ (0599) 4134
Open: 1 Apr–31 Oct Mon–Sat 12noon–9pm, Sun 12.30–8.30pm

This bright modern restaurant is situated beside the main road about a mile from the ferry. A typical lunch of farmhouse pâté, gammon steak or the crofterburger (home-made ¼lb beefburger) followed by cheesecake will keep you within the budget. Snacks are always available and the afternoon menu features basket meals. The varied dinner menu also offers excellent value.

♫ P

LANARK
Strathclyde *Lanarkshire*
Map **11** NS84

Silver Bell 26 Bannatyne St
☎ (0555) 3129
Open: Mon–Sat 11am–9pm, Sun 12.30–2.30pm, 4–8pm

Situated in the centre of a town that boasts its own racecourse, the Silver Bell takes this as its theme with prints of racehorses decorating the walls. Highbacked chairs and dark beamwork add character, and the warm, relaxed atmosphere is enhanced by the friendly local waitresses. A table d'hôte lunch menu offers three courses such as home-made soup, beef steak pie, followed by pear belle Hélène. Tea or coffee is included in the price. Bar lunches and quick snacks are also available. The à la carte dinner menu is more extensive and may take you over the limit. You may prefer high tea which includes a main course such as farmhouse grill or French-fried chicken and bacon, tea, scones, cakes and bread.

C P

The Tavern Riverside Rd, Kirkfieldbank
☎ (0555) 3163/2537
Open: Mon–Sat 12noon–3pm, 6.30–9pm

Ideal for the motorist, this white-painted tavern has a very popular lounge bar with a small wood-panelled restaurant adjoining. The à la carte lunch and supper menus are very reasonably priced, with the emphasis on grills. French fries, garden and peas and carrots are included in the price of all main courses. A plateful of mouth-watering beef steak pie is a popular dish. Basket meals are also available.

C ♫ P

LANCASTER
Lancashire
Map **7** SD46

Old Brussels 53 Market St
☎ (0524) 69177
Open: Mon–Sat 8am–6pm

Old Brussels is a family-owned and run restaurant serving freshly-cooked foods, reasonably priced and nicely presented. Home-baked pizzas, burgers, farmhouse grill and meat and potato pies are hot favourites. Morning coffee, fruit scones and lemon meringue pie are also specialities.

C ♫ P S

The Country Pantry Co-operative Department Store, Church St
☎ (0524) 64355 ext38
Open: Mon–Sat 9am–5pm

Situated on the first floor of the Co-op in the city centre, this bright, self-service pantry is furnished in pine with country-kitchen collages decorating the walls. Pot plants (the genuine thing) act as divides between tables. There is a good selection of hot dishes and salads all at very low prices. A typical meal could be soup, quiche with either jacket potatoes or chips, followed by a cake or pastry. Sorry, no dividend stamps though.

P ♧ **VS**

Squirrels 92 Penny St ☎ (0524) 62307
Open: Mon–Sat 11.30am–2pm, 6.30–10pm, Sun 7–10pm

The smart brown-and-cream exterior of this city-centre wine bar attracts hungry shoppers and wine buffs alike. Inside, the cavernous, cellar-like atmosphere has a pleasing effect and complements the good range of food. Main courses include beef steak and oyster pie with filled baked potatoes, pâté and salads as possible (and cheaper) alternatives. With home-made soup as your starter or a slice of full-cream gâteau for sweet, you have a tasty and wholesome meal.

C ♬ P S ♧

LARGS
Strathclyde *Ayrshire*
Map **10** NS25

Green Shutter Tearoom
28 Bath St ☎ (0475) 672252
Open: Mon–Sun 10am–6pm. Closed Oct–Mar

Just across the promenade from the sea, this restaurant commands a unique view of the beautiful Isle of Cumbrae. A three-course meal is excellent value – home-made soup of the day is available and a wide selection of grills includes haddock with peas and chips or gammon steak with peach. Sweets include home-made apple tart with cream. A special 'Kiddies Corner' menu (for kids of 10 and under) offers beefburgers, sausages, or fish-fingers with peas and chips and ice cream novelties.

P ♧ **VS**

Nardini's Esplanade ☎ (0475) 674555
Open: Mon–Sun 12noon–3pm, 3.30–8pm

A popular seaside establishment catering mainly for holidaymakers in the season; but the enterprising proprietor of Nardini's keeps his winter trade going by offering a three-course meal at rock-bottom prices. Just what you get for your money depends upon the day of the week – fish and chips on Monday, steak and kidney pie on Wednesday, for instance, but there is a selection of grills, omelettes, salads etc, if you do not fancy the 'dish of the day'. The menu also includes a range of children's meals. You can get dinner here too, served from 8pm to 10pm, but the bill would almost certainly exceed our budget.

♬ P ♧

LAUDER
Borders *Berwickshire*
Map **12** NT54

The Black Bull Hotel ☎ (05782) 208
Open: Mon–Sun 8am–9.30pm and normal licensing hours

The jangle of harness and sound of posthorns no longer announces the arrival of travellers in need of rest and refreshment, yet The Black Bull retains the atmosphere of a coaching inn. Built in the 18th century, it survived the coming of the railways and has been revived and modernised to cope with the swing back to road transport. In the elegant dining room you can enjoy lunch and dinner with five or six main dishes including roasts. For a cold meal or snack, try the Harness Room Grill, where you can feast your eyes on relics of coaching days whilst enjoying your choice from the bar menu. This includes a three-course lunch well within our limit, or sample a ploughman's.

♬ P ♧

LEAMINGTON SPA (ROYAL)
Warwickshire
Map **4** SP36

Parkes 19 Park St ☎ (0926) 23741
Open: Mon–Sat 12noon–2pm, 7–11pm

A décor of pink, green and white, with lots of plants and mirrors, sets the scene for this bright, lively restaurant. Open your meal with Parkes' special mushrooms, or a bowl of chili, or *crudités* with a selection of dips. Main courses, all served with Parkes' own special sauces, are reasonably priced, and a plate of lasagne and side salad offers good value. Fresh fish from the local trout farm is also on the menu. For dessert, there are home-made ice creams and should diners feel the need for exercise, there is a small dance floor.

The Regent Hotel★★★ Regent St
☎ (0926) 27231
Open: The Vaults Restaurant: Mon–Sat 12.30–11pm
Chandos Restaurant: Mon–Sat 12.30–2pm, 6.45–8.45pm, Sun 12.30–2pm, 7–8.30pm
Fast Food Bar: normal licensing hours

The imposing Regent Hotel in the centre of this famous spa was the largest hotel in Europe when it was built in 1819 and renowned for its VIP visitors, including Queen Victoria and Napoleon. Today it boasts three excellent eating places. The Vaults and the elegant Chandos Restaurant are, unfortunately, out of our price range, but the Cork and Fork Bar offers light meals at very reasonable prices. Soup followed by steak and kidney pie or piquant chicken and brandy snaps Chantilly are some of the choices on the menu.

C ♬ S ♧ **VS**

LEDBURY
Hereford & Worcester
Map **3** SO73

Applejack 44 The Homend
☎ (0531) 4181
Open: Mon–Sat 12noon–2.30pm, 7.30–10.30pm

The cosy 'old inn' atmosphere is retained here at Applejack where owner Bob Evans has converted this 17th-century inn into a snug two-storey restaurant and wine bar. A racing driver, Bob started the restaurant as a hobby. The Wine Bar offers a variety of intersting dishes including grilled sardines, wholemeal pizza and home-made apple pie. The restaurant offers an evening meal from a more extensive menu, though some of the main courses will take you over our limit. Try cream of almond soup followed

For entry see Bude page 52

by noisettes of lamb in garlic and rosemary. Situated in the main shopping street of Ledbury, this black and white inn is convenient for shoppers and business people.

C S ☘ VS

LEEDS
West Yorkshire
Map **8** SE33

The Allerton Nursery La, Alwoodley
☎ (0532) 680240
Open: Mon–Fri 12noon–2pm, 7.15–11pm, Sat 7.15–11pm

The tasteful restaurant is dominated by the ceiling, which is buttressed by low, shallow arches. The table d'hôte lunch is excellent value and includes a choice of four starters, seven main courses and sweets from the trolley. In the evening the price of the main course includes a sweet from the trolley. Dishes include steak and kidney pie, gammon and southern fried chicken.

C P

Ken Marlow's Fish Restaurant
62 Street La ☎ (0532) 666353
Open: Tue–Fri 12noon–2pm, 5–10pm, Sun 4.30–10pm

Fish is the order of the day at this restaurant set in a modern development close to the northern ring road. A small bar with a few seats leads to an open-plan restaurant with bold décor. All main courses feature fish – fried or grilled, except when in salad form, and chipped potatoes are included. No fancy fare is offered, but a wholesome three-course meal can be enjoyed at a very reasonable price.

S VS

New Inn Wetherby Rd, Scarcroft
☎ (0532) 892029
Open: Mon, Wed–Sat 12noon–2.30pm, 7–10.30pm, Sun 12noon–2pm, 7–10pm

This modern pub and restaurant stands by the roadside and has extensive lawns. The fawns and browns of the pleasant décor blend well with the exposed brickwork and coloured spotlights. Pictures of Falstaffian scenes decorate the walls. Only the set lunch menu qualifies for the limited budget meal as the à la carte menu would need very careful choice to keep within our limit. For lunch, starters include ravioli au gratin and Florida cocktail, with roast pork or lambs liver with onions for main course.

C ♫ P ☘

The Milano ✕✕ 621 Roundhay Rd
☎ (0532) 659752
Open: Mon–Fri 12noon–2.30pm, Sat 7–11.30pm

On the main road into the town stands this smart, ground floor restaurant; an oasis in the desert of shops around it. Food is English and Italian – expensive in the evening but well within our means for lunch. A table d'hôte menu offers a choice of nine starters and eight main-course dishes served with vegetables of the day. A sweet from the trolley or cheese completes a very substantial meal.

C P S ☘

The Traveller's Rest Harewood Rd, East Keswick ☎ (0937) 72766
Open: Mon–Sun 12noon–2pm, 7–10.30pm

This first-floor restaurant enjoys a prime location overlooking the beautiful Wharfe Valley. The small Tudor-style room with its dark wood beams and furniture, partitioned cubicles and rich red carpeting provides a cosy, restful eating place for about 50 people. Main courses comprise grills and fries, with a choice of steaks at the top end of the price scale. It is possible to overdo the limit here, but it is also quite easy to stay within the limit with a meal such as soup, followed by lamb cutlets or a choice from the sweet trolley.

C ♫ P ☘ VS

LEEK
Staffordshire
Map **7** SJ95

The Jester At Leek 81 Mill St
☎ (0538) 383997
Open: Mon–Sun 12noon–2pm, 7–10pm

This beige, pebble-dash restaurant has an inviting, cottagey interior. A good variety of wholesome basic English fare is available and a three-course Sunday lunch with a choice of seven starters, eight main courses and sweets from the trolley comes within our limit. The à la carte menu, with starters, grills and roasts at reasonable prices, includes a lot of fish and seafood. Try fresh salmon or golden seafood platter. Budget meals at lunchtime include home-made steak and kidney pie, breaded plaice and a dish of the day.

P ☘

LEICESTER
Leicestershire
Map **4** SK50

Du Cann's Wine Var 29 Market St
☎ (0533) 556877
Open: Mon–Fri 11.30am–2.30pm, Sat 11.30am–3pm, Wed–Sat 5.30–10.30pm

In one of the city's many little side streets is this popular split-level wine bar. The attractive ground-floor room offers self-service selection of a variety of cold carvery items (turkey, ham, beef etc and some speciality seafood dishes) against a background of plain green walls, livened up by old prints, shelves of crock casks and old wine bottles. A varied three-course meal can be had within our price limit. Below it is the white-walled cellar with its glimpses of original brick, where a full waitress service operates. In the evenings a number of home-made dishes, including chili con carne, are available to supplement the cold selection. During the 'Happy Hour' 5.30–6.30pm Wed–Sat £1 is taken off the price of any bottle of wine.

♫ S ☘

The Good Earth 19 Free La
☎ (0533) 26260
Open: Mon–Thu 12noon–3pm, Fri 12noon–3pm, 7–11pm, Sat 12noon–6pm

Tucked away in narrow Free Lane is this inviting first-floor wholefood restaurant. Inside all is natural wood, with displays of farming implements, hanging brass lanterns and a large farmhouse dresser with old plates and storage jars of preserved fruits, vegetables and grains. Help yourself to hot or cold dishes from the buffet display which includes a selection of soups, hot savoury dishes or roasts, savoury rissoles, a variety of nourishing salads, home-made cakes, fresh fruit and natural goat's milk yoghurt. Parties of 20 or more can arrange to eat an evening meal on nights other than Friday.

P S VS

The Hayloft, Holiday Inn ☆☆☆☆ St Nicholas Circle ☎ (0533) 531161
Open: Mon–Sun 11am–10.30pm

In striking contrast to the modern hotel accommodation, the Hayloft restaurant has an old tithe barn atmosphere, with suitable décor of a hay cart, horse and oxen trappings, and enough room for 120 people. Try the farmhouse soup (fresh made from the cauldron) followed by a 'good and wholesome salad' or chicken casserole. Desserts include crème caramel or pie or gâteau from the pastry shop. Coffee is served from a bottomless pot for one charge. A special attraction on Sundays is the 'splosh and nosh' menu where you can enjoy a sauna and swim in the hotel pool, followed by a three-course meal with coffee though this is just over our price limit. If you find swimming a little too energetic, the regular weekend dinner dances might be just your thing.

C ♫ P ☘

The Post House Hotel ☆☆☆ Branstone La East ☎ (0533) 896688
Open: Barge Coffee Shop: Mon–Sun 7am–10.30pm

Longboat owners will feel very much at home in this bright and original coffee shop, where the ceiling is curved to resemble an abstract version of an upturned boat, and the walls sport a colourful mural of a bargee family and their craft. Cream paintwork and a scattering of pictures depicting canal scenes complete the atmosphere. The imaginative menu gives excellent scope for a satisfying two-course meal. Tasty starters and grills supplement the quick-

and-easy hamburgers, salads and omelettes. A children's menu is available on request, children under five eat free, those under 14 may choose full adult portions at half price. Place mats and lollipops with the famous 'munch bunch' cartoon characters make this a very popular place for all young guests.

C P ♿

A Spanish Place 38A Belvoir St
☎ (0533) 542830
Open: Mon–Sat 9am–6pm

An orange awning and pot plants gives this small modern restaurant a continental flavour. Inside, the emphasis is on home-made cuisine and a friendly, hospitable atmosphere, heightened by the fresh posy of flowers on each table. Snack foods and main meals are available throughout the day. Sandwiches and toasted snacks are made from freshly baked bread and a tasty two-course meal could include fried chicken, peas and jacket potato and home-made fruit pie with fresh cream. Business lunch boxes are made up by Susan and Josef Arroyo, the proprietors, to suit individual customers' requirements.

S

Swiss Cottage Restaurant 52–54 Charles St ☎ (0533) 56577
Open: Mon–Sat 9.30am–7pm

Opened about 19 years ago, this smart restaurant with attractive exposed brickwork, dark wood-effect tables, copper light shades and waitresses dressed as Swiss maids, was the first of six similar restaurants which have sprung up in Leicester. Each site has been chosen for its ease of access for shoppers and business people in the city centre. At lunch-time, chops, steaks, home-made steak and kidney pie, chicken and gammon steak are available. There is an excellent choice of home-made pies served with fresh cream. Sister establishments are located in Churchgate, Lee Circle, Odeon Arcade and the Haymarket. Except for Swiss Cottage, Charles Street, all the restaurants are now licensed for serving wines and beers.

P S

Tower Restaurant Lewis's, Humberstone Gate ☎ (0533) 23241
Open: Mon–Sat 11.30am–3pm

The sleek, 137-foot tower of Lewis's store, topped with coloured lighting was the talk of Leicester and district in 1936, when it was built. The fourth floor restaurant takes its name from this and its interior décor is based on one of the Queen's ships of the Thirties – all turquoise and gold with a rich, red patterned carpet. A special shopper's lunch is available or try the table d'hôte menu which offers excellent value. There is a choice for each course and a typical meal would be soup, followed by grilled ham and pineapple with sweet of the day to finish. The à la carte menu is extremely reasonable, with main courses such as roasts and sweets from the trolley. There is a special children's menu for under 11s. There is no service charge and VAT is included.

C P S ♿

Upstairs, Downstairs Main St, Glenfield (4m NW of Leicester City Centre off A50)
☎ (0533) 312215
Open: Mon–Fri 12noon–2pm, 6.30–10pm, Sat 6.30–10pm, Sun 12noon–2pm

Situated in the grounds of the Tudor Rectory Guest House this pleasant restaurant was opened in 1982 after being converted from premises which were once a church school. 'Downstairs' (the ground floor) houses a comfortable bar and the split level restaurant is 'Upstairs' on the first floor. At lunchtime salads, omelettes, kebabs and steak and kidney pie are popular dishes, and a traditional Sunday lunch offers a good selection of roasts. The dinner menu is outside the scope of this guide.

♫ P ♿ **VS**

LEIGHTON BUZZARD
Bedfordshire
Map **4** SP92

The Cross Keys ✕ The Market Square
☎ (0525) 373033
Open: Mon 10am–2.30pm, Tue–Sat 10am–2.30pm, 7–10pm, Sun 12noon–2.30pm

Opposite the famous 15th-century Market Cross, this pub food bar serves a selection of hot and cold snacks at budget prices. On fine days you can bring the children and enjoy food on the paved forecourt. A special children's menu operates – including egg salad and half-portion scampi and chips. Hot snacks for adults are either served with chips or vegetables and potatoes – plaice, curried chicken, veal escalopes or hot dish of the day such as hot-pot or beef stew are examples. Cold buffet meats, fish, pâtés and salads are reasonably priced along with desserts such as gâteaux with fresh cream.

[C] [P] [S] **VS**

LEVEN
Fife *Fife*
Map **11** NO03

Osborne Lounge and Grill 101 Commercial Rd ☎ (0333) 25626
Open: Summer Mon–Sat 9.30am–12mdnt, Sun 3pm–12mdnt, Winter Mon–Sat 9.30am–12mdnt

This smart, town-centre restaurant offers efficient friendly service with the owners, Mr and Mrs Herd always in attendance. At lunch-time the menu offers roast meat salads and grills. The dinner menu ranges from herring fillets in oatmeal to steaks and there is a choice of starters and desserts.

[♫] [P]

LEWES
East Sussex
Map **5** TQ41

Lunch Counter 7 Station St
☎ (07916) 77447
Open: Mon–Sat 10am–3pm. Closed Sun, Bank Hols, Christmas and New Year

A colourful and cheerful family restaurant which offers hot dishes such as rich fish pie with prawns and fennel, pork ratatouille and lasagne served with your choice of salads. Desserts include chocolate mousse and a variety of home-made cakes and gâteaux.

[♫] [P]

LHANBRYDE
Grampian *Morayshire*
Map **15** NJ26

Tennant Arms Hotel St Andrews Rd
☎ (034384) 2226
Open: Mon–Sat 12noon–2.30pm, 5–9.30pm, Sun 12.30–2.30pm, 5–9.30pm

You will receive the personal attention of the owners, Mr and Mrs Bryce, at this family-run modernised coaching inn, with its cosy little restaurant and attractive bar areas. A three-course bar lunch with main courses such as scampi and chicken in cream sauce is excellent value. The restaurant offers an à la carte menu in the evening.

[P]

LINCOLN
Lincolnshire
Map **8** SK97

Crusts Restaurant 46 Broadgate
☎ (0522) 40322
Open: Mon–Sat 11.30am–2.30pm, 7pm–12mdnt

Only the name 'Crusts', printed in bold lettering on the window distinguishes this restaurant from the quaint little shops on either side of it. Business lunch is a must for the budget-conscious as you can have three courses at a very reasonable price.

[C] [♫] [P]

The Duke William 44 Bailgate
☎ (0522) 30257
Open: Mon–Thu 11.30am–3pm, 6.45–10.30pm, Fri–Sat 11.30am–3pm, 6.45–11pm, Sun 12noon–2pm, 7–10.30pm

This charming 18th century pub stands in the oldest part of the city, close to the famous cathedral. Lunch here is a homely affair with dishes such as home-made steak and kidney pie, grilled plaice or ham salad. A 'business special' is available most days which offers a three-course lunch at a very reasonable price. The dinner menu is too expensive for us.

[C] [P] [🍷] **VS**

Harvey's Cathedral Restaurant
1 Exchequer Gate, Castle Sq
☎ (0522) 21886
Open: Mon–Sat 11.30am–2pm, 7pm–12mdnt. Closed Sun

In the shadows of Lincoln Cathedral and Lincoln Castle is Bob and Adrianne Harvey's bright, split-level restaurant. Lunch here any day and you will receive excellent value for money and a good choice of well-prepared food. The two-course menu of the day coulf include coq au vin or roast lamb.

[C] [P] [S] [🍷] **VS**

Straits Wine Bar 8–9 The Strait
☎ (0522) 20814
Open: Mon–Sat 12noon–2.30pm, 7–11.30pm, Sun 11am–3pm

A simple, but cosy wine bar standing at the bottom of a steep hill in the shadow of the famous Cathedral. There is a good selection of salads and the hot dishes (which vary daily) could include spicy tomato pork chops and lasagne – all at reasonable prices. Sherry trifle is a popular dessert. There is a pleasant terraced garden and patio.

[C] [🍷]

The Wine Barge Brayford Pool
☎ (0522) 39278
Open: Tue–Sat 11am–3pm, Tue–Thu 7.30–11pm, Fri & Sat 7–11pm, Sun 7–10.30pm. Closed Mon

'Prudence', once a working barge carrying grain and cocoa beans on local waterways, has been converted into a wine bar and is now moored in historic Brayford Pool. There is ample seating below decks in the pine-clad salon and further seating on the deck. The menu lists a limited selection of inexpensive bar snacks and light meals. Hot dishes include chicken curry and spaghetti bolognaise. The wine list includes an exclusive range of German wines.

[P] [🍷]

LINLITHGOW
Lothian *West Lothian*
Map **11** NS97

Lochside Larder 286 High St
☎ (050684) 7275
Open: Mon–Thu 9am–6pm, Fri–Sat 9am–6pm, 7–9.30pm, Sun 11am–6pm

This small, neatly decorated restaurant and adjoining take-away bar is situated in a small shopping and residential complex between the main road and the banks of Linlithgow Loch. Both snacks and full meals are available. The lunch menu includes pizza, scampi and a dish of the day and fish and chicken feature on the dinner menu.

[C] [♬] [P] [S] [🍷] **VS**

LITTLE CHALFONT
Buckinghamshire
Map **4** SU99

The Copper Kettle Cokes La
☎ (02404) 3144
Open: Tue–Sat 9.30am–5pm

Simplicity is the keynote here, with polished tables and wheel-backed chairs for about 20 people. The lunch is home-cooked, just as mother used to make it and three courses are available at a very reasonable price. Soups or fruit juices are offered as appetisers. Main dishes served with a variety of fresh vegetables include steak or chicken and mushroom casseroles, roast pork and apple sauce or home-baked pies or flans. Cherry and apple sponge is a typical sweet.

[P]

LIVERPOOL
Merseyside
Map **7** SJ39

Casa Italia Temple Court, 40 Stanley St
☎ 051-227 5774
Open: Mon–Sat 12noon–10pm

This bright, bustling pizzeria, surrounded by more sombre city buildings, instantly commands attention. The menu lists a dazzling selection of pizzas and pastas at very reasonable prices and a range of delicious sweets.

[♬] [P] [S]

Everyman Bistro Hope St
☎ 051-708 9545
Open: Mon–Fri 12noon–11.30pm, Sat 11am–11.30pm

This interesting bistro is situated in the basement of the Everyman Theatre in the centre of town. Blackboards display a menu based on fresh produce and it is easy to eat three courses here and stay within the budget. Home-made soup or quiche Lorraine are two of the starters with dishes such as spicy Caribbean pork, broccoli cheese, salads and casseroles as main courses. There is a selection of home-made sweets, various cheeses and live yoghurts to finish with. Wine to accompany your meal is available by the glass.

[S] [🍷]

La Grande Bouffe 48A Castle St
☎ 051-236 3375
Open: Mon 10am–3pm, Tue–Fri 10am–11pm, Sat 11am–3pm, 7–11pm

La Grande Bouffe is a typical French-style basement café. French pictures adorn the walls. The menu is on a blackboard and dishes include home-made soup such as potato and watercress, quiches, beef sausage-meat and spinach pie and Armenian lamb. Desserts are also home-made. It is a self-service operation – ideal for a quick, tasty meal. The à la carte evening meal is likely to be beyond our limit.

[C] [♬] [P] [S]

McCartney's Atlantic Tower Hotel, Chapel St ☎ 051-227 4444
Open: Mon–Fri 12noon–12mdnt, Sat 12noon–3pm, 7–12mdnt, Sun 7–12mdnt

Those of us who lived through, or joined in, Beatlemania will be our element here with Beatles pictures, Beatles piped music and the name (and is that telephone number deliberately chosen for the 'Fab Four'?). The menu continues the theme with such items as Eleanor Rigby Salad, Octopus' Garden Platter (seafood of course), 'I am the Egg, Man' omelettes and Twist and Shout Kebabs. For dessert Strawberry Fields is an obvious choice, and who could resist 'McCartney's Wonderful' banana split?

C ♫ P ⚘

St George's Hotel★★★★ St John's Precinct, Lime St ☎ 051-709 7090
Open: Buttery: Mon–Sat 10am–10pm

The stylish modern coffee shop of this sumptuous hotel serves a comprehensive range of food. For a quick snack, toasted sandwiches, hamburgers of all varieties, chicken and egg dishes are on the huge menu. There is also plenty of scope for a three-course meal within our budget. A choice of six starters includes minestrone with Parmesan. A good selection of fish and grills make a substantial main course.

C P S ⚘

LIZARD
Cornwall
Map **2** SW61

Housel Bay Hotel Housel Cove
☎ (0326) 290417
Open: Mon–Sun12noon–1.30pm, 8.30–9.30pm

Situated in its own delightful gardens this hotel has superb sea views. Although the set five-course dinner is above our limit, there is an excellent choice of bar snacks which include a variety of salads and hot meals such as chicken, scampi, cottage pie or Madras curry. There is also a home-made meat loaf on the menu. For an extra 50p a head at lunchtime the bar snacks can be served in the dining room.

C P

LLANDUDNO
Gwynedd
Map **6** SH78

Coffee Shop and Poolside Bar, Empire Hotel★★★ Church Walks
☎ (0492) 79955
Open: Mon–Sun 11am–3pm, 6–10pm

Starters range from fruit juice to prawn cocktail. A variety of salads, fresh Conwy plaice and barbequed chicken are just some of the main courses that enable you to keep within the budget. Desserts include fresh fruit salad and cherry brandy cake.

C P

Plas Fron Deg Hotel 48 Church Walks
☎ (0492) 77267
Open: Mon–Sun 12.30–2pm, 6.30–7.30pm

Lunch and dinner menus offer a real choice, with dishes such as salmon mousse, coq au vin and ratafia trifle to tempt the taste buds. 'A Taste of Wales' dishes are a feature of Plas Fron Deg, too, and well worth trying. The à la carte menu is likely to be out of our price range.

C **VS**

LLANGERNYW
Clwyd
Map **6** SH86

The Bridge Inn ☎ (074576) 672
Open: Mon–Sat 12noon–3pm, 7–11pm (late dining room licence Fri and Sat); Sun 12noon–2pm, 6–10.30pm

Colin and Jean Morris run this 18th-century beamed inn mid-way between Abergele and Llanrwst. Everything is home made, the speciality being pies, or choose from delicious baked ham, chicken or a variety of burgers. A good selection of starters and sweets will ensure that you have a satisfying and tasty meal. Real ale is served as well as French and German wines.

♫ P ⚘ **VS**

See advertisement on page 112

LLANGOLLEN
Clwyd
Map **7** SJ24

Gale's Wine and Food Bar 18 Bridge St
☎ (0978) 860089
Open: Mon–Sat 12noon–1.45pm, 6–10pm (also Sun Jun–Oct)

There are more than a hundred wines on offer at Richard and Jill Gale's Wine and Food Bar, including one vintage port. The atmosphere is very friendly and welcoming, the menu written on a blackboard behind the bar. The food is outstandingly good for this kind of operation and very reasonable, with home-made soups, a choice of pâtés and a hot dish of the day. Very popular are pork and apple Stroganoff and beef in Guinness.

P S

LLANGORSE
Powys
Map **3** SO12

Red Lion Inn ☎ (087484) 238
Open: Mon–Sun 12noon–2pm, 7–9.30pm

A warm Welsh welcome is assured in this two hundred-year-old inn close to the famous Llangorse lake. Situated deep in the heart of the Brecon Beacons National Park, it is an ideal holiday stopping-place. Meals in the bar include snacks such as Chef's terrine or beef kebabs, more substantial meals such as veal Cordon Bleu are also available. À la carte meals are served in the dining room, but they may be priced over our limit.

P

LLANSANTFFRAID-YM-MECHAIN
Powys
Map **7** SJ22

Lion Hotel ☎ (069181) 207
Open: Mon–Sat 11.30am–2pm, 6.30–10pm (10.30 Fri), Sun 12noon–2pm, 7–10pm

This family-run country hotel was formerly a courthouse and jail, but they don't need to lock people up to get them here these days – the menu is arresting enough. A good selection of dishes includes home-made pies, trout, Welsh lamb cutlets, chili con carne and chicken chasseur. Home-made fruit pie with cream is a popular dessert. The real ale is from Woods of Shropshire.

C P

LLANYNYS
Clwyd
Map **6** SJ16

The Lodge Llanrhaeadr, near Denbigh
☎ (074578) 370
Open: Mon 10am–5.30pm, Tue–Sat 9am–5.30pm

The Lodge combines the display of fashions (from many parts of the world) and objets d'art with the provision of tasty inexpensive food. The accent is on light meals with filled baps, Welsh rarebit, hamburger, and several other items, but there are more substantial dishes including salads (cheese, ham, prawn or chicken) and savoury pancakes or omelettes. Sweets and pastries are home-made. A wide variety of beverages is available and a table license has been applied for.

C P **VS**

LLOWES
Powys
Map **3** SO14

Radnor Arms ☎ (04974) 460
Open: Mon–Sat 12noon–3pm, 7–10.30pm

This small, pleasant country pub is a converted house with white-painted walls. The atmosphere in the dining area with its high, beamed ceiling, is informal and relaxed. A good selection of food is chalked up on the blackboard menu including home-made soups, quiches, various ploughman's, Cheshire pork and apple pie, and mackerel in white wine. Delicious home-made bread accompanies some dishes and there is a huge choice of mouthwatering sweets.

P

LOCHEARNHEAD
Central *Perthshire*
Map **11** NN52

Craigroyston Lochside, ☎ (05673) 229
Open: Apr–Oct Mon–Sun 10am–10pm

This hotel, situated on the edge of Loch Earn, allows diners to enjoy views over the Loch, including the watersport activities which take place on the Loch. There are a variety of snacks and full meals available all day. Try the open sandwiches, served with salad, or a baked potato with cheese filling. For a full meal, soup, steak pie and sherry trifle comes within our limit.

P

LOCHINVER
Highland *Sutherland*
Map **14** NC02

Caberfeidh Bridgend ☎ (05714) 321
Open: Apr–Oct Mon–Sat 12noon–8pm

This simple, but pleasantly decorated little restaurant is located close to the shore on the east side of the village and is very popular with visiting family tourists. The menu offers starters such as local fresh scallops, while main courses include Scampi, Veal escalope, steak and kidney pie and pizza. For dessert try the Hot Choc Fudge Cake. There is a very reasonably priced children's menu and wine is available by the glass or carafe.

♫ P ♤ **VS**

LOCHTON
Grampian *Kincardineshire*
Map **15** NO79

T'Mast Lochton House (A957, 6m SE of Banchory) ☎ (033044) 543/585
Open: Summer Mon–Sun 12noon–2.30pm, 4.30–10.30pm

Formerly a grocer's shop, then a tearoom, this pub-cum-restaurant with its sun lounge extension now acts as a modern oasis for Grampian travellers. Lunchtime prices here are exceptionally low and the menu includes roast pork with apple sauce and peach Melba. A typical high tea offering is gammon with pineapple, including a hot drink, toast and cakes. Prices for dinner and supper may be over our limit.

P ♤

LONDON

The West End

St Marylebone

Ikaros 36 Baker St ☎ 01-935 7821 Plan4 **52**B4
Open: Mon–Sat 12noon–3pm, 6–11pm

This small Greek restaurant has an authentic air. The charcoal grill wafts the most delicious smells to the diner and gives a flavour to the food not found in normal cooking. Interesting Greek starters such as taramasalata or longaniko sausage are available, and main dishes include doner kebab and moussaka. Vegetables are priced separately and there is a choice of sweets. This is another restaurant where it would be all too easy to exceed the limit, but for central London the prices are not unreasonable.

C ♫ S ♤

Ristorante Alpino 42 Marylebone High St ☎ 01-935 4640 Plan4 **1**B4
Open: Mon–Sat 12noon–11.30pm

A typical Alpino this, with décor in the chalet style; skis on the wall, and the standard Alpino menu including scampi and escalopes of veal cooked in Marsala. A very friendly little restaurant, managed with Italian flair and Italian charm. An accordionist plays light music to aid the digestion of the supper trade. Madame Tussaud's is close by.

C ♫ S ♤

The Rose Restaurant Dickins and Jones, Regent St ☎ 01-734 7070 Plan2 **74**B1
Open: Mon–Sat 9.30am–5.30pm

Judging by the starched linen tablecloths, heavy cutlery, thick carpets and cool, green plants hanging in baskets from the elegant supporting pillars, Dickins and Jones work hard to maintain the old traditions. There is both a cold carvers table a hot carvers table, and but they are out of our price range. Hot dishes of the day such as chicken kebab or fillet of plaice are popular or try one of the grills. There is a mouth-watering selection of freshly-made gâteaux, trifles and pastries on the buffet, and a good range of ice cream-based sweets.

C S ♤

Paddington

The Gyngleboy 27 Spring St ☎ 01-723 3351 Plan1 **50**A2
Open: Mon-Fri 11am-3pm, 5.30–9pm

The 'Gyngleboy' was a leather bottle, or black jack, lined with silver and ornamented with little silver bells 'to ring peales of drunkeness'. So now you know. Conveniently close to Paddington Station, this is a very superior wine bar offering a substantial choice of cold dishes – game pie, smoked chicken and smoked salmon specials, are among the choices. But start with the soup – that's piping hot. The cellar is extensive and there's a sophisticated range of château bottled vintages.

C S

Linda's 4 Fernhead Rd ☎ 01-969 9387 Plan4 **56**B3
Open: Mon–Sat 12noon–3pm, 6–11pm. Closed Sun

Very popular with the locals, Linda's is reputed to be the first Vietnamese restaurant in the country. Proprietors Linda and Robin Blaney offer an à la carte menu and three set menu's with a variety of interesting dishes including cooked beef with rice stick soup and spiced spare ribs. Linda's is licensed.

P

Oodles 128 Edgware Rd, Marble Arch ☎ 01-723 7548 Plan 1 **70** A3
Open: Mon–Sat 11am–9pm, Sun 12noon–8pm

You've got to hand it to Oodles Ltd. The name over its restaurant conjures up visions of plenty. And that's just what it offers – large helpings of nourishing country-style dishes, just like Mother used to make them. Coq au vin, moussaka, and chicken curries are available with modestly priced wholesome sweets and starters. Vegetarian dishes are available too. Typical of all Oodles restaurants it has a simple décor – rough wooden tables, bench seats, white stucco walls hung with wooden advertising plates such as used to be seen on horse-drawn delivery carts. See listing under Bloomsbury and The City for other branches.

S ♤

Piccadilly

Lord Byron Taverna 41 Beak St ☎ 01-734 0316 Plan2 **57**C2
Open: Mon–Sat 12noon–3pm, 6pm–3.30am. Closed Sat lunch.

'You have to kiss a helluva lot of frogs before you find Prince Charming'. This is just one of the thousands of comments that decorate the walls and ceiling of this Greek taverna. Hardly Byronic, but most of the graffiti are quite amusing, and if you can think up something better you are welcome to add your piece. The restaurant premises were once lived in by Canaletto, the Venetian painter, and there is a blue plaque to commemorate this above the entrance. Food is almost entirely Greek, starters including a special variety of taramasalata and avgolemono (chicken soup with egg, lemon juice and rice). Main courses include moussaka, dolmades and lamb, and salad and other vegetables are charged extra. There is a wine bar in the cellars serving Greek wines, moussaka and kebabs.

C ♫ S **VS**

Swiss Centre Restaurants Leicester Sq ☎ 01-734 1291 Plan 2 **85** C2
Open: Mon–Sat 12noon–12mdnt, Sun 12noon–11.30pm

Imbiss Snack Bar (entrance in Wardour St)
Open: Mon–Sun 8.30am–11.30pm

There are four separate restaurants at the Swiss Centre, each with its own décor and menu. Of these only the Chesa prices itself out of this book. The other three are predominantly Swiss in style and offer regional specialities, most of which are within our price range. Of special interest are the hors-d'oeuvres (which may be ordered either as an appetiser or as a main dish), herrings cooked in a number of intriguing ways, and a range of sausage meats, bread, ice ream gâteaux and chocolates, all freshly-made on the premises. The Taverne and the Locanda specialise in Fondue, whilst the Rendez-Vous offers a range of Toggeburger (beefburgers), try the Appenzeller (with pineapple and Appenzeller cheese). The Imbiss Snack Bar offers sandwiches, salads and flans.

C ♫ P S ♧

Mayfair

L'Artiste Musclé 1 Shepherd Market ☎ 01-493 6150 Plan 2 **5** D1
Open: Mon–Sat 12noon–3pm, 5.30–11.30, Sun 7–11pm

In the heart of the Shepherd Market lies L'Artiste Musclé, a French wine-bar-cum-bistro in a 19th-century building which at first sight appears to be a well-populated junk shop. Closer inspection discloses that people are actually eating and drinking inside, though with a minimum of ceremony as they rub shoulders with anything from old chests to chamberpots while doing so. The menu is short, but has a real French-peasantish flavour, with items such as jambon quiche and côte de porc or ragout d'agneau.

♫ S

The Chicago Pizza Pie Factory
17 Hanover Sq ☎ 01-629 2669 Plan 2 **18** B1
Open: Mon–Sat 11.45am–11.30pm, Sun 12noon–10pm

This popular pizza restaurant has a very informal atmosphere, the walls lavishly decorated with Chicago memorabilia. The deep-dish Chicago-style pizza originated here: it has a thick crust and rich filling based on mozzarella cheese. Don't go alone however, as the smallest serves two – and is priced accordingly. If you think you can tackle more than a pizza, start with savoury stuffed mushrooms with sherry and garlic and finish with a delicious cheesecake. Owner Bob Payton's great passion, second after pizzas, is music and a sophisticated stereo system keeps his customers entertained while they wait the customary 30 minutes for their culinary masterpiece to appear from the kitchen.

♫ S ♧

Downs Wine Bar 5 Down St ☎ 01-491 3810 Plan 1 **34** C5
Open: Mon–Sat 12noon–3pm, 5.30pm–12mdnt, Sun 12noon–3pm, 7–11.30pm

A wine bar situated in an 18th-century backwater of Mayfair might be expected to price itself into the millionaires-only class, so it is a pleasant surprise to find that you can enjoy a meal here at Down's and still stay within the budget. Try smoked mackerel or rough country pâté, a daily special (barbecued spare ribs for instance) or trout with vegetables, and a sweet such as cheesecake. There is also a well-stocked 'downstairs' cold table.

C ♫ P S ♧

Granary 39 Albemarle St ☎ 01-493 2978 Plan 2 **46** C1
Open: Mon–Fri 11am–9pm, Sat 11am–2.30pm

Baskets of ferns and air-conditioning create a fresh, cool atmosphere in which to enjoy your meal in this delightful restaurant. Choose what you fancy from the tempting array of food on display, and one of the attentive waiters will carry it to your table. The menu is chalked up and is sure to include a choice of nine main dishes. Prawn provençale, beef Stroganoff and steak and kidney pie are likely choices. Salads are available, and there is a delicious array of sweets.

S **VS**

Soho

Apollonia Restaurant and Taverna
17A Percy St ☎ 01-636 4140 Plan 2 **2** B2
Open: Mon–Sun 12noon–1am (12mdnt on Sun)

Traditional home-made Greek dishes are offered in this very friendly restaurant with its Hellenic murals. The taramasalata is particularly recommended along with the dolmades and moussaka – all served with rice, potatoes and a crisp Greek Salad. In the evenings the basement taverna is alive with Greek dancers and musicians and the traditional plate-throwing that proves they're all having a good time.

C ♫ S

Crusting Pipe 27 The Market, Covent Garden ☎ 01-836 1415 Plan 2 **29** C3
Open: Mon–Sat 11.30am–3pm, 5.30pm–11pm. Closed Sun.

This popular basement wine bar with a sawdust-strewn floor and candle-lit tables offers both bar snacks and waitress service. The limited, but well-prepared menu, includes freshly-cut meats, salads with a choice of dressing, and charcoal grilled rib of beef and steak. The service is friendly and informal and there is a good selection of wines available by the glass.

♫ P S 🍷

Hobson's Wine Bar 20 Upper St Martin's La ☎ 01-836 5849 Plan 2 **51** C3
Open: Mon–Fri 11am–3pm, 5.30–11pm, Sat 5.30–11pm, Sun 7–10.30pm

This wine bar, close to Covent Garden, is located below ground and is on the whole candlelit with the occasional modern discreet light. There's bags of equine atmosphere here with wood-panelled walls, a 'Horse-Box' window and even sawdust. Of the various starters the home-made pâtés are highly recommended. Main course options are fish-biased and include smoked trout and fresh prawns. If you fancy spoiling yourself with some wine, on this occasion you'll find Hobson's choice from the wine cellars immense.

C P

Plummer's Restaurant 33 King St, Covent Garden ☎ 01-240 2534 Plan 2 **71** C3
Open: Mon–Fri 12noon–3pm, Mon–Sat 5.30pm–12mdnt

Victoriana epitomised by old photographs, prints and large mirrors, characterises this eating house, one of the original of the 'new wave' of restaurants in Covent Garden. Dishes include home-made steak and kidney pie, Californian chili served with Chef's salad and Plummer's Superburgers (8oz 100% pure Scottish beefburgers topped with bacon, egg and melted cheese).

S

Rasa Sayang 10 Frith St ☎ 01-734 8720 Plan 2 **72** B2
Open: Mon–Sat 12noon–3pm, 6pm–12mdnt

Attentive waiters at this cool, airy South East Asian restaurant, with its tasteful wood and wicker décor, will help you to select dishes from the intriguing menu. Starters include a variety of soups and a host of main courses is offered – seafood, chicken, beef, pork and vegetarian dishes. Speciality of the house is 'satay' – tender skewers of chicken and beef marinated in Malaysian spices, gently grilled and served with fresh cucumber, rice cakes and a rich savoury peanut-based sauce – all this at a very reasonable price. Desserts include kolak pisang – banana slices in coconut milk sweetened with brown sugar or seasonal fresh fruits. Side dishes are extra, so you will have to select with care to remain within the budget.

C ♫ S

Solange's Wine Bar 11 St Martin's Court ☎ 01-240 0245 Plan 2 **82** C3
Open: Mon–Sat 11am–3pm, 5.30–11pm

A great attraction of this large, unpretentious wine bar is the excellent food, which is prepared in the famed neighbouring two knife and fork restaurant, *Chez Solange*, The four rooms can accommodate 200 people and more on the white-painted garden furniture outside. The menu changes daily, and is written on a blackboard. As an appetiser you could sample one of about a dozen cold dishes – champignons à la Grecque, pâté maison or ratatouille are tasty examples. Hot dishes of the day might include coq au vin, veal or spare ribs – delicious with a serving of cauliflower cheese. Desserts such as fruit salad or cheesecake, are popular.

C ♫

Westminster

The Scallop Restaurant Central Hall, ☎ 01-222 3222 Plan 2 **77** E3
Open: Mon–Sat 12noon–2.30pm, 3.15–5.30pm

Occupying the whole of the basement under the vast Central Hall, The Scallop caters for large numbers yet manages to present well-cooked, appetising food at modest prices. The à la carte menu includes grills and omelettes, fish and chips or salad, and a selection of sweets. The special lunchtime menu offers soup or fruit juice, a choice of five main courses such as a roast, steak and kidney pie or a pasta dish and a sweet. There is also a three-course set lunch which is very good value.

VS

Victoria

Strikes 124 Victoria St ☎ 01-834 0644 Plan 2 **84** E1
Open: Mon–Sun 11.30am–11.30pm

Just why a group of American-style eating houses should be named after a British general strike is hard to fathom, but arrive at Victoria Station feeling hungry and you may be glad to see a Strikes restaurant opposite the main exit. Inside, you'll find a long narrow room with tables along one side, decorated with pictures of the 1926 strike, and there's a staircase twisting down to a second dining area. Starters vary from soup to avocado pear and prawns and you may choose a main course from a wide selection of hamburgers, steaks, salads and platters. Whichever you choose you'll be offered a choice of relishes and sauces at your table. Desserts are all variations on the theme of ice cream, and magnificent concoctions some of them are.

C S 🍷

Vecchia Parma 149 Strand ☎ 01-836 3730 Plan 2 **88** C4
Open: Mon–Sat 12noon–3pm, 5.30–11pm

In the best traditions of Italian restauranteurs, the Ronchetti family do a grand job in running this restaurant close to London's theatreland – Signor Ronchetti is the barman and his wife is also behind the bar. Of their two sons, Sergio cooks and Silvano produces the 'service with a smile' of which they are so proud. Apart from the usual pasta and pizza dishes, there are several tasty grills, omelettes, fish and salad choices.

C ♫ P S 🍷

Bloomsbury and The City

Bloomsbury

Ganpath 372 Grays Inn Rd ☎ 01-272 1938 Plan 4 **44** B4
Open: Mon–Sat 12noon–3pm, 6–10.15pm (10.45pm Fri and Sat). Closed Sun.

This simple restaurant is adjacent to Kings Cross Station and offers a range of southern Indian dishes and some English food – all freshly cooked. Try Sag Rosht – lamb and spinach with spices, or biriani.

C S

Oodles 113 High Holborn ☎ 01-405 3838 Plan 2 **67** B4
Open: Mon–Fri 11.30am–9pm, Sat 11.30am–2.30pm

Apart from staying open more hours in the week than the others, this branch of Oodles is no different from any other, but catch the flavour of its menus by reading the description in the entry under Paddington.

S

Oodles 42 New Oxford St ☎ 01-580 9521 Plan 2 **68** B3
Open: Mon–Fri 11am–9pm, Sat 11am–8pm, Sun 12noon–7pm

The frontage may be reminiscent of 'Ye Olde Tea Shoppe', but inside this eating house is unmistakably Oodles. See under Paddington for a full description.

S

Tuttons 11–12 Russell St ☎ 01-836 1167 Plan 2 **87** B3
Open: Mon–Sat 9am–11.30pm, Sun 12noon–11.30pm

This cream-decorated brasserie with plain pine furniture offers a good range of snacks and salads, and some unusual main dishes such as vegetables and spices wrapped in pastry and baked, or smoked chicken and avocado salad. You are welcome to drop in for a late breakfast, or perhaps just a coffee.

C S 🍷

The City

Balls Bros Moor House, London Wall
☎ 01-628 3944 Plan 3 **8** B2
Open: Mon–Fri 11.30am–3pm, 5–7.30pm

Don't look for an evening meal here, because you won't find it. The lunchtime menu is a typical one for the Balls Bros chain, with hot and cold dishes as well as sandwiches and salads. Portions are generous, and service excellent, and the atmosphere very friendly. As with all the BB outlets, the long-staying staff know their customers and it's nothing to see a City gent waiting for 'his own' waitress to be free to serve him.

C P

Balls Bros 6–8 Cheapside
☎ 01-248 2708 Plan 3 **7** B1
Open: Mon–Fri 11.30am–3pm, 5–7pm

This is a typical Balls Bros City outlet, with food at lunchtimes only, but an excellent wine list including some very reasonable half-bottles. The ground floor bar and basement restaurant serve satisfying snacks and sandwiches, a range of good salads and one hot dish daily. This is a friendly and comfortable little bar, with a faithful following among City folk.

C P S ♧ **VS**

Balls Bros 42 Threadneedle St
☎ 01-283 6701 Plan 3 **9** B3
Open: Mon–Fri 11.30am–3pm, 5–7pm

This is the smallest Balls Bros wine bar and (at the time of writing, at least) the only licensed premises in Threadneedle Street. Very popular with stockbrokers, this intimate little wine bar has only 16 covers and offers a varied menu. Sandwiches are available in the evening.

C

Bow Wine Vaults 10 Bow Churchyard
☎ 01-248 1121 Plan 3 **15** B2
Open: Restaurant Mon–Fri 12noon–3pm
Wine bar Mon–Fri 11.30am–3pm, 5–7pm

The minimum charge of £4 for lunch at the Bow Wine Vaults would buy you baked Scotch salmon with mayonnaise or perhaps you would prefer smoked poussin salad. Starters include chilled watercress soup and smoked salmon mousse. For a sweet you might choose chocolate and strawberry surprise or strawberry fool. The restaurant is a converted warehouse with whitewashed walls, but a Victorian atmosphere is created by the furnishings and bric-à-brac. There is a good range of wines.

VS

The City Boot 7 Moorfields High Walk
☎ 01-588 4766 Plan 3 **20** A2
Open: Mon–Fri 11.30am–3pm, 5–8.30pm

You can buy extremely fine sandwiches here, as well as a plate of ham, game pie or roast beef. Starters include pâté and smoked mackerel and there is a choice of desserts to complete you meal. The food side of the operation (lunchtime only) is small and simple but very good. One Davys treat is the serving of grouse, partridge, pheasant and Scotch salmon when in season.

C

The Coffee Shop, The Brewery, Chiswell St ☎ 01-606 4455 Plan 3 **21** A2
Open: Mon–Fri 10am–3pm

The large brewery complex houses this bright little restaurant with its country-kitchen atmosphere and quaint cobbled courtyard. Simple food is served here, with at least one hot dish such as chicken à la king available daily to supplement the many salads.

♧

Corts 84–86 Chancery La
☎ 01-405 3349 Plan 2 **22** B5
Open: Mon–Fri 11am–3pm, 5.30–8pm

You are less likely to meet criminals here than in the Old Bailey Corts, but lawyers abound as the wine bar is handy for the Strand Law Courts and is not far from the various Inns of Court. Here you will find an air-conditioned basement self-service bar and a ground-floor restaurant in which olive green and red blend with polished wood to create a warm ambience which is matched by the pleasant and helpful waitresses. Food is on the same lines as the original Corts (see below) and starters include items such as smoked mackerel or avocado pear vinaigrette or potted shrimps. Duck and walnut pie is a popular main course.

C ♬ S

Corts 33 Old Bailey ☎ 01-236 2101
Plan 3 **23** B1
Open: Mon–Fri 11.30am–3pm, 5–8.30pm

Rub shoulders with lawyers (and possibly criminals too!) in this comfortable wine bar near the Central Criminal Court. Food at lunchtime is straightforward and enjoyable, with soup, a selection of quiches, pies and cold meats and cheesecake, chocolate gâteau or apple pie.

C ♬ S

The George and Vulture 3 Castle Court
☎ 01-626 9710 Plan 3 **45** B2
Open: Mon–Fri 12noon–3pm

Charles Dickens stayed at The George and Vulture and made it famous in his 'Pickwick Papers'. But even without Dickens it has a claim to fame as probably the oldest tavern in the world, for it is known to have existed in 1175 although only one wall remains of the old structure. The present building retains the Pickwickian aura. You can't stay there now, but you can have a substantial lunch at a very reasonable price. There is a good selection of starters, and mixed grill is a popular main course. For a sweet there is, in season, fresh strawberry flan, and other items. Stilton cheese is recommended, but there is plenty of choice from the cheese board. The restaurant is available in the evening for private functions – just telephone for menu details.

C ♬

Grapeshots 2–3 Artillery Passage
☎ 01-247 8215 Plan 3 **48** B3
Open: Mon–Fri 11am–3pm, 5–7pm

For a wine bar in Artillery Passage Grapeshots is an appropriate name, but put out of your mind the fact that grapeshot was produced by dropping lead from a height into water – the grapes here are of a more fruity variety. This Davys of London wine bar, on the ground and basement floors of a building round the corner from Petticoat Lane, is rather on the small side but with an intimate relaxed atmosphere. The menu is limited and largely cold but good value. An enormous helping of cold meat, with a mixed salad is a substantial main course. Game, salmon and strawberries are sold in their proper seasons.

C P S

Mother Bunch's Wine House Old Seacoal La ☎ 01-236 5317
Plan 2 **64** B5
Open: Mon–Fri 11am–3pm, 5.30–8.30pm

Under the railway arches in Old Seacoal Lane, hard by Ludgate Circus, this Davys of London wine bar does a nice line in Buck's Fizz. Food (do book for the place is extremely popular) is mostly cold but very tasty and good value. A generous plate of finest ham off the bone or game pie with mixed salad or hot potatoes is very reasonably priced. Seafood is a speciality here. Starters and sweets are available.

C P S

Oodles 31 Cathedral Pl ☎ 01-248 2550
Plan 3 **69** B1
Open: Mon–Fri 11.30am–7pm

Although it's in a new building, this Oodles has succeeded in retaining the character of all the others, even though this branch is unlicensed. See under Paddington for full description.

P

Slenders Wholefood Restaurant and Juice Bar 41 Cathedral Pl
☎ 01-236 5974 Plan 3 **81** B1
Open: Mon–Fri 8.30am–6.15pm

Situated in a quiet backwater of the City, and with an equally quiet décor of natural brick, wood and hessian, Slenders is tremendously popular. There is seating for over 100 in separate booths. At lunchtime it is extremely busy. The menu is vegetarian and you can obtain a good wholesome meal well within the budget. Everything is prepared on the premises, including the wholemeal bread. Main courses include a good mixed salad, a hot dish such as vegetable and cheese flan and stuffed peppers. Chocolate mousse or fresh fruit salads are popular sweets.

♬ P S ♧

Whitechapel

Nick's Place 137 Leman St
☎ 01-488 9908 Plan 4 **65** C5
Open: Mon–Fri 10am–11pm, Sat 6–11pm, Sun 12noon–3pm, 6–10.30pm

You have heard of French and Italian bistros, and here is the first English bistro which offers good home cooking using traditional British recipes. The lunch menu offers a variety of hot and cold food from substantial snacks to full meals. The evening menu offers a choice of 10 pies, all very different and four other dishes. Try the John Bull pie, a mixture of steak, mushroom and onion with a soft suet crust, or Fish Porters' pie, a fascinating Billingsgate fishmarket recipe. From the range of starters we recommend the home-made game soup and to finish, try bread and butter pudding.

[C]

Kensington and Chelsea

Knightsbridge

The Chicago Rib Shack 1 Raphael St, Knightsbridge Green ☎ 01-581 5595 Plan 1 **19** C4
Open: Mon–Sun 11.45am–11.30pm

After successfully introducing the deep-dish Chicago-style pizza to London at the Chicago Pizza Pie Factory (see under Mayfair) Bob Payton decided to tempt Londoners with genuine American barbecue ribs at the Chicago Rib Shack. The generous portions can be accompanied by coleslaw, salad, Hilary's Onion Loaf and filled potato skins, and if you can't quite clear your plate then use a 'doggy-bag' to take the food home. Although the food is American the décor is definitely British and includes a bar that originated in a Glasgow pub and stained glass windows from a chapel in Lancashire.

[C] [♫]

The Green Man Harrods, Knightsbridge
☎ 01-730 1234 Plan 1 **49** D4
Open: Mon–Sat 11.30am–3pm

They say that there's nothing you can't buy at Harrods – at a price, and that's true even when it comes to finding a tasty meal. Located next to the Men's Department, the air is distinctly pubby and masculine in the Green Man restaurant. Pleasant and fast service is one bonus to the excellent food, with seafood platter the most expensive item on the menu. A cold buffet displays a choice of salads, cold meats and a very good game pie. Apple pie or cheesecake are examples of desserts.

[P] [S]

Kensington

The Ark Restaurant 122 Palace Gardens Ter ☎ 01-229 4024 Plan 4 **4** C3
Open: Mon–Sat 12noon–3pm, 6.30–11.30pm, Sun 6.30–11.30pm

You won't need to walk into The Ark two by two, but it is advisable not to arrive with a large family party unannounced. The Ark is a small, intimate bistro in the true French tradition. It has plain tables and a warm, friendly staff. The plat du jour, though not entirely French, ranges from crevettes roses (a shrimp concoction), to moules marinières for starters. For the main course, coq au vin or foie de veau à l'ail (calf's liver with garlic) linger in the memory – and on the palate. Follow on with profiteroles, or a gigantic portion of sorbet.

[C] [S]

Daquise 20 Thurloe St, South Kensington
☎ 01-589 6117 Plan 1 **31** E3
Open: Mon–Sun 10am–12mdnt

Full meals can be obtained here at any time between midday and midnight, so if you fancy goulash for tea you can have it. You can buy a selection of other dishes at this Polish restaurant, from meat Pierozki – a savoury pasty – to Wienerschnitzel as well as straightforward salads and omelettes. Vegetables are extra. Ice cream and pastries are available if you want a sweet to finish the meal. From noon until 3pm, set-price two-course lunches are served. Downstairs there is a small licensed restaurant where the atmosphere is cosily intimate.

[S]

Finch's Wine Bar 120 Kensington Park Rd ☎ 01-727 4093 Plan 4 **39** C3
Open: Mon–Sat 11.30am–3pm, 5.30–11pm

Only a stone's throw from the Portobello Road antique market is this neat little basement premises, with its plain white walls and pillars forming intimate alcoves. Hot dishes include Chinese spare ribs and chicken tarragon and rice. The cold collation offers such tempting delicacies as fresh prawns and cold meat salads. Continental breakfast is avilable from 8am on Saturdays.

[C] [P] [S]

Tootsies 120 Holland Park Av
☎ 01-229 8567 Plan 4 **86** C3
Open: Mon–Sun 8am–12mdnt, Sun 11.30pm

The menu at Tootsies offers 'Eye Openers': orange juice with raw egg 'for those who did and wish they hadn't' and a full English breakfast 'for those who didn't and wish they had'. This is primarily a hamburger house – a dozen varieties are listed all served with chips (except in the case of the 'calorie counter' version, where bun and chips are replaced by pineapple and cottage cheese) and a selection of relishes. You can get a number of other dishes here – steak, salads, quiches, for example, at very reasonable prices, and there are delectable cakes and ice-cream specialities.

[♫] [S]

Chelsea

Le Bouzy Rouge 221 King's Rd, Chelsea
☎ 01-351 1607 Plan 1 **14** F3
Open: Mon–Sat 11.30am–3pm, 5.30–11pm, Sun 7–10.30pm

A wine and spirits shop on the ground floor and a wine bar in the basement is an excellent combination, and a useful place to find a few yards from Chelsea Antique Market (if you've any money left). Simple foods, such as pork sausage and butter beans and navarin of lamb, are served in ample portions, and salads are available, too. There is a good variety of wines, of course, with the house wine very reasonably priced. Large bags hanging from brass rods provide comfortable backrests to the bench seating. A welcome change is the background of classical music – piped, certainly, but nevertheless a soothing change from the roar of London's traffic.

♫ S

Caravela 39 Beauchamp Pl, Chelsea ☎ 01-581 2366/01-584 2163 Plan 1 **16** D4
Open: Mon–Sat 12noon–3pm, Mon–Sun 7pm–1am

Delicious squid is served at this Portuguese restaurant, so if you're adventurous – or Portuguese – you'll enjoy such novel dishes as grilled squid or highly spiced pork chops. But there are less exotic dishes to choose from in a warm cosy atmosphere, with varnished wood slats cladding the ceiling, walls and arched alcoves. A fine model galleon on the bar, and pictures, continue the theme of ships and the sea. Watch the prices though – vegetables are sometimes charged extra and there's a cover charge of 65p – but it's not expensive for this part of London and it may be useful to know somewhere which is open until 1am every day of the week.

C ♫ P S

Cheyne Walk Wine Bar Pier House, 31 Cheyne Walk ☎ 01-352 4989 Plan 4 **17** C4
Open: Mon–Sat 11.30am–3pm, 6.30–11pm, Sun 12noon–3pm

Behind the graceful statue of David Wynn's 'Boy on a Dolphin' is a wine bar where you can eat until late evening (and drink until midnight) to the accompaniment of live music. The Victorian-style interior in shades of brown and hung with carriage lamps and old prints overlooks a splendidly romantic night view of the illuminated Albert Bridge. The chef provides tantalising starters, main courses such as hot Sussex smokie (smoked haddock in white wine sauce with cheese), or lamb kebabs, and a range of salads and cold meats.

C ♫

Fulham

Crocodile Tears 660 Fulham Rd ☎ 01-731 1537 Plan 4 **27** C3
Open: Mon–Sun 11.30am–2.30pm, 2pm Sun, 6.30–10.30pm

This is no run-of-the-mill wine bar; the décor is original – with a stuffed crocodile dangling from the ceiling – and the food likewise. For an adventurous meal try the gazpacho, seafood kebab and finish with ice cream gâteau or hot treacle tart with cream. All this will be served by pleasant waitresses. If you come here for the wine you won't be disappointed – there are 15 varieties served by the glass.

C S

Hampstead and Highgate

Hampstead

Maxwells 79 Heath St, Hampstead Village, Hampstead ☎ 01-794 5450 Plan 4 **58** B4
Open: Mon–Sun 12noon–12mdnt

Set in the heart of Hampstead this American-style diner offers excellent value for money in informal surroundings. The ground-floor restaurant leads to a large open basement where the seating is arranged on various levels. Start the evening with one of the many cocktails and study the menu which offers such dishes as corn on the cob, 100% beef burgers with french fries and lashings of salad in a spicy dressing, charcoal chicken, kebabs and spare ribs. To finish the meal try hot fudge sundae or freshly-made waffles with ice cream.

C ♫ S

Milk Churn in Hampstead 70 Heath St, Hampstead Village, Hampstead ☎ 01-435 8444 Plan 4 **60** B4
Open: Mon–Sun 11.30am–12mdnt (Sat 1am)

Milk churns feature in this buttery both as seating at the soda bar, where you can get a quick snack and as the bases for the pine-topped dining tables in the restaurant. The food is served in delightful stoneware pottery with a selection of tempting dishes on the menu. Specialities include savoury pancakes and Yorkshire puddings, both served with a side salad and a small brown loaf. For 'afters' the sweet pancakes and sumptuous ice cream specials are guaranteed to ruin any diet. Wash your meal down with a mug of whipped coffee or chocolate or a glass of wine.

♫ S

Belsize Park

Cosmo Northways Parade, Finchley Rd ☎ 01-722 1398 Plan 4 **24** B4
Open: Restaurant Mon–Sun 12noon–11.30pm, last orders, 10.45pm
Coffee shop Mon–Sun 8.30am–11pm

Mainly Continental food is served at this uncluttered restaurant with its large shop-front window. Try chilled fruit soup with macaroons for starters, then move on to Hungarian beef goulash with continental dumpling, or Wiener Schnitzel. The unadventurous might be relieved to know you can get roast pork and vegetables here too. Sweets include real Viennese apple strudel with whipped cream or crème caramel chantilly. Many well-known personalities can be seen here. The Coffee Shop has egg, sausage and chips on the menu.

S **VS**

Maida Vale

Blue Angel 3 Long La, Finchley ☎ 01-349 4386 Plan 4 **13** A3
Open: Mon–Sat 10am–11pm. Closed Sun

Proprietor/chef Robert Laudeuberge originates from Germany and his specialities include Saubraten with noodles (marinated beef in sour cream sauce) and liver dumplings in red wine and onion sauce. Apart from offering three-course lunches and dinners the Blue Angel is also open for morning coffee and afternoon tea – which is much appreciated by local shoppers. The restaurant is licensed and has a friendly informal atmosphere.

P

Elgin Lokanta 239 Elgin Ave ☎ 01-328 6400 Plan 4 **37** B3
Open: Mon–Sun 12noon–12mdnt

The grill-kitchen of this Turkish restaurant is at the front and takeaway kebabs are a favourite of the locals. Mezeler (starters) include deliciously flavoured calves' livers and there are over 20 more starters on the menu. Main courses are all served with pilaf rice. Try one of the lamb specialities such as sis saslik (skewered lamb with mushrooms and onion slices). Honey and walnut baklava is a tempting dessert from the trolley with which to complete your meal. There is a nominal cover charge for which you receive butter, hot pitta and black olives.

C S

Moss Hall Tavern 280 Ballards La, Finchley Plan 4 **63** A4
Open: Mon–Sat 10.30am–2.30pm, 6–11pm, Sun 11am–2.30pm, 7.30–10.30pm

Relax and enjoy simple home-cooking in this comfortable pub which is decorated in the Elizabethan style. Starters and sweets are not generally available, or necessary, as portions of the main dishes are very generous and are served with a choice of vegetables. With a good selection of hot meals, salads and sandwiches the Tavern justly deserves its reputation for offering good food at very reasonable prices. Real ale is available and there is outdoor seating for the children.

P S

Sea Shell 33–35 Lisson Grove ☎ 01-723 8703 Plan 4 **78** B4
Open: Tue–Sat 12noon–2pm, 5.30–10.30pm

Here is a fresh fish restaurant par excellence, where portion control has been abandoned in favour of customer satisfaction. A Rolls-Royce parked outside while its owner queues for a take-away cod and chips, or enjoys a quick sit-down meal in the small restaurant, is not an uncommon sight. Apart from the fried chicken, the menu is devoted entirely to fish such as plaice, cod, halibut, skate, lemon sole and Dover sole. An extremely satisfying meal including

soup and sweet is reasonably priced.
VS

Highgate

La Cresta Restaurant 18 Crouch End Hill ☎ 01-340 4539 Plan 4 **25** A4
Open: Mon–Fri 12noon–3pm, 5.30–11.30pm, Sat 5.30–11.30pm

A family-owned-and-run restaurant, where a warm welcome is assured. The menu is mainly Italian, with a few English fish and steak dishes thrown in for good measure. Highly recommended is the house speciality of veal escalope valdostana – a marvellous concoction of ham, cheese, spaghetti and veal, and the freshly-baked poppy seed bread which complements every dish.

C P S

Dragon Seed Restaurant 66 Highgate High St, Highgate Village
☎ 01-348 6160 Plan 4 **36** A4
Open: Mon–Thu 12noon–2.30pm, 5.30–11.30pm, Fri–Sun 12noon–12mdnt

This modern Chinese restaurant is decorated with coloured ceiling murals and the walls are hung with traditional silk pictures. The food represents very good value with many traditional chinese cuisine dishes on the menu, all freshly prepared and delightfully presented. If you have trouble chosing from the à la carte menu why not try one of the set meals which offer at least five courses and jasmine tea.

C ♫ P S

The Flask Tavern 77 Highgate West Hill, Highgate Village ☎ 01-340 3969 Plan 4 **40** B4
Open: normal licensing hours

Built in 1663, The Flask Tavern has been the haunt of many interesting characters, including the legendary highwayman Dick Turpin and distinguished painters Hogarth, Morlane and Cruickshank. During the summer the natural wood tables, set out in the large stone courtyard, are constantly in use. You may eat a snack in one of the three popular bars, but if something more substantial is preferred, a good three-course meal can be had in one of the bars. Starters include soup or grapefruit, main course sauté kidneys, fried plaice, fried rock salmon or cod and shrimp Mornay. Dessert is a choice of ice creams or banana fritters.

C P S

Greenwich and South East London

Greenwich

Bar du Musee 17 Nelson Rd, Greenwich ☎ 01-858 4710 Plan 4 **11** C5
Open: Mon–Sat 12noon–3pm, 6.30–11pm, Sun 12noon–2pm, 7–10.30pm

This wine bar is on two levels with a cellar bar reached by a spiral stiarcase. Coats of arms and Dickensian prints enhance the décor. There's a good choice of starters but try the soup of the day, with French bread. Hot dishes such as pizza and salad or a 6oz pure beefburger with salad and French fries are recommended. Beef or ham salads are particularly good. Desserts include cheesecakes, gâteaux and profiteroles.

C ♫

Davy's Wine Vaults 165 Greenwich High Rd ☎ 01-858 7204 Plan 4 **32** C5
Open: Mon–Fri 11.30am–3pm, Mon–Thu 5.30–10.30pm, Fri 5.30–11pm, Sat 12noon–3pm, 7–11pm

Under Davy & Co's head office building in Greenwich the old wine cellar is now used as a wine bar and eating house. Victorian touches add to the out-of-the-past aura and help to make this a most popular place. Davy's offer 'fine foreign wines' and 'rare ports of the finest vintages' to wash down their specialities such as avocado pear with prawns or the tempting fresh salmon salad. A cold buffet is also available.

C P

Diks 8 Nelson Rd, Greenwich
☎ 01-858 8588 Plan 4 **33** C5
Open: Mon, Wed–Sat 12noon–2pm, 7–11pm, Sun 12.30–3pm

Value for money is guaranteed at this delightful restaurant. Proprietor Dik Evans cooks all the food, even the bread rolls and mint fudge served with the coffee. The soup and pâté are served in terrines from which you help yourself to as much as you like. At lunch, three courses are priced by the main dish – veal scaloppini Viennoise with fruit juice and meringue glacé is an example.

C

Gachons 269 Greek Rd, Greenwich
☎ 01-853 4461 Plan 4 **43** C5
Open: Wed–Mon 10.30am–5pm, Thu–Sat 7–10.30pm

Young chef/proprietor Marc Gachon-Dyer says his cooking has been greatly influenced by his French mother, and he produces a Cordon Bleu Chef's Special (such as kidneys sautéd in wine with fresh vegetables) every day to prove it. In fact, this quaint little coffee house, with its bright pine furniture, caters for the majority of tastes by offering a selection of pastries and salads to supplement the substantial hot meals, such as home-made quiche and chicken vol-au-vent.

♫ P S

Blackheath

The Barcave Wine Bar 7–9 Montpelier Vale, Blackheath ☎ 01-852 0492 Plan 4 **10** C5
Open: Mon–Sat 12noon–3pm, 5.30–11pm, Fri–Sat 12mdnt, Sun 7–10.30pm

Special feature of this wine bar is the pretty walled terrace garden on two levels with fountains, a fish pond and hanging plants – very restful on a summer evening. Listed on a blackboard are Today's Specials such as minute steak with chasseur sauce and new potatoes, curry or cold chicken and salad. A printed menu offers a choice of eight starters from melon to pâté maison. Cold buffet includes excellent rare roast beef, and quiche and lasagne are examples from the hot buffet. Desserts include gâteaux and cheesecakes.

Kate 2 Bistro 121 Lee Rd
☎ 01-852 3610 Plan 4 **55** C6
Open: Mon–Sat 12noon–2.30pm, Tue–Sat 7–10.30pm

The food at this simple bistro was described as the 'most enjoyable meal tasted in over 30 years of eating out' by one of our inspectors. A varied menu includes home-made quiche and mixed salad, scampi served with mixed salad, or steak pizzaiola as main courses, and a selection of delicious desserts which change daily as shown on the blackboard. Special portions are offered for children.

VS

See advertisement on page 120

The Source 106 Blackheath Rd
☎ 01-691 1010 Plan 4 **83** C5
Open: Mon 12noon–3pm, Tue–Sat 12noon–3pm, 7–11pm

Enthusiastic vegetarians, Keith and Norma Perry ensure that you enjoy wholesome, unadulterated food in pleasant surroundings – pine tables, a Welsh dresser and an old kitchen range set the scene for a gastronomic experience in healthy eating. Appetisers include stuffed vine leaves or mushrooms à la Grecque. The list of main dishes is no less interesting, with stuffed pepper, ratatouille and quiche with salad and potatoes. All the desserts, such as cinnamon apple cake, are served with fresh cream or yoghurt.

♫

Lambeth

Archduke Concert Hall Approach, South Bank ☎ 01-928 9370 Plan 2 **3** D4
Open: Mon–Fri 11am–12mdnt, Sat 5.30pm–12mdnt

A skilful conversion of a railway arch, with the trains still rumbling along overhead. Elizabeth Philip, and Colin Richmond have created a lively wine bar and restaurant, very popular both with local office workers and South Bank culture lovers. On the lunch menu, there is a choice of starters and desserts; main courses include a home-made pie, usually steak and kidney, or fisherman's pie. There is also a daily 'special' and a cold table. Three-course meals are available in the evening, but for something different try the sausage dishes.

[C] [♫] [P] **VS**

Royal Festival Hall Cafeteria South Bank ☎ 01-928 3246 Plan 2 **75** D4
Open: Mon–Sun 12noon–10.30pm

Good places to eat are few and far between once you're south of the river, so it's worth knowing that you can use the Festival Hall cafeteria whether you're attending a performance or not. Quite near to Waterloo Station and not far from Waterloo Bridge, the South Bank complex is aesthetically pleasing even to those who are not too keen on modern architecture. The uncrowded cafeteria overlooks the busy and perennially interesting Thames, and provides a pleasant place to relax and enjoy a meal. Each day there are two hot dishes as well as cold meats and salads, and home-made sweets and good coffee are served.

[♫] [P]

RSJ 13A Coin St ☎ 01-928 4554 Plan 2 **76** D5
Open: Mon–Fri 12noon–3pm, 7–11.30pm, Sat 7–11.30pm

Once a stable but for the last 30 years a cycle warehouse, this newly-converted restaurant occupies a prime position near to the West End and Covent Garden, as well as the South Bank. Decorated in smart brown and white, it is deservedly popular with business-people from the nearby offices. Starters include watercress soup and haddock mousse and main courses offer cold salmon-trout and calf's liver with avocado. For sweets, try Dutch apple pie, strawberries and cream or various sorbets.

[C] [♫] [P] [🍷]

Southwark

Skinkers 40–42 Tooley St ☎ 01-407 9189 Plan 3 **80** D3
Open: Mon–Fri 11am–3pm, 5.30–8.30pm

Built into the railway arches under London Bridge, next door to the London Dungeons horror museum, Skinkers is

London

beautifully cool in summer, very spacious and relaxed, and enormously popular with City folk and local business people. Décor, menu and wine list are in Davy tradition. The buffet offers a range of starters, a plate of finest smoked ham, roast beef or game pie. If you're going on the off-chance, get there early.

Streatham

Rino's Restaurant 82/84 Streatham High Rd, Streatham ☎ 01-769 7916 or 6033 Plan 4 **73** D4
Open: Mon-Sun 12noon–3pm, 6pm–2am (dinner and dance)

A large regular clientele haunts this very busy Italian trattoria – and not just because Salvatore Polumba, one of the proprietors, otherwise known as Rino, is always chatting with the diners. The menu is very extensive – 14 starters and five soups offer an interesting choice including snails, tunny fish and Italian hors d'oeuvres. Pastas, pizzas and omelettes are available, and Rino's specialities, served with two vegetables of the day, include pollo principessa (chicken with white wine, cream and asparagus tips) or piccatina al Marsala (veal escalopes cooked in butter and Marsala wine). Sweets such as zabaglione el Marsala or lemon sorbet, complete a very substantial meal. This restaurant does a roaring late-night trade.

[C] [♫] [S] [🍷]

Dulwich/Penge

Mr Bunbury's Bistro 1154 London Rd, Norbury ☎ 01-764 3939 Plan 4 **61** D4
Open: Mon–Fri 12noon–2.30pm, 7–11pm, Sat 7–11pm. Closed Sun

A small bistro with Victorian décor and a cosy atmosphere enhanced by the oil lamps and old photographs and prints. Owner Kenneth Williams keeps busy in the kitchen preparing such delights as Bunbury pie (a large individual pie filled with lean chunks of beef, mushrooms, onions, and carrots topped with flaky puff pastry). The set lunch is excellent value. Vegetables are plentiful and served in separate earthenware dishes; the puddings (always generous helpings) are home-made.

[C] [♫] [S] [🍷]

Joanna's 56a Westow Hill, Upper Norwood ☎ 01-670 4052 Plan 4 **53** D4
Open: Mon–Fri 12noon–2pm, 6–11.15pm, Sat 6–11.30pm

Very appealing décor, with hanging plants, large photographs of film stars and smart check tablecloths, is complemented by an atmosphere kept fresh by two huge ceiling fans. Burgers are a speciality of the house – 100% beef served in a toasted sesame bun plus potatoes and fresh salad. There are six varieties – 'Gourmet' is dressed in wine and mushroom sauce. There is also a good selection of prime steaks and 'specials' such as grilled jumbo shrimps and fried chicken with plum sauce (served with side salad and french fries). Starters and delicious desserts such as 'Joanna's Special' – hot waffle with maple syrup and whipped cream or ice cream sundaes are available.

[C] [♫] [P] [S] [🍷]

Eltham

Bistro 22 1 West Park, Mottingham ☎ 01-851 2233 Plan 4 **12** D6
Open: Mon–Sat 7–11.30pm

French posters, bright tablecloths and candles lend an authentic air to this unpretentious bistro, where the menus are written in French and English. A host of interesting dishes are on offer, but care will be needed if you are to pick two courses for around £5, since vegetables are individually priced. Try diced chicken cooked in a wine, tomato and mushroom sauce followed by gâteau. A three-course menu of the day is a little over our limit.

[C] [♫] [P] [🍷] **VS**

Mellins Wine and Food 90 Eltham High St, Eltham ☎ 01-850 4462 Plan 4 **59** D6
Open: Mon–Sat 12noon–2.30pm, 7–11pm, Sun 7–10.30pm

Mellins the apothecary stood here for about 200 years and the wine bar has retained the signs, labels and display cases. An interesting menu offers hot or cold platters such as ham ratatouille, fish pie, chicken basquaise and pork n'peppers. Banana mousse is one of the many tasty desserts.

Putney and South London

Putney

Emandel Pizzeria 1 Kew Rd
☎ 01-940 1165 Plan 4 **38** C2
Open: Mon–Sat 12noon–2pm, 5.30–11.30pm. Closed Sun

Popular with Richmond theatre-goers this clean and freshly-decorated pizzeria offers piping hot food served in individual dishes by pleasant, Spanish staff. Apart from the usual pasta dishes and an extensive range of pizzas, specialities also include trout baked in foil and chargrilled meats. Wine, to accompany your meal, is available by the glass.

[C] [P]

La Forchetta 3 Putney Hill
☎ 01-785 6749 Plan 4 **41** C3
Open: Mon–Thu 12noon–2.45pm, 6.30–11.15pm, Fri–Sat 6.30–11.30pm

You'll find this bright little Italian restaurant at the bottom of Putney Hill. You can buy a cheap pasta dish here, a more elaborate meal could exceed budget but won't if you take care. Starters include soup or pâté which could be followed by fried squid or chicken casserole. Vegetables are extra. A sweet from the trolley will complete you meal. There is a cover charge of 50p. A good place for a tête-à-tête dinner.

[C] [♫] [P] [garden] **VS**

Mr Micawber's 147 Upper Richmond Rd
☎ 01-788 2429 Plan 4 **62** C3
Open: Mon–Fri 12noon–3pm, 5.30–11pm, Sat 12noon–3pm, Sun 7–10.30pm

There's sometimes a small queue for food, but you won't have to wait too long for something to turn up in Mr Micawber's wine bar. You should be able to heed Mr Micawber's maxim about annual expenditure too, for food is very reasonably priced. Choice is limited; but there is a hot dish of the day, chili con carne and quiches as well as cold meats, pies and salads.

[♫] [S] [garden]

Wimbledon

The Crooked Billet 15 Crooked Billet, Wimbledon Common ☎ 01-946 4942
Plan 4 **28** D3

Open: Mon–Fri, Sun 12noon–2.30pm, Fri–Sat 12noon–2.30pm, 7.30–10.30pm, Evening parties catered for

A building which started life as a barn way back in the 15th century, is now an olde worlde restaurant, retaining some of the bygone features such as timbered beams and pillars. Fare is varied and at sensible prices. Starters feature egg mayonnaise and prawn cocktail. Of the main dishes, beef curry or steak pie with two veg are both good value along with huge egg or cheese salads. Home-made apple pie and Black Forest gâteau make delicious desserts.

[C] [garden]

Downs Wine Bar 40 Wimbledon Hill Rd
☎ 01-946 0344 Plan 4 **35** D3
Open: Mon–Sat 12noon–3pm, Mon–Fri 5.30pm–2am, Sat 7pm–2am

Unobtrusive décor gives an atmosphere of intimacy and informality, both in the cosy cellar bar, with its alcoves and dance floor, and in the ground floor bar, where one can take a quieter meal. A popular new addition is the flower garden restaurant bar for the long summer evenings. The menu is changed daily, but there's always a good selection of both hot and cold dishes. Pâté maison could be followed by hot dishes, such as chicken Kiev, scampi provençale and lamb kebab. House special is chicken caribbean which is stuffed with exotic fruit and served with rice.

[C] [♫] [S] [garden] **VS**

Battersea

Atuchaclass 24 Queenstown Rd
Plan 4 **6** C4
Open: Mon–Sat 6.30–11.30pm

An offshoot to the up-market 'Alonso's' (next-door-but-one), this intimate bistro certainly has a touch of class, from its quarry-tiled floor and a subdued lighting to its imaginative international cuisine and the excellence of its fresh vegetables. The prices are just about within our limit for a two-course meal, which for this type of establishment is surprising in itself. How about this for a meal: chicken liver pâté with herbs, spinach and chutney; Indonesian lamb in pastry (pieces of lamb, prawns, rice, raisins, mushrooms, chutney, light curry sauce) served with a selection of fresh, vegetables; raspberry sorbet and coffee.

[♫] [P] [S]

La Grand Café 25 Battersea Rise
☎ 01-228 7984 Plan 4 **47** C4
Open: Mon-Sat 12noon–3pm, 6pm–12mdnt, Sun 12noon–3pm, 6–11.30pm

You can't miss this modern burger restaurant near Clapham Common: just look for the flashing lights at the entrance which reflect on the silver awning. There are three split-level dining areas and the décor is bright and modern. Starters range from soup to deep-fried clam strips, there are also daily specials. Apart from the burgers there is a range of other dishes including chicken Kiev. For dessert try meringue delight.

[C] [♫] [garden]

Just Williams 6a Battersea Rise
☎ 01-223 6890 Plan 4 **54** C4
Open: Mon–Sat 12noon–3pm, 5.30–11pm, Sun 12noon–2pm, 7–10.30pm

This intimate wine bar, with its pine display counter, colourful check tablecloths and rear garden for the summer months is enthusiastically managed by ex wine merchant Michael Walker. The blackboard menu lists interesting starters such as taramasalata, served with pitta bread. Hot dishes of the day include goulash and boeuf bourguignon. Desserts include cheesecakes and gâteaux such as passioncake – a delicious fantasy of walnuts, apples and cream.

[C] [♫] [P] [S] **VS**

Ealing and West London

Ealing

Crispins Too Wine Bar and Cocktail Bar 46–47 The Mall, Ealing
☎ 01-567 8966 Plan 4 **26** C2
Open: Mon–Sun 11am–3pm, 5.30–10.30pm (11pm Fri & Sat)

The unusual exterior is reminiscent of an old railway station, with its cast-iron-and-glass portico forming a protected area where ironwork tables and chairs are available for patrons. There is a similarly-equipped garden at the back for rain-free days. The bar itself is reputed to be the largest in London, stretching almost the full depth of the premises, with cast iron tables and chairs arranged along one side. In spite of its size it gets very crowded on Friday and Saturday evenings. The interior is French bistro-style, the décor somewhat barn-like with natural wood beams and panels and a quarry-tiled floor. Food is cheap and good. Hot dishes such as moussaka, curry or hotpot with accompanying vegetables are available at lunchtime and cold food such as quiche with salad is available at lunchtime or in the evening. Try the traditional roast on Sunday. There is another Crispins at 14 The Green, Ealing.

[C] [♫] [P] [S]

Crusts Gaff 17 The Green, Ealing
☎ 01-579 2788 Plan 4 **30** C2
Open: Mon–Thu 12noon–11.30pm, Fri–Sat 12noon–12mdnt, Sun 12noon–11.30pm

An abundance of natural wood comes in handy for hanging numerous knick-knacks including a spinning wheel, steel helmets and statues. Walls covered with old prints and mirrors complete the individual décor of this popular bistro. Emphasis is on good, wholesome food. Starters include soup and pâté. Main dish specialities include lasagenand spare ribs. Meat and cheeseburgers are rock bottom budget items and there is a selection of competitively-priced salads. Sweets include apple pie and crème caramel.

C ♫ P S

North China 305 Uxbridge Rd, Acton ☎ 01-992 9183 Plan 4 **66** C2
Open: Mon–Thu, Sun 12noon–2pm, 6–11.30pm, Fri–Sat 12noon–2pm, 6–12mdnt

Proprietor Lawrence Lou specialises in Peking cuisine – particularly in Peking Crispy Aromatic Duck – a rare delight which can be enjoyed whole or in portions. Special dinners on offer for two people are good value – mixed hors d'oeuvres, spare ribs, Peking duck, prawns in chili sauce or sweet and sour pork, shredded beef, diced chicken with chashew nuts in yellow bean sauce and Chinese-style toffee apple or banana is one example. The usual baffling à la carte menu with hundreds of dishes is also astonishingly reasonable.

Shireen Tandoori✕ 270 Uxbridge Rd ☎ 01-749 5927 Plan 4 **79** C3
Open: Mon–Sun 12noon–3pm, 6–11.30pm

You can drink an aperitif and nibble spicy Indian nuts at the bar and seating area at the far end of this smart little restaurant, just 10 minutes' walk from Shepherds Bush roundabout. Attractive Indian prints are displayed against matt black walls, and the natural wood of the ceiling is echoed in the herringbone-patterned latticework which screens diners from the main road. Main courses include Tandoori Chicken and Jhinga tandoori, a prawn speciality.

C ♫ P S ♁

Chiswick

Fouberts Wine Bar 162 Chiswick High Rd ☎ 01-994 5202 Plan 4 **42** C3
Open: Mon–Sat 12noon–3pm, 7–11pm

This is a small basement wine bar which uses both wooden and cast-iron furniture to give a slightly Bohemian air. Italian dishes such as lasagne are good here, or if you prefer English no-frills food you can get steak and chips. A large selection of wines includes several which can be bought by the glass. Italian, German, French and Portuguese varieties prove popular with cosmopolitan visitors.

♫ S ♁

Index to London Establishments

London

	Establishment	Area	Page	Plan
36	Dragon Seed	Highgate	119	4 A4
37	Elgin Lokanta	Maida Vale	118	4 B3
38	Emandel Pizzeria	Putney	121	4 C2
39	Finch's Wine Bar	Kensington	117	4 C3
40	Flask Tavern	Highgate	119	4 B4
41	Forchetta, La	Putney	121	4 C3
42	Foubert's Wine Bar	Chiswick	122	4 C3
43	Gachons	Greenwich	119	4 C5
44	Ganpath	Bloomsbury	115	4 B4
45	George and Vulture	The City	116	3 B2
46	Granary	Mayfair	114	2 C1
47	Grand Cafe	Battersea	121	4 C4
48	Grapeshots	The City	116	3 B3
49	Green Man (Harrods)	Knightsbridge	117	1 D4
50	Gyngleboy	Paddington	113	1 A2
51	Hobson's Wine Bar	Soho	115	2 C3
52	Ikaros	St Marylebone	113	4 B4
53	Joanna's	Dulwich/Penge	120	4 D4
54	Just William's	Battersea	121	4 C4
55	Kate 2 Bistro	Blackheath	119	4 C6
56	Linda's	Paddington	113	4 B3
57	Lord Byron Taverna	Piccadilly	113	2 C2
58	Maxwell's	Hampstead	118	4 B4
59	Mellins Wine and Food	Eltham	121	4 D6
60	Milk Churn in Hampstead	Hampstead	118	4 B4
61	Mr Bunbury's Bistro	Dulwich/Penge	120	4 D4
62	Mr Micawber's	Putney	121	4 C3
63	Moss Hall Tavern	Maida Vale	118	4 A4
64	Mother Bunch's Wine House	The City	116	2 B5
65	Nick's Place	Whitechapel	117	4 C5
66	North China	Ealing	122	4 C2
67	Oodles (High Holborne)	Bloomsbury	115	2 B4
68	Oodles (New Oxford St)	Bloomsbury	115	2 B3
69	Oodles	The City	116	3 B1
70	Oodles	Paddington	113	1 A3
71	Plummers	Soho	115	2 C3
72	Rasa Sayang	Soho	115	2 B2
73	Rino's	Streatham	120	4 D4
74	Rose	St Marylebone	113	2 B1
75	Royal Festival Hall	Lambeth	120	2 D4
76	RSJ	Lambeth	120	2 D5
77	Scallop	Westminster	115	2 E3
78	Sea Shell	Maida Vale	118	4 B4
79	Shireen Tandoori	Ealing	122	4 C3
80	Skinkers	Southwark	120	3 D3
81	Slenders Wholefood	The City	116	3 B1
82	Solange's Wine Bar	Soho	115	2 C3
83	Source, The	Blackheath	119	4 C5
84	Strikes	Victoria	115	2 E1
85	Swiss Centre Restaurants	Piccadilly	114	2 C2
86	Tootsies	Kensington	117	4 C3
87	Tuttons	Bloomsbury	115	2 C3
88	Vecchia Parma	Victoria	115	2 C4

London
Plan 1

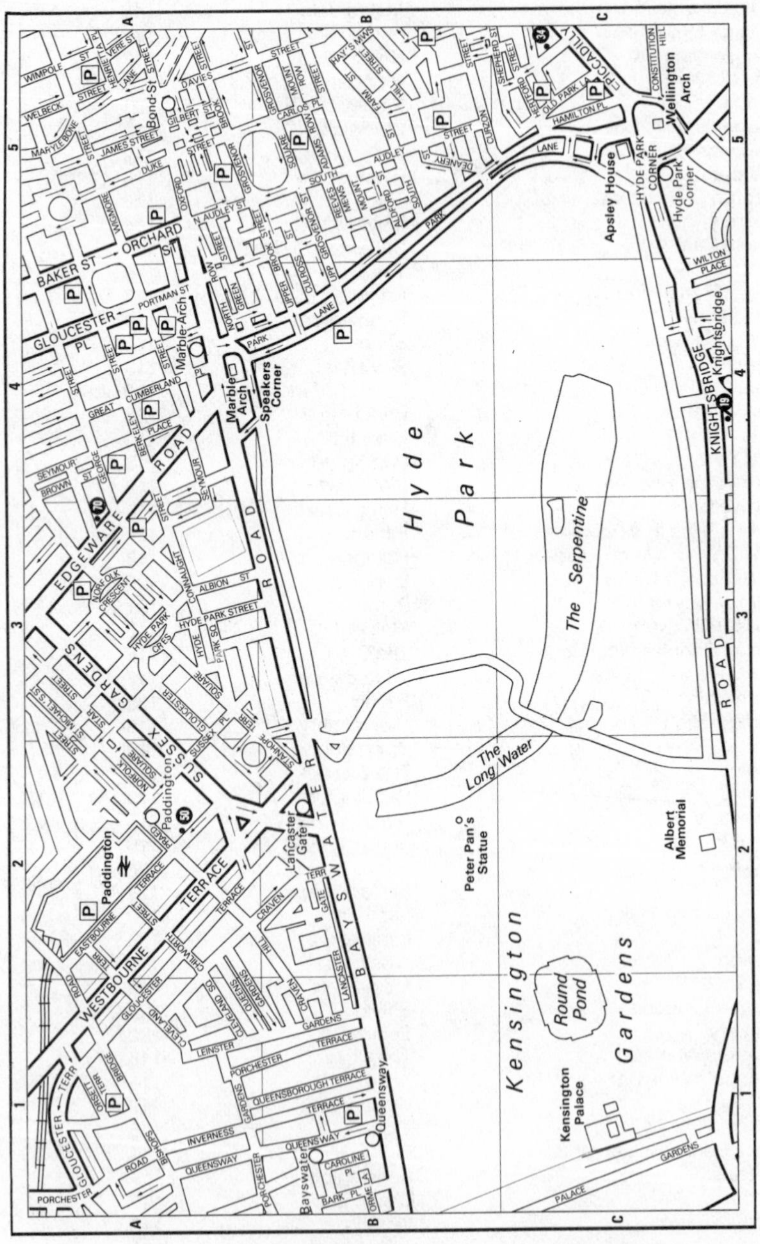

London
Plan 1

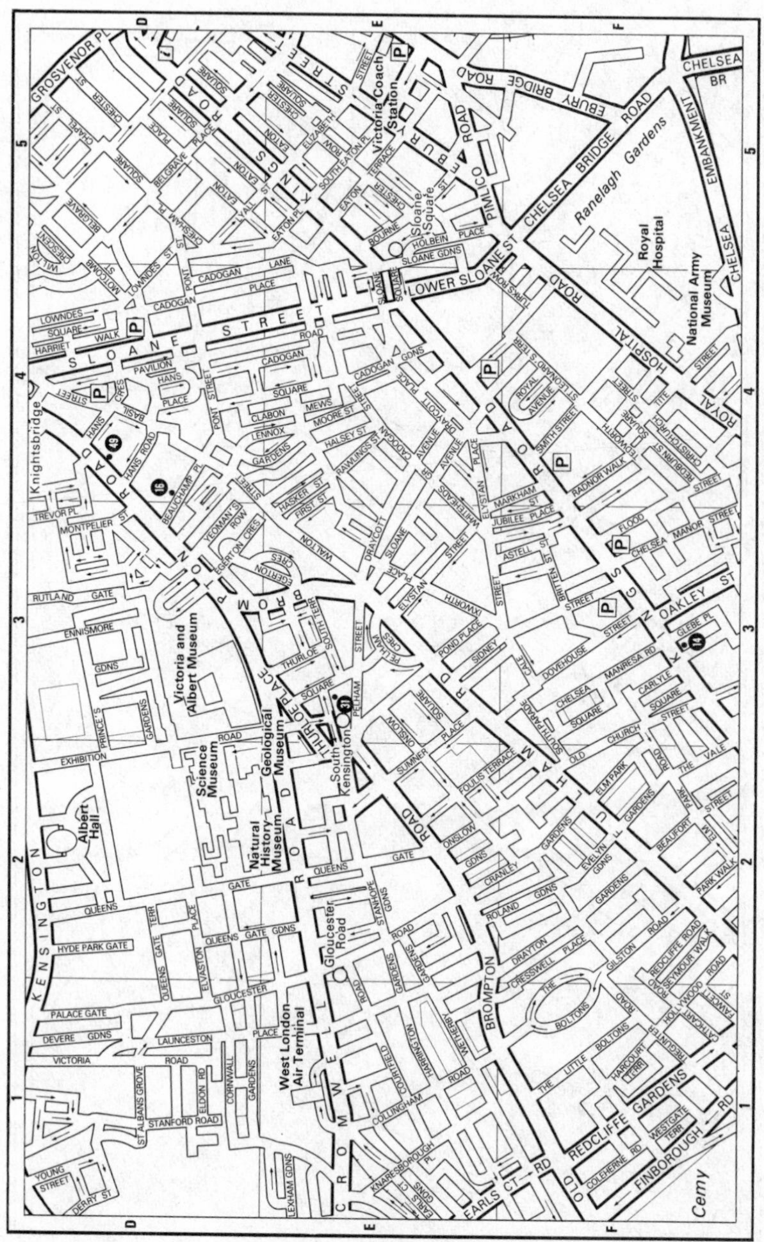

London
Plan 2

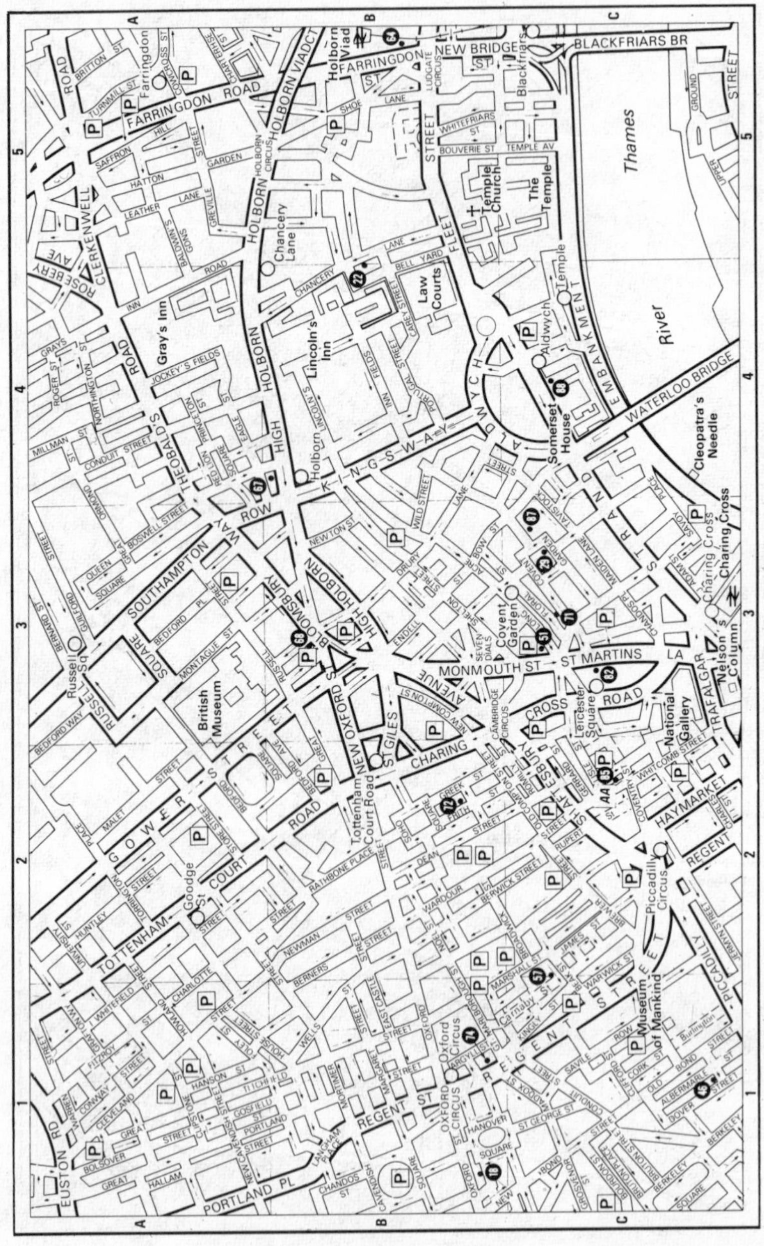

London
Plan 2

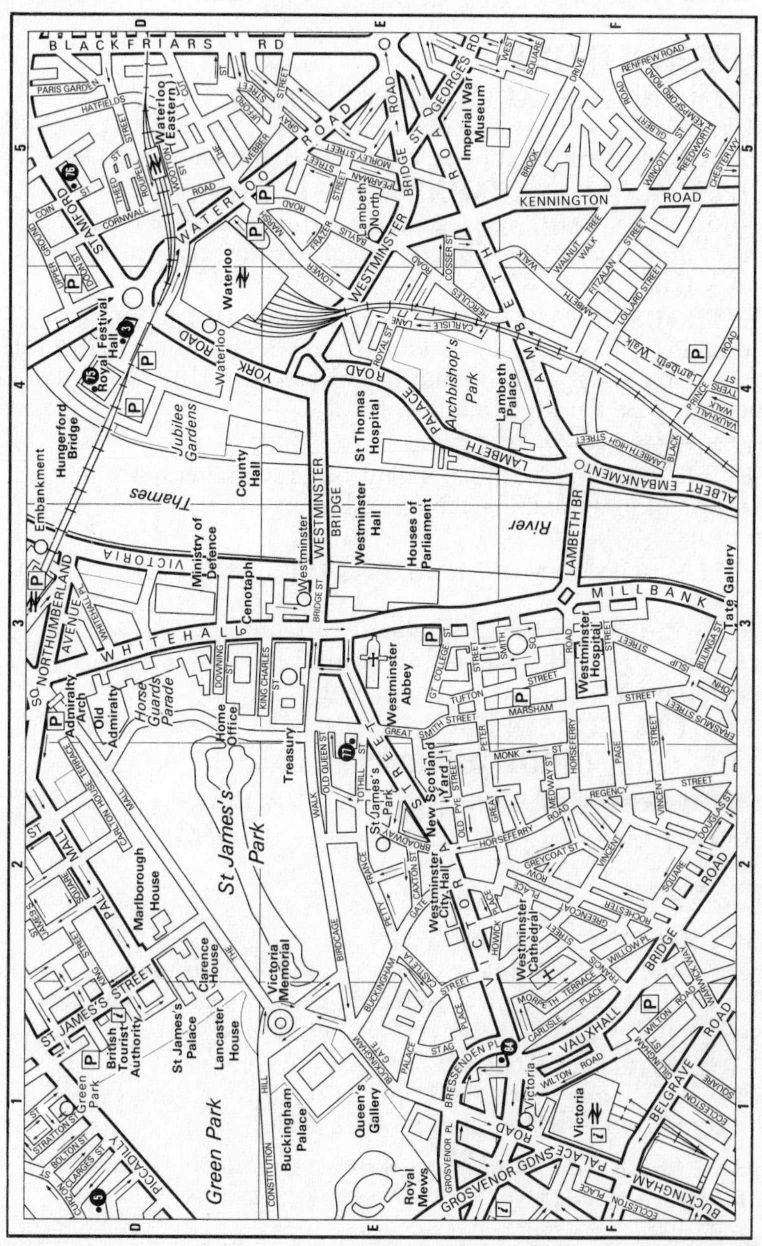

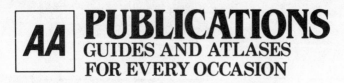

London
Plan 3

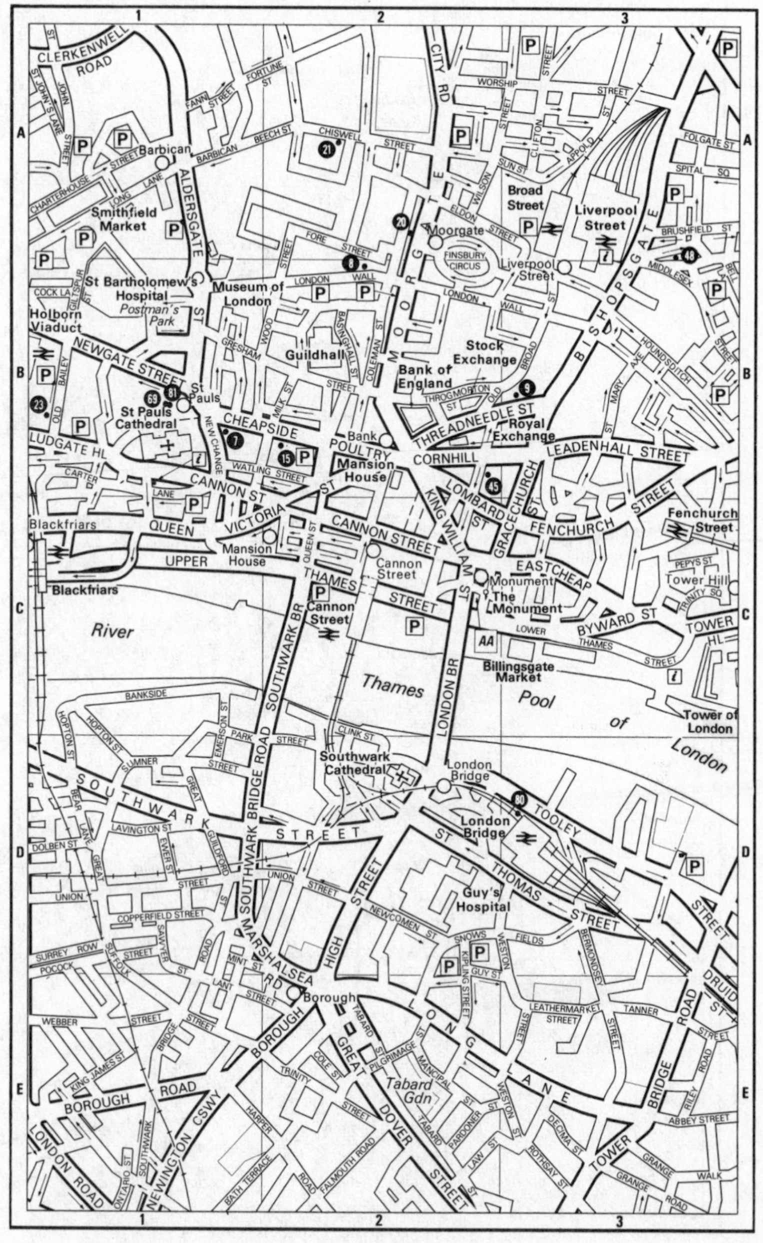

London
Plan 4

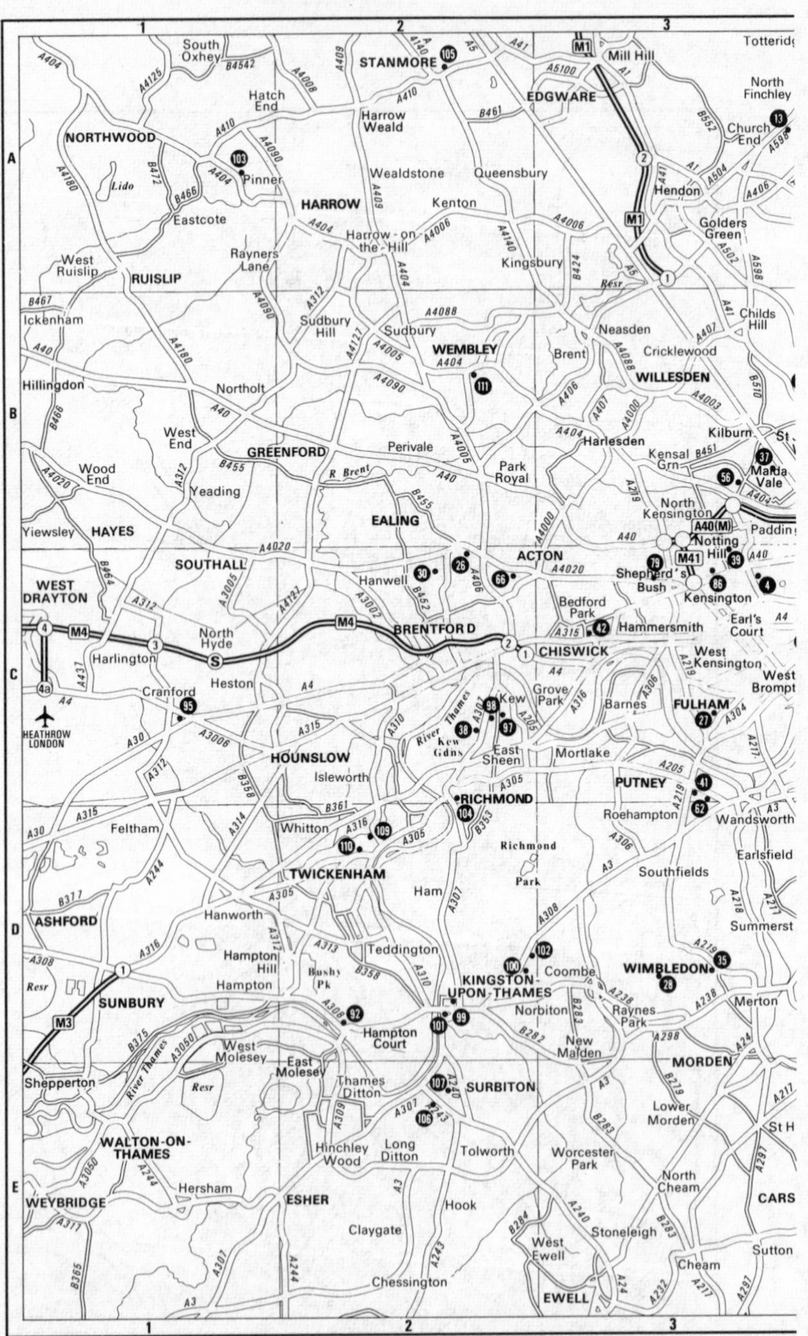

London
Plan 4

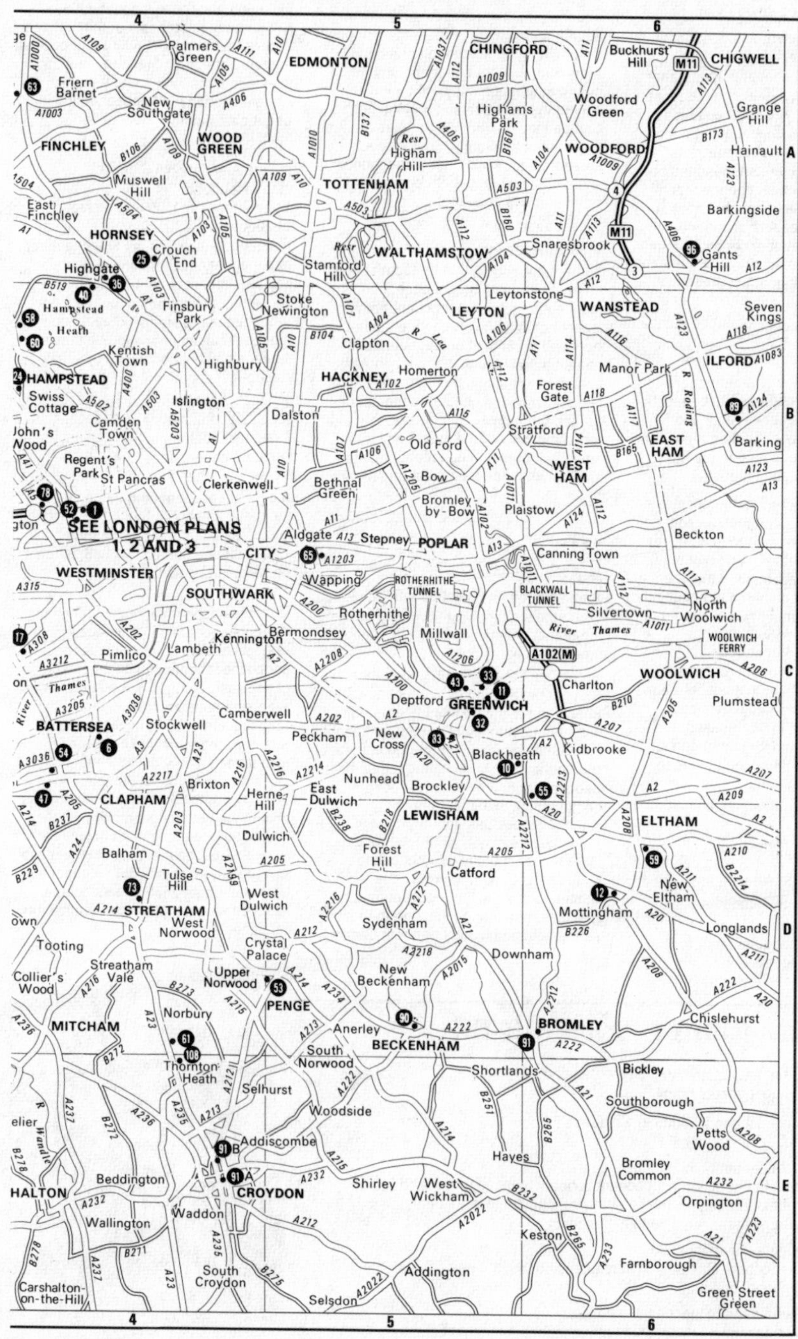

LONGFRAMLINGTON
Northumberland
Map **12** NU10

Besom Byre ☎ (066570) 627
Open: Tue–Sat 11am–2.30pm, 7–11.30pm. Closed Mon and Sun.
Adjacent to the Besom Barn Restaurant (which is over our price limit) the Besom Byre offers a delicious and imaginative selection of bar meals. Everything is home made from the Besom Broth – chicken and vegetable soup – to the pork and venison pie or loin of pork in cider, and the sherry trifle you might choose to round off your meal. All this can be enjoyed in the cosy surroundings of white rough cast walls, beams, scrubbed white wood tables and a woodburning stove.
[P] [&]

LOSTWITHIEL
Cornwall
Map **2** SX15

The Tawny Owl Restaurant 19 North St ☎ (0208) 872045
Open: Summer Mon–Sat 9am-9pm, Sun 11am–5.30pm, Nov–Easter Tue–Sat 9am–5pm. Closed Sun and Mon.
This informal, licensed restaurant in the centre of historic Lostwithiel has softly coloured walls adorned with the work of local artists. Emphasis is on home cooking which characterises the whole range of delicious dishes, savouries, gâteaux and pastries. The lunchtime hot 'dish of the day', served with fresh vegetables is excellent value. Specialities include beef provençale and steak and kidney pie. Quiches, omelettes and salads are available with special vegetarian dishes. In high season evening meals could feature pork chop braised in ginger beer or beef goulash.
[P] [S] [&]

LOWESTOFT
Suffolk
Map **5** TM59

Denes Hotel Corton Rd ☎ (0502) 64616
Open: Mon–Sun 12noon–2pm, 7–10.30pm
This pleasant and popular resort hotel caters for both business and tourist visitors and offers good value bar snacks as well as a carvery restaurant. Bar meals include home-made shepherds pie, curry, burgers, omelettes and fish, and even a steak meal will not exceed our limit. In the carvery a selection of roasts and pies are offered with a choice of vegetables or salads, followed by a sweet from the trolley, all for a set price well within our budget. Children's portions are available.
[C] [♫] [P] [&]

Victoria Bar Buttery, Victoria Hotel★★★ Kirkley Cliff ☎ (0502) 4433
Open: Mon–Sat 12noon–2pm
A well-stocked cold buffet table holds roast Norfolk turkey, ox tongue, beef, ham and prawns in cocktail sauce with a serve-yourself salad. Hot meals include grilled minute steak, breaded scampi or fillets of Lowestoft plaice, but the Chef's special (changed daily) is warmly recommended. At the cheap end of the scale are sandwiches, a ploughman's lunch or hamburgers with salad garnish.
[C] [P] [&]

LUDLOW
Shropshire
Map **7** SO57

Eagle House Corve St ☎ (0584) 2325
Open: Oak Room: Mon–Sun 12noon–2.30pm, 7–10pm
Pine Room: 9am–7pm
Known as 'The Eagle and Child' when it was first built in the 17th century as a coaching inn, this half-timbered building still retains evidence of a cobblestoned blacksmith's yard. In the entrance, traces of wattle and daub plastering have been exposed to show the original construction. Extremely fine oak panelling in the Oak Room restaurant came from nearby Acton Scott Hall and Bitterley Court and is an outstanding feature. The three-course lunch is remarkable value – you could start with grapefruit and orange cocktail, then savour roast lamb and finish with Queen of Puddings – though there are several other choices for each course. Table d'hôte dinner offers a wide selection including roast duckling and chicken à l'espagnole. With careful choice, the à la carte menu could be within our budget. If you are after a quick snack, then climb the stairs to the Pine Room, where anything from a pot of tea to steak and chips is available.
[P] [S] [&]

Penny Anthony✕ 5 Church St ☎ (0584) 3282
Open: Mon–Sat 10.30am–2pm, 7–10pm
Close to the castle entance, a charming Georgian-style building houses this popular little restaurant. There are three set menus, the one which comes within the scope of this guide includes soup, lagagne and dessert. If you prefer a lighter meal then choose from the à la carte.
[C] [P] [S] [&] **VS**

LYDDINGTON
Leicestershire
Map **4** SP89

Marquess of Exeter Inn ☎ (0572) 822477
Open: Mon–Sat 12.15–11.45pm, 7.30–9.45pm, Sun 12.15–1.45pm (open Sun evenings in summer only, 7.15–9.30pm)
The name of this charming 17th-century inn is unique – it is the only establishment in England to be granted the use of the title by the Marquess of Exeter. The comfortable lounge and bar areas reflect the proprietor's past association with horse-racing with lots of pictures and souvenirs. Although the à la carte restaurant is above our limit, there is an interesting selection of bar snacks including devilled whitebait, cheese and onion fritters and home-made pies. A choice of desserts from the trolley will complete the meal. A good choice of real ales are available including Ruddles Bitter and County, Bateman's Tripple XXX, Abbott Ale and Litchborough Bitter.
[C] [♫] [P] [&]

LYDFORD
Devon
Map **2** SX58

The Castle Inn Lydford ☎ (082282) 242
Open: Mon–Sun 12noon–2pm, 7–9.30pm (last orders)

Close to the beautiful Lydford Gorge and next to the castle ruins is this superb example of a 16th-century English pub. The Foresters' Bar, where meals are served, has low lamp-lit beams and a great Norman fireplace ablaze with vast logs in winter or with a profusion of flowers in summer. At lunchtime, apart from a selection of soups, pâtés and basket meals, a sumptuous help-yourself buffet luncheon table is available which includes soups, roast chicken, duck, beef, home-cooked ham, crab, mackerel, smoked salmon, smoked trout, hot home-made steak and kidney pie, cold meat pies, salads, cheeses, sweets and coffee. The extensive à la carte evening menu could exceed our budget.

C P

The Manor Inn Hotel★ Lydford Gorge ☎ (082282) 208
Open: Mon–Sun 12noon–2pm, 7.30–9.30pm and normal licensing hours

French-style cuisine is the hallmark of this pleasant old inn, where Richard Squire prepares an enormous variety of fare. Satisfying bar meals include curry, scampi, a variety of omelettes or Manor Hot Pot, but if you catch a whiff of the sumptuous aroma, wafting from the restaurant you will find it difficult to resist. The à la carte menu includes 18 starters and main course Manor Specialities such as Devonshire pork cooked with sliced apples and local cider, finished with cream and served in apple cases or boned chicken legs stuffed with creamed chicken and herbs.

C P **VS**

LYMM
Cheshire
Map **7** SJ68

The Bollin Restaurant Heatley, 2m NE of Lymm on A6144 ☎ (092575) 3657
Open: Mon–Fri 12noon–2pm, 7–9.30pm, Sat 7–9.30pm, Sun 12noon–2pm

Mrs Jean Barker runs this enterprising restaurant and catering business as well as the village Post Office and you can be assured of a warm welcome from Jean or her General Manager Peter Davies. The three-course table d'hôte lunch menu offers excellent value with main courses such as pork loin and cider apple sauce and rainbow trout. A similar evening menu is too expensive for us. As an alternative try the excellent light lunches and evening meals vailable Monday to Friday. There is a special family lunch on Sunday.

C ♫ P ♧ **VS**

LYNDHURST
Hampshire
Map **4** SU30

The Bow Windows Restaurant 65 High St ☎ (042128) 2463
Open: Summer Mon–Sun 10am–10pm, Winter Mon–Wed 10am–6pm, Thu–Sun 10am–10pm

The little town of Lyndhurst is on a major holiday route in the heart of the New Forest . . . and gets very busy in the tourist season. With this in mind, Bow Windows is particularly conveniently placed opposite a large free car park. Behind those bow windows is an interior decorated with mirror tiles and large murals of forest scenes. The menu is extensive and conventional.

P S ♧

LYNTON
Devon
Map **3** SS74

The Blue Ball Inn Countisbury Hill, Countisbury ☎ (0684) 263
A mile E of Lynton on the A39
Open: Mon–Sun 11am–2.30pm, 6–11pm

The Blue Ball Inn stands amid some of North Devon's most beautiful countryside, just over a mile from the picturesque village of Lynton and Lynmouth. The inn still retains the charm and character of its 17th-century hostelry days with beams, real ale and a welcoming open log fire. In the evening familiar bar snacks such as ploughman's, ham sandwiches and salads are served, along with a selection of more substantial meals like rump steak or breaded plaice, rainbow trout, all at reasonable cost.

♫ P ♧

The Greenhouse Restaurant Lee Rd ☎ (05985) 3358
Open: Summer Mon–Fri and Sun 10.30am–5pm, 6.30–9.30pm. Winter Mon–Fri and Sun 10.30am–5pm. Closed Sat

Originally a greenhouse in the grounds of a hotel, this restaurant has a Victorian theme, from the delightful illustrations on the menu cards to the range of good, wholesome dishes at reasonable prices. It is run in conjunction with a bakery which makes most of the bread, pies and cakes served here. At lunchtime try the home-made steak and kidney pie or locally cured gammon, or a bar snack such as quiche, pasty or lasagne. The evening menu is more extensive with specialities such as roast duck, steak or Vienna Schnitzel. Morning coffee or afternoon tea can be accompanied by lovely fresh cream cakes or apple pie and clottted cream.

C ♫ P ♧

LYTHAM ST ANNES
Lancashire
Map **7** SD32

Corky's 39–41 The Square ☎ (0253) 712513
Open: Mon–Fri 9.15am–5pm, Sat 9.15am–5.30pm. Closed Sun.

This first-floor coffee shop is spacious and bright with its green and cream décor, whicker chairs and pot plants. Anything from a cup of coffee to a three-course meal is available and dishes offered include Danish open sandwiches, filled jacket potatoes, goulash and vegetarian spinach flan. Desserts, or coffee-time snacks, include a variety of cakes and gateaux. Corky's is licensed.

S ♧

Lidun Cottage Barbecue 5 Church Rd ☎ (0253) 736936
Open: Mon–Sun 11.30am–2.30pm, 5–12mdnt

This pleasant licensed restaurant, with attractive bow windows, offers mainly spit-roasted dishes (half a chicken or barbecued loin of pork). There are also 100% beefburgers. Starters include soup of the day and try 'hot from the oven' Lidun Cottage apple pie for dessert.

C P ♧

Tiggis Express Bldgs 21–23 Wood St ☎ (0253) 711481
Open: Mon–Sun 12noon–2pm, 6–11pm (11.30pm on Sat)

A little piece of Italy in Lancashire here in this spacious pizzeria on two levels. Red walls, green ceiling and lights, marble topped tables and Italian piped music create the right atmosphere for such traditional dishes as home-made minestrone, fettucine alla crema, lasagne, and a range of spaghetti and pizza dishes. The menu is extensive and what better to round off the meal than Italian ice cream. Half-portions are available for children.

C ♫ P ♧

MACCLESFIELD
Cheshire
Map **7** SJ97

Da Topo Gigio 15 Church St ☎ (0625) 22231
Open: Tue–Sat 10am–2pm, 7–10.30pm

Half-way down the quaint, cobbled street of this old silk-manufacturing town is this informal restaurant, named after the famous Italian mouse. Morning coffee is served with pastries and scones. Fresh produce is put to good use in the thick minestrone soup – almost a meal in itself – chicken carbonara or grilled lemon sole can be followed by one of the home-made sweets.

P S ♧ **VS**

MADINGLEY
Cambridgeshire
Map **3** TL36

The Three Horseshoes
☎ (0954) 210221
Open: Mon–Sat 12noon–2.15pm, 6–10pm, Sun 12noon–2pm, 7–10pm

Set in attractive parkland in the quiet village of Madingley this thatched village inn is popular with visitors to the nearby American Services Cemetery. The ✕✕ restaurant is out of our price range but the bar snack menu offers a considerable variety of dishes which can be enjoyed in the comfortable lounge areas. Pot-roasted wood pigeon served with bubble and squeak and red mullet in tomato and olive sauce are two of the more unusual dishes available.

[C] [P] [♣]

MAIDENHEAD
Berkshire
Map **4** SU88

The Bacchus Swiss Restaurant
St Mary's Walk ☎ (0628) 36638
Open: Mon–Sat 12noon–2.30pm, Tue–Sat 7–10.30pm

The restaurant is decorated in the style of a Swiss chalet, with sloping wooden ceilings. A selection of cheese, meat and fish fondues are available along with other Swiss specialities including Raclette Valaise and Veal Zurichoise. There is a good choice of starters and sweets. All prices are subject to VAT. The newly-opened wine bar offers a range of dishes including a daily 'special'.

MAIDENS
Strathclyde *Ayrshire*
Map **10** NS20

Malin Court Restaurant ☎ (06553) 457
Open: Summer Mon–Sun 12.30–2.30pm, Mon–Sat 7–9.30pm, Sun 7–8pm
Winter Mon–Sun 12.30–2.30pm, Fri & Sat 7–9.30pm

Situated on the A719 between Maidens and Turnberry the restaurant and lounge bar are ideally suited for the elderly and disabled. Bar lunches offer exceptional value with an emphasis on fish dishes such as grilled fresh salmon steak and poached turbot. Meat dishes include pork chops and medallions of beef à la creme. The dinner menu is, unfortunately, too expensive for us.

[C] [♫] [P] [♣]

MAIDSTONE
Kent
Map **5** TQ75

The Pilgrim's Halt 98 High St
☎ (0622) 57281
Open: Tue–Sat 12noon–2.30pm, 7–10.30pm, Sun 12noon–2.30pm

Winner of our 1981 thousandth entry competition, The Pilgrim's Restaurant offers excellent value for those who will join the search for imaginative meals served in pleasant surroundings throughout the coming year. Daily specials of traditional English dishes represent best value for money, but fried fillet of haddock or grilled gammon and sausage won't break the bank. Finish with vanilla ice cream with hot chocolate fudge sauce.

[C] [♫] [P] [S] [♣] **VS**

MANCHESTER
Gt Manchester
Map **7** SJ89

The Cafe 3–5 Princess St, Albert Sq
☎ 061-834 2076
Open: Mon–Sun 11.30am–4am

Just the place for the late-nighter, this modern-fronted steak and burger restaurant is in the city centre. As well as the char-grilled steaks and pure beefburgers there is a good selection of 'Café Extras' such as poussin Continental – baby chicken cooked in a rich wine sauce with a hint of garlic. For the vegetarian there is the veg-burger and the Café-casserole. Sweets include fresh cream Black Forest gâteau, rum baba, sorbets and cheesecakes.

[♫] [P] [S]

Danish Food Centre Royal Exchange Bldgs, Cross St ☎ 061-832 9924
Open: Copenhagen Restaurant Mon–Sat 12noon–3pm, 6–12mdnt
Danmark Inn Mon–Sat 8am–6pm

This popular Danish eaterie is situated in the city centre, within the Royal Exchange Buildings. A beautifully-decorated three-tier cold table provides the centrepiece of the main restaurant, though a help-yourself choice to as much as you like from the appetising array of dishes offered here will pass the limit a little. Of course, you can always plump for the nourishing open sandwich known as smørbrød. Schnapps and a good wine list are available, although the Danish lagers are enthusiastically recommended!

[S]

Farmhouse Kitchen Fountain St (behind Lewis's) ☎ 061-236 5532
Open: Mon-Sat 9am–7pm

A sister to the restaurant of the same name across the city, but somewhat smaller. Pine tables and partitioning make for a fresh, bright atmosphere. Food is listed on a daily-changing blackboard menu which could feature roast beef salad and steak and kidney pie. Prices are modest and a three-course meal comes well within the budget.

[♣]

Farmhouse Kitchen 42 Blackfriars St (near Deansgate) ☎ 061-832 7001
Open: Mon–Sat 9am–7pm

This Farmhouse serve-yourself Kitchen attracts shoppers and business people to its convenient location in the city centre. Hot and cold dishes are available at very reasonable prices and the excellent salad selection has proved particularly popular. Of the hot meals, the chicken in wine sauce is worth trying as are the fried haddock and cheese and potato savoury or quiche.

[P] [S]

Harper's 2 Ridgefield ☎ 061-833 9019
Open: Mon, Tue, Thu, Fri 10am–7pm, Wed & Sat 10am–11pm

This popular coffee shop/restaurant lies in a small back street close to St Annes Square. Mr Shapiro, the owner, is rightly proud of his venture which is as refreshing in style as the bright green and white décor. The buffet menu changes daily and includes soup, open sandwiches, salads and hot dishes. There is a delicious choice of puds to end your meal. Harper's is licensed.

[C] [P] **VS**

The Lancashire Fold Kirkway, Alkrington, Middleton ☎ 061-643 4198
At the junction of Mount Rd and Kirkway and near M62 junction 20
Open: during normal licensing hours
Restaurant Tue–Fri, Sun 12noon–2pm, 7–10pm, Sat 7–10pm

For those who prefer to get away from the city centre, The Lancashire Fold may provide the answer. This modern extension to a pub has a brick-and-timber décor and comfortable furnishings. Although the à la carte menu is not cheap, it is possible to choose a two-course meal within the limit. Choose chilled melon and suprême de poulet Maryland with additional vegetables, sweets are available from the trolley. At lunchtime you can get a good table d'hôte meal.

[C] [♫] [P] [S] [♣]

Market Restaurant 30 Edge St
☎ 061-834 3743
Open: Tue–Sat 6.30–10.30pm

Energetic owners Su-Su Edgecombe and Elizabeth Price have breathed new life into an almost-dead part of the city with their delightful new restaurant. Pale primrose walls offset with dark green woodwork and simple stone flooring create a plain but pleasing effect, with a smattering of pictures, prints and bric-à-brac to add interest. Candles on the tables and lace curtains are the finishing touches. A starter such as chilled Lebanese cucumber soup made with yoghurt, cream and fresh mint could be followed by spinach and mushroom pancakes au gratin. Desserts include apple sorbet and lemon walnut tart, both served with cream.

Oscars 11 Cooper St ☎ 061-236 6752
Open: Mon–Fri 10.30am–3pm. Closed Sat, Mon–Sun 5.30–10.30pm. Late opening Wed–Sat, until 2am

This city-centre, self-service restaurant has a popular pub-type atmosphere, particularly at lunchtime. Mock beams and rough-cast walls give a friendly 'local' feel – as does the regular clientele. At lunchtime choose from a blackboard menu such dishes as traditional roast, kidney turbigo or chicken and mushroom pie. There is a self-service salad selection and a choice of sweets. In the evening you can have a sirloin steak chasseur or, further down the scale there's Spanish omelette.

C

Pizzeria Bella Napoli 1 Kennedy St
☎ 061-236 1537
Open: Mon–Sat 12noon–11.30pm, Sun 6.30–11.30pm

This friendly basement eating house has typical Italian-style décor, stuccoed walls and tiled floors. Being much smaller than the Pizzeria Italia, its sister restaurant across the city, tables can be hard to come by at peak periods. The slick young staff serve a variety of pastas and pizzas, such as cannelloni ripieni (pancakes filled with beef, eggs and spinach) or pizza marinara (mozzarella cheese, anchovy, olices, tuna and prawns in tomato sauce).

P S

Pizzeria Italia 40–42 Deansgate
☎ 061-834 1541
Open: Mon–Sat 12noon–11.30pm, Sun 6.30–11.30pm

A corner-sited pizza house on two floor-levels, Pizzeria Italia is decorated in the true Italian style with tiled floors and lusty pot plants. Low-priced dishes including soups, fish and chicken supplement the enormous and varied plate-sized pizzas and are excellent value. Service is snappy, operated by well turned-out and efficient all-Italian staff.

P S

Rajdoot Restaurant✕✕ St James House, South King St
☎ 061-834 2176/7092
Open: Mon–Sat 12noon–2.30pm, 6.30–12mdnt, Sun 6.30–12mdnt

One step inside the door of the Rajdoot Indian restaurant is a step into a different world. Waiters in their national costumes wait to greet you – the atmosphere is sultry and authentic. An extremely wide and varied menu is available and the specialities of the house are the Tandoori murghi, Tandoori fish and Makhan chicken and lamb pasanda. A set meal of Tandoori murghi, shish kebab, nan, rogan josh, prawn masalla, rice, dessert and coffee is excellent value though a little over our limit.

C ♫ S ♧

Sam's Chop House✕ Back Pool Fold, Chapel Walks ☎ 061-834 8717
Open: Mon–Fri 12noon–3pm

If you enjoy a lunch in a place which oozes in friendly charm, Sam's Chop House is a must for you. Set in a back alley, below street level, the décor is plain and simple. Stone walls are adorned by large prints and hanging mock oil lamps enhance the cosy atmosphere. Friendly waitressses serve you with good standard English fare: various steaks, lamb cutlets and roast chicken garni are examples. Extra large portions of scampi or plaice are served for gluttons.

♧

Wild Oats 88 Oldham St
☎ 061-236 6662
Open: Thu–Sat 6–11pm

Our inspector was very enthusiastic about this small wholefood restaurant just a short distance from Piccadilly Gardens. It is furnished with a varied collection of tables and chairs, old mirrors and posters (proclaiming 'Look After Yourself'). The menu concentrates on wholefood and vegetarian dishes but there are also a couple of meat and fish dishes on the menu. The menu changes constantly to take advantage of fresh seasonal produce, but typical main courses could be cream and walnut lasagne, fennel and mushroom cheese bake or beef casserole in wine. Desserts include delicious home-made ice cream. Fruit wines such as damson and elderberry are available. It is advisable to book in advance.

♫ P ♧

MARLBOROUGH
Wiltshire
Map **4** SU16

Attilio's Wine Bar 13 New Rd
☎ (0672) 52969
Open: Mon–Wed, Fri–Sat 12noon–2pm, 7-10.30pm, Sun 7–10.30pm (closed Bank Hols)

A cheerful aura of Italy in a corner of rural Wiltshire, Attilio's interior is simple and attractive, with an emphasis on natural textures – rush, cane, brick and wood. The excellent pizzas – with fresh tomatoes and oozing with cheese – can form a filling base for a within-the-budget three-course meal. Lunchtime meals and snacks are reasonably priced. Our inspector was impressed by the home-made crusty rolls, served with a large dish of creamy butter. You'll need a bit of mental juggling to keep the price of an à la carte selection down.

C P S

MARLOW
Buckinghamshire
Map **4** SU88

Burgers The Causeway ☎ (06284) 3389
Open: Mon 9am–12noon, Tue–Sat 9am–5.45pm

Opposite Marlow Park, this 17th-century building has been in the Burger family since 1942. The restaurant is on two levels. A simple, homely menu offers well-cooked food at very reasonable prices. Dishes include liver pâté or egg mayonnaise as a starter, steak and kidney pie or chicken and ham vol-au-vents with potatoes and vegetables, plus fruit pies and custard or Black Forest gâteau and cream to finish.

P S ♧

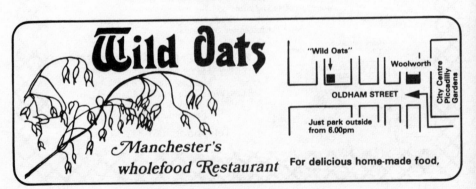

MARPLE
Gt Manchester
Map **7** SJ98

Woodheys Farm Glossop Rd
☎ (04574) 2704
Open: Tue–Sat 11.45am–2pm, 7–10pm, Sun 11.45am–2pm
On A626 between Glossop and Marple

The impressive stone-built Woodheys Farm occupies an idyllic setting overlooking the beautiful Etherow Valley, and once you've feasted on the views outside, an equally impressive culinary triumph awaits you indoors. Unfortunately, the evening carvery is too expensive for us but a similar set-price lunch buffet (a little over out limit on Sundays) is displayed in a 'help-yourself' central cabinet. Appetisers include chilled melon and smoked mackerel, followed by traditional roast joints or pies with vegetables, potatoes and salad. Remember to leave room for one of the scrumptious desserts such as fresh cream gâteau, fresh fruits in season or the speciality – brown bread and brandy ice cream. Coffee is served with mints and home-made sweetmeats.

C P ☘

MARTOCK
Somerset
Map **3** ST41

The George Inn ☎ (0935) 822574 2m off the A303
Open: Mon–Sat 10.30am–2pm, 6.30–11pm, Sun 12noon–2pm, 7–10pm

The George first appeared in church records way back in 1512 and there's a list of licensees dating from 1677 on display. However, most people will be more concerned with the food, of which there is a wide selection at reasonable prices. At the bar, try the 'George Special' of tender steak with onions and mushrooms in a butter bap, or alternatively you might prefer a modest cheese and pickle sandwich or the venerable ploughman's. The small restaurant, adjacent to the bar, was once the local bakery. It has been converted into a cosy eating place where you can enjoy a three-course meal during the day and choose from the extensive menu available in the evening. A three-course Sunday lunch is available.

C P ☘ **VS**

MAUCHLINE
Strathclyde *Ayrshire*
Map **11** NS42

La Candela 5 Kilmarnock Rd
☎ (0290) 51015
On the A76 to Dumfries
Open: Mon–Sun 12noon–2pm, 6.30–1am (last orders 10.30pm)

Despite the evident Italian influence, the extensive menu is quite cosmopolitan, with the French and English getting a decent look in. The décor is continental and romantic, with alcoves to ensure privacy. The lunchtime choice is adequate but fairly basic and reasonably priced. The dinner menu is à la carte.

♬ P ☘

MELKSHAM
Wiltshire
Map **3** ST96

Mr Bumble's Restaurant Conigre Farm Hotel, Semington Rd ☎ (0225) 702229
Open: Mon–Sat 12noon–2pm, 7–10.30pm, Sun 12noon–2.30pm

Formerly a farmhouse, this attractive stone-built hotel/restaurant still retains plenty of old world charm with low-beamed ceilings and oak furnishings. Lunches represent good value for money with the 'Chefs Carvery Lunch' of three courses plus coffee and the 'Mr Bumbles Light Luncheon Repast' which offers dishes such as herbed cottage flan and Conigre Farm pâté. A traditional Sunday Lunch is available. The dinner menus are outside the scope of this guide.

C P ☘

The West End Semington Rd
☎ (0225) 703057
Open: Mon–Sun 12noon–2pm, Sun 1.30pm, 7–10pm

This attractive mellow stone and tile hostelry has an interior with a farmhouse look – beamed ceiling, open-stone fireplace and scrubbed table tops. A limited menu offers simple but well-prepared dishes with emphasis on succulent steaks, all with interesting names. You may wrap your lips around the 'Farmer's Daughter' (a 8oz sirloin steak) or perhaps you'd prefer a Ploughboy's lunch or Hungry Horse?

C P

MELTON MOWBRAY
Leicestershire
Map **8** SK71

Cervino Ristorante Italiano 1–3 Leicester St ☎ (0664) 69828
Open: Mon–Sat 12noon–2pm, 6.30–11pm, 11.30pm Sat

Unmistakably Italian, this pleasant restaurant is rich in memorabilia from the empty Chianti bottles that hang from the ceiling to the many picture postcards and posters of the home country which adorn the walls. An all-Italian menu offers such specialities as home-made pâté, breast of chicken stuffed with cheese, and apple tart and cream.

C ☘

MENAI BRIDGE
Gwynedd
Map **6** SH57

Bridge End Restaurant Telford Rd
☎ (0248) 714864
Open: Summer Mon & Wed–Sun 12.30–2.30pm, Mon & Wed–Sat 7–10.30pm, Sun 7–9.30pm, Winter Mon & Wed–Sun 12.30–2pm, 7–9.30pm. Closed Tue and January

This mid-19th-century property, on Anglesey near Telfords Menai Bridge, is now a pleasant restaurant which has three separate dining rooms (one for non-smokers) and a cocktail bar. Main courses range from freshly-carved roast of the day to rump steak, and with vegetable soup to start with and a choice of sweet you can enjoy a satisfying meal at a very reasonable price. The menu also has a range of children's meals.

C ♬ P ☘

MEVAGISSEY
Cornwall
Map **2** SX04

Mr Bistro ☎ (0726) 842432
Open: Mon–Sun 12noon–2pm, 7–12mdnt

This pleasant, family-owned bistro is located at the harbour's edge in what used to be an old 'bark house' (where a preservative for coating fishing nets was made from crushed bark and resin). Hence, an old local expression for strong tea is 'like bark water'. Such tea would not be served at Mr Bistro, which caters for everyone's palate and pocket. Lunchtime fare starts with cook's own soup or freshly pressed orange juice, followed by an interesting range of home-produced main dishes, with emphasis on seafood; examples are, seafood platter, fried squid, smoked salmon pâté and prawn quiche. A selection of desserts is available and a children's menu should satisfy any beefburger fan. The evening menu, whilst appealing to the most discerning diner, is generally beyond the bounds of this book.

C ☘ **VS**

MIDDLESBROUGH
Cleveland
Map **8** NZ42

Rooney's Garden Restaurant 23 Newport Rd ☎ (0642) 223923
Open: Mon–Sat 11am–11pm. Closed Sun

The first-floor of this converted town-centre building has been transformed by the attractive display of plants and flowers in this fish restaurant. Cod, haddock, plaice and skate can be served with either chips or side salad and in the evening the gourmet selection includes a fish platter and deep-fried scampi. A limited choice of starters and sweets are available and there are special meals for children.

♬ P ☘

MILFORD-ON-SEA
Hampshire
Map **4** SZ29

Bay Trees 8 High St ☎ (059069) 2186 or from early 1984 ☎ (0590) 42186
Open: Tue–Sat 12noon–2pm, 7–9pm, Sun 12noon–2pm

This charming restaurant has a conservatory and beautiful gardens where you can enjoy your pre-meal drinks. The lunch menu provides traditional British fare (roast beef is a speciality of the house). The food is fresh and carefully cooked to ensure excellent value. The evening à la carte menu is a little over our limit. The restaurant is very popular with the locals and it is advisable to book in advance or arrive early to be sure of getting a table.

C P

MILNTHORPE
Cumbria
Map **7** SD48

Crooklands Hotel Buttery and Jakes
☎ (04487) 432
Two minutes from the M6 (No. 36 interchange) on the A65 going towards Kendal town centre.
Open: Mon–Sun 7.30am–2.30pm, 6.30–10.30pm

The Buttery of the Crooklands Hotel is a small, bright and cheerful restaurant, well worth knowing about. You can get a good lunch here, including home-made soup with roll and the 'pie of the day'. A three-course meal with coffee includes some traditional choices such as hot pot and liver and onions. Jakes, the American Winer Diner has steaks, burgers and giant American Spider Crab Claws on the menu and there are a selection of American beers and wines.

C P **VS**

MINEHEAD
Somerset
Map **3** SS94

The Good Food Inn 34 The Avenue
☎ (0643) 4660
Open: Summer Mon–Sun 10am–10pm, Winter closed Mon

Very few restaurants can boast of a service to equal the Good Food Inn: a staggering comprehensive menu of à la carte family fare offered for 12 hours a day and all extremely good value for money. Starters include speciality gourmet soups. Steaks, seafood and poultry are offered in many guises and all may be served in an appropriate wine sauce for a little extra, or if you prefer a lighter meal then try one of the pizzas, omelettes, burgers and salads on offer. Sweets include a vast range of fancy pancakes, some served with liqueurs. Special two- and three-course simple grills are available for children. As a special bonus, if you order and complete a three-course meal between 2.30–4pm, soup and sweet are offered free.

C S **VS**

Northfield House Hotel★★★ HL
Northfield Rd ☎ (0643) 5155
Open: Mon–Sun 12.45–1.30pm, 7–8.30pm

Built at the turn of the century as a tea planter's mansion, this splendid hotel has spectacular views of the sea and the Brendon Hills to the south. The magnificent three acres of garden were designed by Sir Edwin Lutyens and Miss Gertrude Jekyll – the ideal setting for a lunch to remember. The four-course lunch is exceptional value, with choices for each course. After a meal of cream of vegetable soup, roast chicken and salad, lemon layer pudding and fresh fruit or cheese, what better than a stroll around the tranquil gardens? A bonus to non-resident guests is the 9-hole putting green.

C P

MONMOUTH
Gwent
Map **3** SO51

King's Head Hotel★★★ Agincourt Sq
☎ (0600) 2177
Open: Mon–Fri 12.30–2pm, 7–9pm, Sat 12.30–2pm, 7–10pm, Sun 12.30–1.45pm, 7–9pm
Coach House Mon 6.30–11pm, Tue–Sat 12noon–3pm, 6.30–11pm, Sun 12noon–2pm, 7–10pm

Informal lunches well within the budget are served in the cocktail bar – a cold buffet selection with interesting, fresh salads is reasonably priced and hot dish of the day might be a casserole, pasta dish or steak and kidney pie. To the rear of the main hotel, is the Coach House. Colourful plants are arranged on the very pleasant patio area. Try the pub-snack menu or the grill room where the usual selection of grills is enlivened by Barnsley chop or Polynesian prawn and pineapple curry.

P S

MONREITH
Dumfries and Galloway *Wigtownshire*
Map **10** NX34

Glen Roy ☎ (09887) 466
Open: Tue–Sun 12noon–11pm. Closed Mon

The relatively simple facade of this small converted cottage hides a delightful interior full of charm and character. A full range of meals is provided in the two small dining rooms from a snack lunch to high tea, dinner and supper. A three-course lunch could consist of soup followed by haddock and fruit pie, whilst the supper menu offers main courses such as turkey breast Cordon Bleu and special gingered pork.

P 🍷

MONTROSE
Tayside *Angus*
Map **15** NO75

Corner House Hotel★★ High St
☎ (0674) 3126
Open: Mon–Sun 12noon–2pm, 4.30–9pm

This attractive hotel-restaurant is run efficiently by friendly waitresses who will serve you a three-course lunch with coffee and a glass of wine at a very reasonable price. The daily changing menu features the old favourites such as fried haddock, lasagne, roasts and omelettes. Later in the day a high tea menu is available with main courses such as gammon steak and chips or cold York ham salad, home-made scones, cakes and tea. The à la carte menu is generally our of our price range.

P S 🍷

MORECAMBE
Lancashire
Map **7** SD46

Coffee Shoppe 35 Princes' Crescent, Bare ☎ (0524) 414867
Open: Summer Mon-Sat 9.30am–5.30pm, Sun 10.30am–5.30pm, Winter Mon–Sat 9.30am–4.45pm

This typical, pleasant little tea shop is set in a row of shops, just off the sea front. Salads, home-cooked meat pies, cakes, pastries and sandwiches are available along with very reasonable and tasty three-course meals. Try home-made soup, followed by cottage cheese and peach salad then finish with one of Heather Millen's luscious creamy cakes.

P 🍷 **VS**

MORETONHAMPSTEAD
Devon
Map **3** SX78

White Hart Hotel The Square
☎ (064740) 406
Open: Mon–Sat 12noon–2pm, 6–8.30pm, Sun 12noon–1.30pm, 6.30–8.30pm

During the Napoleonic Wars, French officers on parole from Dartmoor Prison met at the White Hart. By then, this 300-year-old building was already established as a coaching inn. Its simple, elegant exterior is distinguished by the figure of a hind above the portico. The interior is unpretentious and comfortable. Lunchtime bar snacks are excellent and reasonably priced (try the chef's steak and kidney pie). As part of the 'Taste of England' scheme, the restaurant menu offers some good basic English dishes (including Devon apple cake) and a three-course tourist menu which is a little over our limit. An effort is made to use fresh local produce wherever possible. Afternoon teas are served to non-residents in the hotel's charming lounge.

C P

MOUSEHOLE
Cornwall
Map **2** SW42

Carn Du Hotel★★ ☎ (0736) 731233
Open: Mon–Sun 12noon–2.30pm, 7.30–8.30pm

Carn Du is set high above Mousehole and enjoys panoramic sea views from St Michael's Mount to the Lizard. Jill and Allan King specialise in hearty British dishes using local fresh fish wherever possible – crab mousse and fresh skate with black butter are just two examples. Other dishes include beef in red wine and home-made steak and kidney pie. There is a range of delicious desserts to end your meal. If you want something lighter then try one of the bar snacks or a Cornish Cream Tea.

C P 🍷 **VS**

MUMBLES
(nr Swansea) West Glamorgan
Map **2** SS68

La Gondola 590 Mumbles Rd
☎ (0792) 62338
Open: Tue–Sun 12noon–2.30pm, 6.30–11pm

Apart from his native Italian, Proprietor Aldo Grattarola speaks English very well, and gets by in French and German so it follows that he should keep a cosmopolitan menu. À la carte choices include veal dishes, fillet Stroganoff, Dover sole meunière and lasagne verdi al forno – a pretty cosmopolitan bag, you'll agree! More modest is the set lunch menu offering four choices of roast, plaice, trout or steak and kidney pie with vegetables and potatoes, plus a sweet and starter.

C P **VS**

MUSSELBURGH
Lothian *Midlothian*
Map **11** NT37

Caprice 198 High St ☎ 031-665 2991
Open: Summer Mon–Sat 12noon–12mdnt, Sun 4pm–12mdnt, Winter Mon–Sat 12noon–2.30pm, 5.30–12mdnt, Sun 4pm–12mdnt

'Our succulent pizzas are cooked in the traditional manner in a wood-fired oven to give them that extra taste of quality. Even the wood used, Scottish pine, is chosen because it adds the required flavour. . . .' That's how Cavalier Victor Alongi introduces his customers to his pizzeria cum Italian restaurant. The 16 different home-made pizza specialities have deservedly gained Victor and his son Alfredo a renowned reputation. A medium-sized pizza (12in diameter) provides a very generous meal for the average eater, but for those with voracious appetites the large pizza (15in) will prove a challenge. Choose from the extensive à la carte menu or the cheaper table d'hôte lunch menus.

♫ P S 🍷

See advertisement on page 140

NESSCLIFFE
Shropshire
Map **7** SJ31

The Old Three Pigeons ☎ (074381) 279
Open: Mon–Sat 10.30am–2.30pm, 6.30–10.30pm, Sun 12noon–2pm, 6.30–10pm

You'll find more than just a good food and ale at this 15th-century roadside inn. For pre-dinner entertainment you can enjoy tales of philanthropic highwayman Humphrey Kynnaston who supped many a jar at The Old Three Pigeons, his favourite retreat. The country-style décor features a grandfather clock and large Welsh Dresser. Home cooking is the order of the day.

P 🍷

NETTLEBED
Oxfordshire
Map **4** SU78

Dog and Duck Highmoor (2m S on B481)
☎ (0491) 641261
Open: Mon–Sun 12noon–2pm, 7.30–9.45pm

A 17th-century inn in a rural setting with small, but cosy bars and a restaurant. Bar snacks can be served in the dining-room at lunchtime (when the restaurant is usually closed) if there are children in your party. The limited dinner menu features grills with a few specials such as venison casserole and leek and cheese quiche. Brakspears real ale is served.

P 🍷 **VS**

See advertisement on page 140

NEWBURY
Berkshire
Map **4** SU46

Cromwell's Wine Bar 20 London Rd
☎ (0635) 40255
Open: Mon–Sat 10.30am–2.30pm, 6–10.30pm, 11pm Fri–Sat

Though a Courage Brewery-owned wine bar, Cromwell's avoids any big business anonymity, thanks to friendly table service from Colin and Jo Maddock and a relaxed, warm interior. Bare floorboards, pew seating and checked tablecloths are the setting for 'no frills' fare. There's a good selection of hot and cold dishes on display, including pizza and salad, daily specials, and grilled rump steak with salad. A choice from the sweet flans and gâteaux or cheeseboard, will keep you well within budget.

[C] [P]

The Hatchet Market Pl ☎ (0635) 47352
Open: Mon–Sat 12.30–1.45pm, 6.30–9.45pm, Sun 7.30–9.45pm
Newbury Race Days: Open 12noon

By the Corn Exchange in this attractive market town, you'll discover this interesting restaurant, with its unique ceiling of wattle sheep-pen fencing. Emphasis is on grills and roasts at competitive prices. Rump steak, lamb cutlets or shallow-fried rainbow trout are all on the menu. A good selection of starters include seafood cocktail and there are tempting sweets from the trolley to complete the meal.

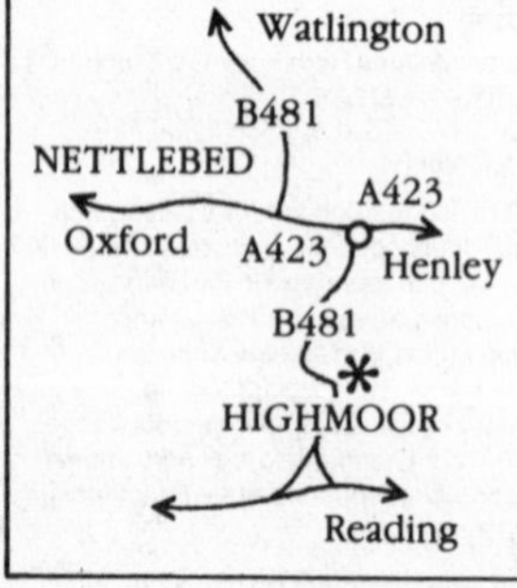

[C] [♫] [P] [S]

NEWCASTLETON
Borders *Roxburghshire*
Map **12** NY48

The Dormouse Main St, on B6357
☎ (054121) 694
Open: Mon–Sat 10am–5pm, Sun 11am–6pm, Wed, Fri & Sat 7.30–8.30pm

Home-cooking and baking at their best are the trademarks of this little country-cottage restaurant/tea-room. Whether you stop for morning coffee, afternoon tea with home-made scones and cakes, or a full lunch or dinner you'll find the quality second to none and the service friendly. For lunch, try the home-made soup, a rainbow trout served with a selection of vegetables and profiteroles. The dinner menu could include home-made pâté, pork fillets à la Dormouse (cooked in cream sauce, with wine, green peppers and herbs), and whiskied oranges with brandy-snaps. It is essential to book for dinner.

[P] [🍷] **VS**

NEWCASTLE UPON TYNE
Tyne and Wear
Map **12** NZ26

Blackfriars Restaurant and Brasserie
Monk St ☎ (0632) 615945
Open: Mon–Sat 8am–4.30pm, Sun 9am–4.30pm

The restaurant is part of a complex housed in Blackfriars, a restored 13th-century Dominican Friary. The brick and stone walls and quarry tiled floor help create an atmosphere in keeping with its history. The wholesome and interesting food is cooked on the premises and crêpes, both sweet and savoury are a speciality – try a filling of beef cooked with green peppers, rice wine and ginger.

[♫] [S] [P] [🍷]

Brahms and Liszt City Vaults La, Bigg Market ☎ (0632) 320801
Open: Mon–Sun 11am–3pm, 5.30pm onwards. (Food served lunchtime only, 12.30–2.30pm)

The lunch menu at this friendly and informal wine bar lists char-grilled steak sandwich (the house special), roast suckling pig and fish kebabs. Snacks include stuffed potatoes with a large selection of fillings and a range of open sandwiches. You can enjoy 'live jazz' every Sunday lunchtime when a traditional Sunday lunch is served at the bar. There is a good range of wines, imported beers and real ale to accompany your meal.

[♫] [S] [P]

Cavalier Steak Bar, Denton Hotel West Rd ☎ (0632) 742390
Open: Mon–Sun 12noon–2pm, 7–10.30pm

The impressive Denton Hotel's steak bar has a bright cocktail bar and an intimate, beamed restaurant with subdued lighting. Soup can be followed by a fine choice of steaks, fish and poultry and a sweet from the trolley. A 'Junior Cavalier Menu' is available for children.

[C] [♫] [P] [S] [🍷]

City Vaults 13 Bigg Market
☎ (0632) 327497
Open: Mon–Sun 11am–3pm, 5.30pm onwards. (Food served lunchtime only 12.30–2.30pm)

This elegant wine bar with wood panelled walls, intimate lighting and thick carpets has a separate area set aside for diners. For a description of the lunch menu see 'Sloanes' entry. There is live jazz every Sunday when a traditional Sunday lunch is available.

[♫] [P]

Coffee House and Bar, Avon Hotel★★★ Osborne Rd
☎ (0632) 817881
Open: Mon–Sun 10am–11pm

The Coffee House serves morning coffee and fresh cream teas in the afternoon, but from mid-day until 11pm snacks, grills and full three-course meals are available. Home-made soup of the day and a main dish such as gammon steak and pineapple or grilled plaice can be followed by a generous slice of fresh cream gâteau. Bar facilities are also available.

Dante and Piero 8 Douglas House, Neville St ☎ (0632) 324035
Open: Mon–Fri 11.30am–2.30pm, 5.30pm–1am, Sat 11.30am–1am, Sun 7–10.30pm

There is a nice, intimate atmosphere in this restaurant which is created by soft lights and background music. There is dancing in the evening, but those wanting a quiet corner will not be disappointed in this large restaurant. The Italian menu offers pizzas, pastas and a range of meat dishes. There is a selection of starters and home-made desserts.

[C] [♫] [🍷]

See advertisement on page 142

Eldon Coffee Shop Blackett Bridge, Eldon Sq ☎ (0632) 617084
Open: Mon–Sat 8am–6pm (Fri 8pm). Closed Sun

This smart little coffee shop is enclosed in a glass bubble in a covered shopping precinct. Everything on the blackboard menu is home-made including soups, spaghetti, casseroles, stuffed potatoes, salads, open sandwiches, sticky buns and a range of sweets.

[S] [P] [🍷]

Emperor Bewick St ☎ (0632) 328856
Open: Mon–Sun 12noon–11.30pm

A pleasant Chinese restaurant with bamboo décor, Chinese lanterns and soft, strumming background music. The excellent value businessman's lunch offers a starter, main course and coffee, or try the à la carte menu with the usual extensive range of poultry, fish and meat dishes at prices to suit all pockets.

[C] [P] [🍷]

The Falcon Prudhoe ☎ (0661) 32324
Open: Mon–Sat 12noon–2pm, 6.30–10pm, Sun 12noon–1.45pm, 7–10pm

The grill room of this modern pub has picture windows the full length of one wall, giving a view of the surrounding countryside. Clean lines and simple furnishings, with an open grill bar give a feeling of uncluttered elegance. The menu is unpretentious and you can get a good three-course meal very reasonably. A typical meal could be smoked mackerel followed by pork chop and a sweet from the trolley. For children there is a special 'Mr Menu' which includes a main meal, an orange and ice cream (and the colourful menu itself).

C P VS

The Golden Bengal Restaurant 39 Groat Market ☎ (0632) 320471
Open: Mon–Sat 12noon–2.30pm, 6–11.30pm, Sun 7–11pm

Soft Indian background music and a décor of Indian murals capture an Oriental atmosphere in this city centre restaurant. Soup or fruit juice are followed by chicken curry, keema pillau with vegetable curry or roast chicken and vegetables, with a sweet or fruit to complete the meal. The à la carte menu contains a wealth of Indian specialities – curries mild and hot, medium hot or very hot, biriani and Tandoori clay oven dishes. Fruit such as guava or mango are served with fresh cream.

C P S

Jade Garden 53 Stowell St
☎ (0632) 615889
Open: Mon–Thu 11.30am–11.30pm, Fri & Sat 11.30am–12mdnt, Sun 12noon–11.30pm

Alex Chung has created a garden effect with green trellis and potted plants in his Cantonese restaurant. Interesting appetisers on the extensive menu include hot and sour soup and stuffed crabs claws with main courses such as roast duck with fried noodles and a range of barbecued dishes.

C P

Legends Grey St ☎ (0632) 320430
Open: Mon–Sun 11am–3pm, 5.30pm onwards. (Food served lunchtime only 12.30–2.30pm)

The walls of this basement wine bar are decorated with mirrored panels which help to create a spacious and comfortable atmosphere. For a description of the menu see 'Sloanes' entry.

P

Mother Tuckers 6 Bigg Market
☎ (0632) 326590
Open: Mon–Sat 7am–7pm. Closed Sun

A simple, self-service restaurant with rough-cast walls displaying large mirrors each with a print of 'Mother Tucker' – a smiling old lady with glasses and a mob cap. Only fresh produce is used and everything is home-made – including the bread. A typical meal could be soup followed by steak and kidney pie and sherry trifle.

C P

Ristorante Roma ✕ 22 Collingwood St
☎ (0632) 320612
Open: Mon–Sat 12noon–2.30pm, 7–11.30pm, Sun 7–11.30pm

A Spanish guitarist entertains guests every night in this charming restaurant. As a gesture to Italian culture the menu has everything from chariot races to Chianti bottles and offers Sophia Loren (a juicy steak dish) and Gina Lollobrigida – the Chef's secret on a plate in the à la carte menu. Who could ask for more? Further temptations are artichoke hearts in a cream sauce and lobster mornay, plus a star-studded list of sweets headed by crêpes suzette and banana, peach or pineapple flambés. Midday budget items include lasagne, cannelloni, chicken and sirloin steak.

C P S

Sloanes Hancock St (at the rear of the Civic Centre) ☎ (0632) 815653
Open: Mon–Sun 11am–3pm, 5.30pm onwards. (Food served lunchtime only 12.30–2.30pm)

A sophisticated, purpose-built wine bar on two floors, the upper floor has a large conservatory and extensive balcony seating for sunny days. The lunch menu includes open sandwiches, poachers pie, chargrilled steak and a daily Chefs special. Hot roast beef sandwich is a popular dish – homebaked wholemeal bread topped with an enormous portion of roast beef and served with salad. Wines, imported beers and real ale are available.

P

NEWPORT

Isle of Wight
Map **4** SZ48

Corkers 11 High St ☎ (0983) 521487
Open: Mon–Sat 11am–3pm, 7–11pm. Closed Sun

True wine bar décor with scrubbed floorboards and tables, wooden chairs and masses of bottles (full and empty) gives a very clean and neat impression. The food is all fresh and home-made with dishes such as stuffed pancakes and chicken Italienne supplemented by a range of fish dishes. Puddings include hot bananas baked in rum and French apple flan. Whilst there are no special meals for children most dishes can be adapted to suit their needs. 'Burts', a locally-brewed real ale, is available.

S P

NEWPORT PAGNELL

Buckinghamshire
Map **4** SP84

Glovers 18–20 St John St
☎ (0908) 616398
Open: Tue-Sat 10.30am–2.30pm, 6.30–11pm. Closed Mon, Sun, Bank Hols, Xmas–New Year

This wine bar is housed in a converted stables and has old church pews as seating. Start your meal with home-made soup or taramasalata then choose from one of the imaginative salads or a hot dish such as steak and kidney pie. Sweets include gâteau and cheesecake.

C P

NEWQUAY

Cornwall
Map **2** SW86

Cross Mount Hotel ★★ Church St, St Columbo Minor ☎ (06373) 2669
Open: Mon–Sun: normal licensing hours. Restaurant: 12.30–1.30pm, 6.30–9.30pm
Bar: 12noon–2pm

The Cross Mount Hotel is just on the outskirts of Newquay but enjoys a village environment. The building is basically 17th century and combines a small residential hotel with restaurant and bar. Burnt orange, toning with the mellow natural stone walls, is the basic colour in the dining room, giving a warm and cheerful setting for a well presented meal. Table d'hôte dinner (available 6.30–7.15pm) is good value, as is the traditional Sunday roast. The 'tourist menu' all-in à la carte dinners (a little over our limit) give a wider choice, and orders are taken until 9.45pm. Bar snacks include basket meals, sandwiches, salads and omelettes.

C P S

The Lower Deck 26 Fore St
☎ (06373) 6520
Follow signs for Fore Street and Harbour
Open: Summer Mon-Sun 12noon–3pm, 5.30–10.30pm, Winter weekends only

A Pugwash character in a boat – the restaurant's distinctive logo – indicates your arrival at the Lower Deck. The seaside theme is continued inside the part pine-panelled, open-plan restaurant, slung with fishing nets and adorned with prints of old Newquay. The Lower Deck's a place for the family on holiday, with a children's menu and a good basic choice of food. Try a ploughman's, fisherman's lunch, fish and chips, home-made pies and quiches, followed by one of the home-made sweets. The evening menu consists of steak, chicken, gammon, chops and a roast dinner and a selection of the chef's specialities. The Upper Deck, open in the evenings, offers a more expensive à la carte menu.

C ♫ ♧

NEW RADNOR
Powys
Map **3** SO26

Red Lion Inn Llanfihangel Nant Melan
☎ (054421) 220
Open: Mon–Sun 12noon–2pm, 7–11pm

A warm welcome always awaits visitors to this 300-year-old roadside inn. Situated on the A44 between Leominster and Rhayader, the building retains its olde-worlde character and charm while also benefiting from modern comforts inside such as the cosy wood-burning stove in the lounge. Dennis and Pauline, the proprietors, pride themselves in offering homely fare and you can enjoy a wholesome lunch of soup and an 8oz sirloin steak with the trimmings and a cup of coffee and still stay within the budget. Sunday lunch is also available. Tasty bar snacks, served day or evening, include scampi or steak and kidney pie and a cold buffet, served from the terrace, is a big attraction.

C P ♧

NEWTON ABBOT
Devon
Map **3** SX87

The Dartmoor Halfway Bickington
☎ (062682) 270
Open: Mon–Sat 11am–2.30pm, 6–10.30pm, Sun 12noon–2pm, 7–10.30pm

A 'change' house in coaching days, this 17th-century cob and stone inn, three miles west of Newton Abbot, has a garden and patio where one may enjoy a meal on hot days. The large, open-area bar is furnished in oak, with wood panelling and hessian-covered walls. Here you may sample one of nine starters, a particular favourite being 'grotti nosh', almost a meal in itself. Follow this with seafood risotto or steak and kidney pie, and complete the treat with fruit pie and cream washed down with fresh coffee and cream with a Turkish delight or mint chocolate.

C P

NEWTON MEARNS
Strathclyde *Renfrewshire*
Map **11** NS55

The Coffee Club 114 Ayr Rd
☎ 041-639 6888
Open: Mon–Sat 10am–10.30pm

You'll have to come early for lunch or dinner to this popular, cosy little coffee shop, as demand far outweighs the seating availability. Situated in a block of 10 shops on the main A77 road to Ayr, the soft brown interior with cork tiles and lots of pot plants offers shoppers and travellers alike a peaceful haven in which to relax and enjoy a meal such as soup of the day, egg, cheese and bacon flan served hot with salad and coleslaw, cheesecake and Viennese coffee. The Coffee Club is unlicensed but coffee is, of course, a speciality of the house.

♫ P S

NEWTOWN
Powys
Map **6** SO19

Bear Hotel ★★★ Broad St
☎ (0686) 26964
Open: Mon–Sun 12.30–2pm, 6.30–9.30pm

Formerly a coaching inn, the Bear has all the atmosphere anyone could wish for. Food is available in the bars, the Spinning Wheel Grill Room and the Severn Restaurant. A cold buffet lunch is available (Mon–Sat) in the cocktail bar and the Severn Restaurant serves an excellent three-course lunch. A table d'hôte and an à la carte menu are available in the evenings with dishes such as Anglesey eggs and roast chicken Welsh style.

C ♫ P S ♧ **VS**

See advertisement on page 144

NORTH PETHERTON
Somerset
Map **3** ST23

Walnut Tree Inn ☎ (0278) 662255
Open: Mon–Sat 11am–2.30pm, 6–11pm, Sun 12noon–2pm, 7–9pm

A 19th-century coaching inn, this hotel has recently been renovated by its owners, Richard and Hilary Goulden, to make it a welcome overnight stop for the modern traveller. Prices are surprisingly low and choices on the menu range from omelettes to steak. Snacks and light meals are available in the bar and there's a very accommodating children's menu, featuring all the old favourites.

C P ♧ **VS**

NORTH TAWTON
Devon
Map **3** SS60

L'Escargot Bistro Kayden Arms
☎ (083782) 242
Open: Summer Mon–Sun 12noon–2pm, Tue–Sat 7.30–11pm, Sun evening bookings only; Winter Fri–Sun 12noon–2pm, Tue–Sat 7.30–11pm, Sun evening bookings only

Since taking over the Kayden Arms in 1983 Mr and Mrs Kaye have opened this small bistro which is decorated with memorabilia from the racing world. The table d'hôte lunch menu offers good value with casserole of beef as a typical main course. The dinner menu offers dishes such as home-made pâté and soup, jugged hare and lemon sole stuffed with prawns.

C P [symbol]

NORWICH
Norfolk
Map **5** TG20

Le Bistro 2A Exchange St
☎ (0603) 24452
Open: Mon 11.30am–2pm, Tue–Fri 11.30am–10pm, Sat 11.30am–2.30pm, 5–10pm

Table d'hôte at Le Bistro is very good value with three-course English and French set menus available for both lunch and dinner, or choose from the à la carte menu. Veal Lyonnaise is a popular choice; other favourites include sole Normandy and duck with orange sauce. The first and second floor restaurants are pleasant and comfortable (once the stairs are negotiated), with fresh flower arrangements set against brocade-patterned wallpaper and oak tables.

C ♫ P S [symbol]

Mano 72 Prince of Wales Rd
☎ (0603) 613143
Open: Mon–Sat 7–11.30pm

The bright orange and white exterior of this bistro proclaims its presence on the corner of Prince of Wales Road and Cathedral Street. As a striking contrast the interior is a faithful reproduction of a Parisian café with dark red paintwork, red velvet café curtains on brass rails and French posters. Green and white tablecloths cover the 10 cast-iron tables which provide seating capacity for 34 people. Contrary to appearance, owner Mano is in fact Turkish and his restaurant boasts a truly international menu. A typical meal could be whitebait, followed by duck pilaff plus pears in burgundy.

S

Rembrandt Restaurant Easton
☎ (0603) 880241
Open: Tue–Sat 12noon–2.15pm, 7–10.15pm, Sun 12noon–2.15pm

Proprietors Bruno (who is also the chef) and Trudie Riccobena extend a warm welcome to all, and have a wide range of menu styles to suit all tastes, including one for children. The restaurant also has facilities for invalids. Without careful selection, the à la carte can easily exceed our limited budget, but the special 'Business Lunch' and 'Holidaymaker's Lunch' are very good value. Main course might be gammon, calves' liver, minute steak, omelette or salad. Under the Rembrandt chef's 'Taste of England' series, steak, kidney and mushroom pies, in particular, are selling like hot cakes! A traditional Sunday lunch is also available.

C ♫ P [symbol] **VS**

Savoy RestaurantXXX 50 Prince of Wales Rd ☎ (0603) 20732
Open: Mon–Sun 12noon–2.30pm, 6pm–1.30am

The Athenian Room on the ground floor is elegantly green with chandeliers, Greek pictures and small booths. The windows overlook an enclosed patio with vines and plants galore. Downstairs is the Cellar Taverna, seating over 100 on two levels, complete with a small dance floor and nightly live music. Three-course table d'hôte lunch in the Athenian Room is excellent value. Main course choices are particularly good – roast beef or chicken, moussaka, kebabs, plaice or ham salad. The à la carte menu is very extensive, with Greek, English, Italian and French cuisine, but you will have to select your meal carefully to stay around the limit.

C ♫ P S [symbol] **VS**

Tatlers 21 Tombland ☎ (0603) 21822
Open: Mon–Sat 6–11.30pm, Sun 12.30–2.30pm, 7–11pm

You'll find Tatlers amongst the beautiful buildings of Tombland. A group of young people have converted an old house into this attractive restaurant, with a bar upstairs, and have succeeded in creating an air of Victorian opulence by the use of floral wallpaper, red curtains, Victoriana lamps, and mirrors. High-backed settles arranged around plain wooden tables provide a degree of privacy and seclusion. All food is prepared on the premises, the accent being on traditional Norfolk dishes prepared from local produce. Starters include pâté or mussels in white wine. More unusual dishes include rabbit in mustard and rosemary or pigeon, duck and orange pie. Sweets (the list includes syllabub and chocolate fudge cake) are reasonably priced.

♫ P S

NOTTINGHAM
Nottinghamshire
Map **8** SK54

Ben Bowers 128 Derby Rd
☎ (0602) 413388
Open: Mon–Fri 12noon-2pm

A sister to its namesake in Derby, this restaurant offers a good value two-course meal (main courses include chili con carne, minute steak au poivre and Almond Malakof) well within our price range. Below in the basement, Betty's Buffet Bar has a wide range of snacks and a cold meat and salad 'help yourself' buffet. Next door in the basement is Palms 'Freehouse' bar and restaurant serving home-made snacks and bar meals and three-course meals.

C **VS**

Eviva Taverna and Kebab House 25 Victoria St ☎ (0602) 580243
Open: Taverna: Mon–Sat 7pm–2am
Kebab House: Mon–Sat 10.30am–12mdnt

If you want to let off steam you can buy plates for smashing here. First, though, enjoy your meal in this basement restaurant transformed by white walls, vines, bunches of grapes and olive branches to a little bit of Greece in the heart of England. There are a few grills and roasts on the menu, but the chef's specialities – stifado (a rather special beef stew), kleftiko (lamb cooked with herbs) and dolmas (stuffed vine leaves) are particularly good and won't break the bank. Starters and sweets (including paklava) are reasonably priced. For two people dining together a half bottle of wine is provided free of charge, or you may choose from the list and have £1 knocked off the wine bill, which really is a worthwhile concession. Having enjoyed all this, listened to Greek music and watched Greek dancers in an adjoining room, you may feel like showing your appreciation by a bit of plate-smashing. Above the taverna is a kebab house run by the same proprietor, Mr Kozakis. This is a pleasant place to stop for a snack or for lunch, and the doner kebab is specially recommended.

C ♫ P S **VS**

Farmhouse Kitchen 14–20 Listergate
Open: Mon–Sat 9am–7pm. Closed Sun

A sister restaurant to the two establishments in Manchester, this large, modern Farmhouse Kitchen is situated beneath the W H Smith store in a pedestrianised city centre street. Run on a self-service basis, the menu offers a wide variety of hot and cold dishes including a good selection of salads.

Lasagne and chicken are examples of the hot dishes.

S ♧

Food for Thought 6 Hurts Yard, Upper Parliament St ☎ (0602) 46888
Open: Mon–Sat 12noon–2.30pm

Simple, good taste is the hallmark of this lunchtime restaurant, tucked away in a narrow alley dating back to Georgian times. Habitat furniture, posters, pictures and plants create a 'trendy' air. Food is cheap, home-made and varied. Starters include chili con carne, soup of the day and deep fried mushrooms. FFT specials include chickebab (chicken pieces with herbs on a skewer, served with French fries) pizza and lasagne. A 'help yourself' buffet, salads and burgers are also available along with chef's specials which change daily. Super desserts such as South Sea Bombe or Bananarama will ruin any diet.

C ♫ S ♧ **VS**

La Grenouille Restaurant✕ 32 Lenton Boulevard ☎ (0602) 411088
Open: Mon–Fri 12.30–1.30pm, 7.30–9.30pm, Sat 7.30–9.30pm

Imagine white-painted tables (only seven of them), white chairs with black cord upholstery, placed on black and white vinyl flooring against brick-red hessian walls highlighted with French posters; then add red tablecloths and matching table napkins. There you have La Grenouille – a little corner of France on the corner of a terrace of large Victorian houses. Young owner Yves Bouanchaud provides superb French food using mainly fresh products. Don't chance the à la carte menu if you're really hard up but it's worth going a bit over the limit to enjoy a meal here if you can afford it. The table d'hôte menu offers a starter of home-made soup or terrine, a main dish such as boeuf bourguignon with vegetables and salad (this changes daily) and a sweet such as fruit salad or chocolate gâteau with cheese as an alternative.

♫ P ♧

Moulin Rouge✕ 5 Trinity Sq
☎ (0602) 42845
Open: Mon–Sun 12noon–2pm, 6–10.30pm

Not strictly a French restaurant but very much a Continental haunt, the Moulin Rouge is close to the Victoria shopping centre and the Theatre Royal. The sparkling restaurant has predominantly red décor, with crisp white table linen and banquettes. The à la carte menu includes appetisers, soups, fish, omelettes, entrées, poultry, curries, grills, salads and desserts, with a wide range of prices. A daily main course 'Special' is excellent value and you can enjoy a two or three-course meal within our budget if you avoid the steaks. If you cannot find the meal you crave 'the menu is only a suggestion, our chef is at your command'.

C P S

The Savoy Hotel★★★ Mansfield Rd
☎ (0602) 602621
Open: Colonial Restaurant: Mon–Sat 12noon–2.15pm, 7–9.30pm, Sun 12noon–2.15pm
Steak Bars: Mon–Thu 12noon–2.15pm, 6–11pm, Fri–Sat 12noon–2.15pm, 6–11.30pm, Sun 12noon–2.15pm, 7–10.30pm
Salad Bar: Mon–Fri 12noon–2pm

One of the most popular eating places in Nottingham, this large, luxurious hotel has a sumptuous restaurant and richly decorated steak bar on the ground floor. The lower ground floor houses a second steak bar with exposed stonework and a salad bar with exposed wall and ceiling timbers. Food is excellent value for money. The restaurant offers a three-course lunch with an extensive choice for all three courses. A five-course dinner with even more choice is a little over our limit. The steak bars provide, efficiently and quickly, a wide range of inexpensive quality meals. The 'all in' price includes a starter, main course and sweet. T-bone steak with all trimmings is a popular choice. A children's menu is available as well as half portions on certain dishes.

P ♧

Swiss Cottage 18 Chapel Bar
☎ (0602) 411050
Open: Mon–Sat 9.30am–7pm

Peter and Bernard Morritt have made this modern, canopied premises in a cul-de-sac the seventh of their family chain of restaurants. Amidst the exposed brickwork and copper lighting it is possible to sample anything from the most simple sandwich to the tastiest rib steak (with all the trimmings, chips and vegetables) preceded by a choice of soups. Finish with a delicious strawberry pancake topped with fresh whipped cream, home-made cherry pie or cheese and biscuits. The restaurant is unlicensed so you will have to forgo a glass of house wine. There is a sister establishment at 15 St Peter Gate.

♫ P S ♧

The Waterfall 7–8 Hurt's Yard, Upper Parliament St ☎ (0602) 42235'Open: Mon–Fri 12noon–2.30pm, 7–11pm, Sat 10am–5pm, 7–11.30pm

It's well worth the search for this interesting little restaurant nestling in the Georgian shopping centre, reached by means of a narrow flagstoned alleyway by the side of the Fox Inn. A wide bow window fronts the restaurant which seats about 60 within its three sections, each with a distinctive olde worlde atmosphere. The waterfall forms part of a cool and splashing grotto which provides an attractive focal point. The dark-wood tables take on a more sophisticated look in the evenings with the addition of Nottingham lace tablecloths and flickering candles. An interesting and reasonably-priced à la carte menu offers a traditional selection of dishes including minute steak. The three-course business lunch offers such dishes as home-made soup, roast lamb or pork cutlet chasseur, sweet plus coffee. If your taste is for the more exotic, you may choose veal cordon bleu or fillet of sole Monte Carlo from the speciality à la carte menu – but beware, prices are high and you'll have to be selective.

C ♫ S ♧

NUTBOURNE

West Sussex
Map **4** SU80

Cedar Tree Restaurant On A27 near Bosham ☎ (0243) 573149
Open: Tue–Sun 12noon–2.30pm, 7–10.30pm

David and Sue Ullah have successfully converted a one-time transport café, on the main Emsworth–Chichester road, into a thriving little restaurant. The set three-course lunch includes roast of the day and home-made steak and kidney pie, plus salads as a lighter option. During the evening the five-course set dinner is a little over our limit (available Tue–Fri) or try the one-course evening meal.

S ♧

OAKFORD

Devon
Map **3** SS92

Higher Western Restaurant
☎ (03984) 210
On the A361, 1½m W of Oakford
Open: Tue–Sun 12noon–2pm, 3–5.30pm, 7–10pm

This small, attractive restaurant is recommended mainly for its good lunchtime bar snacks, from a range of open sandwiches (such as chicken, prawns and salami) to pâté and salad, lasagne, home-made steak and kidney pie or lamb chops and chicken escalope. You can have a three-course meal, including soup and roll and a sweet. Within our budget. There is a set Sunday lunch but dinner is too expensive for us. Many a motorist will be relieved to find a good pull-in at such a remote spot.

P

OBAN

Strathclyde *Argyll*
Map **10** NM83

The Box Tree 108 George St
☎ (0631) 64641
Open: Apr–Nov Mon–Sat 9am–10pm, Sun 6–10pm

Simplicity is the attraction of this unlicensed restaurant. Uniformed staff give friendly, attentive service in a floral wall-papered environment. Sit in your individual dining booth and choose from the short, simple menu. Lunch has an emphasis on salads, although fried Hebridean haddock is also available. The dinner menu is more varied and lists scampi and grilled gammon or veal T-bone steak but will still come within our limit for the three courses. Pâté with oakcakes for a starter sounds a pleasant departure from the norm. Burger snacks and sandwiches are also served.

S

The Gallery Restaurant Argyll Sq
☎ (0631) 64641
Open: Apr–Oct Mon–Sun
9.30am–10pm

Iain Reid is justly proud of his smart little restaurant situated in the busy town centre. Open all day, the Gallery offers hot or cold snacks and full three-course meals. In the evening the atmosphere is transformed as lights sparkle on the attractive watercolours adorning the cream walls. The special three-course 'farmhouse' dinner has choices such as scampi or roast chicken. The two-course lunch menu is excellent value with a choice of salads and hot dishes.

P S

McTavish's Kitchen George St
☎ (0631) 63064
Open: Restaurant Summer Mon–Sun
12noon–2.30pm, 6–10.30pm
Self-service Summer Mon–Sun
9am–10pm, Winter 9am–6pm

James and Jeremy Inglis' large, modern, premises overlooking the sea, houses a downstairs self-service food bar, seating 150 and a clean and bright upstairs restaurant with room for 270, as well as the Laird's Bar and the predatorily named Mantrap Bar. Food in both restaurant and self-service is very good of its kind and not expensive. As you might expect, this is the place for Scottish specialities including 'haggis and neeps'. Table d'hôte lunch and evening meal menus enable you to select three courses and coffee within the budget. During the summer Scottish Evenings feature piping and highland dance. Helpings are generous and the dishes such as pork chop or haddock and chips are well-cooked and presented with flair.

S

Soroba House Hotel ☎ (0631) 62628
Open: Mon–Sun 12noon–2.30pm,
7–11pm

Take the A816 Lochgilpead road out of Oban for approximately 1 mile to David and Edyth Hutchinson's Soroba House Hotel, standing in nine acres of its own grounds with commanding views over Oban to Mull. Rebuilt after a fire, this hotel has an attractive restaurant and bar. The restaurant offers a good choice of well prepared and presented food. The lunch menu offers extremely good value and a typical meal could be iced melon, fresh salmon mayonnaise followed by a sweet from the trolley. Only very careful choice from the dinner menu will keep you within our limit. Afternoon tea is served between 3.30 and 5pm; high tea between 5 and 6pm, and excellent bar meals are available from 7–11pm.

P

Studio Family Restaurant Craigard Rd
☎ (0631) 62030
Open: Mid-March–mid Nov: Mon–Sun
11.30am–4pm, 5–10pm

You'll find this popular licensed restaurant on a steep hill just off the main street. The lunch menu includes a variety of roasts, tempting salads, fresh fish, shell fish and burgers – all at reasonable prices, only the steaks will stretch our budget. The special three-course dinner (available 5–7pm) is excellent value and children's portions are available. Some of the choices on the evening à la carte menu come within our price range.

C S

The Thistle Hotel, Restaurant
Breadalbane Pl ☎ (0631) 63132
Open: Apr–Sep Mon–Sun
12noon–2.30pm, 5–9.30pm

Whatever you do, don't come to Oban without trying the excellent locally-landed seafood. And Robert Silverman's Thistle Restaurant is the place for it. The table d'hôte menu offers a good choice of starters and 14 main courses including fish, roast beef and chicken, minute steak and salads; and a variety of sweets. A two-course special light meal is available between 5–6.30pm.

P ☘

OKEHAMPTON
Devon
Map **2** SX59

Bearslake Restaurant Lake, Sourton, 5m SW of Okehampton on the A386.
☎ (083786) 334
Open: Tue–Sun 10am–2pm, 7–10pm

The choice of bar food at lunchtime ranges from an open prawn sandwich to spicey beef casserole with baked potato. A three-course meal with coffee and a traditional Sunday roast are excellent value. After your meal you can enjoy a stroll in the fresh air (weather permitting) as the restaurant has open access to the moor. The à la carte menu offered in the dining room is rather beyond our price limit.

C P ☘

OLDHAM
Gt Manchester
Map **7** SD90

Mother Hubbard's 270 Manchester St
☎ 061-652 0873
Open: Mon–Sun 11.30am–11.30pm

The cupboard is far from bare at this modern, detached fish restaurant. A variety of fresh fish, delivered daily from Grimsby, ensures that you're in for a piscine treat. A smart interior features spindled wooden divisions (to allow that little bit of privacy at tables) and a Georgian-style bar. The friendly waitresses serve a simple starter, plus main fish dish (scampi, halibut, haddock or plaice with all the trimmings, and a coffee) with ice-cream to finish.

C P ☘

OLLERTON
Nottinghamshire
Map **8** SK66

Rose Cottage Rufford ☎ (0623) 822363
Open: Mon–Sun 12noon–10pm

Two miles south of Ollerton on the A614 and almost opposite the entrance to Rufford Abbey is this quaint brick cottage with small leaded windows, surrounded by an immaculate garden. Inside is all wood panels and beams, with three separate areas for dining. A wide range of fare is available from midday throughout the week. A three-course table d'hôte lunch could include minestrone soup, braised lamb chops and vegetables and ice cream gâteau. A more sophisticated menu is used in the evening, when care will be needed to avoid exceeding the budget.

♫ P ☘

OLNEY
Buckinghamshire
Map **4** SP85

The Olney Wine Bar 9 High St South
☎ (0234) 711112
Open: Mon–Sat 12noon–2.30pm, 7–10.30pm, Fri–Sat 11pm, Sun 12noon–2pm

The charming Georgian shop front of this wine bar leads into a room with an attractive open fireplace. The original bakehouse ovens are still to be seen in the back room. Bill of fare is on a blackboard and includes prawn pil pil and pâté with bread, lasagne, spaghetti bolognese and chili and rice. Desserts include chocolate, rum and raisin cheesecake. Traditional Sunday lunches are available with smaller portions for children. Live music on Wednesdays.

♫ P S **VS**

ORMSKIRK
Lancashire
Map **7** SD40

Tower and Steeple 15 Church St
☎ (0695) 72017
Open: Mon–Fri 10am–2.30pm, 7–10.30pm, Thu 10am–4pm, 7–10.30pm, Sat 10am–4pm, 7–11pm, Sun 12noon–2.30pm

Lunches are particularly tempting here, with lasagne and other Italian dishes at very reasonable prices. A three-course Sunday lunch offers a variety of roasts and desserts from the trolley. The dinner menu includes a host of seafood starters and a variety of steaks and grills. Special 'family' dinners are also available.

P S ☘

OSWESTRY
Shropshire
Map **7** SJ22

The Good Companion 10 Beatrice St
☎ (0691) 655768
Open: Tue–Sat 11am–3pm, 7–11pm. Closed Mon & Sun

Standing amongst the shops and cafés of this Oswestry street this delightful wine bar has a wealth of exposed beams and a large, old pine counter. The owners, Christopher and Denise Hickman, are justifiably proud of the home-made dishes they produce. The soup – served with hot crusty bread and virtually a meal in itself – is highly recommended, or try the shepherds pie or lasagne. Vegetarians are catered for with dishes such as aubergine and tomato bake.

P

OTTERY ST MARY
Devon
Map **3** SY19

King's Arms Hotel★ Gold St
☎ (040481) 2486
Open: Mon–Sat 12noon–2pm, 7–9.30pm, Sun 12noon–1.30pm, 7–9.30pm

Built in 1756, the King's Arms Hotel was originally an old coaching inn. Now the cream painted building commands a central position in this picturesque little town. The oak-decorated Tar Barrel Bar offers an excellent range of food – either snacks or a full three-course meal. Following soup of the day, steak pie, plaice fillets, chicken or beef curry, cider-baked Devon ham, and ham or beef salads are some of the choices for a main course. A good choice of sweets is available to finish your meal. The à la carte dining room menu is pricey, but still good value and children are catered for.

C P S ☘

OUNDLE
Northamptonshire
Map **4** TL08

The Falcon Inn Fotheringhay (4½m N of Oundle off the A605) ☎ (08326) 254
Open: Mon–Sun 12.30–2pm, Tue–Sun 6.45–9.30pm

The Falcon Inn, built in 1820, is situated in the middle of a picturesque and historic village. The popular village pub restaurant has an excellent reputation for good food at very reasonable prices – so be warned, table reservations are required for all meals, with some evenings booked solid for three months. The menus vary daily, hot food is not served Mon, Sat and Sun lunchtime – but an appetising cold buffet is available. A three-course meal could include iced gazpacho, roast duckling with orange and almonds, and fresh peach melba.

P ☘

OXFORD
Oxfordshire
Map **4** SP50

Burlington Bertie's Restaurant and Coffee House 9a High St
☎ (0865) 723342
Open: Mon–Sun 10am–12mdnt

Look above the covered market in Oxford High Street, and there's Bertie's – all plants, pub mirrors, cane-bottomed chairs and highly-polished tables with wrought-iron pedestals. You can get a meal or any kind of drink here at any time. The cuisine is English and Continental, the service fast and efficient, the welcome warm and friendly. A wide variety of meals are available including salads, moussaka, pasta dishes and meat and fish main courses. Desserts include 'specials' such as pancake delight. The three-course set menu is excellent value.

S ☘ **VS**

Maxwell's 36 Queen St
☎ (0865) 242192
Open: Mon–Sun 11.30am–12mdnt

A bright and breezy first-floor restaurant where the high ceiling, iron girders and steel supports give an aircraft-hangar effect. American-style food is efficiently served in an informal atmosphere. Specialities such as lamb kebab, chili and chicken supplement the hamburgers, which come with French fries, tossed salad and a choice of dressings. Ice cream sodas and milk shakes continue the American theme.

[♫] [S] [🍷]

The Nosebag 6–8 St Michael's St
☎ (0865) 721033
Open: Mon–Sat 10.30am–5.30pm, Fri–Sat 6.30–9.30pm, Sun 12noon–5.30pm

Inelegant its name may be, but this upstairs, split-level restaurant, with its oak-beamed ceiling and bright and homely décor, has a certain charm all of its own. The lunchtime hot dish of the day is likely to be moussaka, chicken à la crème or herrings in oatmeal, or try one of the tempting salads. With soup as a starter and apple pie for dessert a three-course lunch is a bargain. And on Friday and Saturday evenings the Nosebag offers an excellent three-course meal with exciting main courses such as mackerel with gooseberry sauce.

[♫] [S]

Opium Den✕ 79 George St
☎ (0865) 248680
Open: Mon–Sat 12noon–2.30pm, 6–12mdnt, Sun 1–2.30pm, 6–12mdnt

Don't let the name discourage you, the only addictive thing sold at the Opium Den is the food. Cantonese with a few Pekinese dishes, the specialities of the house are the sizzling dishes brought piping hot to your table on wooden platters. Lunchtimes are always busy, with a budget-priced table d'hôte menu. The à la carte is extensive with prices to suit all pockets. Set dinners are particularly reasonable.

[C] [♫] [P] [S]

OXTED
Surrey
Map **5** TQ38

The Old Bell High St ☎ (08833) 2181
Open: Mon–Sat 11am–2.30pm, 6–10.30pm (11pm Fri & Sat) Sun 12noon–2pm, 7–10.30pm

Dating from the 15th century this charming pub, with leaded windows and original oak beams, offers home-cooked food and prompt, efficient service. The three-course lunch and dinner daily specials, displayed on the blackboard menu, represent excellent value for money and include a glass of wine in the price of the meal. The steak and kidney pie is especially recommended. There is an à la carte menu, but it is rather more expensive.

[C] [P] [🍷]

PAIGNTON
Devon
Map **3** SX86

Chez Michel 107 Winner St
☎ (0803) 556100
Open: Mon–Sun 12noon–2pm, 7–12mdnt (11.30pm Sun)

The atmosphere is very continental at Chez Michel, when you dine by candlelight in the central courtyard at scrubbed pine tables bedecked with fresh flowers. The restaurant offers an impressive menu with a European flavour but for our budget-conscious readers the wine bar is the place. Charcoal-grilled chicken, steaks, rainbow trout or porc en brochette are available with a jacket potato and self-serve salad. Fruit salad or cheese and biscuits with coffee will complete your meal. Go along on Monday evenings if you enjoy live folk music.

[C] [♫] [S]

Lalkin 33 Hyde Rd ☎ (0803) 551005
Open: Mon–Sun 12noon–2pm, 5.30–11.30pm

The unusual marble-look frontage and smoked glass, 'porthole'-style door is an incongruous entrance to this Chinese restaurant in the main shopping area. Inside, the décor is more appropriate, with Chinese lanterns illuminating black chairs, white cloths and sparkling cutlery. Chicken with cashew nuts and fried rice followed by apple, banana or pineapple fritters and syrup is on the à la carte menu, and the three-course business persons lunch (always available) is excellent value. Chinese or Russian tea is served, as well as coffee.

♫ P S **VS**

La Taverna 53 Torbay Rd
☎ (0803) 551190
Open: Summer Mon–Sat 10.30am–2.30pm, 5.30–11pm, Sun 12noon–2pm, 7–10.30pm, Winter Mon–Thu 10.30am–2.30pm, 5.30–10.30pm, Fri–Sat 10.30am–2.30pm, 5.30–11pm, Sun 12noon–2pm, 7–10.30pm

A bit of the Mediterranean on the English Riviera. The canopied front is set back from the road far enough to allow tables and sunshades to be placed outside in fine weather; wrought ironwork, white-rendered walls with painted murals and Italianate tiled floor in the dining area complete the illusion that the Italian sun shines outside. The family of the owner, Ernest Pelosi, has lived in Paignton since 1903, so it may be with a sense of nostalgia that the Mediterranean scene has been so carefully created. Pizza and pasta dishes are specialities and there is a short list of other main dishes including steaks, chicken, fish and salads. Sausages, egg, beans and chips and ploughman's lunch are popular bar snacks.

S

PAINSWICK
Gloucestershire
Map **3** SO80

The Painswick Hotel★★★ Kemps La (4m N of Stroud on A46)
☎ (0452) 812160
Open: Mon–Sun 12.30–2pm

This elegant hotel with a country-house atmosphere is recommended here for its buffet luncheon and a traditional Sunday lunch. The buffet is laid out in an anteroom to the comfortable bar lounge which overlooks the garden. You can choose from the hot dish of the day (which could be lasagne, canelloni, boeuf bourguignon or steak and kidney pie) with vegetables or cold meats and salads. Dessert with fresh cream and coffee will complete your meal. The buffet is not served on Sunday. The four-course Sunday lunch is over our limit.

C P 🍷

PAISLEY
Strathclyde *Renfrewshire*
Map **11** NS46

Cardosi's 46 Causeyside St
☎ 041-889 5339
Open: Mon–Thu 11am–7.30pm, 4.30–11pm

After about 20 years of running the same restaurant in the same town, the Cardosi family has had plenty of time to get to know its clientele and how to please them. They cater for all tastes by operating a café and take-away counter as well as the first-floor restaurant and dispense bar, where it's possible to get a good three-course business lunch at a very low price. A typical choice of dishes from this menu would include cream of asparagus soup, 'haggis, neeps and tatties' and banana crumble and custard. A reasonably-priced à la carte menu is always available, along with its list of chef's specialities – Mexico steak, chicken Kiev or Napoli steak with all the trimmings.

♫ P S 🍷

PARKGATE
Cheshire
Map **7** SJ27

Chompers The Parade ☎ 051-336 1567
Open: Mon–Fri 12noon–3pm, 5.30–11.30pm, Sat & Sun 12noon–11.30pm

Set on the promenade (the sea deserted Parkgate years ago) is this fascinating restaurant having uninterrupted views across the Dee to Wales. Polished wood floors and tables and brick walls are a backdrop to a 'cacophony' of bric-à-brac, plants and old metal advertising boards. The menu is bright and appetising too, with lots of choice. Start with corn on the cob, home-made pâté or stuffed pepper, followed by one of the burgers, pizzas or perhaps a chili or lasagne. Desserts include chocolate fudge cake, banana split or the 'Belly Buster' prepared for two or more diners – a mountain of ice cream, fruit, chocolates and whipped cream lit up with sparklers.

C P 🍷

PATELEY BRIDGE
North Yorkshire
Map **7** SE16

Bridgeway Restaurant 1 High St
☎ (0423) 711640
Open: Tue–Fri, Sun 12noon–5pm

This first-floor restaurant overlooks the valley of the River Nidd in upper Nidderdale where the road bridge spans the river. Dark oak tables, wheelback chairs, light oak-clad walls and a beamed ceiling complete the rustic feeling. Home-made country fare is a special feature, from lentil soup to English kidneys braised in red wine sauce, home-made beef steak, kidney and mushroom pie, roast topside and Yorkshire pud and roast Nidderdale turkey. Home-made fruit pies with fresh cream are popular desserts.

P 🍷

PENARTH
South Glamorgan
Map **3** ST17

Rabaiotti's, Caprice Restaurant✕✕✕
The Esplanade ☎ (0222) 702424
Open: Mon–Sat 10.30am–2.30pm, 7–10.30pm, Sun 10.30am–2.30pm

Situated below the Caprice Restaurant (superb cuisine but too expensive for us!) Rabaiotti's operates from the same kitchen and offers good, unpretentious food at very reasonable prices. A typical meal could be home-made soup, followed by lamb cutlets, peas and chips and gâteau. The three-course Sunday lunch is very good value, the price list for the main course being inclusive of starter and sweet. Rabaiotti's also boasts an interesting cocktail bar open to non-diners which proves popular.

C ♫ P S 🍷

PENRITH
Cumbria
Map **12** NY53

Waverley Hotel Crown Sq
☎ (0768) 63962
Open: Summer Mon 10am–2pm, 6.30–8.30pm, Tue–Sat 10am–8.30pm, Sun 12noon–2pm, 7–8.30pm Winter Mon–Sat 12noon–2pm, 7–8.30pm
Coffee Shop Summer only

On the fringe of the town centre is this very popular hotel dining room with a small, intimate cocktail bar. The attraction is very reasonably-priced home-made food and fresh vegetables. The main menu includes barbecued spare ribs, steak and kidney pie, beef curry and a selection of pizzas. There are also various 'dishes of the day' and a cold buffet table.

C P S 🍷

PENSHURST
Kent
Map **5** TQ54

The Leicester Arms Hotel★★
☎ (0892) 870551
Open: Mon–Sun 12.15–2pm, 7.30–9pm

This 17th-century inn with its exposed beams, wheel-back chairs and copperware is just what you'd expect to find in picturesque Penshurst. Although the restaurant is over our limit, the delicious bar meals are prepared by the same chef, Luigi Carugati, who is also the Manager. Try his Pasta alla Parmigiana or the Osso Bucco Milanaise – veal in a sauce with saffron rice. For the less adventurous there is plaice and chips, salads or minute steak and vegetables, with an assortment of desserts to finish off the meal.

C P 🍷

PENZANCE
Cornwall
Map **2** SW43

Admiral Benbow Chapel St
☎ (0736) 3448
Open: Mon–Sun 12noon–2pm, 7–10pm

In the early 18th century, bands of smugglers known as the 'Benbow Brandy Men' made the Admiral Benbow Inn their headquarters. Here it was that the surplus tea, 'baccy, perfume, silk and brandy were hidden. Today, it boasts an equally desirable list of goodies to be chosen from the 'Vittals Chart', such as Cornish lobster, smoked mackerel pâté, roasts, grills and various curries. Ice creams are the speciality – try the 'gooseberry lagoon' (coffee ice, gooseberries and iced fruit syrup) or the Southern Star (banana, paw-paw, peach and iced fruits), and wash it all down with a shot of finest rum. Buffet lunches are available in the bar upstairs.

C 🍷

Smuggler's Hotel and Restaurant
Newlyn Harbour ☎ (0736) 4207
Open: Mon–Sun 6.30pm–12mdnt

This 270-year-old character restaurant overlooks picturesque Newlyn Harbour, choc-a-bloc full of fishing boats, nets and weatherbeaten fishermen. Legend has it that there was once a secret tunnel direct from the restaurant's cellar bar to the harbour side, and the one-eyed smuggler whose sinister portrait acts as the restaurant's sign certainly looks as though he once drank his fair share of boot-legged brandy. Freshly caught mackerel makes a tempting starter, followed by piping hot lamb barbecue, port Marsala or Mexican chicken. Sweets are generously served from the trolley. David and Ann Reeve, resident proprietors, are always at hand.

C 🍷

PERSHORE
Hereford & Worcester
Map **3** SO94

Sugar and Spice High St
☎ (0386) 553654
Open: Mon–Sat 9.30am–5.30pm

Painted pink, this eaterie stands out from its more sober-fronted high street neighbours. In true teashop tradition, you'll find the cheerful restaurant by walking through a patisserie and extensive gift shop. At the rear there is an attractive patio setting for when the weather's fine. Start with soup with roll and butter followed by one of the no-nonsense main course dishes such as cottage pie with potatoes and peas or a ploughman's lunch. For dessert, there's a large counter of mouth-watering confectionery to delight the most discerning gâteau gourmet.

C P S

PERTH
Tayside *Perthshire*
Map **11** NO12

Hunter's Lodge Bankfoot 8m N of Perth off A9 at Bankfoot services turn-off
☎ (073887) 325
Open: Mon–Sun 12noon–2pm, 5–9pm

This country restaurant, only eight miles north of Perth on the main road to Inverness, makes a speciality of traditional Scottish fare, both in the à la carte and bar menus. The award-winning bar food features Hunter's Lodge pâté, home-made beef steak pie and curry – all firm favourites. Children's own menu 'Toy Town Special' is also available. In the dining room traditional Scottish high tea is nothing short of a slap-up dinner or try the à la carte menu.

C P 🍷 **VS**

Kardomah St John's Sq ☎ (0738) 25093
Open: Mon–Sat 9.30am–6pm

These Trusthouse Forte restaurants are favourites with many people. This one is certainly quick and convenient if you are shopping or sightseeing. Supplementing the usual THF menu of omelettes, grills and salads is a table d'hôte lunch (either two or three courses) and a high tea (including tea and toast).

C S 🍷 **VS**

Olde Worlde Inn, City Mill Hotel West Mill St ☎ (0738) 28281
Open: Mon–Sun 12noon–2.30pm, 5–10.30pm

Convenient, fast food of the steaks, chicken and haddock variety is served in a 19th-century mill which has been converted into a modern hotel of the Reo Stakis organisation. The mill stream and wheel can be seen through plated glass in the hotel's lounge bar and reception area. Main course prices include a starter, but sweets or cheese are extra.

C P 🍷

The Pancake Place 10 Charlotte St
☎ (0738) 28077
Open: Summer Mon–Sat 10am–5.30pm, Sun 11.30am–5.30pm (open till later in the summer)

This specialised restaurant, with its informal tea-room atmosphere, was the first to pander to pancake fans in central Scotland (other sister restaurants have since opened at Edinburgh, Kirkcaldy and St Andrews). After fruit juice or soup of the day, you can sample a giant burger, chicken and pineapple or any one of six crispy salads. And to follow? How about 'Florida' – a large pancake topped with ice cream, peaches and fresh whipped cream – just one of a dozen exotic desserts guaranteed to ruin your diet!

S 🍷

Pizza Gallery 32–34 Scott St
☎ (0738) 37778
Open: Mon–Sat 10am–11pm. Closed Sun

This bright, modern pizza restaurant opened in December 1982 and is already as popular as its sister restaurant in Dundee. The pizzas (named after famous artists) come with various toppings including sea food – the Michaelangelo. The limited range of starters and sweets includes corn-on-the-cob and apple pie.

♫ S S 🍷

Tudor Restaurant [Windsor (Perth) Ltd] 38 St John St ☎ (0738) 23969
Open: Mon–Fri 10am–7pm, Sat 10am–7.30pm, Sun 4–7pm

This is a first-floor restaurant in a complex of bars, restaurants and function rooms, with comfortable seating, and highly polished wooden tables. Home-made lentil soup, lasagne with green salad, creamed chicken pie all served with boiled or french fried potatoes and

vegetables of the day, offer good value for money. For dessert choose from peach condie or perhaps sherry trifle and cream. Children can choose from their own menu, cheeseburger with side salad, Windsor pizza or sausage, bacon and egg.

[C] [♫] [P] [S] [♧]

PETERBOROUGH
Cambridgeshire
Map **4** TL19

Costers, Great Northern Hotel Station Rd ☎ (0733) 52331
Open: Mon–Sun 10am–10pm

The 'barrow boy' theme of this restaurant is emphasised by an original costermonger's barrow which is piled high with a 'help yourself' selection of freshly-made salads, cheeses, pâtés and fruit. A three-course meal can be chosen from the small à la carte menu or the daily table d'hôte menu. If you want something lighter, then try one of the snacks (pizza, pasty, quiche, scrambled eggs served on muffins, and pancake rolls). The hotel car-park fee can be recovered when buying your meal.

[C] [♫] [P] [S] [♧] **VS**

Mr Pickwick's Wine Bar 15 Westgate Arcade ☎ (0733) 41552
Open: Mon 11.30am–3pm, Tue–Sat 11.30am–3pm, 7.30–11.30pm. Closed Sun

An olde worlde Dickensian atmosphere is created in this intimate wine bar by pictures and trivia of that period. The seating arrangements are particularly unusual in that the tables have been converted from Singer sewing machines. Starters include French onion soup and devilled prawns and there is a good selection of main courses. Fish dishes include simple plaice fillet or a more complex cod and prawn gratin, while speciality dishes might be chili con carne, lasagne, moussaka or steak and kidney pie, with a good range of sweets to follow. If you only want a light repast there are ploughman's, omelettes, pizzas and salads at very reasonable prices.

[♫] [S] [P]

PETERHEAD
Grampian *Aberdeenshire*
Map **15** NK14

Coffee Shop Fraserburgh Rd
☎ (0779) 71121
Open: Mon–Sun 7.30am–11pm

Inside Peterhead's newest and most modern hotel, the Waterside Inn, you will find this glowing Coffee Shop. A variety of sandwiches are available otherwise a three-course meal of soup, haddock and apple turnover are just a few of the dishes on the menu. A three-course evening meal is served from 6.30–11pm featuring a daily main course choice, soup as a starter and ice cream or cheese and biscuits. There is a special menu for children.

[C] [♫] [P] [♧]

PETERSFIELD
Hampshire
Map **4** SU72

The Punch and Judy Restaurant High St ☎ (0730) 62214
Open: Mon–Sat 8.30am–5.15pm

This attractive olde-worlde building dating from 1613 has plenty of charm and combines a bakery, coffee shop and small restaurant. A set menu of good basic English fare could include smoked mackerel, roast beef and apple pie or prawn cocktail, chilli con carne and gâteau. There is also a dish of the day on offer such as roast loin of pork served with a good selection of well-prepared vegetables.

[C] [P] [S] [♧] **VS**

PETWORTH
West Sussex
Map **4** SU92

Lickfold Inn Lodsworth ☎ (07985) 285
Open: normal licensing hours

A very attractive old inn between Lickfold and Lodsworth about six miles from Petworth, the Lickfold Inn has earned itself quite a local reputation for good food. Lunches and evening meals are served and there is a mouth-watering selection of dishes. Examples are lamb cutlets reform, or fillet of haddock filled with crab meat and served with bearnaise sauce. At lunchtime it is possible to get fisherman's pie or chicken princess as well as a wide range of salads. The bar is in two parts, one around a huge open fire and the other part is used as a dining area. A good selection of real ales is available and is marked up on the beams near the bar. There is also a separate room at the back for children.

[C] [♫] [P] [♧]

PEWSEY
Wiltshire
Map **4** SU15

The French Horn Marlborough Rd (on A345) ☎ (06726) 2443
Open: Mon–Sat 10am–2pm, Sun 12noon–1.45pm, Mon–Thu 6–10pm, Fri & Sat 6–10.30pm, Sun 7–10pm

This attractive inn, which lies adjacent to the Kennet and Avon Canal, was converted from old cottage and a smithy. The menu is not over-elaborate, but large portions of good, wholesome dishes are provided. For starters, try a tasty home-made soup or prawn cocktail. For your main course home-made steak and kidney pie, scampi and chips and salads are all within our price range. The home-made fruit pies are excellent value. A set Sunday lunch includes a glass of wine.

[P] [♧]

See advertisement on page 154

PIDDLETRENTHIDE
Dorset
Map **3** SY79

Brace of Pheasants Plush, 2m NE of Piddletrenthide off B3143 ☎ (03004) 357
Open: Mon–Sat 11.30am–2.30pm, 7–10.30pm, Sun 12noon–2pm, 7–10.30pm

This thatched free house dates from the 16th century. The proprietor Joan Chandler has a wide experience of catering and provides an excellent choice of meals in the Buttery Bar, well within the price range of this guide. The blackboard menu lists, amongst other dishes, home-made soup, home-made pâté, cold meat platter with a range of salads, smoked salmon platter and a range of hot dishes. Sweets and coffee are also available and there is a children's menu.

[P] [🍷] **VS**

PINNER
Gt London

The Old Oak 11 High St ☎ 01-866 0286
Plan 4 **103** A1

Open: Mon–Fri 12noon–2pm, 7–10.30pm, Sat 12noon–2pm, 7–11pm, Sun 12.30–2.30pm, 7.30–10pm

Business person's lunch starters include delicacies such as avocado and grapefruit salad, Waldorf salad (apple, celery and walnuts in sour cream) or crevettes aioli (peel-yourself prawns and garlic mayonnaise). There is a wide choice of main dishes: meat which could be pork in an apple, sage, cider and cream sauce, or a spicy dish such as chili con carne or curry de volaille aux bananes. To finish a satisfying repast, sweets include rum and coffee mousse and Old English flummery, or you might prefer Brie or Camembert to keep the meal memorably continental.

[C]

PITLOCHRY
Tayside *Perthshire*
Map **14** NN95

The Brown Trout Pitlochry Festival Theatre ☎ (0796) 3054
Open: May–Sep Mon–Sat 10am–5pm, 6.30–10pm. Closed Sun

In 1981 Scotland's 'theatre in the hills' moved to its present location on the banks of the River Tummel on the outskirts of town. The Brown Trout Restaurant is housed in the impressive new building and enjoys panoramic views of the surrounding countryside. Morning coffee and afternoon tea are available and at lunchtime there is an attractive cold buffet and a choice of two hot dishes. The table d'hôte dinner menu is outside our budget.

C P

The Luggie Rie-Achan Rd
☎ (0796) 2085
Open: Apr–early Nov Mon–Sun 10am–9pm

A 'luggie' is a milkmaid's bucket – appropriate since this quaint little restaurant was originally the byre of an old dairy farm. Inside, the raftered roof, white-painted rough-cast walls and stone fireplace are very welcoming. Ian and Diana Russell, the owners, ensure that home-baking and local produce are a main feature of all the fare. Lunchtime offers the choice of a self-service cold table and an excellent selection of cold meats, duck, salmon and smoked mackerel, accompanied by a variety of original salads, assorted gâteaux and fresh fruit salads, or hot dishes such as grills which are served at the table. The dinner menu offers a much wider choice of hot dishes but the price is likely to bring the full meal outside our budget.

PLYMOUTH
Devon
Map **2** SX45

The Barbican Steps Serenade Arts, Castle St, The Barbican
☎ (0752) 267655
Open: Mon–Sat 10am–5pm

This small restaurant in Plymouth's picturesque Barbican area is run by American former food writer Louis Meeks and his English wife Dawn. Mr Meeks' speciality is oriental cookery, a fact which becomes apparent in his daily 'specials'. One example is Thai chicken – a mixture of pieces of breast of chicken with peanuts and spring onion on a bed of garlic rice. Gâteaux and home-made ice cream are examples of desserts available and morning coffee and afternoon tea are also served.

C P

The Khyber Restaurant✕✕
44 Mayflower St ☎ (0752) 266036
Open: Mon–Sun 12noon–2.30pm, 6–11pm

Pass the Khyber and you will miss the chance of enjoying a friendly, well-established Indian restaurant run with family pride since 1960. Décor and furnishings are very Indian, cuisine is authentic and of a high standard. Table d'hôte lunch includes a starter such as shami kebab (delicious round pats of finely chopped meat with spices and onions), a selection of curries and English dishes, and a sweet – try guavas and clotted dream – to follow. The reasonable prices allow you the pick of the à la carte menus.

C P

Merlin's Restaurant★ 2 Windsor Villas, Lockyer St ☎ (0752) 28133
Open: Mon–Sat 12noon–2pm, 6.30–9.30pm

There's often something extra going on in this small hotel close to the city centre. Barbecues, Hallowe'en night parties, French or Greek evenings and beggar's banquets are Anne and Bill Proudman's specialities, but a no-nonsense lunch or dinner is always readily available. You'll be pleasantly surpriseed at the low prices of the well prepared dishes, served in an atmosphere of intimate friendliness. The à la carte menu offers, for example, delicious home-made soup, chicken chasseur with fresh and tender vegetables, and a sweet from the trolley; and much of the more exclusive à la carte menu is also within our budget – bar the lobster!

C ♫ P S

POCKLINGTON
Humberside
Map **8** SE84

Bayernstubl 4–6 Market Pl
☎ (07592) 2643
Open: Tue–Sun 12noon–10.15pm, (10.45pm Sat)

This converted pantiled cottage in the centre of town is furnished in natural wood to emphasise the Bavarian atmosphere. The popular lunch-time menu is basically English fare with sandwiches, home-made fruit pies and gâteaux at extremely reasonable prices. The main 'Speisekarte', written in German with English subtitles, offers krabben salat (prawn cocktail), then sample a rich, spicy German dish such as paprika huhn (paprika roasted chicken) and round it off with apfel strüdel and cream.

P S

POLEGATE
East Sussex
Map **5** TQ50

The Wishing Well Wilmington, 2m W of Polegate on the A27 ☎ (03212) 5956
Open: Mon–Sun 10am–6pm (hot food is served 12noon–2.30pm)

Teas have been served in the gardens for over 100 years. The Wishing Well is now under the personal supervision of Fay Steadman, whos is assisted by her mother. Sussex cream teas, mini teas and a variety of snacks are served all day. Lunches include hamburgers, chicken and a range of salads, home-made soup is a tasty starter and a range of desserts is available. Whether you decide to have a full meal or a snack you can choose to eat either in the attractive gardens or the restaurant. The restaurant is licensed.

♫ P

POLPERRO
Cornwall
Map **2** SX25

Crump's Crumplehorn (¾m N on A387)
☎ (0503) 72312
Open: Mon–Sun 10.30am–5.45pm, 7.30–10pm

Mike and Wendy Costello's tea room and bistro, in this most picturesque of Cornish fishing villages, is a low-beamed 250-year-old farmhouse, furnished in the late Victorian/Edwardian style and offering a range of cuisine to suit all tourist tastes. Daytime meals are pâtisserie-style; snacks and light dishes. The set lunches of freshly prepared salads with crab or duck or home-made pizza and quiche include fruit juice or melon as appetisers with ice-cream or cheese and biscuits for dessert. The bistro atmosphere is enhanced in the evening with white tablecloths and candles. In addition, the Family Wine Bar serves light dinners, similar in choice to the daytime menu.

P

PORLOCK WEIR
Somerset
Map **3** SS84

The Pantry Cottage Hotel and Restaurant ☎ (0643) 862749
Open: Mon–Sun 12noon–6pm

This attractive buttery, whose entrance is located by the Cottage Hotel garden, serves a good selection of meals and snacks throughout the day. A satisfying three-course meal can be had for a price well within our budget. For starters you could choose prawn cocktail or home-made chicken liver pâté served with French bread, and a main course of home-made cottage pie with garden peas; for dessert try the fruit salad with cream.

C P

PORT GAVERNE
Cornwall
Map **2** SX08

Port Gaverne Hotel★★
☎ (020888) 244
Open: Summer Mon–Sat 12noon–2.15pm, 6–10pm, Sun 12noon–1.45pm, 7–10pm, Winter Mon–Sat 6–10pm, Sun 12noon–1.45pm, 7–10pm

This 17th-century restored inn nestles in a sheltered Cornish cove. Its interior is full of charm and character and the staff are friendly and welcoming. An appetising range of home-made dishes are on offer including crab soup, Cornish fish pie, steak and kidney pie and gammon. There is also a selection of bar snacks and half-portions are available for children.

C P

PORTISHEAD
Avon
Map **3** ST47

The Peppermill Restaurant 3 The Precinct ☎ (0272) 847407
Open: Mon–Thu 9.30am–3pm, Fri–Sat 9.30am–10.30pm

Enterprising female proprietors occasionally give cookery demonstrations at this bright, clean restaurant in Portishead's town-centre precinct, and the results of their endeavours go on sale to the public. At mid-day a business lunch is available along with grills, omelettes and other dishes. There is a good variety of home-made sweets. A lunch and dinner 'speciality' three-course meal is over our limit.

[C] [P] [S] **VS**

PORTPATRICK
Dumfries & Galloway *Wigtownshire*
Map **10** NX05

The Old Mill House ☎ (077681) 358
Open: Apr–Oct Mon–Sun 10.30am–11pm

This picturesque, whitewashed old mill house, set amid beautiful gardens complete with trout steam and heated outdoor pool, ground its last barley in 1929 and the miller is said to haunt the premises still. Food includes a table d'hôte menu of good British fare, or try Galloway steak with chips and salad and a sweet which is available all day. The dinner menu includes local steaks and salmon. High teas vary in price according to the main dish chosen and there is a good range of hot and cold dishes (including a special children's meal) on the bar menu.

[P]

Crown Hotel ☎ (077681) 409
Open: Mon–Sun 12noon–2pm, 6–10pm

Walk through the bars of this harbour-front hotel to a room at the back where the coffee house is decorated in art nouveau 1920s style, with oval tables and willow chairs. At the far end is a lovely small conservatory area with doors leading out into the garden. Service is informal and the food is excellent. A typical three-course meal could consist of hearty soup, beef hot pot and profiteroles. The restaurant also offers a selection of toasted sandwiches or Danish open sandwiches on brown bread.

[P] [S]

PORTSCATHO
Cornwall
Map **2** SW83

Smugglers Cottage of Tolverne King Harry Ferry, Roseland Peninsula
☎ (087258) 309
Open: May–Oct Mon–Sun 12noon–2pm, 3–5.30pm, 7.30–10pm

Sailing and boating enthusiasts can drop anchor and pop in to sample the delicious home-made cuisine offered by Elizabeth and Peter Newman at this picturesque thatched cottage nestling close to King Harry's Ferry. Part of the cottage and the beach were used by the Americans in the preparation and planning of D-Day in the last war. At lunch-time there's an attractive cold buffet of home-produced quiches, fish mousses and meats, accompanied by original fresh salads. Barbecue evenings at the Boathouse Bar-B-Q are ideal for the children. Informal suppers are superb value. Starters include stockpot soup or smoked trout. For your main course your selection could be savoury pancakes or a casserole. Gooseberry fool or apple pie are a couple of the tempting desserts.

[P]

PORTSMOUTH AND SOUTHSEA
Hampshire
Map **4** SZ69

The Hungry One 15 Arundel Way, Arundel St ☎ (0705) 817114
Open: Mon–Sat 9.30am–5pm

For the very best kind of snack bar, in clean, comfortable, purpose-built surroundings, try Michael See's Hungry One. Fresh salads are a speciality of the house and the varieties range from Cheddar cheese to red salmon. There is a good selection of substantial snacks including chicken and chips, and a range of delicious desserts. No alcohol, but finish with the locally-esteemed coffee with fresh cream.

[♫] [P] [S]

POYNTON
Gt Manchester
Map **7** SJ98

Herbs 43 Park La ☎ (0625) 876666
Open: Mon–Sat 12noon–3pm (last orders 2pm), 7pm onwards (last orders 10pm) Sun 12noon–2pm

Outside this small, elegant restaurant Mr Frank Thornley, the proprietor, has created an attractive paved garden with raised beds containing small plants. The entrance door is especially wide, and with no steps to negotiate there is easy access for the disabled (there is also a unisex toilet suitable for the disabled in the restaurant). The lunch menu offers a good choice of dishes and is changed daily. The à la carte menu is more expensive. Real ale is available at the bar.

[C] [♫] [P]

PRESTBURY
Cheshire
Map **7** SJ97

Prestbury Place New Rd
☎ (0625) 828423 and 828156
Open: Tue–Sat 7.30–10pm

Built at the end of a row of 17th-century cottages, this 'home from home' is friendly, relaxed and informal with a simple green décor. The menu, chalked up on a blackboard, includes smoked trout and salad, game pie, salad and jacket potato, Alabama chili or chicken on rice and an excellent hot chocolate fudge cake. Early evening reservations are taken.

[P] **VS**

PRESTON
Lancashire
Map **7** SD52

Alexanders Winckley St
☎ (0772) 54302
Open: Mon–Fri 12noon–2.30pm, 7–10pm

Originally a 19th-century coach house and stable, this elegant building is set in a courtyard in the centre of town. A sumptuous atmosphere is created inside with fawn and burgundy suede-look wall covering, dark-wood panels and 'picture' mirrors, and the whole effect is enhanced by subtle lighting from mock-Victorian wall lamps. The very good table d'hôte menu is changed twice weekly and offers superior main courses such as chicken Americaine and grilled gammon with mushrooms. An ambitious selection of dishes appear on the à la carte menu which is rather more expensive – but very tempting.

[C] [♫] [P] [S]

La Bodega 21 Cannon St
☎ (0772) 52159
Open: Mon–Sat 11am–2pm, Tue–Thu 7–10.30pm, Fri & Sat 7–11.30pm

Upturned barrels as tables, wine posters and gingham tablecloths exude a Continental air echoed in the names of dishes such as paella and chicken Basque style. Steak forms the basis of most dishes on the menu, try the Drunken Bull – sozzled in red wine and brandy. Lunchtimes are self-service.

[P] [S] **VS**

The Danish Kitchen, The Barbecue and the Coffee Shop 10 Lune St
☎ (0772) 22086
Open: The Danish Kitchen Mon–Sat 9.15am–5.15pm
The Barbecue Mon–Sat 12noon–3pm, 6–11pm
The Coffee Shop Mon–Sat 11am–5.30pm

Bright and refreshing, this town centre Danish Kitchen is gaining in popularity with business people and shoppers, with its choice of eating styles. Upstairs is the budget self-service operation where Danish open sandwiches, salads, omelettes and a hot dish of the day are available. Downstairs is the Barbecue, where you choose your own steak from a refrigerated display, then see it cooked over charcoal while waitresses serve you with a starter. Chops, burgers, chicken, kebabs and trout are also on the menu. Pine tables and beams accentuate the fresh, Continental atmosphere. The

Coffee Shop has a Laura Ashley look with waitress service and offers coffee, quiches, snacks and a wide variety of home-made cakes. All three restaurants are licensed.

[P] [S] **VS**

French Bistro✕ Miller Arcade, Church St ☎ (0772) 53882
Open: Mon–Sat 12noon–2.15pm, 7pm–12.15am, Sun 7pm–12.15am

This small intimate Bistro has two bars. At lunch-time chili con carne, beef bordelaise and various salads are available. In the evening the table d'hôte and à la carte menus offer a range of dishes.

[C] [♫] [P] [S]

The Patio, Trafalgar Hotel☆☆☆
Preston New Rd, Samlesbury
☎ (077477) 351
On A59 E of Preston at junction with Blackburn road
Open: Mon–Fri 12noon–2.30pm, 6.30–10.30pm. Sat 12noon–2.30pm, 6–11pm, Sun 12noon–11pm

The nostalgic French design of the menu, the costumed waitresses, and the opportunity to eat all day long sets the scene. Tiled floors and glass-topped tables, potted plants and a fountain makes a refreshing environment. The menu offers a variety of dishes including crêpes, omelettes, meat and fish dishes and salads. Home-made soup followed by beef in ale with an Italian Ice for dessert makes a satisfying three-course meal.

[C] [P] [♧]

The Tickled Trout☆☆☆
☎ (077477) 671
Open: Kingfisher Restaurant Mon–Sun 12noon–2.15pm, 7–10.15pm

The oak-beamed Kingfisher Restaurant with its alcoves, antiques and views of the River Ribble offers a table d'hôte, three-course lunch and a hot or cold buffet. The à la carte menu is beyond our means.

[C] [P] [♧] **VS**

PRESTWICK
Strathclyde *Ayrshire*
Map **10** NS32

Taj-Indian 141 Main St ☎ (0292) 79464
Open: Mon–Sat 12noon–3pm, 5pm–1am, Sun 5pm–1am

This popular Indian restaurant in Prestwick's main shopping street offers an excellent value three-course businessman's lunch and an à la carte menu. The Tandoori dishes are highly recommended and are available as starters and main courses. Taj specialities include Biryanies and a range of curries.

[C] [♫] [S] [♧]

PRINCETOWN
Devon
Map **2** SX57

Fox Tor Two Bridges Rd
☎ (082289) 238
Open: Apr–Oct: Mon–Fri, Sun 9.30am–5.30pm, later times by arrangement

Just a little more than a stone's throw from the famous Dartmoor prison, this licensed restaurant specialises in fresh, home-made fare ranging from scones and Devon cream to full three-course meals. Appetisers include egg mayonnaise or soup of the day with home-made bread. For your main course you can enjoy sirloin steak with mushrooms, tomatoes, peas and buttered new potatoes. Sweets such as fruit tart or Devonshire junket are served with cream.

[P] [♧]

RALEGH'S CROSS
Somerset
Map **3** ST03

Ralegh's Cross Inn Brendon Hills, Watchet ☎ (0984) 40343
Open: Summer Mon–Sat 10.30am–11pm, Sun 11am–10.30pm

This old Exmoor inn has one large bar which serves a variety of snacks and light meals including curries, venison sausages and chips and smoked mackerel salad. The cold carvery, though tempting, is a little over our limit.

[C] [P] [♧]

READING
Berkshire
Map **4** SU77

Beadles Wine Bar 83 Broad St
☎ (0734) 53162
Open: Mon–Sat 10.30am–2.30pm, 5.30–10.30pm

This popular basement wine bar is situated on the one-time site of Simmonds Brewery and the original globe lights are still a splendid feature. An interesting selection of food includes 'snacks for the peckish or starters for the starving' such as pâté with hot garlic bread and a side salad. Main courses served with salad could be roast beef, turkey, chicken, dressed crab or prawns, depending on their availability or a hot dish such as Taunton pork, served with green beans and sauté potatoes. Delicious home-made sweets follow.

[♫] [S]

The George Hotel★★ King St
☎ (0734) 53445
Open: Mon–Sun 12noon–2.30pm, 6–11.30pm, Sun 7–11pm

The historic, timbered George Hotel complete with cobbled courtyard and stagecoach has obscure origins, but appears in a rent roll dated 1578. Today it boasts two steak bars of distinctive character and an extensive hot and cold snack bar. Rump steak, fish or chicken can be followed by Dutch apple pie or cheesecake.

[C] [♫] [P] [S] [♧]

Heelas Restaurant Broad St
☎ (0734) 55955
Open: Tue–Sat 9.30am–5pm, 6.30pm Thu, 5.30pm Sat

Still a haven in one of Reading's most popular department stores, Heelas' licensed restaurant offers a relaxing break from the hustle of a busy day's shopping. Predominantly green and white décor with lots of leafy green plants is complemented by the classy contemporary prints which line the walls. Smart waitresses provide swift service and the food tastes all the better for being served on modern Wedgwood bone china. There are meals to suit everyone, from a half portion of fish and chips for children and a Danish open sandwich, piled high with meat or cheese and salad, for the weight-conscious to the Chef's choice roast beef and Yorkshire pudding.

[P] [S] [♧]

Mama Mia 11 St Mary's Butts
☎ (0734) 581357
Open: Mon–Fri 12noon–2.30pm, 6–9.30pm, Fri 10pm, Sat 12noon–10pm

The trattoria Mama Mia serves only Italian food and wines in an almost operatic setting of rough-cast, white-painted walls, crowned by rafters hung with clusters of Chianti bottles and strings of onions and other vegetables. Home-made soups, pastas and pizzas offer excellent value, although weight-watchers are advised to resist the entrées.

[C] [♫] [P] [S] [♧]

See advertisement on page 158

Sweeney and Todd 10 Castle St
☎ (0734) 586466
Open: Mon–Sat 11am–3pm, 5.30–10.30pm, Fri–Sat 11pm

Through the Victorian pie shop, up sawdust-strewn steps, is this small saloon-type restaurant, with church-pew seating, copper curtain-rails and gilt globe lighting. Meals are also served below in the cellars. Lunchtime specials such as roast suckling pig with fresh vegetables are popular. Imaginative home-made pies include steak and oyster, kidney and fennel and poachers (mixed game). 'Vicars' lunches consist of a plate of cold meat with French bread, pickles and salad. Home-made treacle tart, apple pie and crumble and fresh fruit with cream are some of the home-made desserts on offer.

[P] [S] [♧]

REDBOURN
Hertfordshire
Map **4** TL11

Aubrey Park Hotel☆☆☆ Hemel Hempstead Rd, Redbourn, St Albans
☎ (058285) 2105

Open: Ostler's Room Sun–Sat 12.30–2pm, 7–10pm, Sat 7–10.30pm

The warmly-glowing Ostler's Room, with its glazed brickwork and low-beamed ceilings, is dedicated to the serving of traditional English dishes in an atmosphere of medieval jollity. A wholesome two-course meal can be picked from a choice of country vegetable broth or onion flan followed by Angler's Pie, pork loin chops baked with cider and apples and finishing with pastries and puddings from the cook's pantry.

[C] [♫] [P]

REDHILL
Surrey
Map **4** TQ25

Crocks 33 High St ☎ (0737) 61177
Open: Summer: Mon–Thu 11am–2.30pm, 5.30–10.30pm, Fri & Sat 11am–2.30pm, 5.30–11pm, Sun 12noon–2pm, 7–10.30pm; Winter: 10am–4.30pm

Green awnings and a stylish interior distinguish this recently modernised eating place where quality and comfort are ensured. The same high quality applies to the food which, although simple, is all fresh and home cooked. The menu changes daily, but might include beef and mushroom hot-pot, cottage pie or sweet and sour pork. Bar snacks include ploughman's, salads and jacket potatoes while the desserts consist mainly of luxury concoctions of ice cream with sauces and trimmings.

[S] [P]

REDRUTH
Cornwall
Map **2** SW74

Penventon Hotel★★★ West End
☎ (0209) 214141
Open: Mon–Sun 12noon–2pm, 7–9.30pm

This haven just off the A30 is set in 11 acres with ample parking. Lunch is available in the 'Top Bar' which has a range of bar snacks and the hotel restaurant which provides three-course meals. The bar snacks range from sandwiches to fresh Newlyn crab Thermidor with roll and salad. In the summer the restaurant provides a three-course lunch with coffee and petits fours, and there is a free glass of wine (there is a charge for the wine in the winter). In the evening the small cellar bistro provides starters, a choice of seven main courses, curry, steak and fish dishes, and a range of sweets.

[C] [♫] [P]

REIGATE
Surrey
Map **4** TQ25

Cobbles Wine Bar Brewery Yard, Bell St
☎ (07372) 44833
Open: Mon–Sat 12noon–3pm, 7–11pm. Closed Sun

You may have to look hard to find this small wine bar, tucked away in an alley off the High Street, but you'll be glad you made the effort. Good farmhouse home-cooked dishes are brought in fresh each day and might include beef carbonnade, chicken supreme, and steak and kidney pie. A good selection of home-made desserts will round off a hearty meal. Real ale is available.

[C] [P]

Home Maid 10 Church St
☎ (07372) 48806
Open: Mon–Sat 6.45am–6pm, Sun 10am–3pm

As the name suggests, the atmosphere is homely, the food simple. The staff have a warmth and courtesy that is almost old-fashioned. Black beams offset cool white walls and checked tablecloths. Two three-course lunch menus, served from 11.30am, are of the grill, roast or fried variety, with fresh vegetables when available. Traditional puds follow, including steamed sponges and rice pudding. Individually-priced grills and snacks are also available throughout the day, giving a café-style service, although Home Maid is licensed.

New Hong Kong 27 Bell St
☎ (07372) 43374
Open: Sun–Fri 12noon–2pm, 5.30–11.30pm, Sat 12noon–mdnt

Skilful fresh cooking and attentive service are the hallmarks of this family-run Chinese restaurant. The restaurant is modern and spacious, with a small foyer bar lounge and there is also a take-away service. As usual with a Chinese restaurant there is an extensive à la carte menu on which few of the dishes would exceed our limit and of the chef's specialities Rice paper wrapped chicken or squids with green pepper and black bean sauce are particularly good value. There is also an excellent three-course special luncheon at a very reasonable price.

C S P

RENFREW
Strathclyde *Renfrewshire*
Map **11** NS56

The Armoury Restaurant, Stakis Normandy Hotel, Inchinnan Rd
☎ 041-886 4100
Open: Mon–Sun 10am–10.30pm

Another of the Stakis steakhouses, but there's not the olde worlde décor here that you'd expect. This is very much an up-to-date restaurant, featuring a circular wood ceiling with ultra-modern lighting. Still, as a contrast, the armoury itself has several medieval wall-hangings and drawings. Starter choices here are country pâté, prawn cocktail, farmhouse broth or fruit juice, and are included in the price of thę main course. Most of the favourites are on the menu, such as gammon steak, half-chicken and fillet of haddock with a good range of desserts to follow. There's a very good deal for children, too. Soup, a choice of three main courses with ice cream and strawberry sauce to follow, plus a fizzy drink, all at a very reasonable price.

C P **VS**

RICHMOND
North Yorkshire
Map **7** NZ10

The Black Lion Hotel Finkle St
☎ (0748) 3121
Open: Mon–Sun 12noon–2pm, 7–9.30pm

Once a coaching inn, this quaint 17th century building has a restaurant on the first floor with a low, beamed ceiling, white décor, wheelback chairs and 19th century prints. Meals are honest-to-goodness English fare, well-prepared, pleasantly served and excellent value. A typical lunch could be soup followed by roast beef or steak and kidney pie with apple pie as dessert. The dinner menu has Beef Wellington and noisette of lamb as main course dishes, but is priced a little over our limit.

RICHMOND-UPON-THAMES
Gt London

Mrs Beeton's 58 Hill Rise
☎ 01-940 9561 London Plan 4 **104** D2
Open: Mon–Sun 10am–5.30pm, Wed–Sun 6.30pm–12mdnt (Closed Sun evening in winter)

This village-style restaurant has a craft shop in the basement selling local crafts and kitchen items. The informal restaurant is run by a co-operative of women who are each allocated to a day to prepare and serve the food, which is home-made and excellent value for money. Starters include minted cucumber soup or liver pâté with toast. Cheese and courgette quiche with a salad, fricassée of chicken and mushrooms with rice or lasagne are popular main courses. A huge choice of desserts includes a very light chocolate layer cake.

S

RICKINGHALL
Suffolk
Map **5** TM07

Hamblyn House ☎ (037 989) 292
Open: Tue-Sat 12noon–2pm, 7–10pm, Sun 12noon–2pm

This delightful beamed restaurant forms part of a fine 16th century proprerty. Imaginative meals, from bar snacks, through to the elaborate à la carte, are enhanced by fresh vegetables grown in the garden and prepared by chef Keith. A typical bar snack would be small Dover soles with chips and salad or steak and kidney pie with potatoes and two veg. A three-course table d'hôte menu is available and there are children's meals. The à la carte menu offers a good choice but the prices are over our limit.

C P

RICKMANSWORTH
Hertfordshire
Map **4** TQ09

The Chequers Restaurant 21 Church St
☎ (0923) 72287
Open: Mon–Sun 12noon–2pm, 7–10.30pm

The Chequers Restaurant, built in 1580, is the oldest building in this old town. Another Four Pillars Group venture, the menu and prices are comparable with those at the Pinner restaurant, though during any particular week the actual dishes available are different. There is a separate, more expensive steak menu. A table d'hôte lunch is available at a very reasonable price.

C

RINGWOOD
Hampshire
Map **4** SU10

Peppercorns Restaurant 9 Meeting House La ☎ (04254) 78364
Open: Tue–Thu 10am–2.30pm, Fri–Sat 10am–2.30pm, 7.30–9.30pm, Sun 12noon–2pm

Hanging flower baskets, bright against the whitewashes walls, pick out Peppercorns. Exposed beams and hunting prints create a relaxed cottage atmosphere, enhanced by displays of fresh flowers. At lunchtime you can choose from a variety of roasts or fish dishes, a daily special such as cottage pie or try the Cold Buffet. An à la carte menu on Friday and Saturday evenings offers a good range of dishes, but you will have to take care to stay within the budget. Sunday lunch is a special feature, with a choice of four starters, two roasts or fish, two hot sweets or a selection of desserts (it is adviseable to book in advance). Home cooking with the maximum use of fresh vegetables is a speciality.

[P] [S]

RISCA
Gwent
Map **3** ST29

Michael's 39–41 Tredegar St
☎ (0633) 614300
Open: Tue–Sat 9.30am–4pm, 7.30pm–12mdnt, Sun 12noon–2pm

The restaurant seats about 50 people and also has a snack bar. Two- and three-course lunches are available, but the evening 'Chef's Specials' and the extensive à la carte menu are generally outside the scope of this guide.

[C] [P] [S]

ROCHDALE
Gt Manchester
Map **7** SD91

Mario's Pizzeria 115 Yorkshire St
☎ (0706) 46286
Open: Mon–Sat 12noon–2.30pm, 6–11.30pm

Mario Andreotti and his English wife make their cellar pizzeria a warm, welcoming haven for the hungry. Gingham tablecloths, padded benches and plain white rough-cast walls help to give the place a simple charm which compensates for the fairly predictable menu of pizzas and pastas. The most expensive dish – a sirloin steak cooked in Chianti – may exceed the budget when ordered with a starter or sweet but you should be able to enjoy a three-course meal if you stick to the modest Italian fare.

ROLLESTON ON DOVE
Staffordshire
Map **8** SK22

The Brookhouse Inn★★ Brookside
☎ (0283) 814188
Open: Mon–Fri 12.30–2pm, 7.30–10pm, Sat 7.30–10pm. Closed Sun

This Grade II listed building, originally a farmhouse, dates from the 17th century and has been tastefully converted into a fine country hotel. Oak beams, antiques, polished brass and copper and lots of fresh flowers create an atmosphere which demands good food. Unfortunately an à la carte dinner would exceed our limit but the table d'hôte luncheon is very good value. This might consist of smoked mackerel with gooseberry sauce or egg mayonnaise followed by medallions of pork fillet à la creme or grilled fillet of trout almondine, a sweet from the trolley or cheese and buscuits – all within our price limit.

[C] [P]

ROSS-ON-WYE
Hereford & Worcester
Map **3** SO62

The Old Pheasant 52 Edde Cross St
☎ (0989) 65751
Open: Easter–Sept: Mon–Tue, Thu–Sat 10.30am–5pm, Sun 2–5.30pm

Step into this brightly painted cottage-style restaurant and enjoy a snack or lunch, personally prepared by Meryl Taylor. Many of her recipes have been gleaned from her Welsh forbears, for example, chocolate orange drizzle cake and rice cake. At lunchtime there is a small choice of home-made hot meals, including steak pie, chicken, mushroom and ham pie, served with new potatoes and two fresh vegetables and a range of salads.

[P]

RUGBY
Warwickshire
Map **4** SP57

The Carlton Hotel Railway Ter
☎ (0788) 3076
Open: Mon–Fri & Sun 12noon–2pm, Mon–Sat 7–10pm

This brightly painted hotel, close to the railway station and the town centre, has a small licensed restaurant which offers a three-course luncheon. There is a choice of six starters including smoked mackerel and asparagus omelette. Main courses include a roast, steak, kidney and mushroom pie and a Punjab dish prepared by Mrs Singh who runs the hotel with her husband. The evening meal just exceeds the budget and there is also an à la carte menu.

[P] [C]

RYE
East Sussex
Map **5** TQ92

The Peacock Wine Bar Lion St
☎ (0797) 223161
Open: Summer Mon–Sat 11.30am–2.30pm, 6.30–11pm, Sun 12noon–2pm, 7–10.30pm; Winter: as above except Sun–Thu evenings, opening hours for these days to be displayed at Wine Bar

This period, cottage-style restaurant/wine bar has a small separate bar and is under the personal supervision of the owner, Jane Edgar, who does most of the cooking. For starters, try the excellent home-made soup or the pâté. Light snacks are available but for those wanting something more substantial, home-made steak and kidney pie, pork and turkey pie, moussaka and chili con carne are all reasonably priced. There is a good range of desserts and for a small charge you can have all the freshly-made coffee you can drink.

[C] [P]

SAFFRON WALDEN
Essex
Map **5** TL53

Eight Bells Bridge St
☎ (0799) 22790/22764

Open: Restaurant Tue–Sun 12.30–2pm, Mon–Thu 7.30–9.30pm, Fri–Sat 7–10pm; bar food normal licensing hours

Situated in a comfortable spot on the edge of town, like the noble old sentinel it is, this 400-year-old inn retains its original pub sign and a good deal of olde worlde charm. The table d'hôte lunch menu is of an extremely high standard and includes a main course of roast ribs of beef carved from a silver trolley, you can keep within the budget if you forego a sweet. There is also a selection of hot and cold meals available in the bar including steak and oyster pie and a quarter honey-roast duckling. The à la carte menu is beyond the scope of this guide.

[C] [P] [🍷] **VS**

ST ALBANS
Hertfordshire
Map **4** TL10

Aspelia 17 Heritage Close
☎ (0727) 66067
Open: Mon–Sat 12noon–2.30pm, 6.30–10.30pm. Closed Sun, Christmas Day and Boxing Day

This comfortable basement wine bar, off the Cathedral gardens, has an intersting décor and an interesting array of food. Start with houmous or perhaps Tzatsiki (yoghurt, cucumber and garlic) before sampling such main courses as squid in red wine sauce, Stifado or kebabs. There should still be room within our budget to sample a Greek dessert such as Baklava (pastry with almonds and syrup) or Kataifi – described on the menu as 'like shredded wheat with nuts and honey.' Some English dishes are available too.

[C] [♫] [S] [P]

Black Lion Hotel Fishpool St, St Michaels Village ☎ (0727) 51786/64916
Open: Mon–Fri 12noon–2pm, 7–10pm, Sat 12noon–2pm, 7–10.30pm, Sun 12noon–2.30pm

Modernisation has not stripped the interior of its character and old beams and brickwork abound. In the bar an impressive cold buffet is on display and hot dishes include chicken Provençale and turkey and mushroom vol-au-vents. A table d'hôte menu in the restaurant is priced by the main dish – lamb sweetbreads with banana is just one option. Appetisers include corn on the cob, ham and cottage cheese coronet and a selection of home-made soups. Choice from the sweet trolley is good.

[C] [P] [🍷]

Scotts 30 London Rd ☎ (0727) 30385
Open: Mon–Sat 12noon–3pm, 7–11pm. Closed Sun

Converted from a shop, this wine bar has a large basement restaurant with a colourful décor, large mirrors and prints and lots of plants. The menu includes a good range of starters such as taramasalata with pitta bread, pâté or smoked salmon which can be followed by one of the many varieties of char-grilled burgers or a 'dish of the day' from the blackboard.

[♫] [P]

Tudor Tavern 28 George St
☎ (0727) 53233
Open: Mon–Sun 12noon–2.30pm, 6–11pm

The special thing about Berni is that it restores and preserves some of this country's most attractive old buildings. The Tudor Tavern is the oldest complete half-timbered building in the ancient city of St Albans. All main-dish prices here include roll and butter, and ice cream or cheese and biscuits to follow, so an 8oz rump steak with chips, tomato and peas is just in our price range.

[C] [♫] [P] [S] [🍷]

ST ANDREWS
Fife *Fife*
Map **12** NO51

Pepita's 11–13 Crails La
☎ (0334) 74084
Open: Mon–Sat 10am–4.45pm, 5.30–11pm, Sun 11.30am–4.45pm, 5.30–10pm

Stone-built cottages built in 1699, have been tastefully converted into a restaurant, situated in a narrow, paved lane in the centre of St Andrews, surrounded by ancient buildings. Start your meal with home-made soup, follow up with seafood risotto, beef in a paprika, cream and red wine sauce with rice, or lasagne, and finish with one of a wide variety of sweets and you should still have change from a £5 note.

[🍷]

The Pancake Place 177–179 South St
☎ (0334) 75671
Open: Mon–Sat 10am–5.30pm, in Jul & Aug, 8am–9pm, Sun 11am–5.30pm

The interior of this attractive speciality restaurant is surprisingly rural, with a beamed ceiling, natural stone and white-painted plaster walls. Pancakes may be sampled as a starter, main course or dessert. Start with soup of the day or a savoury pancake such as ham and peach or haddock Mornay. For a main course you could choose a Rockey Mountain burger. A range of salads is also available including chicken, ham, cheese and egg. There is a choice of a dozen sweet pancakes.

[♫] [P] [S] **VS**

ST ANNES
Lancashire – see LYTHAM ST ANNES

ST AUSTELL
Cornwall
Map **2** SX05

Hicks Wine Bar Church St
☎ (0726) 4833
Open: Mon-Sat 11am–2.30pm

The Tudor frontage of Hicks gives way to a small, intimate wine bar of simple design with wooden tables and stools, and wine racks against the walls. Food is attractively displayed at one end of the bar and dishes can be chosen from a blackboard menu. Main meals are served with a selection of three salads such as curried rice or tomato, cucumber and onion, and an apple and celery mixture. These accompany various salamis, home-made quiche, gala pie or chef's home-made pâté. There is a range of tasty hot dishes such as cottage pie and chicken and ham pie. For dessert choose from Stilton, apple and biscuits, gâteau or cheesecake.

Pier House Hotel★★ Harbour Front, Charlestown ☎ (0726) 5272
Open: Summer Mon–Sun 8–10pm

The Pier House Hotel, magnificently located right at the harbour's edge at the picturesque Georgian village of Charlestown, is well worth a visit though you must choose your dishes with care to keep within budget. The small harbour still exports china clay, and from the split-level restaurant of the charming, period hotel, adorned with masts, riggings and other nautical relics, one can view the complex manoeuvring of ships, laden with china clay, in the outer basin of the tiny docks. À la carte dinner offers good choices of French and English cuisine, such as Charlestown smoked mackerel, followed by fresh local sole or râgout of seafood, rounded off with fresh strawberries or crème caramel, or a good choice of cheeses. Fresh seafood salads are also available.

 [P]

ST HELIER
Jersey *Channel Islands*
Map **16**

La Bastille Taverne 4 Wharf St
☎ (0534) 74059
Open: Mon–Fri 10am–5pm, Sat 10am–3pm. Closed Sun

This small, bustling cellar-style wine bar is very popular with the locals – always an indication of good food. Service is pleasant and informal and Mr Moreira, the proprietor, is always available to ensure satisfaction. The food is generally based on salads – fish, meats and delicious home-made pies. There are no sweets but the cheese basket has a selection of good continental cheeses.

[P]

The Tavern Carvery and Le Pommier Coffee Shop Pomme d'Orr Hotel★★★
The Esplanade ☎ (0534) 78644
Open: Carvery Mon-Sat 12noon–2.30pm. Closed Sun; Coffee Shop Mon–Sun 7am–10.30pm

The Tavern Carvery is situated on the lower ground floor of this large modern hotel. Excellent lunches are available with a choice of the cold buffet, two roasts and daily specials which are chalked on the blackboard. There is a range of starters and cold sweets. The attractive and popular Coffee Shop offers snacks, main courses such as steak, mixed grill, fish dishes and salads – including excellent lobster and smoked salmon salads.

[C] [P] [🍷]

ST MICHAELS-ON-WYRE
Lancashire
Map **7** SD44

The Cherry Tree Grill Garstang Rd
☎ (09958) 661
Open: Mon–Thu 12noon–8pm (last orders), Sat 12noon–9pm (last orders), Sun 12noon–6pm (last orders)

This stone-built end-of-terrace house was once the village smithy and is now a small but pleasant grill restaurant. The three-course lunch is all-inclusive for the price of the main course. A more extensive à la carte menu is available for high tea though sirloin steak and scampi are just over our limit. To finish there is a tempting array of desserts – how about raspberry Pavlova or coupe Jamaica?

[P] [🍷]

ST PETER PORT
Guernsey *Channel Islands*
Map **16**

Ulla's Kitchen 2 Mill St ☎ (0481) 23730
Open: Mon 11am–5pm, Tue–Sat 11am–4.30pm, 6.30–10pm. Closed Sun and Feb

Ulla's Kitchen, situated on the first floor in a shopping area and facing the market, is a combined restaurant, coffee shop and patisserie. There is a display of mouthwatering pastries, cheesecakes, flans, etc., at the entrance of the restaurant all prepared by the proprietor Richard Deutschmann whose efforts have earned him major awards in the island's Culinary Festival. The menu lists Danish open sandwiches, a range of starters and snacks including Gravard Lax (salmon marinated the Scandinavian way) and main courses such as beef curry Creole style.

[C] [P] [🍷]

SALEN
Isle of Mull, Strathclyde *Argyll*
Map **10** NM54

The Puffer Aground✕✕ Aros
☎ (06803) 389
Open: Easter–mid May Tue-Sat 12.30–2.30pm, 6.30–9pm, mid May–mid Oct Mon–Sun 12.30–2.30pm, 6.30–9pm, mid Nov–mid Jan, Fri–Sat (reservations only)

No need to find your sea-legs on this ship, though you may have doubts, as the restaurant's design is strikingly based on that of a Clyde 'Puffer', and maritime paintings line the walls. The restaurant shares its home in a row of converted roadside cottages with a craft shop. Excellent use is made of fresh local produce and as far as possible, each meal is individually prepared. Fisherman's pancake or shellfish soup with brandy and cream live side by side with more conventional, and cheaper starters. Home-made pies, casseroles and salads can be followed by sweets such as baked sponge or fresh peach and cream roll. Service is simple but very friendly.

[P] [🍷]

SALISBURY
Wiltshire
Map **4** SU12

The Greyfisher Ayleswade Rd
☎ (0722) 27511
Open: Mon–Sun 10am–2.30pm, 6–10.30pm

Once a very small pub, The Greyfisher has been turned, like the ugly duckling, from a coot into a heron. Wooden beams and bare brickwork give this three-year-old inn, hard by both cathedral and shops, a character which merges well into the rest of Salisbury. There is a wide range of dishes, from a good home-made steak and kidney pie, beef or chicken curry and rice, to sirloin steak garni. For a snack, or a first course try Wiltshire ham, home-made soup, or prawn cocktail and for dessert, fruit pie and cream or bread pudding and cream make a worthy ending to the meal. Seating is very comfortable and the service friendly and fast.

[♫] [P] [🍷]

Harper's Upstairs Restaurant 7–9 The Market Pl ☎ (0722) 333118
Open: Mon–Sat 12noon–2.30pm, 6.30–10.30pm

Very handy for shoppers, this is a pleasant rendezvous for a quick break or a substantial lunch. Harper's offers good food at very reasonable prices and (with its children's meals offering two courses including fish fingers or beefburgers) is excellent for families. Evening dishes include casserole of beef cooked in Guinness and chicken cooked in tarragon, brandy and cream.

[C] [♫] [P] [S] [🍷] **VS**

Mainly Salads 18 Fisherton St
☎ (0722) 22134
Open: Summer: Mon–Sat 12noon–2.30pm; Winter: Mon–Sat 12noon–2pm. Closed Sun and last two weeks Sep

Proprietors Ron and June Ceresa prepare all the excellent vegetarian dishes offered here. As well as salads there are also such meatless dishes as vegetable curry with brown rice, pizza, quiche and jacket potatoes. Desserts include Dutch apple cake and pavlova. As well as being a no meat establishment there is also no alcohol and no smoking.

[P] [🍷]

Michael Snell 8 St Thomas's Sq
☎ (0722) 6037
Open: Mon–Sat 9am–5pm

No-one should go to Salisbury without trying Michael Snell's superb Black Forest gâteau. In these old, part millhouse premises, the Swiss-trained Mr Snell makes and sells his own chocolate and cakes, besides specialising in the sale of fine teas, coffees, jams, chutneys and local honey. His light lunch menu contains a great variety of dishes including smoked mackerel fillet with

carrot and coleslaw, and cheese flan or home-made pizza with salad. Children's portions are available. Appetisers include soup and a selection of torten and pastries or speciality sorbets completes a satisfying meal. Michael Snell is unlicensed. This restaurant has easy access for disabled people, with some tables on street level.

P S ♿

SAMLESBURY
Lancashire
Map **7** SD52

The Samuel Whitbread Cuerdale La
☎ (077477) 641
Open: Mon–Fri & Sun 12noon–1.30pm, Mon–Sun 6.30–9.30pm

Situated at a crossroads about half a mile from the A59 and close to junction 31 of the M6 this restaurant, built in 1560, has many interesting features including a priest hole. The à la carte lunch menu is equally interesting with spit roasted duckling and loin of pork as house specialities. Other main courses could include sirloin steak and chicken chasseur. The six-course dinner menu offers similar dishes but it is out of our price range.

C P ♿

SAMPFORD COURTNEY
Devon
Map **2** SS60

The Countryman Beacon Cross
☎ (083782) 206
5m N of Okehampton on the B3215
Open: Mon–Sat 11am–2.30pm, 7–10.30pm, 11pm Fri–Sat, Sun 12noon–2pm, 7–10.30pm

This sophisticated, unusual inn in the heart of Devon is frequented as much for its excellent bar food as for its draught beers. A two-course meal from the à la carte menu will just about come within the limit if carefully selected. A choice of ten starters, including pâté à la volaille (chicken pâté with Cognac) may be followed by one of six main fish courses, a grill, poultry, curry or home-made steak and kidney pie. Most of the home-made desserts are served with cream but an ice cream is an alternative. The cold buffet table includes a host of salads, ploughman's lunches and sandwiches.

P

SAMPFORD PEVERELL
Devon
Map **3** ST01

The Farm House Inn Leonard's Moor
☎ (0884) 820824
Open: Mon–Sat 7am–12mdnt, Sun 12noon–10.30pm

This restaurant is a conversion of two cottages and set back off the road in its own grounds. Cooking is predominantly of the wholesome English variety and all meals from breakfast through morning coffee, lunch, afternoon tea, dinner and supper are served here. At lunchtime, as well as the à la carte choice, there is a special 'dish of the day' and there is a three-course Sunday lunch, featuring traditional roast beef, in the restaurant. If you prefer a lighter meal, a cold buffet is set out in the attractive bar.

C ♫ P ♿

SANDBACH
Cheshire
Map **7** SJ76

The Old Hall Hotel Newcastle Rd
☎ (09367) 61221
Open: Mon–Fri 12.30–2pm, 7–10pm, Sat 7–10pm, Sun 12.30–2pm

Said to be one of the last genuine 'black and white' buildings to have been completed in England, the Old Hall Hotel is of great historical and architectural interest. The Jacobean Room, with its superb panelling, fireplace and priest hole, now serves as the restaurant where a good table d'hôte lunch can be enjoyed. This could consist of seafood cocktail, gammon and pineapple, fresh vegetables and a sweet from the trolley. The table d'hôte dinner and the à la carte menu both break our budget, but there are a good range of bar snacks at very reasonable prices.

C P ♿

SANDWICH
Kent
Map **5** TR36

16th Century Tea House 9 Cattle Market
☎ (0304) 612392
Open: Mon–Sun 9am–5.30pm, Sat 7–9.30pm

Set in the market square of the picturesque old town is this historic 16th century building with a quaint, beamed restaurant. A three-course lunch includes Normandy pâté with toast or hors d'oeuvres. Home-made steak and kidney pie or sweet and sour chicken with special fried rice are two of the five main courses on offer, and desserts such as chocolate nut sundae or baked lemon curd roll complete the meal. A suggested evening dish is grilled gammon steak Hawaiian style.

P S ♿

SAVERNAKE
Wiltshire
Map **4** SU26

The Savernake Forest Hotel★★
Savernake ☎ (0672) 810206
Open: Mon–Sun 12noon–2pm, Tue–Sat 7–9pm, Sun 7.30–9pm

On the fringe of the beautiful Savernake Forest, this charming old hotel specialises in home-prepared dishes. The Buttery Grill menu offers soup and mackerel fillets as starters and main courses include lasagne, chicken curry, cold meats and salads. The traditional Sunday lunch and an ambitious à la carte menu are available in the restaurant – unfortunately beyond the scope of this guide. Last orders 9pm.

C P ♿

SCUNTHORPE
Humberside
Map **8** SE81

Amina Indian Restaurant 25–27 Cole St
☎ (0724) 840823
Open: 12noon–2.30pm, 6pm–12mdnt (1am Thu, Fri & Sat)

Curry and Tandoori dishes are the speciality in this spacious restaurant where the décor is predominantly red with brass table lamps. The menu is extensive with a good variety of starters including soups, prawn cocktail and Tandoori kebab. Persian, Biriani and fish dishes are among the main courses, along with the curries, vegetables and rice dishes.

♫ P

SETTLE
North Yorkshire
Map **7** SD86

The Little House Duke St
☎ (07292) 3963
Open: Tue–Sun 12noon–2pm, 6–10.30pm (11.30pm Fri & Sat). Closed Mon except Bank Hols.

Built in 1780, The Little House has been converted into a bright clean wine bar with a collection of antique Yorkshire wooden tables and old photographs of local scenes. The accent here is on 'home-made' and its frequently changing menu might include steak and mushroom pie, cheese and onion pie, pizzas, pasta and burgers.

C ♫ ♿

SHANKLIN
Isle of Wight
Map **4** SZ58

Cliff Top Hotel★★★ Park Rd
☎ (098386) 3262/3
Open: Restaurant Mon–Sun 1–2pm, 7–9pm
Coffee Shop Mon–Sun 10am–6pm (summer only)

Cliff Tops calls itself the 'good food' hotel and takes a great pride in its English and French cuisine. The three-course table d'hôte lunch here is not expensive and dinner is reasonably priced also.

C P S

The Cottage Eastcliffe Rd
☎ (098386) 2504
Open: Mon, Tue & Thu–Sat 12noon–2pm, 7.30–9.45pm, Sun 12noon–2pm. Closed Wed and mid Feb–mid Mar

A popular, quaint restaurant built of natural stone in one of the oldest streets on the island. The table d'hôte lunch menu offers excellent value for money, with a good choice of dishes, a typical meal could be soup, roast lamb and apple pie. Grills and steaks feature on the dinner menu.

C ♫ S P

The Tudor Rose Restaurant 59 High St ☎ (098386) 2814
Open: Tue–Sun 10am–9pm

A long, mock-Tudor building originally a bakery and tea-rooms, in which proceedings are supervised by proprietor John Barrymore Simpson. Lunchtime fare consists of mainly traditional English roasts, but fresh salmon, cold meats and flans are also available, and can be followed by a choice from the sweet trolley. Starters include pâté and home-made soup.

C ♫ S ♨ **VS**

SHEFFIELD
South Yorkshire
Map **8** SK38

Ashoka 307 Ecclesall Rd
☎ (0742) 686177
Open: Mon–Thu 12noon–2pm, 6–12mdnt, Fri–Sat 12noon–2pm, 6pm–1am, Sun 12noon–2pm, 7–12mdnt

What the Ashoka lacks in ethnic décor and atmosphere it more than compensates for by the range and quality of its Indian cuisine. Main courses, all eastern variations on a theme of chicken, fish or meat, are reasonably priced. Two or more people could dine in style by sharing a selection of dishes. For that special celebration, a party of six can order a lamb massallam – a leg of lamb marinated in a rich sauce with herbs and spices, roasted and then carved at your table. It is served with ghee rice and costs around £30. But you'll have to warn the chef you are coming – he requires two days' notice if he is to prepare this masterpiece to your satisfaction. Authentic starters and sweets complete the menu.

VS

The Crosspool Tavern Manchester Rd
☎ (0742) 662113
Open: Mon–Thu 12noon–2pm, 7–10pm, Fri 12noon–2pm, 7–10.30pm, Sat 7–10.30pm. Closed Sun

Exposed stonework and carved oak woodwork are reminiscent of an ancient banqueting hall and the dark oak refectory tables and panelled cubicles add to the effect. The restaurant is run as a carvery, with starters and sweets served by waitresses, the main course carved for you by the chef. This might be roast rib of beef, an alternative roast or poultry, or the Chef's Speciality of the Day. A sweet or cheese from the trolley is included in the set price.

♫ S P

Dam House Restaurant Crookes Valley Park ☎ (0742) 661344
Open: Mon–Fri 12noon–2.30pm, Tue–Thu 7–11pm, Fri–Sat 7pm–2am

The 18th century Dam House is set in a lush green valley overlooking a boating lake. Food is predominantly Continental with some English dishes, with the traditional Yorkshire pudding with onions and gravy featuring as a starter. Main dishes on the three-course lunch menu include the tried-and-true favourites, beef and kidney hotpot and home-made steak and kidney pie. The à la carte menu and the dinner menu are outside the scope of this guide.

C ♫ P S

Edward's Restaurant 344–6 Abbeydale Rd ☎ (0742) 585194
Open: Mon–Fri 12noon–3pm, 7pm–12mdnt, Sat 7pm–12mdnt, Sun 12noon–3pm

Although this restaurant has comprehensive à la carte and table d'hôte menus, most are outside our limit and it is for the Business Lunch that we include it here. This will provide a starter of soup, pâté, melon or egg mayonnaise, followed by a main course which could be chicken, steak or fish, a pie of the day or a salad. Round it off with a sweet from the trolley and you will still remain within our limit.

C ♫ P

Gangsters 11–17 Division St
☎ (0742) 22861
Open: Mon–Thu 12noon–11.45pm, Fri 12noon–12mdnt, Sat 11.30am–12mdnt, Sun 4–11.45pm

An imaginative décor sets the Gangster scene here with mellow brown paintwork, pictures of movie gangsters and their molls, American car number plates and corrugated black iron roof rafters. Floodlighting focuses on rotating mirrors to complete the atmosphere. A huge variety of burgers and pizzas are available and a children's menu is aptly named 'Bugsy Malone'. Lots of mouthwatering desserts are on offer including ice creams, apple strudel, fudge gâteau and passion cake. A comprehensive list of beers, spirits and cocktails is available as well as wines and soft drinks.

♫ P 🍷

Nameless 16–18 Cambridge St
☎ (0742) 29751
Open: Mon–Sat 11am–12mdnt

This pizza-biased restaurant is located in the city centre and boasts an authentic Victorian atmosphere. The food, however, is bang-up-to-date with a wide variety of burgers, pizzas and other Italian dishes. Leaving aside sirloin and T-bone steak, you'll soon see that it's difficult to reach the limit – even if you sample a delicious Tia Crêpe dessert (ice cream plus Tia Maria folded into a crêpe, topped off with whipped cream). A special kiddies' meal consists of a mini pizza, ice cream and a fizzy drink.

♫ P S 🍷

Raffles Charles St ☎ (0742) 24921
Open: Mon–Sat 12noon–2.30pm

A small entrance between shops in busy, down-town Sheffield leads to this first-floor restaurant. A grotto-like staircase takes you, via goldfish tanks, to a pleasant green-ceilinged room with mood-setting floodlights. Glass-topped bamboo tables are interspersed across a green-striped carpet. Random fishing nets and glass floats set the scene for a predominantly seafood menu. Prawns, oysters, mackerel and crab are all available with side-salad, with meat salads and curries has alternatives for non-fish lovers. In the evenings there's a disco here, but the menu soars out of our range.

♫ S 🍷

Waggon and Horses Abbeydale Rd, Millhouses ☎ (0742) 361451
Open: Mon–Sun 12noon–2pm, 7–10pm

Part of the Falstaff Taverns group, this two-storey, stone-built inn overlooks a pleasant recreation area. A three-course lunch is served here daily, when you can sample a plain but wholesome range of dishes against a charming background of exposed stone walls, oak beams and wrought-iron screens. Typical choices from the menu would be soup, pâté or melon followed by rump steak, plus a sweet from the trolley. The Sunday lunch menu, offering two roast dishes and other choices is inexpensive.

C P 🍷

SHEPTON MALLET

Somerset
Map **3** ST64

King's Arms Leg Sq ☎ (0749) 3781
Open: Tue–Sat 12noon–2pm, 7–10pm, Sun and Mon 12noon–2pm

Situated in the oldest part of Shepton Mallet, the King's Arms has been a pub since 1680 and has been owned by the Showering family for some 300 years. The present tenants, Beryl and Peter Swan provide lots of good home cooking including pies, lasagne, curries and goulash. Real ales on offer include Halls Harbest Bitter, Wadworths 6X, Burton Ale and Draught Guinness.

P 🍷

SHERBORNE

Dorset
Map **3** ST61

Swan Inn Cheap St ☎ (0935) 814129
Open: Mon–Sun 12noon–2pm, 6.30–9.30pm

The Swan Lounge and Steak Bar is to be found through an archway on a pedestrian short cut, leading from the main car park close to the town centre. This quaint hostelry offers a selection of satisfying grills, including scampi and rump steak, all served with garni and French fries, peas and mixed vegetables. Grills may be supplemented with appetising starters such as pâté, whitebait, smoked salmon and prawn cocktail, and sweets such as home-made fruit pie.

C P S 🍷

SHOEBURYNESS

Essex
Map **5** TQ98

Shore House Restaurant Ness Rd
☎ (03708) 3408
Open: Mon–Sun 12noon–3pm (last orders for food 2pm), 7–11.30 (last orders for food 10pm)

If the fresh air gives you an appetite you'll find this sea-front eating place a very tempting proposition. However, the plush restaurant with its warm red décor is likely to just tip our limit in the evenings. An interesting à la carte lunch menu is available along with excellent choice of dishes. The buttery is open at lunchtime for bar snacks and salads.

C ♫ P 🍷

SHREWSBURY

Shropshire
Map **7** SJ41

Cornhouse Restaurant and Wine Bar
59A Wyle Cop ☎ (0743) 241991
Open: Mon–Sat 11.30am–2.30pm, Mon–Thu 6.30–10.30pm, Fri–Sat 6.30–11pm, Sun 7–10.30pm

This restaurant occupies the ground and first floors of a warehouse built in the mid 1800s, a few minutes walk from the town centre. Stripped pine furniture, polished floorboards, potted plants and a beautiful wrought-iron spiral staircase help to create a pleasant atmosphere. Customers may choose to eat a light meal or snack in the ground floor wine bar, or go upstairs to the restaurant for a more substantial meal. There is live music on Sunday evenings.

C ♫ P 🍷

Delany's St Julians Craft Centre for Shropshire, off Fish St ☎ (0743) 60602
Open: Mon–Sat 10am–5pm (evenings for party bookings)

A more unlikely place for a restaurant than the vestry of a church is hard to imagine, but Delany's – a vegetarian's delight – looks quite at home among the original wood panels and highly-polished boards and beams. Soups instead of sermons are the order of the day now the old church has become a restaurant and craft centre. Tasty and original dishes such as Syrian aubergine and lentil casserole and cauliflower and pea nut-crumble are served on the cheerful green-and-white clothed tables, each equipped with flowers, a pot of fresh ground rock salt, dishes of soft brown sugar and unsalted butter. The menu is not extensive but all the dishes are inexpensive so why not enjoy a glass of wine with your meal.

♫ S 🍷

The Dickens Restaurant, Lion Hotel★★★ Wyle Cop ☎ (0743) 53107
Open: Mon–Sat 12.30–2pm, 7–10pm, Sun 12.30–2pm, 7–9pm

The popular, elegant 18th-century Lion Hotel stands in the centre of Shrewsbury. Distinguished visitors have included Disraeli, Paganini and, of course, Dickens. Roast of the day, carved at the table, and including coffee is reasonably priced. The four-course table d'hôte meal, including coffee is too expensive for us.

C P S 🍷

Dun Cow Abbey Foregate
☎ (0743) 56408
Open: Mon–Sun 12noon–2pm, 6.30–10.30pm

You're not likely to find a more historic eating house than the Dun Cow, reputed to be one of the oldest pubs in England, dating from circa 1085. Thanks to the research efforts of the owners, you can read about its amazing history including the sightings of a ghost in the dress of a

Dutch cavalry officer, from the special leaflet they have produced. The dining room is more modern than the rest of the premises but an effort has been made to capture the 'olde worlde' atmosphere with exposed beams, rough plaster walls and some exposed stonework. Dishes on the interesting à la carte need careful selection as some prices will exceed our limit. Trout Sabrina – two trout dressed with almonds and lemon and kebabs are two of the main courses.

C ♫ P ♘ VS

Just Williams 62–63 Mardol
☎ (0743) 57061
Open: Mon–Sat 11am–11pm

Not far from Shrewsbury's main street is this wine bar which is undergoing a major face-lift. New additions include the Raven Real Ale Bar and a dance floor. The food includes home-made soups, salads, a range of hot dishes and snacks, and char-grilled steaks. Around 20 wines are available by the glass as well as farmhouse cider and glühwein (in the winter months).

C ♫ P S ♘

The Old Tudor Steak House Butcher Row ☎ (0743) 53117
Open: Tue–Sat 12noon–2.15pm, Tue–Fri 7–10.30pm, Sat 7–11.30pm

The Old Tudor Steak House occupies the second floor of fine 16th-century black and white timbered premises. The 'olde worlde' restaurant and bar have an authentic Tudor atmosphere which is warm and relaxing. Table d'hôte lunch is very good value. Three courses include soup of the day, a choice of eight main courses such as chicken in red wine and a sweet of the day. The à la carte menu offers Continental dishes and grills and though more expensive, with care two courses can be enjoyed for around £5.

C P S ♘

Steak and Pizza Bar 50 Mardol
☎ (0743) 4834
Open: Mon–Sat 11.30am–2.30pm, Mon–Sun 6–11pm

A large bay window and a vivid sign announce these charming little premises, ideally situated for cinemagoers, shoppers and riverbank walkers. The walls are dotted with posters of Italian landmarks and bright red and white gingham cloths cover the tables. All beefburgers and pizzas are freshly made on the premises, and represent excellent value for money. French and Italian wines feature on the wine list.

C ♘ VS

SIBSON
Leicestershire
Map **4** SK30

Millers Main Rd ☎ (0827) 880223
Open: Mon–Sat 11am–2pm, 6–10.30pm (11pm Fri & Sat) Sun 12noon–2pm, 7–10.30pm

Ray and Rita Holland have converted this early bakery into a fine country hotel which retains many original features and also has the added attraction of a working water mill. Our main interest here is the extensive range of bar meals with the emphasis on good British cooking. Steak and kidney pie, potato cake and bacon, faggots and pease pudding and soused herring are just a few of the choices on the menu. The restaurant meals are, unfortunately, outside the scope of this guide.

C P ♘

SIDCOT
Avon
Map **3** ST45

Sidcot Hotel ★★ ☎ (093484) 2271
Open: Tue 7–10pm, Wed–Sat 12.30–2pm, 7–10pm, Sun 12.30–2pm

Set high in its own grounds and overlooking the beautiful Winscombe Valley, this imposing stone-built mansion has a pleasant dining room offering excellent value three-course table d'hôte lunches and dinners to non-residents. Home cooking is the norm here, and house specialities include fresh cream pavlovas. An extensive and reasonably-priced à la carte menu also operates.

[C] [♫] [P] [&]

SIDMOUTH
Devon
Map **3** SY18

Applegarth Hotel★ Sidford
☎ (03955) 3174
Open: Mon, Wed–Sun 12.30–1.30pm, Mon–Sat 7–9.30pm

The Applegarth dates back to the 16th century when it was used as a staging post for monks who transported salt from the mines of Salcombe Regis to Exeter. The 'olde-worlde' character pervades the building to this day, not least in the restaurant with its beamed ceiling. The cuisine is always new and exciting – Barbara being a Cordon Bleu cook. For lunch, her array of dishes such as pâte Strasbourg, veau a la crème flambée and trout Applegarth will tempt the most discerning palate. More conventional dishes such as braised steak and chicken with honey and lemon sauce are available. Desserts are the responsibility of young chef Tracey, who produces tasty concoctions with the aid of fresh cream, sherry, brandy or liqueurs.

[C] [P] [S] [&]

Bowd Inn Bowd Cross ☎ (03955) 3328
On A3052 2m from Sidmouth seafront
Open: Mon–Thu 11am–2.30pm, 6–10.30pm, Fri–Sat 11am–2.30pm, 6–11pm, Sun 12noon–2pm, 7–10.30pm

Strategically placed at Bowd Cross *en route* to Sidmouth is this attractive 12th century inn, set in a welcoming shrub and flower garden. Low ceilinged, beamed bars are cosy and inviting and the choice of food is excellent. Starters such as whitebait, melon frappé or home-made soup are on offer. Main courses include home-made quiche Lorraine and crab, tongue, ham or beef platters. Fish dishes, roast duckling and steak are also available. All dishes include potaotes or French fries and salad or vegetables of the day. Home-made sweets are reasonably priced.

[P] **VS**

Tudor Rose 34 High St
Open: Mon–Sat 10.30am–2.30pm, 6–11pm (10.30pm in winter), Sun 12noon–2pm, 7–10.30pm

This charming Free House occupies a listed 17th-century building, originally the proprietors own cottage. It is full of character with its collection of copper kettles and an antique penny-farthing suspended (safely) from the ceiling. The menu is extensive, both for the restaurant and for bar snacks and includes ploughman's, lasagne, burgers, grills and fish dishes. Everything except the steak meals come within our price limit.

[C] [♫] [P] [&]

SKEGNESS
Lincolnshire
Map **9** TF56

The Copper Kettle Lumley Rd
☎ (0754) 67298
Open: Summer Mon–Sun 9.30am–10pm, Winter Mon–Sat 10am–5.30pm. Closed Jan–Feb

Set amongst the shops in one of the town's busiest streets, you could easily dismiss this brown, bow-windowed restaurant as yet another gift shop. However, once inside, you can forget the hurly-burly world of amusement arcades and trumpery, and relax in the peaceful atmosphere created by rich green carpeting with subtly contrasting white plaster and plain brick walls. Modern lights, masquerading as old-style oil lamps, hang from the ceiling at strategic points between the pine tables. The fare is limited, but will prove very good value for money. Starters include pâté and prawn pil pil, with main courses such as Somerset Pork. Desserts are home made.

[♫] [P] [S] [&] **VS**

The Vine Seacroft ☎ (0754) 3018
Open: Mon–Sun 12.30–2pm, 7–9.15pm

The Vine, a large brick-built inn dating back to 1660, stands in two acres of attractive, peaceful grounds ½ mile south of the hustle and bustle of the town centre. Tennyson was a regular customer and reputedly wrote 'Come into the Garden Maude' here. The friendly and efficient staff offer a 'value for money' table d'hôte lunch menu with main courses such as grilled gammon, a roast and liver and onions; hot and cold bar snacks and an à la carte menu to suit most appetites and pockets.

[C] [P] [&]

SKIPTON
North Yorkshire
Map **7** SD95

Herbs 10 High St ☎ (0756) 60619
Open: Mon, Wed–Sat 9.30am–5pm

This bright, clean, wholefood and vegetarian restaurant can be found above the Heathilife Natural Food Centre at the top of the High Street. Green and white décor with pine tables and chairs give the place a nice fresh feel. The menu offers good home-made dishes with a variety of salads. There are 12 different fruit and vegetable juices available and a range of desserts. Also included on the menu are 16 different herbal teas, so if you have never tried this type of tea before – here's your chance!

[P] [S] [&]

SLEAFORD
Lincolnshire
Map **8** TF04

Carre Arms Hotel★ ☎ (0529) 303156
Open: Mon–Sun 12noon–2pm, 6.30–8pm

The red-brick public house built in 1906 is on the edge of the town centre near a level crossing. The bright, well-maintained dining room offers a good selection of mainly grill and roast dishes at reasonable prices. Even if you do splash out on a steak with a starter or sweet you should still stay within the budget. Bar snacks are also available.

[C] [P] [S] [&] **VS**

SOLIHULL
West Midlands
Map **7** SP17

Bobby Brown's 183 High St
☎ 021-704 9136
Open: Mon–Sat 12noon–2.30pm, 7–11pm

Chris, Caroline and Annie are three young friends who met while working in someone else's wine bar. They decided to stay together as a team and open their own restaurant. The result of their labours is this cosy, informal place with a courtyard where spontaneous barbecues are often held. Salads, hot dishes such as Chilli Alabama and coq au vin are available along with the daily 'specials' which are listed on the blackboard. Bobby Browns is licensed.

♫ S

SOLVA
Dyfed
Map **2** SM72

Harbour House Solva ☎ (0437) 721267
Open: bar meals Mon–Sun 12noon–2pm, 6.30–9pm

The Canby-Lewis family run this small hotel with obvious enjoyment. The 'Lite Bite' menu (available in the bar and restaurant at lunchtime, bar only in the evening) offers cawl a caws, a large bowl of home-made soup served with a tasty cheese roll and butter, home-made steak and kidney pie and crispy fried apple turnover along with a range of other dishes. The house specialities are Captain's Murphy and Ham Murphy – jacket baked potatoes with a tasty filling served with salad. A children's menu is available in the restaurant at lunchtime. The à la carte and table d'hôte menus available in the restaurant in the evenings (check for opening times) are outside the scope of this guide.

P ♧ **VS**

SOUTHAMPTON
Hampshire
Map **4** SU41

Golden Palace✕ 17 Above Bar St
☎ (0703) 26636
Open: Mon–Sat 11.45am–12mdnt, Sun 12noon–12mdnt

Slap in the middle of Southampton's modern shopping area, this colourful Chinese restaurant oozes Eastern calm. Prettily decked out with coloured lanterns, tiles, high archways and pillars to give a 'palatial' effect, it is immensely popular with the local orientals, and every encouragement is given to Western diners to use chopsticks. Dishes from the Tim Sum menu such as prawns Cheung Fun or meat rolls and duck's webs (available from 12noon–5pm only) prove to be the best loved and are all reasonably priced. A two-course à la carte dinner should keep you within the budget.

C ♫ P S ♧

La Margherita 4–6 Commercial Rd
☎ (0703) 333390
Open: Mon–Sat 12noon–2.30pm, 6pm–12mdnt, (11pm Mon–Thu)

A popular nightspot, particularly with theatre and cinema folk from the nearby Gaumont, is Franco Fantini's La Margherita. 'Let's Go Marghereating' is the house motto, with a choice of starters ranging from hot garlic bread to Parma ham and melon. There are made-to-order pizzas, and main dishes such as fresh fish.

C ♫ P **VS**
See advertisement on page 170

Mister C's Park La, off Cumberland Pl (entrance along lane on the left of the Southampton Park Hotel)
☎ (0703) 332442
Open: Mon–Sat 12noon–2pm, 6.30–11pm

This lively, fun-eating place is not recommended for those with small appetites. The full range of starters from farmhouse soup to fresh prawns on shell can all be served with salads, baked potato or chips if required. The main course specialities and pies include some dishes within our price range (such as Worzels Pie or Lasagne) or choose from the daily 'specials' on a blackboard. A range of cocktails is available.

C P ♧ **VS**

Oscars 8A Commercial Rd
☎ (0703) 36383
Open: Mon–Sat 12noon–2pm, 7–11.30am. Closed Sun

A popular restaurant with 1930's Hollywood décor and appropriate background music. The extensive menu includes a range of appetizers, fish and vegetarian dishes, Oscars 'Bistro' Range (including chicken and mushroom profiteroles and real crêpes), 'Specialities' such as Lambs Kidneys Rosemary and mouthwatering sundaes and sweets. It is advisable to book in advance for dinner.

C ♫ S P ♧

Piccolo Mondo 1 36 Windsor Ter
☎ (0703) 36890
Open: Tue–Fri 10am–8pm, Sat & Mon 10am–7pm

Very handy for top-of-the-town shopping and the Hants and Dorset bus station, Salvatore La Gumina and Domenico Bibbo's Piccolo Mondo incorporates bakery and snack bar. A good cup of coffee, freshly-baked cheesecakes and cream cakes, and freshly-cut sandwiches are available. Hot snacks include home-made lasagne alla Romana and the cooked-to-order pizzas.

♫ S **VS**

Pizza Pan 28A Bedford Pl
☎ (0703) 23103
Open: Mon–Sun 10am–3pm, 6pm–1am

This enterprising bistro-cum-restaurant has boldly-written outside menus and an eye-catching window display of bottles to tickle the palates of passers-by. Inside (where a personal welcome awaits you). Ercol-style tables and chairs, with check tablecloths, fill the large eating area. Most appetisers here tend to be rather expensive, but this is compensated by the reasonably priced pastas and pizzas.

C ♫ P S
See advertisement on page 171

Simon's Wine House Vernon Walk, Carlton Pl ☎ (0703) 36372
Open: Mon–Thu 11.30am–2.30pm, 7–10.30pm, Fri–Sat 11.30–3pm, 7–11pm, Sun 7–10.30pm

This simple Simon wine house, with its dark wood, bare bricks and bowls of shiny green palms is located in Southampton's bohemian back-street area. Dishes chalked on a blackboard include home-made pâté or chicken curry, and Simon's game pie (a speciality of the house), with home-made sweets such as gâteau, cheesecake and trifle.

♫ P S

SOUTHEND-ON-SEA
Essex
Map **5** TQ88

Chinatown 28 York St ☎ (0702) 64888
Open: Mon–Thu 12noon–2.30pm, 5pm–12mdnt, Fri–Sat 12noon–2.30pm, 5pm–1am, Sun 12noon–12mdnt

This cosy Chinese restaurant close to the town centre offers an enormous choice of traditional Chinese and English dishes at budget prices. Well-cooked and pleasantly served by Ken, the owner's son. Wan Tun soup is extremely tasty and roast duck Hong Kong style, decorated with Chinese mushrooms and peppers is highly recommended. Chop suey and chow mein dishes are excellent value for money. A special set dinner for one person, which includes coffee, is excellent value for money when you consider the amount of time spent in preparing the dishes.

P S

The Pipe of Port 84 High St
☎ (0702) 614606
Open: Mon–Thu 11am–2.30pm, 6–10.30pm, Fri–Sat 11am–2.30pm, 6–11pm, Sun 12noon–2pm

This wine bar is situated just off the High Street in a basement premises underneath Greenfields. There is a good menu with some interesting starters, such as the toasted fingers topped with anchovy, sardine or Stilton. A three-course meal of soup, chicken and chestnut pie and fresh fruit salad is a very satisfying and nutritious repast. Daily 'specials' feature dishes such as poached salmon salad and haggis, tatties and neeps.

C P S

Spencer's 20 High St, Hadleigh
☎ (0702) 558166
Open: Mon–Sat 10am–2.30pm, 6–11pm, Sun 12noon–2pm, 7–10.30pm

This wine bar is easily spotted by the attractive pavement patio. Comfortable banquette seating and French cane-back chairs enable to you to take your ease while absorbing the intersting reading on the walls. Chalkboards display the menu, offering plenty of choice with dishes such as pâté, lasagne. local seafood pie and pork in ginger beer. A selection of toasted sandwiches is also available.

C ♫ P S

SOUTH PETHERTON
Somerset
Map **3** ST41

The Pump Room Oaklands Palmer St
☎ (0460) 40272
Open: Mon–Sun 12noon–2pm, 7–10pm

This attractive little food and wine bar lies at the back of Oaklands Restaurant (a good à la carte AA-appointed restaurant with menus above our limit). A variety of tempting dishes ranges from home-made port and chicken liver pâté, gammon steak with pineapple or home-made turkey and herb pancakes. There is a variety of home-made desserts.

C P

SOUTHPORT
Merseyside
Map **7** SD31

The Grape Escape 367 Lord St
☎ (0704) 37231
Open: Mon–Thu 10am–10.30pm, Fri & Sat 10am–11pm, Sun 12noon–10.30pm

This wine bar in fashionable Lord Street is on two levels with a spiral staircase leading up to the balcony (there is also a lift which the disabled may use). There is an attractive salad bar, and hot dishes, listed on the blackboard menu, include individual pies and lasagne – the house specialities. Home-made tomato soup makes a tasty starter.

♫ P

Pizzeria-Ristorante Paradiso 120 Lord St ☎ (0704) 40259
Open: Mon–Sat 12noon–3pm, 5.30–11pm, Sun 5.30–11pm

Main courses range from pizzas and pasta dishes to beef stroganoff. There is a good choice of starters, and sweets are available from the trolley.

S 🍷

Vesuvio 329 Lord St ☎ (0704) 42275
Open: Mon–Sat 12noon–2.30pm, 6–11pm

Set in a small alleyway leading off Lord Street, this diminutive, attractive restaurant offers a whole range of dishes, from pizzas and pastas to scampi provençale. Venetian pictures and bric-à-brac are complemented by cream and brown walls and Chianti bottles. Particularly tempting is a three-course menu, available at lunchtime and in the evening. A choice of four starters includes minestrone soup. Main dishes offer a choice of English or Italian – plaice or chicken for patriots or lasagne, spaghetti bolognese or cannelloni for those with a more exotic palate. Desserts are apple pie, crème caramel or ice cream.

C ♫ P S

SOUTH STAINLEY
North Yorkshire
Map **8** SE36

Red Lion Inn Ripon Rd
☎ (0423) 770132
Open: Summer Mon–Sat 12noon–2pm, 6.30–10pm, Sun 12noon–1.45pm, 7–10pm. Winter as summer except Mon–Fri evenings 7–10pm

Situated on the A61 with good parking facilities, this old-established inn has a beer garden and a children's play area. Bar snacks include a daily roast, home-made steak and mushroom pie and a range of salads. Grills are the main feature on the menu in the Cavalier Restaurant and all main courses are served with vegetables and a 'help yourself' selection from the salad bar. There is a good choice of hot and cold starters and sweets. Real ale is available.

C P

SOUTHWELL
Nottinghamshire
Map **8** SK75

Bramley Apple Inn Church St
☎ (0636) 813675
Open: Mon–Sun 12noon–2pm, Tue–Fri 7.30–10pm, Sat 7.30–11pm

This small but pleasant inn takes its name from the famous apple which originated in Southwell. At lunchtime the range of bar snacks includes a tasty stilton ploughmans and home-made farmhouse casserole with hot rolls – these can be served in the dining room if required as the restaurant is normally only open in the evenings. The dinner menu in the restaurant offers a good selection of simple, home-made, wholesome dishes – a typical meal could be soup, followed by country chicken and a sweet from the trolley. A traditional Sunday lunch is available.

P

SOUTH ZEAL
Devon
Map **3** SX69

Oxenham Arms★★ ☎ (083784) 244
Open: bar snacks Mon–Sat 12noon–2pm, 7–9pm, Sun 12noon–1.30pm, 7–9pm
Restaurant: Mon–Sun 12noon–1.30pm, 7.30–9pm

'The stateliest and most ancient abode in the hamlet' is how Eden Phillpotts described this beautiful, beamed inn, which was first licensed in 1477. The hamlet quoted is South Zeal, a cluster of houses found by taking a slight detour off the A30 east of Okehampton. Bar snacks offer an array of fish and seafood including rainbow trout and mixed seafood platter. Home-made fruit pie and cream is a popular dessert. On Sundays cold meals only are served in the bar – salads include roast beef, chicken and cheese. Three-course meals served in the cottagey restaurant are excellent in both choice and value for money. Lunches are priced by the main course and include home-made steak and kidney pie.

C P

STAFFORD
Staffordshire
Map **7** SJ92

Anemos 22 Crabbery St
☎ (0785) 48940
Open: Mon–Wed 9am–5pm, Thu–Sat 9am–5pm, 7.30–11pm

The small upstairs dining room of this shop-fronted Greek restaurant serves a cosmopolitan range of light lunches – omelettes, salads, pizzas, pasta dishes and moussaka. A more substantial lunch can be enjoyed from a choice of 14 starters – including soup of the day or dolmades. Main course could be sofrito (a Corfu speciality of beef in wine sauce served with a side salad) beef Stroganoff or prawn kebab with salad and rice. Desserts include gâteaux. The evening menu is basically Greek and more expensive, but two courses could be savoured for around £5.

S

Annabel's Greyfriars (on A34 ½m N of town centre) ☎ (0785) 54500
Open: Wed–Sun 12noon–2pm, 7–10.30pm. Closed Mon & Tue

The wine bar at the front of the building is ideal for those who enjoy high powered disco music (and occasionally live entertainment) with their food. Here the substantial bar meals include beouf bourgignon and steak. The restaurant to the rear, with striking red and blue décor, has plenty of small alcoves and screening for a more intimate meal. Roast chicken and spare ribs in barbeque sauce are just two choices from the table d'hôte menu ot try the rainbow trout or veal escallop from the à la carte.

C P

STAMFORD
Lincolnshire
Map **4** TF00

The Bay Tree Coffee Shop 10 St Pauls St
☎ (0780) 51219
Open: Tue, Wed & Fri 9.30am–5.30pm, Sat 9.30am–5pm, Sun 1–5pm

This quaint, bow-windowed little coffee shop is located in one of Stamford's quieter streets close to the main shopping area. Horse brasses displayed on dark beams and prints on the cream walls create a pleasant period atmosphere. Emphasis is on home-made fare and prices are astonishingly reasonable. A three-course meal could include soup and roll, home-made steak and kidney pie, fruit pie and cream, coffee and a glass of wine.

S

Ye Olde Barn Restaurant St Mary's St
☎ (0780) 63194
Open: Mon–Sun 12noon–2pm, 6–10pm. Closed Mon evening & Sun all day in winter

Step into the alleyway at the rear of Ye Olde Barn coffee shop and you will find this two-storey restaurant, crowded with fine antiques and gleaming with well-polished copper and brass. The upper floor seats 60 below the rafters of the fine timbered roof, where a small cocktail lounge is also to be found. Downstairs is a slightly smaller restaurant boasting the same low prices and excellent value for money. Traditional English food such as roast beef or trout is on the menu and a large selection of snacks is also available.

P S

STANMORE
Gt London

Peking Duck 35 The Broadway
☎ 01-954 4050 London Plan 4 **105** A2
Open: Mon–Sat 12noon–2.30pm, 6pm–12mdnt, Sun 6pm–12mdnt

For those who understand the language, the extensive Peking Duck menu is in Chinese as well as English. The westernised Chinese dishes, familiarised by a thousand take-aways are there, but supplemented by more convincingly eastern-sounding dishes such as Gota fish with garlic and ginger, or crab meat with straw mushroom. A lunchtime special menu, with six choices of main courses is available, and the restaurant specialises in meals consisting of six to eight dishes. The décor of the first-floor restaurant is pleasantly muted, coloured in shades of cream and brown, with modern Chinese prints on the walls and wicker-shaded lights hanging low over the tables.

C S

STEVENTON
Oxfordshire
Map **4** SU49

Fox Inn (4½m S of Abingdon off A34)
☎ (0235) 831253
Open: Mon–Sun 12noon–2pm, 7–10pm

This old village inn (now modernised) has a separate dining area with banquette seating where you can enjoy plain English cooking. The short menu is chalked on the blackboard and offers salads and well-prepared home-cooked dishes such as steak and kidney pie (with an excellent shortcrust pastry), sausages and bacon, and omelettes. Wine is available by the glass.

P

STEYNING
West Sussex
Map **4** TQ11

The Old Dairy 67 High St
☎ (0903) 815799
Open: Etr–end Sep Mon–Sat 10am–5.30pm (Thu, Jun–Aug only), Sun 12noon–5.30pm; Oct–Etr Mon–Wed & Fri 10am–4pm, Sat 10am–5.30pm, Sun 12noon–2pm. Closed Thu

Hugh and Jill Pollock offer good wholesome home cooking at very reasonable prices at their quaint, cosy farmhouse kitchen. Daily lunches are chalked on the blackboard and include soup with wholemeal bread, lasagne and salad, cheese, onion and tomato flan and a delicious lemon cheesecake. If you are just popping in for a cup of tea you'll have six varieties to choose from and a mouthwatering selection of home-made cakes and biscuits. A traditional roast is available on Sundays.

S ♧ **VS**

STIRLING
Central *Stirlingshire*
Map **11** NS79

Qismat 37 Friars St ☎ (0786) 63075
Open: Mon–Sat 12noon–11.45pm, Sun 3.30–11.45pm

This smartly decorated Asian restaurant stands in a narrow street which leads up to the castle. The menu lists a wide variety of freshly prepared curries including the chicken Quorma and beef Dopiazza, but the restaurant is especially popular for its range of Tandoori dishes – Tandoori Ghinga are grilled and spiced King prawns.

C S P ♧ **VS**

The Riverway Restaurant✕ Kildean ☎ (0786) 5734
Open: Mon–Wed 10.30am–3pm, Thu–Sun 10.30am–7pm

Half a mile from the town centre, on the road to the Trossachs, just off the M9 motorway and yet enjoying a panoramic view of the River Forth, the Riverway Restaurant is well-known for its excellent cuisine at reasonable prices. The three-course table d'hôte lunch offers good nourishing food in ample portions. High tea, the main evening meal including grills, is also available. The Saturday night dinner-dance, with live music is over our limit.

♫ P ♧

STOCKPORT
Gt Manchester
Map **7** SJ88

Georgian House 59–61 Buxton Rd ☎ 061-480 5982
Open: Mon–Sat 12noon–2.30pm, 6–11pm, Sun 12noon–2pm, 5–11pm

The bow-windowed Georgian House restaurant on the A6 doesn't go in for frills but you can get good, reasonably-priced meals there, with half-price portions of certain dishes for children. The special two-course lunch is particularly good value. A half roast chicken, garnished, served with vegetables, roll and butter and a choice of sweet is modestly priced or try the 5oz rump steak. Trout is available on the à la carte menu where the price of the main course includes vegetables, roll and butter and a sweet or cheese and biscuits.

P ♧

STOKE-ON-TRENT
Staffordshire
Map **7** SJ84

Capri Ristorante Italiano 13 Glebe St ☎ (0782) 411889
Open: Mon–Fri 12noon–2.30pm, Mon–Sat 6–11pm

Entering the rear of this little Italian restaurant from the car park has been compared with walking into the famous Blue Grotto of Capri. Blue and green lighting creates the illusion, which is enhanced by scenes of Italy painted on the white stucco walls by proprietor Vittorio Cirillo. Good, home-cooked Italian fare is highly recommended, wtih minestrone or salami to start, lasagne, spaghetti, penne alla arrabiata or penne al ragu as the main course, and delicious desserts such as profiteroles or orange slices with liqueur.

C P **VS**

The Poachers Cottage✕✕ Stone Rd, Trentham ☎ (0782) 657115
Open: Mon–Sun 12noon–2pm, Tue–Sat 7–9.30pm

This black and white cottage is easily located on the A34, close to Trentham Gardens. The cottage atmosphere has been retained inside, with black beams, natural stone and tapestry upholstered chairs. White linen tablecloths and colourful carpets add a touch of luxury. The lunchtime menu has excellent value roasts and grills, try the rollmop herring hors d'oeuvres and roast chicken with trimmings.

P ♧

Rib of Beef, Grand Hotel★★★ 66 Trinity St, Hanley ☎ (0782) 22361
Open: Mon–Sun 12.30–2.30pm, 7–10pm

Situated on the lower ground floor of the impressive Stakis-run hotel close to Hanley city centre, the Rib of Beef restaurant boasts some tasty local favourites. Try the excellent table d'hôte menu. At lunchtime you can choose home-made broth – one of three starters – then take your choice of roast ribs of beef, fish, grilled lamb chops – it's different every day! Try the delicious vegetables and sauces, and if you have room for it, the sweet trolley offers a host of gooey goodies.

C P S ♧

Roosevelt's Restaurant 24 Snow Hill ☎ (0782) 269544
Open: Mon–Sun 12noon–12mdnt

As the name implies, an American-style fast service operates here, the result of owner Philip Crowe's long observations in the States. Judging by the hordes of people that frequent the restaurant, the system is a great success. Brown hessian walls, a quarry-tiled floor and Liberty-print tablecloths create a warm, welcoming effect and the many photographs and posters continue the Americana theme. Having started with, perhaps, corn on the cob, you can choose from several hamburger specials, all with French fries and trimmings. Prices are reasonable so you can afford to splash out on a knickerbocker glory for dessert.

C ♫ ♧ **VS**

STONEHAVEN
Grampian *Kincardineshire*
Map **15** NO88

Creel Inn 1m E of A92, 5m S of Stonehaven ☎ (05695) 254
Open: Tue–Sun 12.30–2.30pm

James and Avril Young's attractive white-painted inn nestles on the clifftop above the tiny harbour of Catterline. In the short period that they've owned the restaurant, the Youngs have considerably enhanced its reputation. As you'd expect from an East Grampian eaterie the accent is on sea-food. After a home-made soup you can try home-cured ham salad or a fresh prawn salad.

C P ♤

STORRINGTON
West Sussex
Map **4** TQ01

Oscars Mill La ☎ (09066) 4618
Open: Mon–Sat 12noon–2.30pm, 6.45–11pm. Closed Sun

The Hollywood theme of this licensed restaurant and coffee house is extended to the menu with dishes listed under the titles of popular films – 'Anchors Aweigh' (starters) include taramasalata and Arbroath smokies. Main courses range from chargrilled burgers to seafood dishes (clam fires, platter of king prawns) and salads. Aunt Anna's cheesecake pineapple log and gâteau are popular sweets. Daily specials and a set three-course lunch are chalked on the blackboard.

C ♫ S P

STOURBRIDGE
West Midlands
Map **7** SO88

The Gallery Restaurant ✕ 121 Bridgnorth Rd, Wollaston
☎ (03843) 2788
Open: Tue–Sat 7.30–9.30pm

Just mention the 'restaurant above the butcher's' to anyone in this area and you will be directed to the popular 'Gallery'. Lamb chops, sole and scampi feature on the à la carte menu, all at reasonable prices. Soup and trolley desserts are also available.

C S

Penny Farthing Restaurant Pedmore House, Ham La ☎ (03843) 3132
Open: Tue–Fri 12.30–2.30pm, Tue–Sat 7–10.30pm

Pedmore House, situated on a busy roundabout, has gained a worthy reputation over the years, and has three restaurants to choose from: The Highlander Restaurant and Grill offers an extensive à la carte menu which is outside the range of this guide; The Regency Bar provides substantial bar meals, but if you want a three-course meal at a reasonable price, then try the Penny Farthing basement restaurant. Fish, pasta, chops and steak and kidney pie are among the dishes on the menu.

C P ♤

Talbot Hotel ★★ High St
☎ (03843) 4350
Open: Mon–Sun 12noon–2pm, 7–9.30pm

This town centre hotel has been popular for many years. The ground floor dining room seats about 70 in comfortable alcoves screened by velvet half-curtains hung from brass rails, and it is here that lunch on weekdays, Saturdays and Sundays is chosen from a buffet with hot and cold dishes. A Chef's Special is also provided. The Sunday lunch menu offers traditional roasts. There is a full à la carte menu in the evening. Prices are very reasonable for both table d'hôte and à la carte.

C ♫ P S ♤

STOW-ON-THE-WOLD
Gloucestershire
Map **4** SP12

Old Farmhouse Hotel Lower Swell 1½m W of Stow-on-the-Wold on A436
☎ (0451) 30232
Open: Mon–Sat 12.15–2pm, Sun 12.30–2pm

A charming and personally run small hotel noted here for its bar lunches and 'Swell Suppers'. The bar lunches include a range of fried fish dishes, omelettes, salads and sandwiches all at very reasonable prices. The 'Swell Supper' menu has some similar dishes and also includes trout. There are a selection of sweets and coffee and mints are available. The Sunday lunch is over our price limit.

C P 🍷

STRATFORD-UPON-AVON
Warwickshire
Map **4** SP25

The Dirty Duck Waterside
☎ (0789) 297312
Open: Mon–Sat 12noon–3pm, 6–12mdnt

This typically English pub-restaurant is a favourite haunt of the theatre world, due to its olde worlde charm, and its nearness to the Shakespeare Theatre. Apart from serving meals before and after performances, they also offer a good lunch here. Main dishes include roast chicken and braised oxtail which could be followed by sweets such as apple pie and cream or fruit sundae.

C S 🍷

Hathaway Tea Rooms and Bakery 19 High St ☎ (0789) 292404
Open: Mon–Sat 9am–5.30pm, Sun 11.45am–5.30pm (later by arrangement)

Although the name suggests otherwise, this impressive building, with its olde worlde atmosphere goes a good deal further back than Shakespeare's era – the original site dates back to 1315. The tea rooms are reached by passing through the shop up the Jacobean staircase to the tiny landing, which houses a superb grandfather clock. Once inside, you will find everything you expected – dark oak beams, white walls, an open fireplace and antique dressers and tables. A good old-fashioned lunch menu offers traditional dishes such as roast beef and Yorkshire pudding, steak and kidney pie and spotted Dick, apple and raspberry tart and banana split.

S

Horseshoe Buttery and Restaurant 33–34 Greenhill St ☎ (0789) 292246
Open: Mon–Sun 9am–10pm

Handy for pre-film and theatre snacks, this bay-windowed, period-style restaurant with its charming mock-Tudor façade lies opposite the cinema and just 50 yards from the famous clock tower. An exceptionally good value table d'hôte lunch offers three courses (e.g. soup, steak and kidney pie, home-made fruit pie), and coffee. A special two-course meal is also available. The dinner menu from 5pm (pre-theatre) offers a good choice of starters, substantial fish and meat grills and a selection of sweets.

P S 🍷 **VS**

The Opposition Restaurant 13 Sheep St ☎ (0789) 69980
Open: Tue–Sat 12noon–2.30pm, Mon–Sat 6–11.30pm

No need to feel bloodthirsty to enjoy the steakburger – Macbeth style. It's innocent enough to look at with its topping of melted cheese. Other varieties (including Texan and American styles) are well worth trying, as they are made to the proprietor's own recipe by a local butcher. Pizzas, spaghetti and pastas are also available, and there's a small list of 'specials' including sirloin, fillet or rump steak, and chicken Kiev, tagliatelle with prawn and wine sauce.

♫ S 🍷

The Thatch Restaurant Cottage La, Shottery ☎ (0789) 293122
Open: Mon–Sun 9am–6pm

Next to the famous Anne Hathaway's Cottage you will find this delightful thatched restaurant with its olde worlde dining room and rustic canopied terrace. Here you can enjoy a fine traditional English lunch with three courses, including roast beef and Yorkshire pudding followed by a slice of home-made apple or lemon meringue pie. Cream teas are good value.

P 🍷

STRATHCARRON
Highland *Ross & Cromarty*
Map **14** NC94

Carron Restaurant (On the A890, at the head of Lochcarron, between Achnasheen and Kyle of Lochalsh)
☎ (05202) 488
Open: In season Mon–Sat 10.30am–9.15pm, out of season, Wed, Fri & Sat 7–9.15pm

A small restaurant that epitomises the best in careful attention and well-prepared food. Local paintings adorn brown hessian walls and, if you like the look of one of the paintings, you can take it home with you as they are all for sale. The tiled floor and large windows, the pine tables, set with locally-made pottery all add to the homely atmosphere. The chicken-liver pâté is well recommended and the minute steak served with salad and French fries is good value (all steaks are charcoal grilled). Choose from a selection of home-made sweets.

C P 🍷

STREET
Somerset
Map **3** ST43

Knight's Tavern☆☆☆ Wessex Hotel
☎ (0458) 43383
Open: Mon–Sat 10.30am–2.30pm, 7.30–10pm, Sun 12noon–2pm, 7.30–10pm

With direct access from the car park, there's no need to go through the hotel to reach the Knight's Tavern, so it is a good place to know about, especially for families with children. Pleasant cheerful service and comfortable modern surroundings make it a worthwhile stopping place. Rest awhile in the King Arthur Bar – aptly named in this Camelot Country, where at lunchtime you can choose from a wide variety of bar snacks, and there are joints from the carvery, charcoal grills, omelettes, curries, fish and many other favourites at budget-prices. You could choose a good dinner in the grill room/restaurant under the limit too, though you could bust the budget if you ignored the menu prices. Fruit juice, followed by fillet of plaice and a sweet from the trolley would come within our limit, leaving plenty over for a glass of wine and a tip – and there are a number of other permutations under our price limit.

C ♫ P 🍷 **VS**

STRETTON
Leicestershire
Map **8** SK91

The Shires on southbound carriageway of the A1 close to its junction with the B668, approx 8m N of Stamford
☎ (078081) 316 and 332
Open: Tue–Sat 7–11.30pm, Sun 12noon–2pm, 7–10.30pm

The Shires is accessible to both north and southbound travellers and there is plenty of space in the grounds for customers with touring caravans. The stone building was originally a rectory and the farmhouse tables in the large, open-plan, ground-floor room can each seat up to 10 diners. Starters include mussels in a cream and wine sauce and the main courses include gammon steak with spiced peaches. There is a choice of sweets.

P 🍷

STURMINSTER MARSHALL
Dorset
Map **3** SY99

The Old Kitchens Henbury Hall
☎ (0258) 577
Open: Mon–Sun 12noon–2pm

Henbury Hall, built in 1730, has been successfully renovated by the present owners, Charles and Sue Maitland, who have opened this restaurant in the old kitchens and servant's hall. The buffet lunch menu (which changes every week) offers a limited range of hot and cold dishes using local produce wherever possible. A starter of soup could be followed by Poole Fishermans Pie or cold meats and jacket potato with a 'help yourself' salad selection. One of the home-made puds will complete your meal. The dinner menu (Mon–Sat) is outside the scope of this guide.

C P 🍷

SUDBURY
Gt London

Terry's Restaurant and Banqueting Suite 763–765 Harrow Rd
☎ 01-904 4409
Open: Mon–Fri 12noon–2pm

The main operation here is catering for large parties, but on weekday lunchtimes the reception area is utilised for serving what could be one of the cheapest three-course lunches in London. There is choice of starters which include items such as melon cocktail and egg mayonnaise, a choice of four main dishes such as roast or meat pie with a good selection of the appropriate, well-cooked vegetables, tasty omelette, or cold meat salad, and a choice of four mouth-watering sweets or cheese and biscuits with which to round off the meal.

P 🍷

SUNDERLAND
Tyne & Wear
Map **12** NZ35

The Melting Pot 9 Maritime Ter
☎ (0783) 76909
Open: Mon–Sat 12noon–2.30pm, 6pm–12mdnt

Peacock blue drapes covering three walls create a comfortable atmosphere in this intimate Indian restaurant situated in Sunderland's pedestrian precinct. The 'lunchtime special' menu, offering a choice of soup or fruit juice, 10 traditional Indian dishes such as chicken or prawn curry, five English dishes including rump steak, plus sweet, is superb value. The extensive à la carte is also well within our budget. Wine is not sold by the glass, but in a minimum of half-bottles so you would be wise to take a friend or two along.

C P S

Sams Bar The Continental, St Thomas St
☎ (0783) 674635
Open: Food served lunchtime only Mon–Sat 12noon–2.30pm. Closed Sun.

As you may have guessed from it's name, the theme of this wine bar is based on the film 'Casablanca' with photos of the stars displayed on the natural brick walls. The chef's specials change daily and include mince and dumplings, a range of curries, lasagne and home-made quiche – all served with salad or vegetables. Grills, steak, and scampi are also available.

P ♨

SURBITON
Gt London

Cars Café 7 Brighton Rd ☎ 01-399 1582 Plan 4 **106** E2

Open: Mon–Fri 6–11.30pm, Sat & Sun 12noon–11.30pm

As the name may indicate motor cars and traffic lights are the focal points of this buttery. The plain brick walls are decorated with prints of motor cars, spot lights and the occasional potted plant. The menu includes a good range of starters, hamburgers, grilled steaks, spaghetti dishes, quiches, chef's specials, salads and desserts. A three-course meal could include soup, steak and kidney pie and meringue glacé.

C ♫ P S ♨ **VS**

The Good Life 3 Central Parade (between Ewell and Brighton Rds) ☎ 01-399 8450 Plan 4 **107** E2

Open: Mon–Sun 12noon–2.30pm. 6.30–11pm

Open-plan, wood-panelled rooms with wall prints lend an authentic air to this popular bistro. Starters include pâté and sauté mushrooms. Steaks (served with French fries or jacket potatoes), boeuf bourguignon, lasagne, spaghetti bolognese and chili con carne are a sample of the main courses. Desserts include apple pie and cream. Coffee and wine are also available.

♫ ♨

SUTTON COLDFIELD
West Midlands
Map **7** SP19

Bobby Browns Bracebridge Pool, Sutton Park (enter Sutton Park at 'Four Oakes' or 'Town' Gates) ☎ 021-308 8890

Open: Mon–Sun 10am–10pm

Sutton Park, with its open spaces, woods, streams and pools, is the setting for this 400-year-old Hunting Lodge – now an attractive and friendly restaurant. A tea-room menu operates in the mornings and afternoons with tea cakes, and scones, etc. Light lunches include filled jacket potatoes and quiche with salad or choose from the à la carte menu (also available in the evening) with dishes such as Rafters Pie and Chicken Teryaki.

♫ P ♨

Pimpernell 59–61 Birmingham Rd ☎ 021-354 9809

Open: Tue–Sat 12noon–2.30pm, 6–10.30pm

Just the place to eat before or after a film at the nearby cinema. Green and red tasteful décor complements the excellent and inexpensive cuisine. The à la carte menu offers dishes from many countries and is well within our budget. Particularly good value fare may be sampled from the Daily Special lunchtime menu.

C ♨

SUTTON-ON-SEA
Lincolnshire
Map **9** TF58

Anchor 12 High St ☎ (0521) 41548

Open: Summer Mon–Sun 10am–5.30pm, 7–10pm, Winter Fri–Sat & Sun 10am–2.30pm, Fri & Sat 7–10pm

A canopied doorway and bow windows pick out this country-style restaurant, converted from an old house reported to be a home to Alfred Lord Tennyson. Food to suit the pocket and palate of any poet is served here. A three-course lunch includes minute steak garni and a three-course dinner plus coffee could include melon, steak chasseur and a sweet from the trolley. The à la carte menu is also very reasonable, with a good choice of starters, roasts, fish dishes, salads, grills and desserts well within our budget. Half portions are available for children.

C P ♨ **VS**

SWAFFHAM
Norfolk
Map **5** TF80

Cork's Wine Bar Ploughwright Pl, The Market Pl ☎ (0760) 23883

Open: Mon–Fri 12noon–3pm, 7pm–12mdnt, Sat 10.30am–5pm, 7pm–12mdnt, Sun 12noon–3pm, 7–11.30pm.

Wheelwrights, blacksmiths and plough manufacturers have been associated with Ploughwright Place since the 18th century. It is now a small shopping precinct which still maintains the character of its past. The food at Corks is very reasonably priced with a simple range of daily specials such as chicken Veronique and steak and kidney pie.

♫ S P

The Red Door The Market Pl, 7 London St ☎ (0760) 21059

Open: Tue–Sat 9am–5pm, Sun 12noon–5pm, Fri & Sat 7–9.30pm. Closed Mon.

This tea shop and restaurant is housed in a listed Georgian building which is part of a conservation area in the market place. Behind the red door you'll find a cottage atmosphere, where morning coffee and afternoon tea are served with a variety of scones and cakes. A special two-course lunch offers dishes such as Lancashire hot-pot and chocolate fudge pudding, or choose from a selection of home-made pies, omelettes, etc. and a range of starters and sweets. A three-course tradtional lunch is available on Sundays and there is also a limited dinner menu. The Red Door is ideal for families with toddlers and babies as high chair and changing facilities are available.

P ♨

SWANSEA
West Glamorgan
Map **3** SS69

The Dragon Hotel ☆☆☆☆ Kingsway Circle ☎ (0792) 51074

Open: The Birch Room Mon–Sun 12.30–2.30pm, 7–9.30pm The Dragon Coffee Shop Mon–Sat 10am–11pm

The Birch Room Restaurant offers a 'Kings Table Luncheon' selection, two courses come just within our limit. An à la carte menu featuring local Welsh dishes is also on offer. The Coffee Shop prices are extremely competitive for a quick meal or snack throughout the day. Bar salads are served in both bars.

C ♫ P S ♨

Home on the Range St Helens Ave ☎ (0792) 467166

Open: Mon–Sat 10.30am–3.30pm, 6–10.30pm. Closed Sun.

This small bistro is run by a co-operative of four young, enthusiastic proprietors, Jenny, Steve, Phil and Isaac, who offer honest and well-prepared meals. A daily special and an attractive and imaginative range of cold meats and home-made quiches are on the menu. Home-made Kiwi fruit meringue is a popular sweet. As yet Home on the Range is unlicensed but you are welcome to bring your own wine. Both a take-away and an outside catering service are available.

P ♨

SWINDON
Wiltshire
Map **4** SU18

Sheraton Suite East St ☎ (0793) 24114

Open: Mon–Sat 12noon–2pm

If ornate surroundings are what you look for in a restaurant, you could do no better than to eat in the red and gold dining-room of the Sheraton Suite. Sit back amidst the chandeliers, velvet-upholstered chairs and flock wallpapers and enjoy the table d'hôte lunch which includes a starter of soup or fruit juice, and eight choices of main dishes such as roasts, steaks, chicken chasseur or fish plus a daily special such as devilled kidneys followed by cheese or a sweet from the trolley. You may, if you prefer, order from the à la carte menu; most dishes obviously fall outside our price range, but two courses such as scampi and gâteau are still within reach. Snacks are available from the bar.

C P S ♨

See advertisement on page 178

TAMWORTH
Staffordshire
Map **4** SK20

Kealeys✕✕ 36 Market St
☎ (0827) 55444
Open: Tue–Sat 12noon–2pm, 7–10pm. Closed Mon and Sun.

This bright, modern restaurant on the approaches to the main shopping area has a ground-floor lounge where you can enjoy an aperitif before climbing the long flight of stairs to the dining room. We are mainly interested in the two lunch menus – the three-course set lunch could offer leek and carrot soup, veal cutlets and bilberry and apple flan, whilst lasagne, Danish open sandwiches and salads are some of the choices on the Bistro menu. The imginative dinner menu is too expensive for us.

C P 🍷

TARPORLEY
Cheshire
Map **7** SJ56

The Loft 69 High St ☎ (08293) 3470
Open: Tue, Thu & Fri 10.30am–2pm, 7–10pm, Sat 7–10pm, Sun 10.30am–2pm. Closed Mon & Wed.

A family-run licensed restaurant which is situated above a stationery shop in this small Cheshire town. The Loft provides simple, inexpensive lunches including steak and kidney pie and omelettes. Dishes from the à la carte menu, available lunchtime and evening, will not break the bank with main courses of crill à l'Americane and fillet de porc en crôute.

C P 🍷

TAUNTON
Somerset
Map **3** ST22

The Crown Inn Creech Heathfield (4½m NE off the A38) ☎ (0823) 412444
Open: Mon–Sat 10.30am–2.30pm, 6–11pm (10.30pm in winter), Sun 12noon–2pm, 7–10.30pm.

You'll find this attractive 13th-century thatched public house tucked away down a quiet residential cul-de-sac. The interior is olde worlde with a flagstone floor, an inglenook fireplace and horse brasses. The menu offers snacks, fish dishes and grills with a range of starters and sweets. The more adventurous daily specialities include king prawns in garlic served with salad.

P 🍷

Heatherton Grange Hotel★ Bradford-on-Tone ☎ (0823) 46777/8 On A38 1m from M5, junction 26
Open: Mon–Sat 12noon–2pm, 7–10.30pm, Sun 12noon–2pm, 7–9pm

This former coaching inn, dating from 1826 or earlier is easily accessible from Taunton or the M5. A wide variety of bar meals include Madras curry, steakburgers, home-made pies and salads (including fresh lobster and crab in season). Most of the á la carte menu presented in the small dining room is within our two-course budget. Basic favourites are supplemented by sweetbreads in sherry sauce, Swiss pork chop (stuffed with oregano, cheese, onions and mushrooms) or breast of chicken in a lovely lemon sauce.

C P ♫ 🍷 **VS**

TAYVALLICH
Strathclyde *Argyllshire*
Map **10** NR78

New Tayvallich Inn ☎ (05467) 282
Open: Mon–Sun 12noon–2pm, 7.30–9pm (bar meals 6–7pm)

Overlooking the moored yachts on Loch Sween, the Tayvallich Inn offers a bar menu which, at lunchtime, may be taken in the garden, the bar or the attractive small restaurant. Specialities include whole prawns in shells with home-made mayonnaise and mussels served with garlic bread. Home-made soup and burgers are two of the more simple dishes on the menu. The prices on the dinner menu exceed our budget, but bar meals are available from 6–7pm.

C ♫ P 🍷

TENBURY WELLS
Hereford & Worcester
Map **7** SO56

The Peacock Inn Worcester Rd
☎ (0584) 810506 1m E of Tenbury Wells on the A456
Open: Mon–Sat 10.30am–2.30pm, 6–10.30pm, 11pm Fri–Sat, Sun 12noon–2pm, 7–10.30pm

Amid the famous hop fields and orchards of the beautiful Teme Valley is this half-timbered, 14th-century inn, run by partners Alastair Hendry and Bernard Bond, who returned to England three years ago after spending almost 30 years in Malaysia. It follows that one of the house specialities should be Malaysian curry, but where they learned to make such marvellous lasagne is quite a mystery. A starter such as smoked salmon mousse or sweet (could be rum and walnut gâteau) will complete your meal.

[P]

TENBY
Dyfed
Map **2** SN10

Hol San Restaurant Tudor Sq
☎ (0834) 2025
Open: Apr–Sep Mon–Sun 12noon–11.45pm, Oct–Dec, Mar Thu–Fri 6–11.45pm, Sat–Sun 12noon–11.45pm

A friendly, enthusiastic Cantonese atmosphere is to be found here in the centre of Tenby. Chopsticks are laid out to test your dexterity and help is at hand should you fail the test. The choice of special dinners is impressive. A four-course dinner and coffee is excellent value, and the three-course menu offers a selection of four main dishes and coffee. Particularly remmended are hot and sour soup and char siu – honey roast pork with Cantonese roast duck and boiled rice. Special facilities exist for mothers with young babies.

The Lion's Den, Royal Lion Hotel★★
High St ☎ (0834) 2127
Open: Summer Mon–Sun 12noon–2.30pm, 7–11pm

The Lion's Den restaurant and bar, with its dark oak settles and intimate atmosphere provides a perfect venue for a relaxing meal. The lunch menu ranges from salads, hot snacks and full meals. The à la carte evening menu specialises in local home-produced food. Seafood is the house speciality, mackerel, plaice and bass are all fully garnished. The sweet trolley provides a good variety of choice to conclude your meal.

[C]

Plantagenet House Quay Hill
☎ (0834) 2350
Open: Etr–Oct Mon–Sun 10am–10.30pm

This 15th-century house boasts a superb example of a Flemish chimney. As well as the more traditional meals, Barney and Tina Stone also offer an interesting selection of vegetarian and wholemeal-based dishes. Dishes include vegetarian quiche and crab or salmon in season with a large mixed salad. Home-made chili con carne with brown rice or a large home-made wholemeal pizza are also available. A lighter meal of open sandwiches or burgers can be had in the downstairs Quay Room. This historical restaurant welcomes families. Children are well-catered for.

[C] [S]

THAME
Oxfordshire
Map **4** SP70

The Coffee House 3 Buttermarket
☎ (084421) 6302
Open: Mon–Tue, Thu–Sat 10am–5pm

This charmingly decorated restaurant with its pine furniture, white walls, large open fireplace and green plants was opened in 1979. A large choice of

hot and cold snack lunches includes ploughmans, filled jacket potatoes and various toasted sandwiches. Desserts include home-made cakes, gâteaux and cheesecakes.

[♫] [P] [S] [☘]

THORNTON HEATH
Gt London

Othello 814 London Rd ☎ 01-684 5253
Plan 4 **108** E4

Open: Mon–Sat 12noon–3pm, Tue–Sat 6pm–12mdnt. Closed Sun.

A small, cosy Greek restaurant which is very popular with the locals and businessmen. The table d'hôte lunch menu represents excellent value with a good choice of English dishes. The à la carte menu features Greek specialities including beef stifato and lamb kebabs and English dishes such as grills and salads.

[C] [P] [S]

THORVERTON
Devon
Map **3** SS90

Dolphin Inn ☎ (0392) 860205

Open: during licensing hours. Meals: Mon–Sun 12noon–1.45pm, 7–10pm

This two-storey inn enjoys a central position amid a picturesque village setting. Décor and furnishing in the Victoria Lounge bar would have pleased even the most discerning Victorian, and the deep-seated armchairs offer a place to relax with an after-dinner coffee. An archway leads through the bar to the attractive Gueridon Restaurant, romantically illuminated with oil lamps to produce a complementary atmosphere in which to enjoy some of the homely fare offered on the extensive menu. House specials include home-made steak and kidney pie with Mackeson. Try the soup (also home-made) to start with, and for dessert there is a choice of cold sweets or ice cream – all reasonably-priced. Traditional bar snacks are available every day – the locally-produced pasty with gravy sounds like a tempting and cheap filler. Lunch can also be taken in the wisteria-clad beer garden or in the separate real ale and wine bar.

[P] [☘] **VS**

THRAPSTON
Northamptonshire
Map **4** SP97

The Court House Huntingdon Rd
☎ (08012) 3618

Open: Mon–Sun 12noon–2pm, 6.45–10pm, 10.30pm Fri & Sat

This restaurant is contained in the old Thrapston court and police station, but grim-faced magistrates handing out fines and sentences have been replaced by smiling waitresses with plates of food. Relics of the former function decorate the dining room, in the shape of police memorabilia, helmets, badges, truncheons and handcuffs. The old cells were demolished to make room for modern bedrooms, so even the worst-behaved guests need have no fear of being locked up for the night! A wide range of food is offered at The Court House; from sandwiches, ploughman's and beefburgers, through to more substantial dishes of steak, fish, gammon etc – all fitting easily into our budget. In the evening try the chef's special which could be carbonnade of beef, chicken supreme or even WPC Buster (no it's not a truncheon but a huge steak and kidney pie).

[C] [P] [☘] **VS**

THURSO
Highland *Caithness*
Map **15** ND16

Pentland Hotel★★ Princes St
☎ (0847) 3202

Open: Mon–Thu 12noon–2pm, 6.30–8.30pm, Fri–Sat 12noon–2pm, 6.30–8.30pm, Sun 12.30–2pm, 6.30–8.30pm

In the bright, cheerful dining room of the Pentland, you can be tempted by an extensive à la carte lunch, dinner, or to combine the best of two meals, a high tea (5–6pm). A three-course lunch may include roast Caithness ribs of beef, or for 'a few dollars more', fresh Thurso salmon. Bar lunches served during the week are again very reasonably priced.

[S]

TIDESWELL
Derbyshire
Map **7** SK17

Madeira House 5 Commercial Rd
☎ (0298) 871176

Open: Tue–Sun 12noon–2pm

Portuguese proprietor Mr Abreu is proud that his restaurant dates from before the discovery of the New World by his fellow countryman Christopher Columbus. So be prepared for the low ceilings, supported by stury oak beams. Although open in the evening when an international cuisine is served, it is for the more simply-priced and prepared lunch and bar meals that Madeira House is noted in this guide. A home-made soup of the day can be followed by a choice of main dishes (such as fish, pizza, or minute steak) all served with salad and chips, and a sweet.

[S] [☘]

TOMINTOUL
Grampian *Banffshire*
Map **15** NJ11

Glenmulliach Restaurant 2m SE of Tomintoul on A939 Braemar road
☎ (08074) 356

Open: Mon–Sun 10am–8pm (last orders)

The Lannagan family have built their dream restaurant from scratch. Father and sons did the building work, mum took over the decorating. The result is a pleasant, modern, cottage-style building set amongst forested hills. Inside, a wood-burning stove, red-pine fittings and a cheerful atmosphere defy the occasional Scottish mist. Food-wise, the emphasis is on home-baking and Scottish fare. A three-course lunch is excellent value and in the evening a two-course meal, with venison as the main course, comes within the budget.

[P] [☘] **VS**

TOPSHAM
Devon
Map **3** SX99

Amadeus Restaurant 62 Fore St
☎ (039287) 3759
Open: Tue–Sun 12.30–2pm, 6–10pm

The recorded music of Amadeus Mozart, after whom the restaurant is named, provides a relaxing atmosphere for meals in this attractive little restaurant in the town centre. Tom and Jose Williams serve a selective luncheon with half portions for children under 13 years. Starters include soup and home-made pâté and there is a good range of main courses such as seafood pilaf with lemon garni, sauté lamb's kidneys on a bed of rice, and a roast. Excellent home-made sweets with rich clotted cream complete a first-class meal. In the summer months cold buffet lunches with salad and potatoes are served and may include delicious local salmon. To avoid disappointment table reservations are essential. The evening meals are à la carte, but are beyond the scope of this guide.

[P]

TORMARTON
Avon
Map **3** ST77

The Vittles Bar The Compass Inn, Tormarton ☎ (045421) 242
Off the A46 Stroud–Cheltenham road, and a few minutes from junction 18 of the M4.
Open: Mon–Sat 10am–2.30pm, Sun 12noon–2pm, Mon–Thu 6.30–10pm, Fri–Sat 7–10.30pm, Sun 7–10pm

This pleasant old country inn has four bars to choose from, but we suggest hungry travellers make straight for the Vittles Bar, where a tempting cold buffet is on display. Hot dishes are listed on a blackboard, and can often include rabbit pie, hot seafood casserole or ham and asparagus in cheese sauce with salad. Starters include prawns with mayonnaise or pâté. Various home-cooked meats with salad and sandwiches are also on offer along with a range of sweets. Full meals can also be taken in the restaurant. Leading off the Vittles Bar is the Orangery, a pretty, glass-enclosed garden which draws families in the summer.

[C] [P]

TORQUAY
Devon
Map **3** SX96

Anstey's 89 Babbacombe Rd, Babbacombe ☎ (0803) 39888
Open: Etr–end Sep Mon–Sun 12noon–3pm, 7pm–12mdnt; Oct–Etr Mon–Sat 12noon–3pm, 7–11.30pm

Set amongst shops on the main road this corner-sited wine bar/bistro has a pleasant mock-Tudor interior with posters and paintings on the walls. Tasty starters include ham and mushroom crêpes, whilst main courses range from pasta dishes to carbonnade of beef. Only wines and aperitifs are served.

[C] [S] [P] **VS**

The Copper Kettle Ilsham Rd, Wellswood ☎ (0803) 23025
Open: Summer Mon–Sun 9.30am–10.30pm, Winter Tue–Sat 10am–5pm

This 'copper kettle' brews up not only for guests enjoying a refreshing cuppa after a meal but also for the picnicker on his way to the beach some yards away. Later in the day, day trippers about to make the long drive home are catered for. This is a special service offered by Leslie Bentham at his neat little Georgian restaurant in the heart of this holiday town. Many a thirsty tourist has had his flask filled to the brim with piping hot tea or freshly-percolated coffee by the enterprising Mr B. His wife, Elaine, specialises in high-standard home cooking– and the well-cooked roast lunch (with a starter) and a Devonshire cream tea (with home-made scones) is very popular. Salads are the house speciality; egg mayonnaise, chicken, fresh crab, salmon and many more – with special reduced prices for children. Evening meals are also served.

[P] [S] **VS**

The Epicure 34 Torwood Rd
☎ (0803) 23340
Open: Summer Mon–Sun 10am–10pm, Winter Mon–Tue, Thu–Sun 10am–5pm, Wed 6.30–10pm

With some 30 years' experience in hotels and catering behind him, proprietor Gary Dowland runs his attractive little restaurant with the emphasis on personal service and quality grill-style fare. Situated some 600yds from the harbour, in a row of shops, The Epicure is one of Torquay's oldest restaurants and instantly recognisable by its green stucco exterior with green woodwork and sun canopy. The deceptively small frontage leads into a long, brightly-decorated dining room. The cool exterior colouring is echoed inside with lush green plants. Best china and cutlery is used here and the walls bear framed prints of old sheet music. An extensive menu of fish dishes and grills is available, with home-made soups a starter speciality. Parents please note the special children's menu with main dishes less than half the standard price.

[P] [S]

Homestead 40 Tor Hill Rd
☎ (0803) 23210
Open: Mon–Sat 12noon–2.30pm, 5.30–9.30pm, Winter Mon–Sat 12noon–2.30pm, Mon–Wed 5.30–7.30pm, Thu–Sat 5.30–9.30pm

This bistro-style eating place has a mixture of English and American dishes on the menu. Choose from salads, fish dishes, American-style burgers, steaks, grills, house specials and a good range of sweets. The steaks may take you over our price limit, but with careful choice you can have a good three-course meal within our budget. A range of bar snacks and children's meals are available.

[P] [S] **VS**

See advertisement on page 181

Livermead Cliff and Livermead House★★★ HL Torbay Rd
☎ (0803) 22881 – Livermead Cliff,
☎ (0803) 24361 – Livermead House)
Open: Lunch 1–2pm, dinner 7–8.30pm

The big attraction here is the marvellous view afforded by these sea-front hotel restaurants. Cream leatherette seats and velour drapes make for a very comfy inside setting and the uniformed staff are keen to ensure that everything is to your satisfaction. A set luncheon menu offers soup or fruit juice as a starter, with a choice of four hot main courses (grilled mackerel, fried lamb's liver, grilled pork chop or prawn omelette) plus a wide range of salads – the pressed ox tongue is delicious. Desserts include apple pie with cream and coupe Andalouse. There are special children's portions. A four-course dinner is served but it is over our price limit. On the seafront you will find Livermead House (300yds distant) – a sister hotel run along almost identical lines.

C P VS

Pizza-King 2 The Terrace, Fleet St
☎ (0803) 24365
Open: Summer Mon–Sun 12noon–12mdnt, Winter Mon–Sat 12noon–2pm, 6–11pm

A cheerful, bright red canopy invites you into this rustic-style restaurant with wood-panelled walls and oak refectory tables. Red-painted chairs add warmth and colour to the simple yet attractive décor. There are 20 really substantial pizzas to choose from. You can make a feast out of the Pizza-King Special which is topped with cheese, tomato, salami, onion, mushroom, ham and pimentoes. An extensive salad bar offers an exciting range of salads (try apple, orange and celery or chicken Waldorf). Home-made soup, quiches and curries are also available. A special lunch for children is exceptional value. Wine is sold by the glass.

♫ S VS

TORRINGTON, GREAT
Devon
Map **2** SS41

Castle Hill Hotel★★ South St
☎ (08052) 2339
Open: bar: Mon–Sat 11am–2.15pm, 7–10.30pm, Sun 12noon–2pm, 7–10.30pm
Restaurant Mon–Sun 12noon–2pm, 7–9pm

Magnificent views over the Torridge Valley and the hills beyond can be enjoyed from the garden of this delightful old hotel. A wide range of snacks is available in the bar, including a hot dish of the day such as curry, cottage pie or pork chops. The table d'hôte three-course lunch, served in the restaurant, offers four or five choices of starter, three hot main courses – a roast and fish dish are always available – and a salad. There is also a generous selection of sweets from the trolley. Cheaper portions are available for children. The extensive evening à la carte menu features grills of all descriptions.

C ♫ P VS

Rebecca's 8 Potacre St ☎ (08052) 2113
Open: Summer Mon–Sat 7.30am–9.30pm (last orders), Winter 10.30am–9.30pm (last orders). Closed Sun

Rebecca's, a double-fronted cottage-type restaurant just off Torringtons shopping area, is named after the young daughter of Gill and Paul Lilly, who own the restaurant. Traditional English dishes, individually prepared to order, are available throughout the day. The menu includes Mistress Duffields chicken, a pair of pork chops with honey and herbs and for pudding iced fudge mousse and orange caramel custard. The 'little bite' menu, available until 7pm, offers a range of afternoon teas, light snacks and simple meals including cold gammon with salad and fried potatoes, omelettes and ploughmans.

C ♫ P VS

TOTNES
Devon
Map **3** SX86

Casa Doro 67 Fore St ☎ (0803) 863932
Open: Mon–Sat 12noon–2.30pm, 7.15 onwards

Catch the distinct Spanish flavour of this small restaurant on the ground floor of a three-storey listed building. Heliodoro Lopez runs the place with the aid of his wife and mother-in-law, and together they produce a marvellous list of goodies. Tasty starters such as 'tropicanas' (layers of grilled ham, cheese and pineapple served on bread) or barquitas de apio (celery boats filled with tuna fish, peppers and olives) make interesting appetisers, with paella, chicken Espanol or a host of imaginative, Spanish main courses to follow. Sweets include delicious figs in brandy.

C P S

Cranks Health Food Restaurant
Dartington Cider Press Centre, Shinners Bridge, Dartington ☎ (0803) 862388
Open: Mon–Sat 10am–5pm

Cranks have made a name for themselves by serving appetising whole-foods while at the same time encouraging crafts by displaying specially-commissioned articles and equipping their restaurants with craftsman-made furniture and pottery. This branch, in the interesting Cider Press Centre, which is dedicated to the encouragement and display of traditional crafts, is run on the usual Cranks lines with a buffet service counter serving soups, salads, and vegetable-based savouries, the accent being on compost-grown vegetables and unchemicalised (their word!) ingredients. All food, including wholemeal bread, is baked on the premises. A substantial three-course meal with coffee includes soup, a hot savoury such as mushroom stroganoff and vegetable crumble, a sweet and coffee. There's outside seating for 30.

P S

The Sea Trout Inn★★ Staverton
☎ (080426) 274
Open: Mon–Sun 12noon–2pm, 7–10pm

The à la carte menu would surely take you beyond our limit, but you need not deny yourself the pleasure of eating in this attractive old inn, for they also serve a comprehensive list of bar meals. A typical meal would be grapefruit cocktail, home-made quiche Lorraine with chips and veg, gâteau or cheesecake. The bar occupies the original part of the building, and with oak furniture, white-washed walls, beamed ceiling and stone fireplace it retains a certain 'olde worlde' look. Bar meals are limited on Sundays when a full lunch is provided in the restaurant, and in fine weather meals can be taken on the patio.

C ♫ P 🏠

The Waterman's Arms Bow Bridge, Ashprington (3m S of Totnes off the A381)
☎ (080423) 214
Open: Mon–Sat 11am–2pm, 6–10.30pm, Sun 12noon–2pm, 7–10pm

Standing adjacent to the old Bow Bridge. deep in the lovely Devonshire countryside lies the 'picturebook' Waterman's Arms Inn. Polished brassware adorns the bar where at lunchtime you can order excellent and very substantial salads with fresh crab, turkey, ham or beef all served with crusty bread and butter. Home-made soup, cottage pie and a few sweets are also available. In the summer you can enjoy your lunch at the tables on the banks of the pretty River Harbourne. More expensive meals are served every night in the restaurant, but they are outside the scope of this guide.

P 🏠

TOTON
Nottinghamshire
Map **8** SK53

Grange Farm Restaurant
☎ (06076) 69426
Open: Mon–Sat 12noon–1.45pm, 7–9pm

A much extended brick-built farmhouse dating back to 1691 is quite a find just two miles off the M1 (exit 25), especially if it offers generous portions of wholesome English fare attractively presented, as this restaurant does. The dining room itself is in one of the oldest parts of the building, where oak beams and white brick abound, and there you can sample a quite superb table d'hôte lunch. A seemingly limitless choice of dishes is available – there are around 19 starters including whitebait, lasagne, melon and pâté, 12 main dishes such as rainbow trout, rabbit pie or supreme of chicken Marengo, all served with two vegetables and both creamed and roast potatoes, and almost 20 different sweets, some rather unusual.

[P]

TREGONY
Cornwall
Map **2** SW94

Kea House Restaurant 69 Fore St
☎ (087253) 642
Open: Apr–Sep Mon–Sat 12.30–2pm, 3–6pm, 7.30–9.30pm, Sun 12.30–2pm, 3–6pm; Oct–Mar Mon–Sat 7.30–9pm (bookings only)

An attractive white-painted stone cottage in the centre of the village houses this open-plan restaurant/café with a bar area. At lunchtime straightforward dishes of steak and kidney pie and cod, etc. are served with chips, with fruit pies and ice cream to follow. There is a similar children's menu. In the evening the menu includes salmon pâté, gammon steak and a range of sweets.

[C] [P] [🍷]

TROON
Strathclyde *Ayrshire*
Map **10** NS33

The Grill Room Marine Hotel
☎ (0292) 314444
Open: Mon–Sat 12noon–2.30pm, 6.30–10.30pm, Sun 12.30–2pm, 6.30–10pm

Forming part of the Marine Hotel with its championship Royal Troon and Portland golf courses, the Grill Room and lounge bar is popular with golfers, locals and tourists alike. The menu offers a good range of dishes including snacks, grills and seafood. A typical meal could be soup with wholemeal bread, chef's special Supreme of chicken Royal Scot and chocolate meringue gâteau.

[C] [♫] [P] [🍷] **VS**

TRUMPET
Hereford & Worcester
Map **3** SO63

The Bistro The Verzons Hotel
☎ (053183) 381
Open: Mon–Sun 10.30am–2pm, 6.30–10pm

Nestling in the peace of the Herefordshire countryside is the busy and popular Verzons Hotel. Originally a Georgian farmhouse, it stands in a lush four acres. In winter bistro diners can wallow in the warmth of an open log fire while supping a plateful of home-made soup followed by a generous portion of lasagne verdi. Summer sees guests enjoying their meal outside in the wooded beer garden. A speciality of the bistro is the home-made desserts which include the mouth-watering crunch cake laced with brandy. A fine range of traditional ales and real local cider adds to the convivial atmosphere created here by owners Philip and Mary Stanley.

[C] [P] [🍷]

TUNBRIDGE WELLS (ROYAL)
Kent
Map **5** TQ53

Bruin's Bar and Ristorante Orso 5 London Rd ☎ (0892) 35757
Open: Mon–Sat 12noon–2.30pm, 7–10.45pm, Sun 12noon–2pm, 7–10pm

Good food, good wine, good ale and great company are what Randy and Gill Brown, owners of Bruin's, view as life's 'bear necessities'. All three are taken care of in the bar, decorated in shades of brown and adorned with an assortment of teddy bears that give the restaurant its name. The first-floor restaurant (orso means 'bear' in Italian) offers a wide choice of Italian specialities, very reasonably priced. In the bar, snacks range from onion soup with bread to steak and kidney pie.

[C] [♫] [P] [S] [🍷] **VS**

Wellington Hotel★★L Mount Ephraim
☎ (0892) 42911
Open: Mon–Sat 12noon–2.30pm. Closed Sun

An elegant, old-fashioned Regency hotel, well positioned overlooking the common. The small buttery has garden access and offers good value lunches with roast turkey and pork chasseur as examples of the main courses, and a range of daily specials. Home-made apple pie and mince pies, both served with cream, are tasty desserts.

[C] [P] [🍷]

TURNBERRY
Strathclyde *Ayrshire*
Map **10** NS20

The Tapple Toorie Dormy House, Turnberry Hotel ☎ (06553) 202
Open: Mar–Nov Mon–Sun 8am–8pm

Situated between the Ailsa and Arran golf courses of the Turnberry Hotel, this smart coffee shop caters predominantly for golfers seeking refreshment between rounds, but all are made equally welcome. An attractive cold buffet and a hot dish of the day are available between mid-day and 4pm. Other dishes on the menu include haddock and deep fried chicken with apple pie and gâteaux as desserts.

[C] [P]

TURVEY
Bedfordshire
Map **4** SP95

The Chicery, The Laws Hotel on the A428 from Bedford to Northampton ☎ (023064) 213
Open: Summer: Mon–Sat 12noon–2pm, 7–9.30pm (Sat 10pm); Winter open evenings only. Closed Sun

A new concept in eating-out, the Chicery offers a limited menu based on gas-fired lava-brick grilling of chicken, cooked with various home-made sauces including Tandoori and Barbecue. Pork kebabs, scampi and steaks are also available. The décor is a garden theme of white and green with metal garden chairs, paving stone-type lino, green garden trellis round the walls with tablecloths to match help to give it an outdoor atmosphere. Start off with pâté, soup or grapefruit cocktail and, if you have a sweet tooth, chocolate fudge cake or meringue glacé.

VS

TWICKENHAM
Gt London

The French Connection (Eddie's Wine Bar) 53 London Rd ☎ 01-892 1650 Plan 4 **109** D2
Open: Mon–Sat 11am–2.30pm, 5.30–10.30pm (11pm Fri & Sat), Sun 12noon–2pm, 7–10.30pm

Cuttings from French newspapers and magazines decorate this wine bar which has the added attraction of unobtrusive live music in the evenings. The appetising menu offers simple, home-cooked dishes including cold meat salads, chicken and mushroom pie and spiced meat loaf. There is a good selection of cheeses or try the old-fashioned bread pudding served with cream.

[♫] [P]

Rugantino Trattoria Italiana 128/130 Heath Rd ☎ 01-892 9875 Plan 4 **110** D2
Open: Mon–Sun 12noon–2.30pm, Mon–Thu 6–11pm, Fri & Sat 6pm–12mdnt

A popular Italian restaurant off Twickenham High Street which specialises in pizza and pasta. The hand-painted wall murals and live music on Friday and Saturday evenings help to create a pleasant atmosphere. The menu offers dishes such as Mozzarella in Carrozza (soft cheese fried in breadcrumbs) for starters, followed by spaghetti with clam, tomato and garlic sauce and assorted ice creams.

[C] [♫] [P]

TYNDRUM
Central *Perthshire*
Map **10** NN33

Clifton Coffee House A82/A85 junction ☎ (08384) 271
Open: Apr–Oct Mon–Sun 8.30am–5.30pm

You'll be pleasantly surprised by the prices at this cheerful eaterie. It is part of a smoothly-run tourist complex that includes craft, book and whisky shops. Inside, the décor is predominantly white with strategically placed hanging baskets and hand-crafted pottery. There is an air of quality here, despite it being a self-service operation. A wide range of starters includes pâté and home-made soup. Various main courses are available throughout the day, such as lamb and beef casseroles, chicken and ham pie and lasagne.

[C] [P] [S]

TYNET
Grampian *Banffshire*
Map **15** NJ36

The Mill Motel★★ ☎ (05427) 233
Open: Mon–Sat 12.30–2pm, 7.30–9pm, Sun 12.30–2pm, 5–6pm

This old mill was converted into a restaurant in 1970 and in recent years 15 letting bedrooms have been added. The original mill wheels form the entrance hall and the mill stones can be seen in the cocktail bar. The dining room offers lunch which could consist of soup, a traditional roast and a choice of sweet. The evening meal is outside the scope of this guide.

[C] [♫] [P] **VS**

TYWYN
Gwynedd
Map **6** SH50

Greenfield Restaurant High St ☎ (0654) 710354
Open: May–Oct Mon–Sun 12noon–2pm, 4–9pm

This small restaurant with bay windows is attached to the Greenfield guesthouse (AA listed) and they are both run by Brian and Cynthia Elson. There are two lunch menus – the 'special', offering soup or juices followed by steak and kidney pie or fish, and the 'fixed price' which has a choice of seven main dishes, mostly grills and fried dishes, and a choice of sweets. A similar menu is available in the evening along with a more expensive à la carte menu. Sunday lunch is available.

[P] [S]

UCKFIELD
East Sussex
Map **5** TQ42

Percy's 119 High St ☎ (0825) 61366
Open: Tue–Sat 12noon–2.30pm, 7–11pm. Closed Mon & Sun

This popular wine bare with a Victorian staircase and a long marble-topped bar is also the home of 'Calao', a huge bird from the Ivory coast. The menu includes starters of soup and aubergine au gratin and main courses of pasta, steak, fish and pies. The choice of puddings varies from day to day. The impressive wine list includes wines from Chile, California and England.

[C] [♫] [P]

ULLAPOOL
Highland *Ross & Cromarty*
Map **14** NH19

Far Isles North Rd ☎ (0854) 2385
Open: Mon–Sun 12noon–2.15pm, 5.30–9.30pm

This attractively decorated, modern restaurant and bar on the northern outskirts of this picturesque little fishing village serves reasonably-priced wholesome food. Dishes include fresh Loch Broom scallops with savoury rice and salad, or escalope of pork Cordon Bleu, French fried and croquette potatoes with vegetables.

[P] [S]

UPMINSTER
Gt London
Map **5** TQ58

The Mill Roomes Department Store, Station Rd ☎ (04022) 50080
Open: Tue–Thu 9am–5pm, Fri–Sat 5.30pm

Recently modernised, this pleasant restaurant, with its attractive wall mural and soft lighting is on the second floor of Roomes department store. Service is personal and friendly and good, no-nonsense food is excellent value for money. The menu changes every day, but particularly recommended is the home-made steak pie, bursting with meat and served with two veg. With a starter and sweet the meal will still come within our budget. Children's portions are available.

[S] **VS**

UPPINGHAM
Leicestershire
Map **4** SP89

The White Hart Inn High St West ☎ (057282) 2229
Open: Mon–Sun 12noon–2pm, Mon–Sat 6–9.45pm, 7–9.45pm

This pleasant, old inn provides good portions of simple fare at reasonable prices either in the lounge bar or the restaurant. The starters can be followed by salads or a range of hot meals and a sweet, all at reasonable prices. Steaks are more expensive.

[P]

UPTON NOBLE
Somerset
Map **3** ST73

The Lamb Inn ☎ (074985) 308
Open: for food Mon–Sat 12noon–2.30pm (limited menu Mon), Tue–Sat 6.30–10.30pm, Sun 12noon–2pm, 7–10.30pm

You can enjoy views of the surrounding

countryside, including King Alfred's Tower, from the bar of this 17th-century free house. Starters of smoked salmon, pâté or deep fried mushrooms could be followed by Mendip steak and oyster pie or lamb kebabs, or sample one of the daily specials chalked on the blackboard. Real ales are available.

[P]

UPTON-UPON-SEVERN
Hereford & Worcester
Map **3** SO84

Cromwells 16–18 Church St
☎ (06846) 2447
Open: Mon–Sat 10am–2pm, 7–9.30pm

Oliver Cromwell is reputed to have waved to a pretty lady at an upstairs window of this charming black-and-white half-timbered cottage. The bistro with exposed brick walls and beams leads on to a walled garden where children may let off steam. Upstairs is 'Oliver's Bar' where diners may sip an aperitif and study the blackboard menu. A typical lunch menu could be home-made vegetable soup prawn and cheese vol-au-vents with a tossed salad and lemon syllabub. The dinner menu offers more choice – 10 possibles for each course including frog's legs as a starter! Stilton and onion soup could be followed by scrumpy chicken and Cromwell gâteau or lemon syllabub.

[C] [ꝏ]

VENTNOR
Isle of Wight
Map **4** SZ57

Four Seasons Wine Bar 15 High St
☎ (0983) 852169
Open: Mon–Sat 12noon–2.30pm, 7.30–11pm, Sun 12noon–2.30pm

Roger and Mavis Clinch's wine bar specialises in good, home-made international and English dishes, all at very reasonable prices. Starters include soup and taramasalata whilst stuffed trout, pork chops in barbecue sauce, prawns Creole and Indian-style chicken curry are examples of the main courses. Banana rum mousse is just one of the delicious desserts. There is live entertainment on Thursday, Friday and Saturday evenings.

[♫] [S] [P]

The Royal Hotel (THF)★★★ Belgrave Rd ☎ (0983) 852186
Open: Mon–Sun 8–9.30am, 7–9pm

The Royal does a limited but reasonably priced à la carte menu, a three-course buffet lunch and a four-course table d'hôte dinner (a little over our limit) as well as a menu of children's favourites.

[C] [P] [ꝏ]

WAKEFIELD
West Yorkshire
Map **8** SE32

The Venus Restaurant 51 Westgate
☎ (0924) 75378
Open: Mon–Sat 12noon–2.30pm, 6.30–11.30pm, Sun 7–11pm

The menu here is rich in English and Greek cuisine with some Greek speciality dishes such as kebabs and afelia (pork fillet cooked in wine sauce with coriander and cream) but the à la carte menu will require careful selection to keep the cost around £5. The three-course table d'hôte lunch is ideal, offering traditional dishes such as fish, roasts or salads, with one Greek special. Though part of the Black Bull Tavern, children are catered for with half portions of selected dishes – at half price.

[C] [♫] [P] [ꝏ]

WALTHAM CROSS
Hertfordshire
Map **5** TL30

Blues 41b High St ☎ (0992) 718633
Open: Mon–Sun 12noon–2.30pm, 7.30–10.30pm (11pm Fri & Sat)

Situated close to the 'cross', this attractive wine bar has maps of French vineyards on the walls and distinctive wooden tables and chairs making it a relaxed and casual rendezvous for lunch or dinner. The blackboard menu offers a hot 'dish of the day', pizzas and salads and a range of sweets. Service is friendly and efficient and in fine weather you can enjoy your food in the peaceful garden at the rear.

[P] [S]

WANSFORD
Cambridgeshire
Map **4** TL09

Haycock Hotel ☎ (0780) 782223
Open: Mon–Sun 12noon–2.15pm, 6.30–10pm

This early 17th-century coaching inn, situated on the River Nene and near the A1, is an ideal stopping place for road and river travellers. There is a good selection of tried and popular bar snacks including grilled rainbow trout and curried turkey leg, served with rice and poppadums. The cold buffet offers a choice of cold meats and salads. A word of warning – try to arrive early as the Haycock Hotel is very popular with locals.

[C] [P] [♤]

WAREHAM
Dorset
Map **3** SY98

The Anglebury Coffee House 15 North St ☎ (09295) 2988
Open: Mon–Sat 9.30am–5pm, lunch served 12noon–2pm (closes at 1.30pm on Wed from Oct–Mar).

The coffee house, situated in an attractive 16th century building in Wareham town centre, offers home-made cakes and light lunches prepared by the proprietors Anne and Rodney Goodhand. Lunches represent good value for money with tasty home-made pies (made with feather-light pastry) quiche and a savoury pizza served with a crisp salad. Start your meal with soup and finish with home-made fruit pie and fresh cream. The beamed interior is bright, attractive and clean and it is said that the Anglebury was once the haunt of Lawrence of Arabia.

[C] [P] [♤]

The Old Granary The Quay
☎ (09295) 2010
Open: Mon–Sat 12noon–2pm, Sun 12noon–3pm, Mon–Fri & Sun 6.30–9pm, Sat 6.30–10pm

This picturesque restaurant, situated on the banks of the River Frome, dates from 1770 and was converted from a grain store. The choice of dishes is extensive, a two-course lunch includes seafood platter, home-made pâté, hot country pie, all served with mixed salad and potatoes or granary roll and butter. The à la carte menu provides a three-course meal for lunch or dinner and with careful selection you can keep within the price limit.

[C] [P] [♤] **VS**

WARMINSTER
Wiltshire
Map **3** ST84

Chinn's Celebrated Chophouse Market Pl ☎ (0985) 212245
Open: Mon–Sat 12noon–2pm, 7–10.45pm (except mid-Oct)

Rabbits, or rather the lack of them, are the reason that this charming little eating place exists today. The Pickford family had for many years carried on a Butchers' and Fish, Game and Poultry business in Warminster, and if it hadn't been for a devastating outbreak of myxomatosis in 1965, they would still be using these cellars for their once well-established trade in rabbits and rabbit skins which were graded and dispatched from here. Braving their misfortune the Pickfords decided to convert the cellars into a restaurant. So, today you will be welcomed by staff dressed in the traditional straw boaters and striped aprons of that original business. With their knowledge of meats, fish and poultry you are assured a good, reasonably-priced meal. Chops, steak, gammon and lemon sole can be followed by a range of sweets including apple pie and peach melba. Smoked mackerel and home-made pâté are among the starters.

[C] [S] [♤]

See advertisement on page 188

WARWICK
Warwickshire
Map **4** SP26

Cindy's 48 Brook St ☎ (0926) 493504
Open: Tue–Sat 9.30am–5pm

Only about 20 people can be seated in this country kitchen style restaurant found above a tempting delicatessen, so booking in advance is advised. Dominated by pine furniture, Lowire prints and paintings for sale by a local artist, it offers freshly prepared dishes attractively displayed on the large pine dresser. During summer, a hot dish of the day, home-made quiches and pies accompanied by a selection of salads and gâteaux are the bill of fare. In the winter months, delicious soup and hot main dishes are available.

[C] [S]

Nicolini's Bistro 18 Jury St
☎ (0926) 495817
Open: Tue–Sun 9.30am–10.30pm

Located on one of the main thoroughfares of the city is this delightful little restaurant with its stripped pine chairs, potted plants and effective spot lighting. A well-stocked glass counter displaying fresh salads and tempting sweets (including ice-cream specialities) immediately attracts the eye, and other dishes are available, such as tasty home-made pizzas.

[C] [P] [S] [♤] **VS**

The Waterman Hatton ☎ (0926) 492427
Open: Mon–Sat 11am–2pm, 6–10pm (10.30 Sat), Sun 12noon–2pm, 7–10pm

This imposing brick inn was built by the famous Arkwright family in 1842. The main bar offers panoramic views of the daunting 21 Hatton locks of the Grand Union Canal. Bar snacks can be enjoyed in the garden when the weather permits. In the restaurant there is a good range of starters and for your main course there is a choice of fish, steaks, salads, chicken and duck. The price of the main course includes a sweet of ice cream or cheese and biscuits. The three-course Sunday lunch is excellent value and all children's portions in the restaurant are half price.

[C] [P] [🍷]

WATERHOUSES
Staffordshire
Map **7** SK05

The Olde Beams ☎ (05386) 254
Open: Tue–Sat 12noon–2pm, 6.30–10pm, Sun 12noon–2pm

In the centre of the village is this charming brick-built house which was originally an inn. It was built in 1746, and the restaurant has exposed ceiling beams, refectory tables and Windsor chairs. All the food on the table d'hôte menu is home-made, including a selection of delicious sweets on the trolley, the soup of the day, and delicious bread rolls. The menu is changed weekly but main courses could include fillet of plaice, escalope of pork Viennoise and steak and mushroom pie.

[P] [🍷]

WELLINGBOROUGH
Northamptonshire
Map **4** SP86

Magee's Bistro 5–7 Queen St
☎ (0933) 226051
Open: Mon–Sun 12noon–2.30pm, 7–11pm

This family-run restaurant displays a collection of authentic enamel advertising signs dating from 1910. The extensive menu offers a wide variety of dishes including a range of pasta and vegetarian meals. Starters of deep fried Camembert or Billingsgate fish soup could be followed by main courses of Mariners tart (a creamy tart of smoked fish) or steak and mushroom pie. Wine is available by the glass or try one of the interesting cocktails.

♫ P ⚘

WELLINGTON
Somerset
Map **3** ST12

Beam Bridge Hotel★★ Sampford Arundel ☎ (0823) 672223
Open: Mon–Sat 11.30am–2.30pm, 6.30–11pm, Sun 12noon–2pm, 7–10.30pm

This small hotel on the A38 is an ideal stopping off place for the motorist. If you are in a hurry, the bar snacks are the thing – try the jacket potatoes with cheese, prawn or curry filling. Bill of fare in the peaceful restaurant offers a very wide choice, with a good range of starters. Deep fried breaded mushrooms with tartare sauce are delicious and reasonably priced. Chicken Kiev or lambs kidneys with herbs and wine sauce are interesting main courses. A host of sweets include crême caramel and black cherry and kirsch ice cream.

C ♫ P ⚘ **VS**

Poachers Pocket Burlescombe
☎ (0823) 672286
6m S of Wellington on the A38
Open: Restaurant: Mon–Sat 12noon–2.30pm, 6–10pm, Sun 12noon–2.30pm
Bar: Mon–Sat 11am–2.30pm, 6–10pm, Sun 12noon–2pm, 7–10pm

This 17th-century inn gives you the choice of a pleasant bar or a peaceful restaurant. The bar offers a wide range of snacks, including chicken or prawn curry, scampi or chicken in the basket, gammon and pineapple, rump steak, giant pasties, salads and sandwiches. In the restaurant, the à la carte menu gives excellent value and you can feast on pheasant cooked in Madeira wine, and a starter such as terrine provençale or apfel strudel with Devon cream for dessert. All main courses include vegetables. Children are welcome and can eat food from the bar menu in the restaurant if their parents wish to eat à la carte.

C P ⚘

WELLS
Somerset
Map **3** ST54

Riverside Restaurant Coxley
☎ (0749) 72411
3m S of Wells on the A39
Open: Mar–Sep Mon–Sun 10am–11pm, Oct–Feb Tue–Sun 11am–2.30pm, 6–10pm

This 10-year-old family-run restaurant was originally an 18th-century cottage which housed the local wheelwright in an adjoining barn. Nestling alongside the River Sheppey, it has retained its simple charm. Children are particularly welcome with a menu to suit their tastes with dishes such as egg and chips or sausage and chips. Main courses offer two house specialities: pollo al cacciatore (chicken with sauce of wine, tomato, mushrooms and pimento) and bistecca alla Siciliana (rump steak in a slightly hot red wine sauce) – all include croquet or chipped potatoes plus vegetables of the day or mixed salad. Coffees include a rum, coffee and fresh cream concoction. Any dishes on the menu may be taken away at slightly less than the normal charge and you can place your order by telephone.

♫ P ⚘

WEMBLEY
Gt London

Peking Castle Restaurant 379 High Rd
☎ 01-902 3605 Plan 4 **111** B2
Open: Mon–Sun 12noon–2.30pm, 6–11.30pm

Apart from the à la carte menu, this quiet haven from the rush of the High Road

for entry see Bleadney

traffic, where hanging Chinese lanterns and a dragon motif evoke the East, offers special dinners for two or more people. A meal composed of soup, crispy duck, chicken in yellow-bean sauce, prawns in chili sauce, vegetables, fried rice and toffee apple comes within our budget. The main menu includes the usual array of fish, poultry and meat dishes, the cuisine is the upper-class Peking style. Economy-minded diners would be well advised to skip wine with their meal, instead drinking china tea, which will be served ad infinitum.

S

WESTBURY
Wiltshire
Map **3** ST85

Whalley's 35 Warminster Rd
☎ (0373) 822551
Open: Mon–Sun 12noon–3pm, Fri & Sat 7.30–11pm

This modern shop-fronted restaurant is on the main Warminster Road through town. The selection of snacks, including pizza, cottage pie, cauliflower cheese and pâté are all reasonably priced. Main dishes include roast lamb, braised beef in ale, steak and kidney pie, fish dishes and salads, and there is a range of sweets. There is an evening à la carte menu on Friday and Saturday but most of the meals are just outside the limits of this guide. Cream teas are also served.

P

WESTERHAM
Kent
Map **5** TQ45

The Henry Wilkinson 26 Market Sq
☎ (0959) 64245
Open: Mon–Sat 12noon–3pm, 7–10.30pm

This new wine bar has a pleasant restaurant with pine tables and a good choice of home-made casseroles and soups, fresh salads, savoury flans and pies. The blackboard menu displays the special hot dish of the day for lunch and supper, which is usually served with potatoes or rice and a green salad. Desserts include meringue glacée and a pudding of the day.

C P S

WEST KIRBY
Merseyside
Map **7** SJ28

The Pancake Kitchen 96 Banks Rd
☎ 051-625 9060
Open: Mon–Fri 12noon–3pm, 7pm–12mdnt, Sat and Sun 12noon–12mdnt

A bright and lively place where the pancakes are served with a wide variety of toppings and fillings. Our inspector tried Chicken Creole – chicken in a wine and creamy cheese sauce with a chopped egg sandwiched between two pancakes and topped with sweetcorn – and described it as delightfully different. The range of sweet pancakes includes the Mississippi Special – pancake topped with chocolate ice cream, hot chocolate fudge, chocolate chips and cream. There is a special menu for children.

C P

What's Cooking? 34 Banks Rd
☎ 051-625 7579
Open: Mon–Sat 12noon–11.30pm, Sun 1–11.30pm

The bright cream and green exterior of this first-floor restaurant is just as inviting as its name. Ideal for shoppers and families, What's Cooking? is located close to the town centre and specialises in American and Continental-style cuisine. Menu selections include beefburgers with a choice of toppings plus home-made dressing, pizzas, steaks and chicken or 'mouth-watering, mammoth salads'. Chili con carne or spare ribs are interesting alternatives.

C S

WESTON-SUPER-MARE
Avon
Map **3** ST36

Chris's Restaurant 8 Alexandra Parade
☎ (0934) 23481
Open: Mon–Sun 12noon–2pm, 6–11.30pm

Chris's Restaurant, formerly known as the Regent Steak House and under the same management, is a small, attractive, fully-licensed eating place with 16 tables in polished dark wood, red/gold-patterned upholstered chairs with elegant green carpet and plush curtains, all of which add warmth to the room. Charcoal-grilled steaks are the house speciality. Other grills, salads or omelettes are plain but less pricey. The 'chef's specialities' are more ambitious creations with tempting sauces, but these are likely to be outside our budget. For the grand finale there are six special coffees, including monk's coffee with Benedictine liqueur.

C ♫ P S **VS**

WETHERBY
North Yorkshire
Map **8** SE44

Alpine Inn (2m N on the A1)
☎ (0937) 62501
Open: Mon–Sun 11.30am–7pm

This roadside inn could have been transported from the Alps with its traditional Alpine décor and furnishings. Here we are mainly interested in the lunch and high tea menus. The three-course lunch menu offers a choice of dishes, a typical meal could be soup, followed by a roast or home-made steak and kidney pie and a sweet. The high tea menu operates from 3–7pm and offers a variety of dishes including lasagne, haddock and salad.

C ♫ P ☺ **VS**

WEYMOUTH
Dorset
Map **3** SY67

The Clarendon Restaurant 52/53 The Esplanade ☎ (0305) 786706
Open: Mon–Sun 9am–11pm

A licensed seafront restaurant near the shopping area which provides day-long refreshment for shoppers, businessmen and families. A three-course meal offers a range of starters, main dishes and sweets, both lunch and dinner are within our price range, or choose from the à la carte menu. Fresh seafood is available daily and the local crabmeat salad is a treat. Children's portions of most à la carte dishes can be ordered but the Pirate's Delight or Cowboy's Brunch are established favourites.

C S ☺

WHITBY
North Yorkshire
Map **8** NZ81

The Georgian 25 St Hilda's Ter
☎ (0947) 603345
Open: Summer Mon–Sun 11.45am–6pm, 7–10.30pm, Winter private functions only

Did you know that many of the horrible deeds of Bram Stoker's Count Dracula actually took place in Whitby? Well, you may rest assured that such fiendish goings on will not trouble you in The Georgian restaurant – it used to be the vicarage. Attractively situated, with fine lawns and rose beds, the restaurant is conveniently placed for access to the town centre. Prices are reasonable and there is a set lunch, with a varied menu.

♫ S ☺

Magpie Café 14 Pier Rd
☎ (0947) 602058
Open: Mon–Thu, Sat–Sun 11.30am–2.30pm, 3.30–6.30pm

Proprietors Sheila and Ian McKenzie claim that their menus provide a meal to suit *all* tastes though a special effort is made to cater for families, with cradles and high chairs provided. A Magpie Special Lunch offers home-made soup of the day as one starter, home-made steak pie, chips and peas and a choice which includes fresh cream sherry trifle or strawberry flan, Black Forest gâteau or apple pie. The Magpie Special Fish Lunch offers a choice of Whitby crab, prawn cocktail or potted shrimps as appetisers, cod or haddock with chips and a selection of about 26 sweets. With both lunches a pot of tea is included, since The Magpie is unlicensed, but since there is a choice of four liqueur mousses in each case, you won't be totally on the wagon! A special children's meal offers sausage, beans and chips, jelly and ice cream and a glass of orange.

☺

WHITCHURCH
Hereford & Worcester
Map **3** SO51

Gallery Restaurant Wayside
☎ (0600) 890408
Open: Mon, Wed–Sun 12.30–2pm, 7.30–10pm

Travellers on the A40 often drive straight past Whitchurch, but at mealtimes, particularly at lunch-time, a detour to the Gallery Restaurant is well worth while. This comfortable and elegant little restaurant provides an excellent table d'hôte lunch menu. The menu varies but there is always a choice of at least three starters and main courses. A typical meal could be cream of mushroom soup, roast rib of beef and a choice of sweet from the trolley. The à la carte menu available in the evening is outside our budget but worth saving for.

C P ☺

WHITEBROOK
Gwent
Map **4** SO50

The Crown ☎ (0600) 860254
Open: Mon–Sun 12noon–2pm, 7–10pm

Situated in a pleasant, hilly, wooded area near the River Wye, the Crown describes itself as 'a French restaurant with rooms'. The gourmet restaurant is too expensive for us but some of the sophisticated restaurant dishes are available in the bar. These include Ballotine de Canard – truffled duck terrine with port, and Ficelles Brestoise – buckwheat pancakes filled with cheese, mushrooms and ham. All dishes are served with home-made rolls and butter. An interesting range of cocktails is available.

C P

WHITMINSTER
Gloucestershire
Map **3** SO70

The Old Forge ☎ (0452) 740875
Open: Mon–Sun 12noon–2pm, 7–10pm

Good home cooking is the order of the day at this small character Free House and restaurant, conveniently positioned adjacent to the A38 and close to the M5 (exit 13). Careful selection of two courses from the à la carte menu may well fall within our budget. However, the bar menu is very popular and offers excellent value with dishes such as steak and kidney pie, giant Gloucester sausage and grilled fresh Alderley trout. Starters and sweets are also available.

[C] [P]

WHITSTABLE
Kent
Map **5** TR16

Pearson's Crab and Oyster House Sea Wall ☎ (0227) 272005
Open: Mon–Sat 12noon–2.30pm, 6–10.30pm, Sun 12noon–2pm, 7–10pm (open until 11pm 1Jun–1Oct)

This attractive 16th-century restaurant and pub, facing the sea, specialises in sea food. Both the crab and lobster are kept in the restaurant's own tanks and along with the Imperial Whitstable oysters, they are expensive – but aren't they everywhere? Try a bowl of hot mussels and follow with whole fresh prawns served with salad. Other dishes include roast beef and cheese salads, and a range of sweets. The restaurant is very popular with the locals – so come early. A bar menu (mainly sea food) is also available.

[🍷]

WHITTINGTON
Staffordshire
Map **7** SO88

Whittington Inn Wine Bar
☎ (038483) 2110
Open: Mon–Sat 12noon–2.30pm, 6.30–10.30pm, Sun 12noon–2pm, 7–10.30pm
On the A449

If you want to know the real story of Dick Whittington the legendary Lord Mayor, you could do not better than to eat a meal in the attractive attic wine bar in his ancestral home. A potted history of the Whittington family dating from 1307, is available for any interested diner to read. The interior of the wine bar is mainly white-painted brick, effectively decorated with old prints and posters, antique bed warmers and armoury and with the original black oak beams and rafters a prominent feature. A selection of food is made either from the mouthwatering array of salads, pies, sweets and cheeses displayed behind a glass counter, or from a blackboard which lists hot or cold specialities such as lasagne or chili con carne.

[P] [🍷]

WICK
Highland *Caithness*
Map **15** ND35

Lamplighter Wellington Guest House, 41–43 High St ☎ (0955) 3287
Open: Summer Mon–Sat 11.30am–1.45pm, Thu–Sat 6–9pm (last orders), Winter Mon–Sat 11.30am–1.45pm

This well-established house has been in operation for 50 years, and now John and Rhona Houston are at the helm to provide an excellent lunch or dinner at their first-floor restaurant, or a good range of snack meals in the ground-floor cafeteria. Lunch of melon and raspberries in sparkling wine, followed by prawns au gratin, plus a home-made sweet from the trolley is a satisfying meal.

[P] [🍷]

WIGAN
Gt Manchester
Map **7** SD50

Roberto's Rowbottom Sq
☎ (0942) 42385
Open: Restaurant Mon–Sat 11.30am–2pm, 7–10pm, Fri 10.30pm
Pizza Bar Mon–Sat 11.30am–2pm

Nestling in what were once the cellars of the local newspaper, this pine-tabled restaurant, with its pot plants and pictures, offers pastas, pizzas and inexpensive 'English' meals of the chicken or plaice and chips variety in a pizza bar next door, and an excellent table d'hôte menu in the restaurant. A three-course lunch could consist of egg mayonnaise, cannelloni and sherry trifle.

[C] [♫] [🍷]

WILMSLOW
Cheshire
Map **7** SJ88

Greyhound Steakhouse Wilmslow Rd, Handforth ☎ (0625) 523193
Open: Mon–Sat 12noon–2.30pm, 6–1.30pm, Sun 12noon–2.30pm, 7–10.30pm

This Schooner Inn steakhouse, about 10 miles south of Manchester, features natural stone combined with timbers from Fleetwood pier. Begin with soup or prawn cocktail. Main courses (the price includes an ice cream sweet or cheese) vary from fillet of plaice with lemon, tartare sauce, peas and jacket potato or chips to chicken Cordon Bleu. Lunchtime snacks such as shepherd's pie or filled rolls are available at the bar.

[C] [♫] [P] [S] [🍷]

WILTON
Wiltshire
Map **4** SU03

Ship Inn Burcombe ☎ (0722) 743182
Open: Mon–Sat 10am–2.30pm, 6–11pm, Sun 12noon–2pm, 7–10.30pm

An old inn of great character, The Ship is run by Ken Price who was once a chef on the Cunard liners, the *Queen Mary* and the *Queen Elizabeth*. If the day is sunny, sit at one of the tables set out in the garden and enjoy your meal out in the open air. The garden also has a trout stream running by it. There is a good menu to choose from and the choice is varied. Starters include country pâté served with hot toast and melon in a boat; main courses include, mushroom or

cheese and tomato pizza, with chips and garni.

[♫] [P] [☘]

WIMBORNE MINSTER
Dorset
Map **4** SZ09

Quinneys West Boro' ☎ (0202) 883518
Open: Tue–Sat 9.15am–5.15pm (lunch served 12noon–2pm)

Quinneys is a delightful old cottage near to the town's main square and the Minster. Various one-course economy meals include avocado pear with prawns and salad and grilled lamb cutlets with three veg. The three-course lunchtime meals are on offer and examples are roast chicken, lamb and gammon, plus the local speciality – Wimborne trout. Quinneys has its own bakery producing home-made gâteaux, cream cakes and a host of original recipe confectionery. There is also an extensive tea menu. Wine is available by the glass.

[P] [S] [☘] **VS**

WINCHELSEA
East Sussex
Map **5** TQ91

The Bridge Inn The Strand
Open: Mon–Sat 10.30am–2.30pm, 6–11pm, Sun 12noon–2pm, 7–10.30pm

This delightful 16th-century inn offers a good choice of meals all at reasonable prices. Seafood platter, salads and home-made steak and kidney pie are just a few of the main courses on the menu. Snacks include jumbo sausage and chips and a range of sandwiches.

[♫] [P] [☘]

WINCHESTER
Hampshire
Map **4** SU42

The Cart and Horses Inn Kingsworthy 2m N of Winchester off the Winchester by-pass ☎ (0962) 882360
Open: during licensing hours Mon–Sun, hot food 12.15–1.45pm, cold food 12noon–2pm, hot food 7–9.45pm, cold food till later

Built in 1540, the Cart and Horses is a traditional beams-and-brasses type of pub. The furnishings are simple, staff friendly and there is a good range of bar food to choose from including a cold buffet and hot dishes such as pan fried liver, bacon and onions and pork and pineapple curry. A range of snacks is also available. The new Carvery offers a choice of roasts and puddings such as Spotted Dick and Jam Rolly Poly. The à la carte menu served in the restaurant is beyond our price range. There is a garden seating for children and if the weather is poor they may use the restaurant (though not the bar).

[C] [P] [☘]

Minstrels Restaurant 18 Little Minster St ☎ (0962) 67212
Open: Mon–Sat 10am–6pm

Situated just off the High Street this friendly restaurant in farmhouse style with pine tables and chairs is a popular venue for shoppers and tourists alike. A delicious range of home-made cakes, sweets and patisserie are on display to accompany your morning coffee or afternoon tea. Hot dishes available throughout the day are quiche, pizzas, savoury pancakes and jacket potatoes. Salad side dishes are available and a selection of these can be formed for a full meal. Other dishes include ratatouille, fisherman's pie and moussaka.

[☘]

Mr Pitkin's Wine Bar & Eating House
4 Jewry St ☎ (0962) 69630
Open: Restaurant Sun–Thu 12noon–2pm, 7–10pm, Fri–Sat 12noon–2pm, 7–10.15pm
Bar Mon–Thu 11am–2.30pm, 6–10.30pm, Fri–Sat 11am–2.30pm, 6–11pm, Sun 12noon–2.30pm, 7–10.30pm

When Tony Pitkin left the hubbub of Fleet Street advertising, he brought a little of the London life to Winchester with him. His wine bar is now one of the busiest rendezvous in the city, with live music one or two nights a week and a pleasantly trendy, Edwardian-style atmosphere. The long, narrow bar has gas-lamp-style fittings and enlarged prints of wine labels; Mr Pitkin blends into the atmosphere well with his bow tie and colourful shirts. Three courses from the appetising slabs of cold meats and smoked fish, hot dishes of the day and good range of starters and sweets will come within the budget. A chef presides over the bar's Sunday roast and Yorkshire pudding. The upstairs restaurant, elegant and intimate with its marble fireplace and russet walls, serves a daily lunch, but beware of the enticing items with a budget-breaking surcharge in brackets. Dinner is too expensive for us.

[C] [♫] [S] [☘] **VS**

The Old Chesil Rectory Chesil St
☎ (0962) 53177
Open: Tue–Sat 12noon–2.30pm, 7.30–10.30pm, Sun 12noon–2.30pm. Closed Mon

The restaurant, set in the oldest building in Winchester, offers Italian and French cuisine. Inexpensive daily lunches include home-made soup, skate in butter sauce, rabbit casserole, sweet and savoury pancakes, cheese and sorbets. The à la carte dinner menu is generally outside the scope of this guide.

[C] [♫] [S] [P]

Old Mill Restaurant 1 Bridge St
☎ (0962) 63151
Open: Mon–Sat 11.45am–1.45pm, 6.45–9.45pm, Sun 11.45am–1.45pm

This small, cosy licensed restaurant standing on the site of the old Eastgate Mill, offers excellent value home cooking and very friendly service. The lunch menu has a good choice of plain, English dishes – all at very low prices. Soup could be followed by roast chicken and home-made apple pie. A more international menu is available in the evenings and dishes include chicken chasseur, duck à la l'orange and beef stroganoff.

[♫] [S] [P]

Splinters✕✕ 9 Great Minster St
☎ (0962) 64004
Open: Mon–Sat 11am–2.30pm

Mike and Fiona Sherret's tastefully decorated Victorian restaurant, with its dark gold wallpaper and 'ball' lights, offers predominantly French cuisine – its à la carte lunches are mainly outside our price range, but it earns a well-deserved place in the guide for the excellent-value lunches served in the brasserie, where soup, hot or cold ratatouille, fresh crab au gratin and a range of meat dishes and desserts are available. If the ground floor is full, you can order the brasserie menu upstairs in the restaurant.

[C] [S]

WINDERMERE
Cumbria
Map **7** SD49

Gibby's 43 Crescent Rd ☎ (09662) 3267
Open: week before Easter–end October, Mon–Sun 11.15am–2.30pm, 4.30–9pm

This small, canopied restaurant, in Tudor style, can be found in Windermere town centre. The daily three-course 'special' for lunch or dinner is excellent value, and children's meals include beefburgers or fish-fingers with chips. There is also a selection of special coffees. This is an unpretentious restaurant, popular with families, holidaymakers and business people alike.

[♫] [P] [S] [☘] **VS**

See advertisement on page 196

WINDSOR
Berkshire
Map **4** SU97

Choices 10 Thames St ☎ (07535) 66437
Open: Mon–Sat 12noon–3pm, 6–11pm, Sun 12.30–3pm, 6.30–10.30pm

Handily placed for a visit to Windsor Castle, this busy restaurant has refreshingly uncluttered floor space. Traditional-style wall-lights interspersed with framed prints make for a pleasant enough décor. Onion soup could be followed by lamb cutlets, but you will have to forego a sweet to stay within the budget.

C S

The Drury House Restaurant 4 Church St ☎ (07535) 63734
Open: Tue–Sun 10am–5.30pm

In this charming 17th-century setting, within a stone's throw of the guardsmen at the gate of the Castle, Joan Hearne serves good, plain English food at no-nonsense prices, with a choice of salads and of main dishes including grilled lamb's liver and bacon. Home-made gâteaux are on sale.

VS

Summerfield's 15–17 Thames St
Open: Mon–Sun 12noon–12mdnt

Situated opposite the castle, Summerfield's offers a range of home-made pizzas and pasta dishes. The house special is Fettuccine served with a tasty cheese, ham and mushroom cream sauce which, like most of the pasta dishes, can be served either as a main course or a starter or child's portion. The deep dish pizzas are freshly made to order with a choice of wholemeal or white crust and a variety of toppings. There is a limited choice of desserts.

♫ P

WINGFIELD
Bedfordshire
Map **4** SP92

The Plough Inn off the A5120 near Toddington ☎ (05255) 3077
Open: Mon–Sat 12noon–2pm, 6–10.30pm, Sun 12noon–2pm, 7–10.30pm

A good place to stop when the weather's good, this Whitbread pub dating from the early 17th century is in pleasant countryside between Houghton Regis and Toddington, and has a garden. A fairly conventional choice of lunches is available Monday to Saturday (roasts, steak, fish, etc), but excellent value. Apart from peas, only fresh, local vegetables are served. Interesting specialities such as venison pie make filling main courses.

♫ P

WINSCOMBE
Somerset
Map **3** ST45

Penscot Farmhouse Restaurant
Shipham ☎ (093484) 2659
Open: Wed–Sat 7–9.30pm, Sun 12noon–2pm. Closed Mon & Tue

Quietly set back from the village green this attractive farmhouse hotel restaurant has a particularly friendly and informal atmosphere. Dishes on the à la carte menu have a Somerset flavour with main courses such as pork chops cooked in local cider and Somerset gammon and apricots. A traditional lunch is available on Sundays. The restaurant is licensed.

P

WISBECH
Cambridgeshire
Map **5** TF40

Dickens Tavern 17 Hill St
☎ (0945) 583476
Open: Tue–Sat 12noon–2.30pm, 7.30pm–12mdnt

Built in the early 18th century, this former private residence was recently converted into the Dickens Tavern – a restaurant and wine bar. The Tavern is on two levels with the wine bar on the ground floor and the main restaurant on the first floor. The tastefully decorated Georgian Room on the ground floor is used by restaurant diners and private parties. Of the two menus on offer, only the Tavern Fare Menu is suitable for this guide. Listed on this menu (all dishes are home-made) are omelettes, salads, spaghetti bolognese, lasagne, moussaka and chicken and chips. Weekly 'specials' could include gammon, steak, seafood platter and steak and kidney pie.

C ♫ P S

WISHAW
Strathclyde *Lanarkshire*
Map **11** NS75

Anvil Steakhouse 254 Main St
☎ (0698) 375546
Open: Mon–Sat 12noon–2.30pm, 5–10pm, Sun 6.30–10pm

In Wishaw's main street, this member of the Stakis Steakhouse chain is a popular lunchtime venue for local business people. The emphasis is on convenience, with good value, standard menus of the chicken, gammon and steak variety. Accompaniments are chips or baked potato and peas.

C ♫ S

WIVELISCOMBE
Somerset
Map **3** ST02

Country Fare 4 High St ☎ (0984) 23231
Open: Mon–Wed & Fri 9am–5.30pm, Sat 9am–5pm, Sun 12noon–2pm

Use Wiveliscombe's free parking and stroll down the High Street to Country Fare! This small 18th-century family restaurant has an extensive range of good, fresh basic food, including home-made cakes and pastries. The Paskin family regard the comfort and satisfaction of their guests as of prime importance; home cooking is prepared and served to high professional standards. The daily 'bargain bite', consists of dishes such as home-made sausage, apple and chutney pie or two beefburgers and chips. A set lunch might include soup, pork chops in cider (locally-brewed, naturally) or a roast, followed by fruit pie and cream.

P **VS**

WOBURN
Bedfordshire
Map **4** SP93

Woburn Wine Lodge 13 Bedford St
☎ (052525) 439

Open: Mon–Sat 12noon–2.30pm, 6.30–10.30pm, Sun 12noon–2pm, 7–10.30pm

Housed in a converted stone cottage with pretty bay windows, the Woburn Wine Lodge offers a range of salads from a display cabinet and a tasty dish of the day which could be roast lamb, or beef and potato pie. There is a self-service barbecue in the garden during the summer (weather permitting).

C P ♧

WOLVERHAMPTON
West Midlands
Map **7** SO99

Le Bistro Steakhouse 6 School St ☎ (0902) 24638
Open: Mon–Sat 12noon–2.30pm, 6–11.30pm

A variety of bottles hanging against white walls, black wrought-iron partitions, and red-patterned carpet create a welcoming atmosphere in this first-floor restaurant. The kitchen is supervised by owner 'Steve' Kyriakou who makes sure that Greek specialities such as moussaka and afelia are cooked to perfection. Lunchtime table d'hôte menus offer a choice of Greek or English food.

♫ S ♧

Pepito's 5 School St ☎ (0902) 23403
Open: Mon–Sat 12noon–2.30pm, 6–11pm

For those who like Italian food, Pepito's offers the real thing in a pleasant modern restaurant with glass partitioning providing a degree of privacy. Owner Mr Catellani supervises the cooking while his wife, helped by two young ladies, looks after the customers. The two-course table d'hôte lunch is good value with a choice of four starters and a main course pasta dish or, perhaps, goulash or a roast – there are seven or eight items to choose from. A three-course meal is also available.

C ♫ P S ♧

WOODSTOCK
Oxfordshire
Map **4** SP41

Brothertons 1 High St ☎ (0993) 811114
Open: Mon–Sun 12.30–2.30pm, 7–10.30pm

This gas-lit wine bar/brasserie offers a set three-course lunch menu which could consist of home-made soup with bread, a chicken dish, and rum truffle cake. The à la carte menu has a vegetarian dish of the day, crêpes, salads and hot dishes such as halibut steak with provençale sauce. A traditional roast lunch is served on Sundays in place of the normal menu.

S P ♧

WOOLHAMPTON
Berkshire
Map **4** SU56

The Rowbarge Station Rd
☎ (93321) 2213
Open: Mon–Sun 12noon–2pm, 7–9pm

Character actor Lawrence Naismith presides over this low-ceilinged inn. The menu changes every day, but excellent examples are home-made rissoles in wine gravy with sauté potatoes or haddock Monte Carlo (served with parsley and egg sauce, poached egg and sauté potatoes). Prices are very reasonable and you can select a three-course meal within our budget. The restaurant offers an à la carte menu.

♫ P ♧

WOOLSTHORPE BY BELVOIR
Lincolnshire
Map **8** SK83

Chequers Inn ☎ (0476) 870250
Open: Mon–Sat 11.30am–2.30pm, 7–10pm, Sun 12noon–1.15pm, 7–9.30pm

A typical red-brick village pub, thought to be around 400 years old, with its own cricket ground used by the village team. Extensive bar menus offer snacks, speciality ploughman's, pâté, etc. and more substantial meals of steak, kebabs, gammon and a daily special.

P ♧

WORCESTER
Hereford & Worcester
Map **3** SO85

The Bear and Ragged Staff Bransford (4m SW of Worcester of A4103)
☎ (0886) 32407
Open: bar meals: Mon–Sun 12.15–2pm, 7–9.30pm
Restaurant: Tue–Sat 12.30–2pm, 7.30–10pm, Sun 12.30–2pm

This restaurant is in a large building in the centre of the peaceful village of Bransford which lies at the foot of the Malvern Hills. Inside you can expect a warm welcome from Ian and Jaqueline Stanton who pride themselves on running a good restaurant. An à la carte menu is available in the restaurant, and bar meals are served by waitresses in a separate room (or the pleasant gardens, weather permitting). On the bar-menu soup can be followed by main courses ranging from roast chicken to pizza, and a choice of sweets. A popular Sunday lunch is also available.

P ♧

Natural Break 17 Mealcheapen St
☎ (0905) 29979
Open: Mon–Sat 10am–4.30pm

Brown-tiled tables and natural pine create an informal, cottagey atmosphere in this popular rendezvous, where proprietors Sandra and Nigel Wolfenden pin notices of local societies' meetings on the wall alongside paintings by local artists which are offered for sale. The board menu lists a choice of eight interesting salads – potato, carrot and cheese, mushroom, apple, celery and walnut – ideal to accompany the home-made savoury flans and quiches. Desserts include home-baked apple pie, meringues and pastries – freshly prepared every day.

S ♧

WORTHING
West Sussex
Map **4** TQ10

Happy Cheese Liverpool Bldgs, Liverpool Rd ☎ (0903) 201074
Open: Mon–Sat 8am–5pm

Two floors are devoted to this modern eating place and bar. A wallboard menu offers such dishes as home-made soup, roast chicken with vegetables, pizzas and salads. A three-course meal should come within our budget.

♫ S ♧

The Mississippi 187 Montague St
☎ (0903) 39712
Open: Summer Mon–Sun 12noon–2.30pm, 6–11pm; Winter Mon–Sat 12noon–2.30pm, 7–10.30pm. Closed Sun

The restaurant's design is based on a river boat with wooden floors and walls and boat motifs on the windows. The menu lists a range of snacks, burgers and house 'specials' including chicken à la creme and shallow-fried turkey breast stuffed with asparagus and ham sauce. One of the sundaes or ice cream coupes will round off your meal. There is a 'ragtime' pianist Friday and Saturday evenings.

C ♫ S P ♧

YARMOUTH
Isle of Wight
Map **4** SZ38

The Bugle Hotel★★ St James's Sq
☎ (0983) 760272
Open: Summer Mon–Sun 12.30–2pm, 7–9pm, Winter Mon–Sun 7–9pm

The 300-year-old Bugle, with its panelled dining room, complete with ancient stone fireplace, has a great deal of character and charm. The cuisine is international and the menu table d'hôte, offers a three-course lunch (dinner unfortunately is outside our budget). The recently-enlarged Galleon Bar, with décor on a nautical theme, has cold meat salads and various snacks available.

C ♫ P S ♧ **VS**

The George Hotel★★ Quay St
☎ (0983) 760331
Open: Mon–Sun 8.30–10am, 12.30–2.15pm, 7.30–9.15pm

Built by the Governor of the Island, during the reign of Charles II, the George is now a comfortable family-owned and run hotel, popular with yachties and locals. A table d'hôte lunch is available in the panelled dining room, but dinner is now a little above our budget. The food is English traditional, with fresh vegetables and is very good. For lunch you can enjoy soup, roast lamb, and a choice of sweet. Bar snacks include hot dishes ranging from sausage and chips to steak and salad. Sandwiches and lighter snacks are also available. A large glass of French house wine is available in the restaurant – a welcome accompaniment to your meal.

[C] [P] VS

YARMOUTH, GREAT
Norfolk
Map **5** TG50

Moments 149 King St ☎ (0493) 2967

Originally two merchants' houses, Moments is an American-style restaurant, serving a range of steaks, hamburgers, spare ribs, club sandwiches, pizzas and pancakes. Starters include clam chowder, Caribbean melon, prawn and tuna cocktail.

[C] [P]

YEOVIL
Somerset
Map **3** ST51

Bountiful Goodness 5 Union St ☎ (0935) 73722
Open: Mon–Sat 9am–9pm

Situated in Yeovil town centre, Bountiful Goodness is a wholefood restaurant enthusiastically run by Liz Morris. Coffee and tea with home-made cakes are available mornings and afternoons. The menu includes quiches, pizzas, salads and moussaka with home-made desserts to follow. Wine and real ale is also served. In the evening there is a take-away next door which is popular with business people.

[S] [P] VS

YORK
North Yorkshire
Map **8** SE65

Bess's Coffee House Royal Station Hotel, Station Rd ☎ (0904) 53681
Open: Mon–Sat 12.30–2.30pm, 6–9pm, Sun 12.30–2pm

The tables here are set between stage coach doors; a highwayman's pistol and a mural depicting Turpin's ride and ultimate capture, line the walls. The menu offers a good range of well-priced dishes and a typical meal might include Yorkshire broth (made from an ancient local recipe), savoury steak and kidney pie and cheesecake with whipped cream. Children can have a main meal of chicken leg and chips or fish fingers and chips.

[C] [P] [S]

Betty's Oakroom Restaurant and Tea Room St Helen's Sq ☎ (0904) 22323
Open: Mon–Sat 9am–5.30pm

The main restaurant in this three-storeyed corner house complex is in the basement and takes its name from the all-oak furnishings. A three-course meal here could include Chef's special cauliflower soup, roast beef and Yorkshire pudding and Swiss sherry trifle to finish. Above, in the cafeteria you can dine on fruit juice, roast beef and Yorkshire pud, plus a gâteau.

[P] [S]

Bibis 115–119 Micklegate ☎ (0904) 34765
Open: Mon–Fri 6–11.30pm, Sat 12noon–2.15pm, 6–11.30pm, Sun 12.15–2.15pm, 6–11pm

Very Italian, this ballroom-sized ground-floor restaurant with its wide selection of pastas and pizzas as well as blackboard-listed specials such as chicken, fish, or steak dishes. Starters include fresh Whitby crab when in season, buttered corn-on-the-cob, and honeydew melon, and there is a selection of home-made desserts and flambé ice creams.

[P] [S]

Charlie's Bistro County Hotel, Tanner Row ☎ (0904) 25120
Open: Mon–Thu 12noon–2pm, 6–11pm, (closed Mon evenings) Fri–Sat 12noon–2pm, 6–12mdnt

This little bistro on the ground floor of the County Hotel is decorated in 1920s style, with pictures of Charlie Chaplin around the walls. The choice of dishes à la carte includes peppered fillet steak with baked potato and salad and York gammon with egg and chips and there are a number of delicious sweets. For a really cheap meal you'd find it hard to beat the two-course lunch.

♫ P S ♧ **VS**

Dreamville King's Sq ☎ (0904) 36592
Open: Mon–Sun 10am–11pm

Dreamville is exactly what it sounds – an American-style food-fantasy, with a colourful gangster theme, and décor reminiscent of the 1920s. The menu lists hamburgers, charcoal-grilled sirloin and T-bone steaks, pizza, pasta and barbecued spare ribs and freshly caught local fish. End your meal with an exotic ice cream sundae. Dreamville is fully licensed.

C S ♧

Punch Bowl Hotel Micklegate Bar
☎ (0904) 22619
Open: Mon–Sat 12noon–2.30pm, 7–10.30pm, Sun 12noon–2pm, 7–10pm

You can imagine yourself in an old coaching inn when you take a meal at the 18th century Punch Bowl. In fact this is what it once was, but it has now been refurbished as a hotel and steak house, offering a very reasonable table d'hôte lunch of starter, main dish and dessert. An example is grapefruit cocktail, roast beef with Yorkshire pudding and apple pie and cream.

C ♫ P ♧

Ruffles Tea Rooms 41 Stonegate
☎ (0904) 29812
Open: Summer Mon–Sat 9.30am–8.30pm, Sun 11am–6pm, Winter Mon–Sat 9.30am–5pm

Apart from the mouthwatering selection of sandwiches, cakes and cream teas which are served all day, the lunch and supper menu includes pâté de campagne as a starter, pizza Marina (seafood special) for main course and a dessert.

C S **VS**

Ristorante Bari 15 The Shambles
☎ (0904) 33807
Open: Mon–Sun 11.30am–2.30pm, 6–11pm

Situated in one of Yorks oldest and most picturesque streets, the Ristorante Bari offers both a quick single course and a full leisurely meal in a relaxed Continental atmosphere. The menu lists 12 varieties of pizza with the usual range of pastas and tempting seafood, chicken, veal and steak dishes. Home-made sweets are available from the trolley.

C ♫ P S ♧

YOULGREAVE
Derbyshire
Map **8** SK26

The Bull's Head Hotel Church St
☎ (062986) 307
Open: Mon–Sun 12noon–2pm, 7.30–10pm

This stone-built coaching inn, situated in the Peak District National Park, dates back to 1674 and offers a simple dining room menu of mainly grill-type dishes including gammon and roast chicken in barbecue sauce. Bar meals range from toasted sandwiches to basket meals. There is a disco Friday evenings. Real ale is served.

♫ P ♧

Establishments participating in the Voucher Scheme

Supplementary Index to London Plan 4

The establishments listed below are located on London Plan 4 although they are listed within the alphabetical gazetteer. Other Greater London establishments can be found on the main atlas pages 4 and 5.

Establishments open all day

Many of the establishments listed in our guide open for lunch and then again for dinner in the evening. Below we list those which are open throughout the day – or at least are open by 10 or 10.30 am and do not close again before 4.30 pm. This does not necessarily mean that a full meal will be available whenever you happen to visit, but a welcome drink and a snack are sure to be offered. Not all of these places are open every day, so do check the gazetteer entry before making a visit.

Aberdeen	Kardomah
	Victoria
Aberfoyle	Old Coach House
Aberystwyth	Caprice
Alfriston	Drusillas Thatched Barn
Alnwick	Maxine's Kitchen
Alyth	The Singing Kettle
Aviemore	Crawfords
Ayr	The Coffee Club
	The Tudor Restaurant
Bala	Neuadd Y Cyfnod
Basingstoke	Perrings Coffee Shop and Wine Bar
Bath	La Creperie
Beauly	The Skillet
Berkhamsted	Cooks Delight
Berwick upon Tweed	Popinjays
	The Rum Puncheon
Bewdley	Back of Beyond Coffee Shop
Bideford	Rose of Torridge
Billingshurst	Old House
Birmingham	The Conservatory, Holiday Inn
	Hawkins Café-Bar
Bishops Stortford	The Swan Restaurant
Blackburn	Kenyon's Studio Buttery
Blackpool	The Danish Kitchen
Bognor Regis	Tudor Rose
Bournemouth	Fortes
Bowness on Windermere	The Quarterdeck
Bridge of Allan	Cranachan
Bridlington	The Old Forge
Brighton	Meeting House
Bristol	Circles
	Dragonara Hotel
	Grand Hotel, Brass Nails Restaurant
	The Guild Restaurant
Broadway	The Coffee Pot
	Cotswold Café and Restaurant
Bude	Red Post
Budleigh Salterton	The Lobster Pot
Burntisland	Copper Kettle
Buxton	Barbecue
Callander	Dalgair House
	Pips
Cambridge	The Roof Garden
	Wilsons Granary
Carlisle	Cumbrian Hotel, Cumbrian Kitchen
Carmarthen	The Old Curiosity
Chester	The Farmhouse
Chichester	The Coffee House
Chiddingfold	Crown Inn Bistro
Chudleigh	The Wheel Craft Centre
Congleton	The Gingerbread Coffee Shop
Corris	Corris Craft Centre
Coventry	Nello Pizzeria
Crail	The Tolbooth
Crieff	Chatterbox
	The Highlandman
Dartmeet	Badger's Holt
Derby	The Lettuce Leaf
	Swiss Cottage
Doncaster	Ristorante il Fiore in Legards
Dorchester	Judge Jeffrey's
Downham Market	Crown Stables, Crown Hotel
Droitwich	The Spinning Wheel
Dumfries	Opus
	Pancake Place
Dunblane	Fourways
Dundee	Pizza Gallery
Dunoon	Woosters (summer only)
Durham	Royal County Hotel, Bowes Coffee House
Eastleigh	Piccolo Mondo 2
Edinburgh	Mr Boni's Ice Cream Parlour
	Cafe Cappuccino
	Crawford's
	Pancake Place
Esher	Julie's Bistro
Eton	The Eton Buttery
Evanton	Foulis Ferry
Exeter	Clare's
Fareham	Gabbies
Fort William	The Angus Restaurant
	McTavish's Kitchen (self service section)
Frome	The Settle
Gateshead	The Griddle
Glasgow	Cul de Sac
	Delta
	Epicures Bistro
	Massimo's
	The Pancake Place
	Pizza Park
Glastonbury	Rainbow's End Café
Gloucester	Comfy Pew
Gorey	Jersey Pottery
Grantham	Catlin's
Grantshouse	Cedar Cafeteria
Gretna Green	The Auld Smiddy
Hale	Village Green
Harrogate	Betty's
	Mr Pickwick
Haslemere	Darnley's Wine Bar
Hatfield	Corks and Crumbs
Hathersage	Bradgate Buttery
Haywards Heath	Country and Wine
Helensburgh	Le Jardin
Henley-in-Arden	The Little French Café
Hereford	Tudor Restaurant
Hungerford	The Tutti Pole
Ilkley	Betty's Café Tea Rooms

Ilkley	Café Konditorei
Insch	The Rothney (summer only)
Inverness	Crawford's
	The Pancake Place
	Pizzaland
Invershin	Invershin Hotel
Irvine	The Coffee Club
Kendal	Cherry Tree
Keswick	Bay Tree
Kew	Maids of Honour
Kilkhampton	The Coffee House
Killin	The Old Mill
Kilmarnock	The Coffee Club
Kingston-upon-Thames	The Farmhouse Kitchen
Kingussie	Wood 'n' Spoon
Kinloch Rannoch	Gitana Grill
Kirkcaldy	Green Cockatoo
	The Pancake Place
Kirkcudbright	The Coffee Pot (summer only)
Kirkmichael	Jock's Coffee Shop
Lancaster	Old Brussels
	The Country Pantry
Largs	Green Shutter Tearoom
Lauder	The Black Bull Hotel
Leicester	The Post House Hotel
	A Spanish Place
	Swiss Cottage
Leven	Osborne Lounge and Grill
Linlithgow	Lochside Larder
Little Chalfont	The Copper Kettle
Liverpool	St George's Hotel Buttery
Llanynys	The Lodge
Lochearnhead	Craigroyston
LONDON	
St Marylebone	The Rose
Piccadilly	Imbiss Snack Bar
Bloomsbury	Tuttons
The City	Slenders Wholefood Restaurant
Whitechapel	Nick's Place
Kensington	Daquise
	Tootsies
Maida Vale	Blue Angel
Greenwich	Gachons
Lambeth	Royal Festival Hall
Lostwithiel	The Tawny Owl
Lyndhurst	The Bow Windows
Lynton	The Greenhouse
Manchester	Farmhouse Kitchen (Fountain St)
	Farmhouse Kitchen (Blackfriars St)
	Harper's
Marlow	Burgers
Minehead	The Good Food Inn
Morecambe	Coffee Shoppe
Newcastleton	The Dormouse
Newcastle upon Tyne	Blackfriars Restaurant and Brasserie
	Coffee House and Bar, Avon Hotel
	Eldon Coffee Shop
	Mother Tucker's
Newton Mearns	The Coffee Club
Nottingham	Eviva Kebab House
	Farmhouse Kitchen
	Swiss Cottage
Oban	The Box Tree
	The Gallery Restaurant
	McTavish's Kitchen (self-service section)
Oxford	Burlington Bertie's
	The Nosebag
Pershore	Sugar and Spice
Perth	Kardomah
	The Pancake Place
	Pizza Gallery
	Tudor Restaurant
Peterborough	Costers, Great Northern Hotel
Peterhead	Coffee Shop
Pitlochry	The Brown Trout
	The Luggie
Polegate	The Wishing Well
Polperro	Crump's
Portpatrick	The Old Mill House
Portsmouth & Southsea	The Hungry One
Preston	The Danish Kitchen
Princetown	Fox Tor (summer only)
Ralegh's Cross	Ralegh's Cross Inn
Reading	Heelas Restaurant
Reigate	Home Maid
Renfrew	The Armour Restaurant
Richmond upon Thames	Mrs Beeton's
Risca	Michael's
Ross-on-Wye	The Old Pheasant
St Andrews	Pepita's
	The Pancake Place
St Helier	La Bastille Taverne
Salisbury	Michael Snell
Sampford Peverell	The Farm House Inn
Sandwich	16th Century Tea House
Shanklin	Cliff Top Hotel Coffee Shop
	Tudor Rose
Shrewsbury	Delany's
Skegness	The Copper Kettle
Skipton	Herbs
Southampton	Piccolo Mondo 1
Southport	The Grape Escape
Stafford	Anemos
Stamford	The Bay Tree Coffee Shop
Steyning	The Old Dairy
Stratford-upon-Avon	Hathaway Tea Rooms
	Horseshoe Buttery and Restaurant
	The Thatch Restaurant
Strathcarron	Carron Restaurant
Sutton Coldfield	Bobby Brown's
Sutton on Sea	Anchor
Swaffham	The Red Door
Swansea	The Dragon Hotel Coffee Shop
Tenby	Plantagenet House
Thame	The Coffee House
Tomintoul	Glenmulliach Restaurant
Torquay	The Copper Kettle
	The Epicure
Torrington, Great	Rebecca's

Totnes	Cranks Health Food
Turnberry	The Tappie Toorie
Tyndrum	Clifton Coffee House
Upminister	The Mill
Wareham	Anglebury Coffee House
Warwick	Cindy's
	Nicolini's Bistro
Wells	Riverside
Weymouth	The Clarendon
Wimborne Minster	Quinney's
Winchester	Minstrel's
Windsor	The Drury House
Wiveliscombe	Country Fare
Worcester	Natural Break
Worthing	Happy Cheese
Yeovil	Bountiful Goodness
York	Betty's Oakroom
	Dreamville
	Ruffles Tea Rooms

Wine Bars

Alcester	The Three Tuns
Alderley Edge	No. 15
Alresford	The Bodega
Alton	Pilgrims
Altrincham	Ganders
Ambleside	De Quincey's
Baldock	The Vintage
Basingstoke	Corks
	Perrings
Bath	Clarets
	Danish
Beverley	Upstairs Downstairs
Birmingham	Dingos
	La Galleria
	Horts
	Maxwell's Plum
	Rock Candy Mountain
Bramhall	Ganders of Goose Green
Bridgnorth	Baileys
Bristol	Le Château
Broadway	Goblets
Canterbury	Alberry's
Cardiff	Ye Olde Wine Shoppe
Castletown	Chabus Cellar
Chelmsford	Corks
Cheltenham	Forrests
	Montpellier
Chepstow	The Grape Escape
Chester	Clavertons
	Pierre Griffe
	Sir Edward's
Cirencester	Shepherd's
Coventry	Corks
Crawley	Solomon's Ancient Priors
Croydon	The Wine Vaults
Dartmouth	The Steam Packet
Doncaster	Maigret's
Durham	Dennhöfers
Edinburgh	Nimmo's
Egham	Maggies
Enfield	Divers
Enville	Granary
Epping	Beatons
Eton	The Eton
Evesham	The Vine
Ewell	The Loose Box
Exeter	Coolings
Farnham	Sevens
Folkestone	Pullman
Glasgow	The Belfry
Guildford	Pews
Hale	Hale
Halstead	Halstead (Pendles)
Hatfield	Corks and Crumbs
Hythe	The Butt of Sherry
Ilford	Harts
Ironbridge	Old Vaults
Keighley	The Vaults
Knutsford	Sir Frederick's
Lancaster	Squirrels
Ledbury	Applejack
Leicester	Du Cann's
Lincoln	Straits
	The Wine Barge
Llangollen	Gales
LONDON	
Paddington	The Gyngleboy
Mayfair	L'Artiste Musclé
	Downs
Soho	Crusting Pipe
	Hobson's
	Solange's
The City	Balls Bros (London Wall)
	Balls Bros (Cheapside)
	Balls Bros (Threadneedle St)
	Bow Wine Vaults
	Corts (Chancery Lane)
	Corts (Old Bailey)
	Grapeshots
	Mother Bunch's Wine House
Kensington	Finch's
Chelsea	Le Bouzy Rouge
	Cheyne Walk
Fulham	Crocodile Tears
Greenwich	Bar du Musée
	Davy's Wine Vaults
Blackheath	The Barclave
Lambeth	Archduke
Southwark	Skinkers
Eltham	Mellins
Putney	Mr Micawber's
Wimbledon	Downs
Battersea	Just Williams
Ealing	Crispins Too
Chiswick	Fouberts
Marlborough	Atillio's
Newbury	Cromwell's
Newcastle upon Tyne	Brahms and Liszt
	City Vaults
	Legends
	Sloanes
Newport	Corkers
Newport Pagnell	Glovers
Olney	The Olney
Oswestry	The Good Companion
Peterborough	Mr Pickwick
Reading	Beadles
Reigate	Cobbles
Rye	The Peacock

(Continued on page 207)

Report Form 1984

You are invited to recommend your favourite restaurant for the 1985 edition of *Eat Out In Britain For Around £5.*

To: The Automobile Association
Hotel and Information Services Department
9th Floor
Fanum House
Basingstoke
Hampshire
RG21 2EA

Name of establishment ______________________

Address ______________________

Telephone number ______________________

Date of visit ______________________

Average price of a two-course meal £

Is the restaurant already listed? YES/NO

If so, do you agree with the classification or recommendation? YES/NO

Name ______________________

Address ______________________

Date ______________ Signature ______________

CUT ALONG HERE

Additional remarks:

St Albans	Aspelia Scotts
St Austell	Hicks
Settle	The Little House
Shrewsbury	Cornhouse
Southampton	Simon's Wine House
Southend on Sea	The Pipe of Port Spencer's
South Petherton	The Pump Room
Southport	The Grape Escape
Stafford	Annabel's
Sunderland	Sam's Bar
Swaffham	Corks
Torquay	Ansteys
Twickenham	The French Connection (Eddie's)
Uckfield	Percy's
Ventnor	Four Seasons
Waltham Cross	Blues
Westerham	The Henry Wilkinson
Whittington	Whittington Inn
Winchester	Mr Pitkin's
Woburn	Woburn Wine Lodge

Acknowledgements

The illustrations which appear on pages 10 to 26 are the work of Leslie Sternberg.

The National Grid

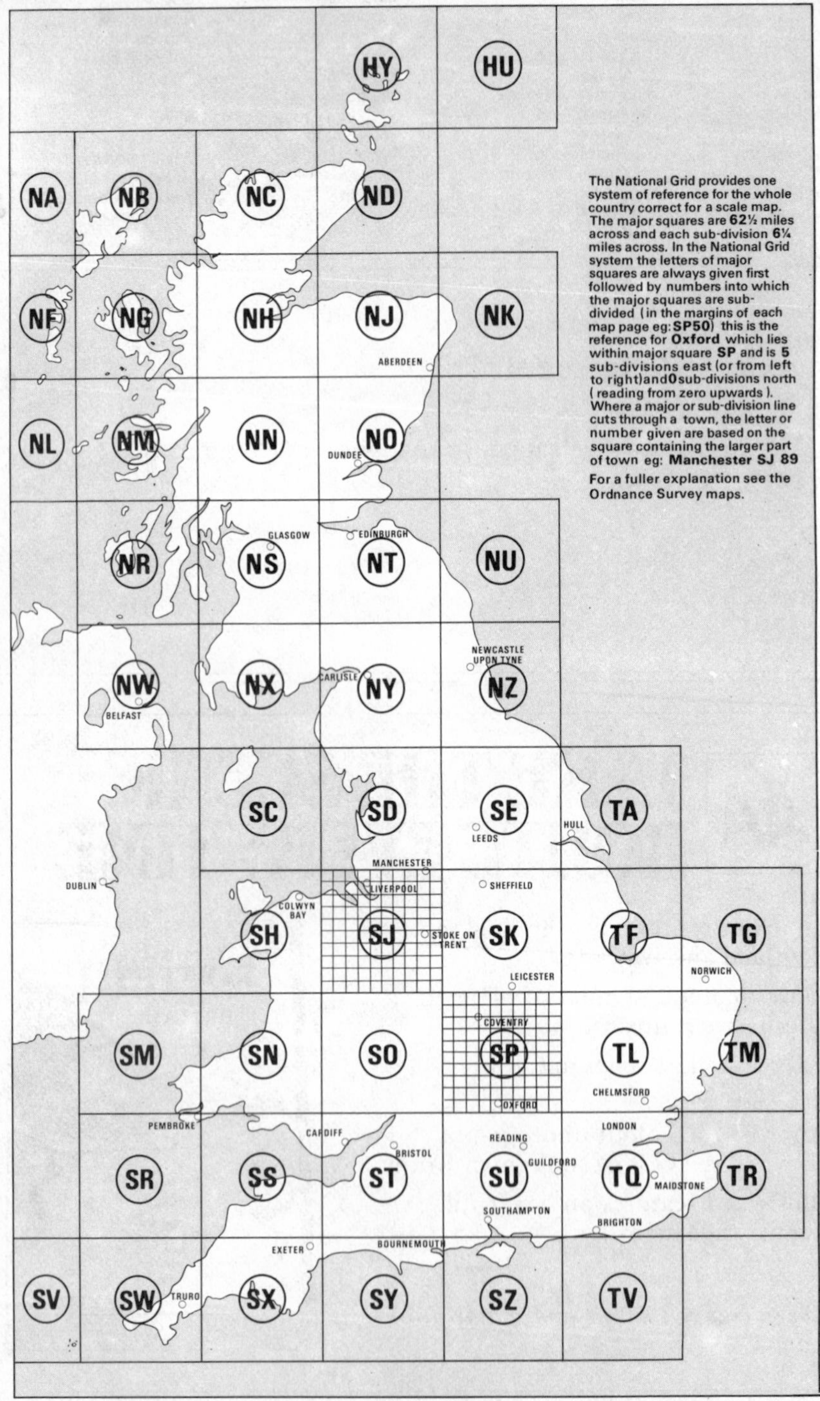

The National Grid provides one system of reference for the whole country correct for a scale map. The major squares are **62½** miles across and each sub-division **6¼** miles across. In the National Grid system the letters of major squares are always given first followed by numbers into which the major squares are sub-divided (in the margins of each map page eg: **SP50**) this is the reference for **Oxford** which lies within major square **SP** and is **5** sub-divisions east (or from left to right) and **0** sub-divisions north (reading from zero upwards). Where a major or sub-division line cuts through a town, the letter or number given are based on the square containing the larger part of town eg: **Manchester SJ 89**

For a fuller explanation see the Ordnance Survey maps.

Key to Atlas

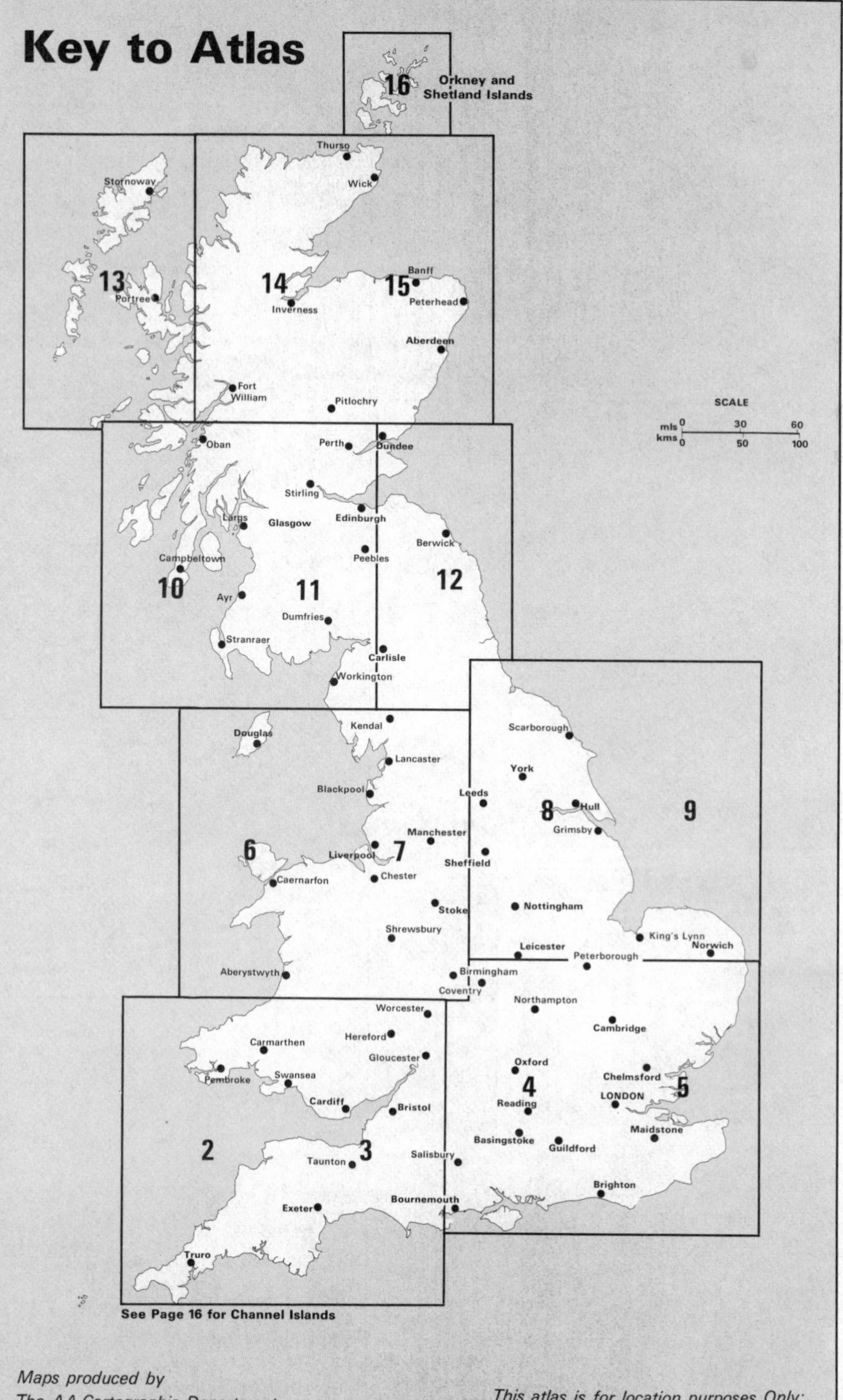

See Page 16 for Channel Islands

Maps produced by

The AA Cartographic Department (Publications Division), Fanum House, Basingstoke, Hampshire RG21 2EA

This atlas is for location purposes Only: see Member's Handbook for current road and AA road services information

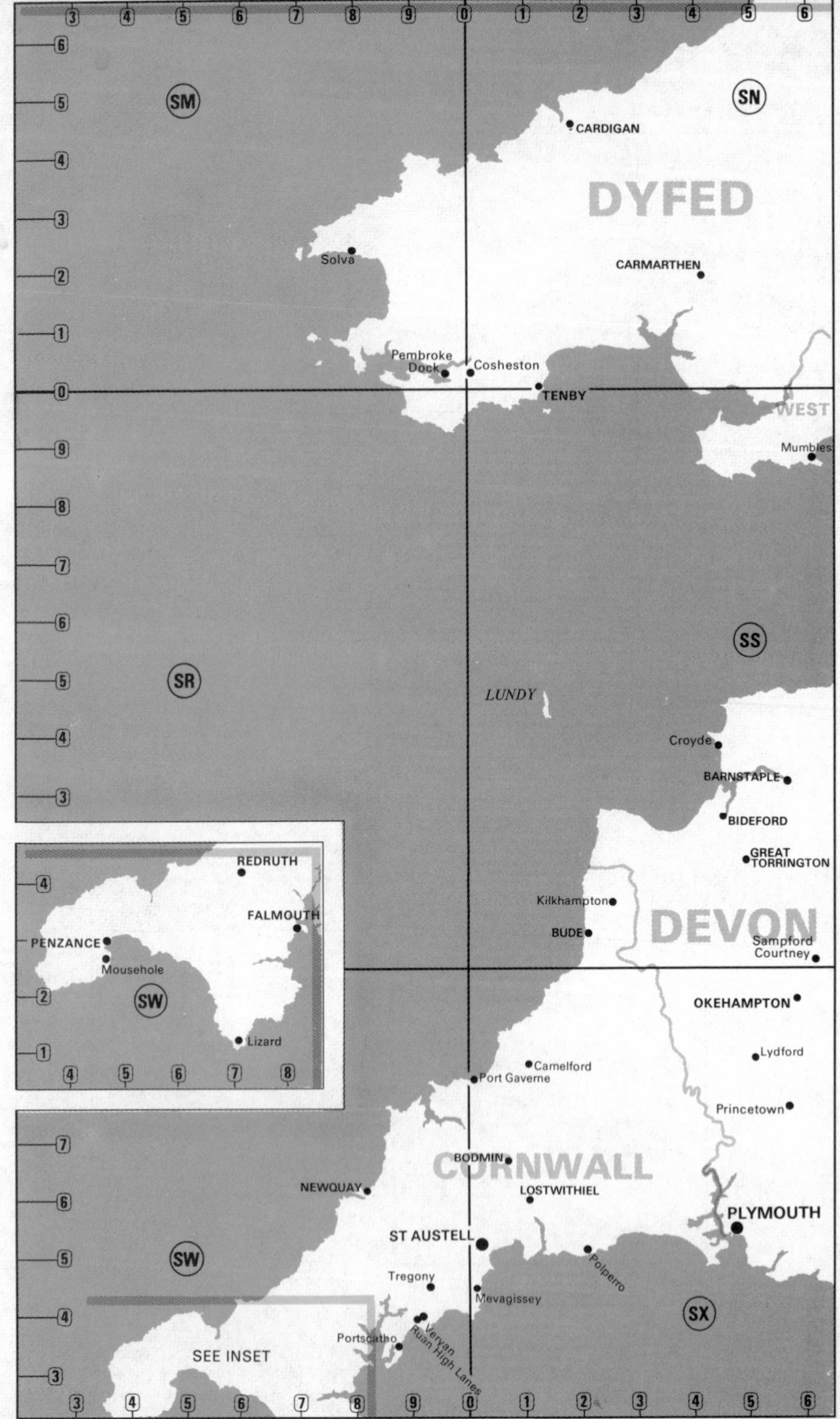

For continuation pages refer to numbered arrows

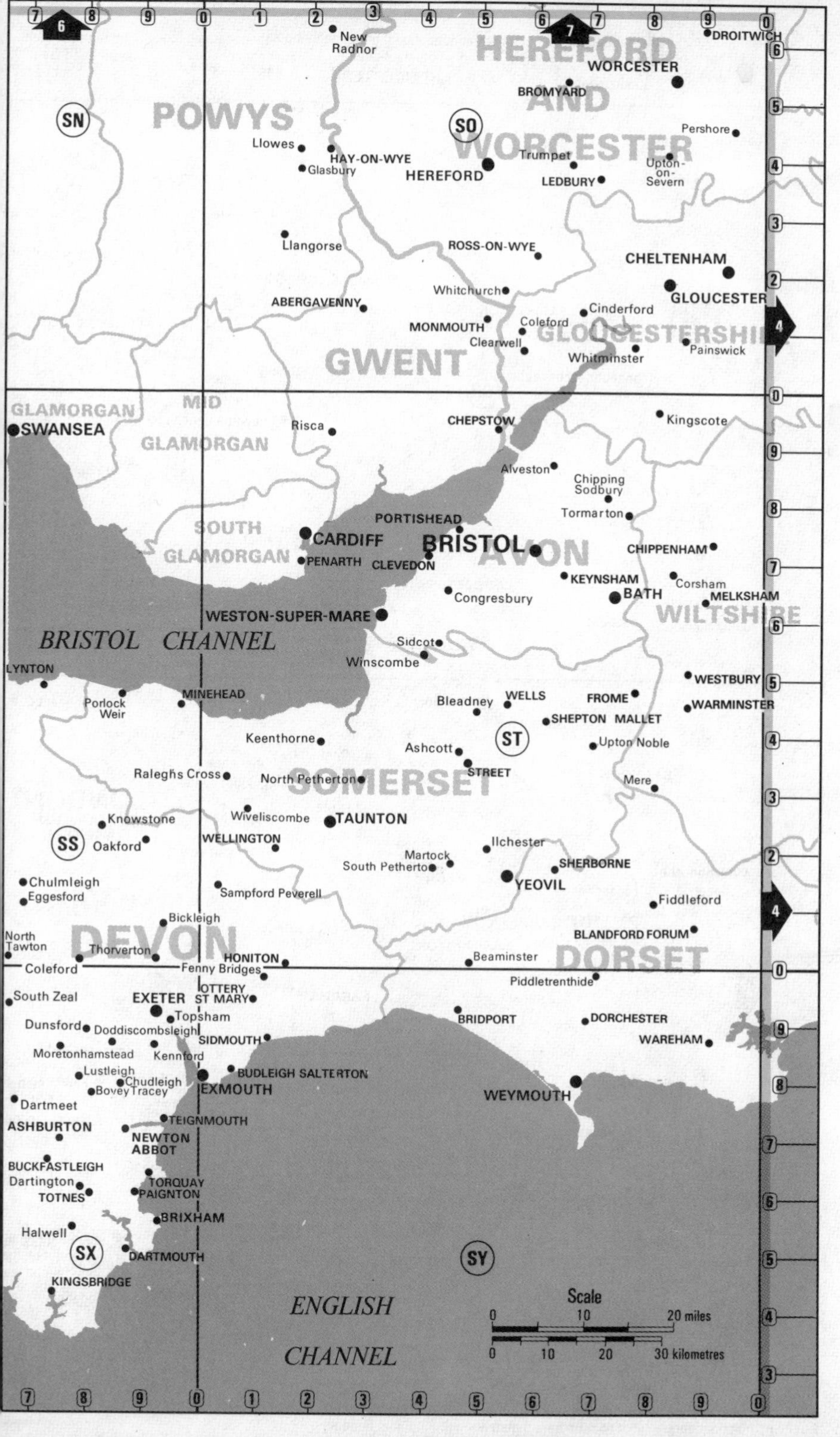
HEREFORD AND WORCESTER
POWYS
GWENT
GLOUCESTERSHIRE
GLAMORGAN
MID GLAMORGAN
SOUTH GLAMORGAN
AVON
WILTSHIRE
SOMERSET
DEVON
DORSET
BRISTOL CHANNEL
ENGLISH CHANNEL
SN
SO
SS
ST
SX
SY
New Radnor
DROITWICH
WORCESTER
BROMYARD
Pershore
Llowes
HAY-ON-WYE
Glasbury
HEREFORD
Trumpet
Upton-on-Severn
LEDBURY
Llangorse
ROSS-ON-WYE
CHELTENHAM
GLOUCESTER
Whitchurch
ABERGAVENNY
MONMOUTH
Coleford
Cinderford
Clearwell
Whitminster
Painswick
SWANSEA
Risca
CHEPSTOW
Kingscote
Alveston
Chipping Sodbury
Tormarton
PORTISHEAD
CARDIFF
PENARTH
BRISTOL
CLEVEDON
CHIPPENHAM
KEYNSHAM
Corsham
Congresbury
BATH
MELKSHAM
WESTON-SUPER-MARE
Sidcot
Winscombe
LYNTON
Porlock Weir
MINEHEAD
WESTBURY
WARMINSTER
Bleadney
WELLS
FROME
SHEPTON MALLET
Keenthorne
Ashcott
Upton Noble
STREET
Raleghs Cross
North Petherton
Mere
Knowstone
Wiveliscombe
TAUNTON
Oakford
WELLINGTON
Ilchester
Martock
South Petherton
SHERBORNE
YEOVIL
Chulmleigh
Eggesford
Sampford Peverell
Fiddleford
Bickleigh
North Tawton
Thorverton
BLANDFORD FORUM
Coleford
HONITON
Fenny Bridges
Beaminster
Piddletrenthide
South Zeal
EXETER
OTTERY ST MARY
Topsham
BRIDPORT
DORCHESTER
Dunsford
Doddiscombsleigh
SIDMOUTH
WAREHAM
Moretonhamstead
Kennford
Lustleigh
Chudleigh
BUDLEIGH SALTERTON
Bovey Tracey
EXMOUTH
WEYMOUTH
Dartmeet
ASHBURTON
TEIGNMOUTH
NEWTON ABBOT
BUCKFASTLEIGH
Dartington
TORQUAY
TOTNES
PAIGNTON
BRIXHAM
Halwell
DARTMOUTH
KINGSBRIDGE
Scale
0 10 20 miles
0 10 20 30 kilometres

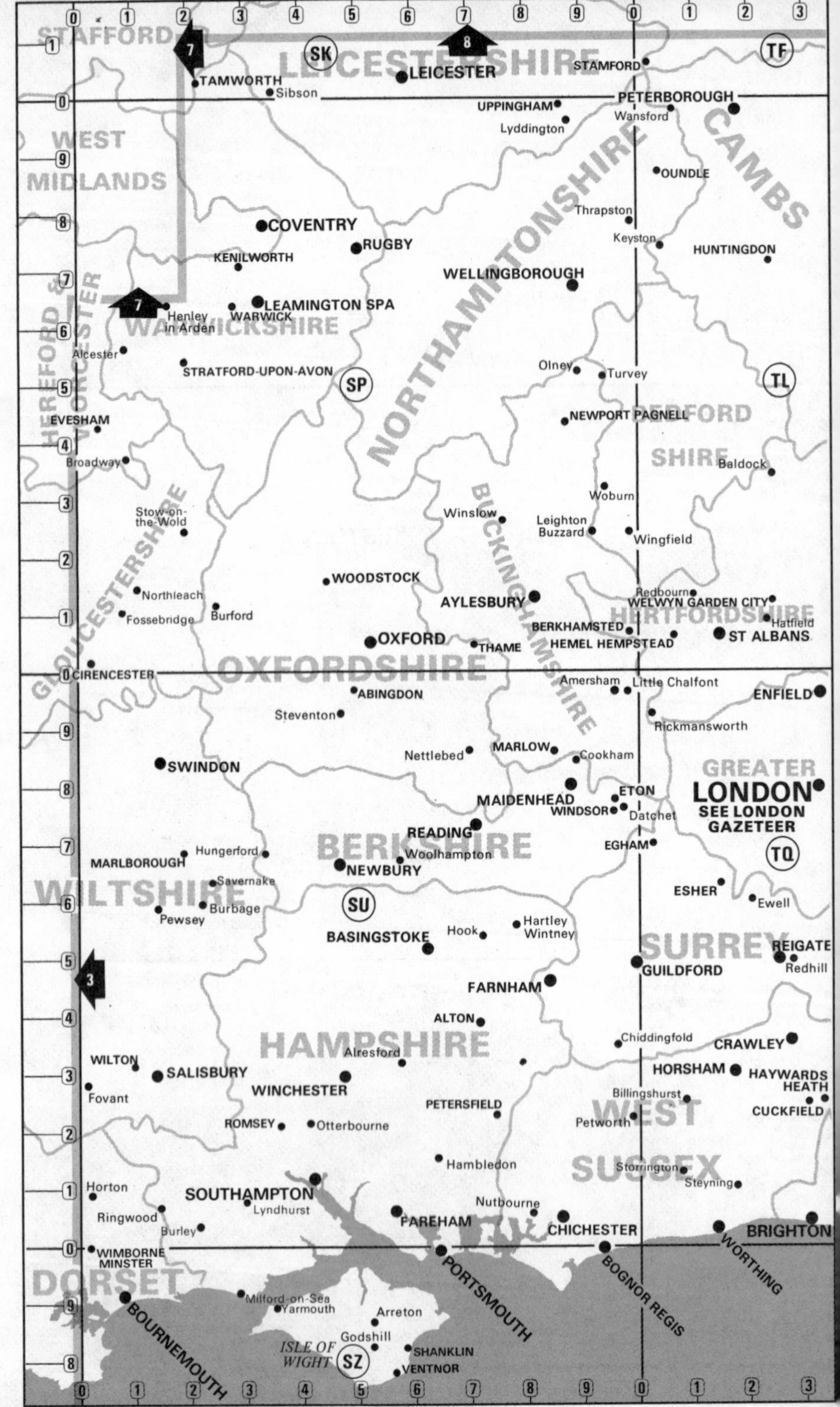

For continuation pages refer to numbered arrows

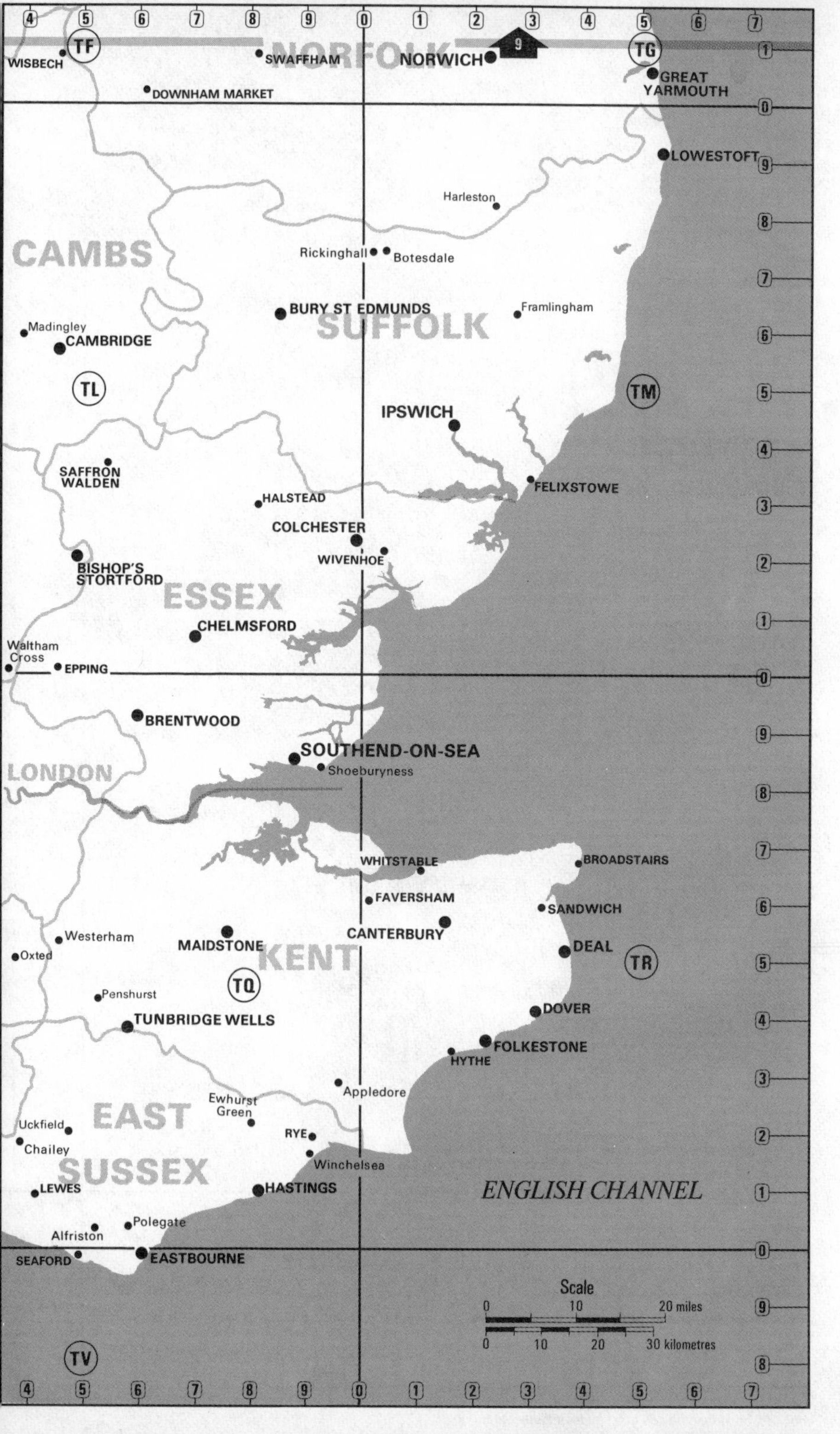
NORFOLK
WISBECH
SWAFFHAM
NORWICH
GREAT YARMOUTH
DOWNHAM MARKET
TF
TG
9
LOWESTOFT
Harleston
CAMBS
Rickinghall
Botesdale
BURY ST EDMUNDS
Framlingham
SUFFOLK
Madingley
CAMBRIDGE
TL
TM
IPSWICH
SAFFRON WALDEN
FELIXSTOWE
HALSTEAD
COLCHESTER
WIVENHOE
BISHOP'S STORTFORD
ESSEX
CHELMSFORD
Waltham Cross
EPPING
BRENTWOOD
SOUTHEND-ON-SEA
Shoeburyness
LONDON
WHITSTABLE
BROADSTAIRS
FAVERSHAM
SANDWICH
CANTERBURY
Westerham
MAIDSTONE
DEAL
Oxted
KENT
TR
TQ
Penshurst
DOVER
TUNBRIDGE WELLS
FOLKESTONE
HYTHE
Appledore
Ewhurst Green
EAST
Uckfield
RYE
Chailey
Winchelsea
SUSSEX
LEWES
HASTINGS
ENGLISH CHANNEL
Polegate
Alfriston
SEAFORD
EASTBOURNE
Scale
0
10
20 miles
0
10
20
30 kilometres
TV

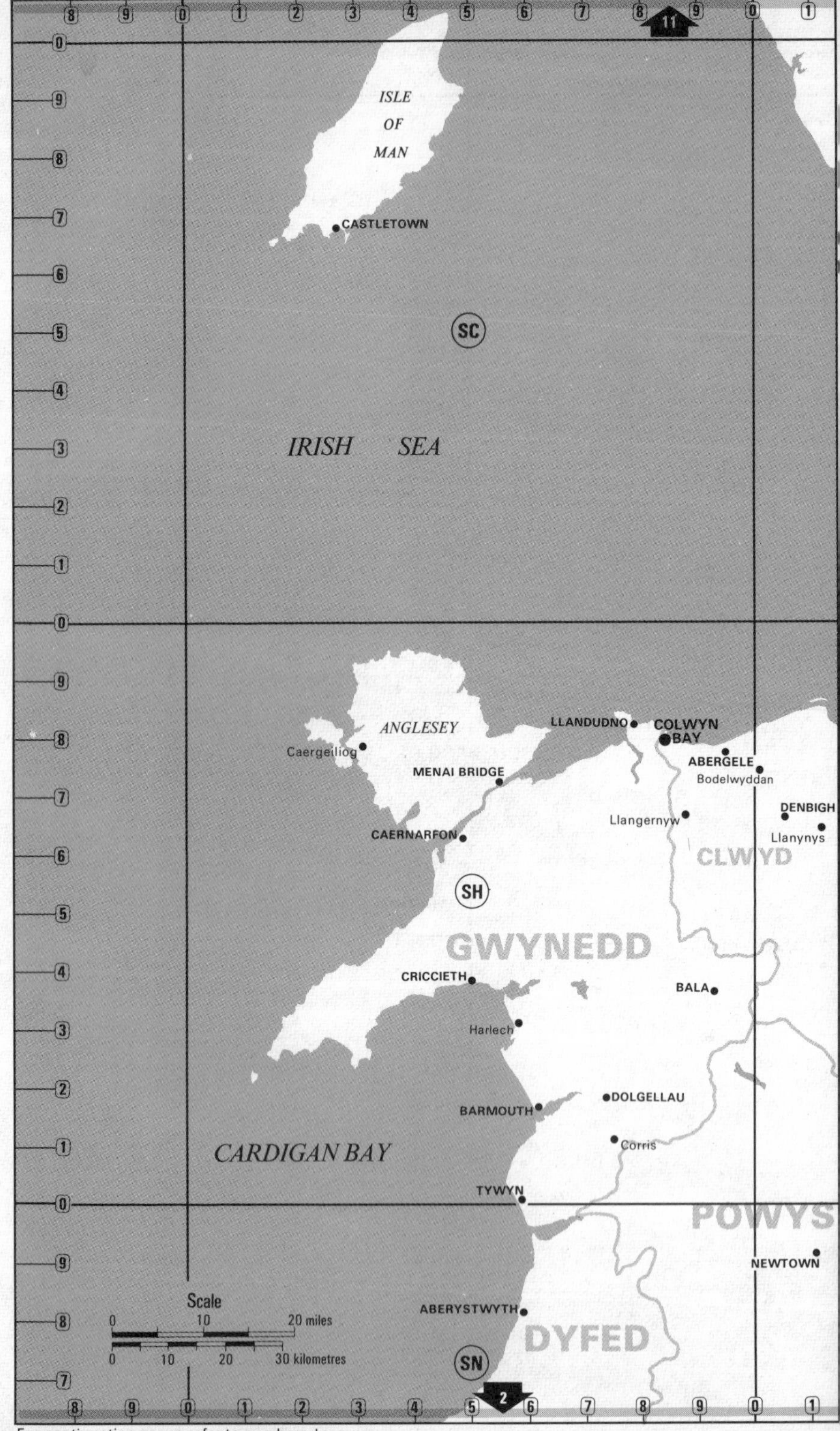

For continuation pages refer to numbered arrows

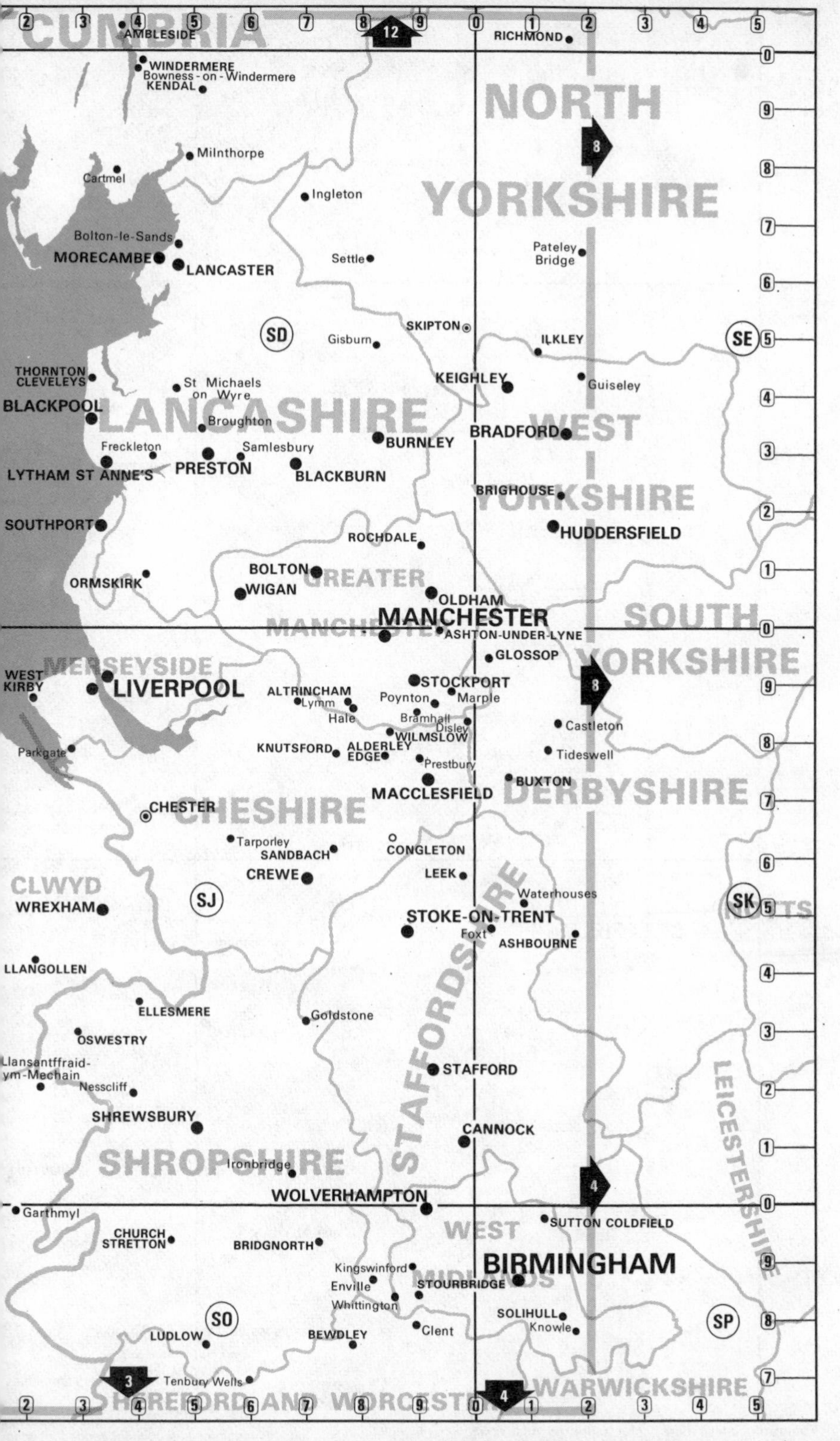
CUMBRIA
AMBLESIDE
WINDERMERE
Bowness-on-Windermere
KENDAL
RICHMOND
NORTH
YORKSHIRE
Milnthorpe
Cartmel
Ingleton
Bolton-le-Sands
MORECAMBE
LANCASTER
Settle
Pateley Bridge
SD
SKIPTON
Gisburn
ILKLEY
SE
THORNTON CLEVELEYS
St Michaels on Wyre
KEIGHLEY
Guiseley
BLACKPOOL
LANCASHIRE
Broughton
BURNLEY
BRADFORD
WEST
Freckleton
Samlesbury
LYTHAM ST ANNE'S
PRESTON
BLACKBURN
BRIGHOUSE
YORKSHIRE
SOUTHPORT
HUDDERSFIELD
ROCHDALE
ORMSKIRK
BOLTON
GREATER
WIGAN
OLDHAM
MANCHESTER
SOUTH
ASHTON-UNDER-LYNE
GLOSSOP
MERSEYSIDE
YORKSHIRE
WEST KIRBY
LIVERPOOL
ALTRINCHAM
STOCKPORT
Lymm
Poynton
Marple
Hale
Bramhall
Disley
Castleton
Parkgate
KNUTSFORD
ALDERLEY EDGE
WILMSLOW
Prestbury
Tideswell
BUXTON
MACCLESFIELD
DERBYSHIRE
CHESTER
CHESHIRE
Tarporley
SANDBACH
CONGLETON
LEEK
CREWE
CLWYD
Waterhouses
WREXHAM
SJ
SK
NOTTS
STOKE-ON-TRENT
Foxt
ASHBOURNE
LLANGOLLEN
STAFFORDSHIRE
ELLESMERE
Goldstone
OSWESTRY
Llansantffraid-ym-Mechain
STAFFORD
Nesscliff
LEICESTERSHIRE
SHREWSBURY
CANNOCK
SHROPSHIRE
Ironbridge
WOLVERHAMPTON
Garthmyl
SUTTON COLDFIELD
CHURCH STRETTON
BRIDGNORTH
WEST
Kingswinford
BIRMINGHAM
Enville
STOURBRIDGE
MIDLANDS
Whittington
SO
SOLIHULL
Knowle
SP
Clent
LUDLOW
BEWDLEY
Tenbury Wells
HEREFORD AND WORCESTER
WARWICKSHIRE
12
8
8
4
3
4

For continuation pages refer to numbered arrows

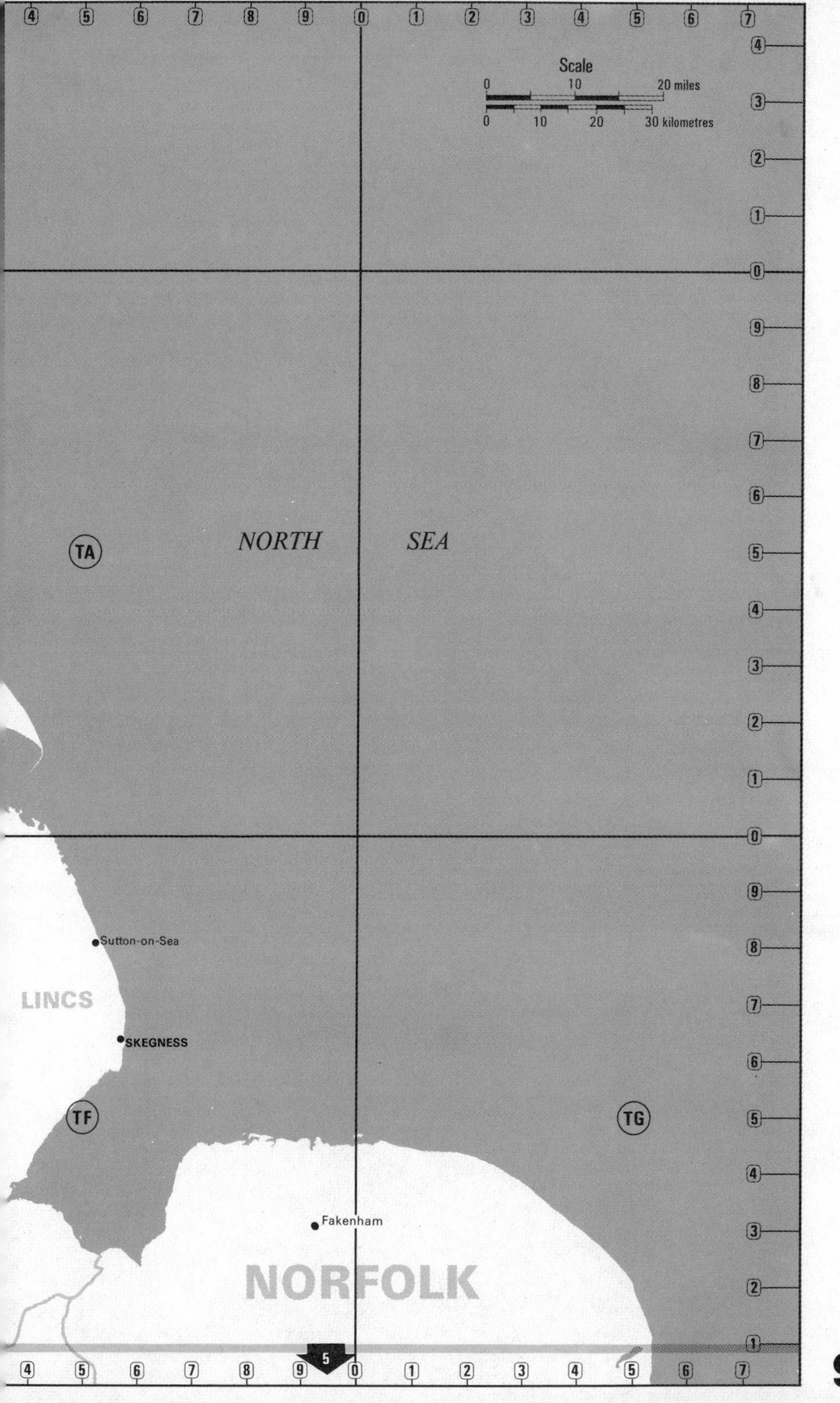
Scale
0
10
20 miles
0
10
20
30 kilometres
NORTH
SEA
TA
TF
TG
Sutton-on-Sea
LINCS
SKEGNESS
Fakenham
NORFOLK
5

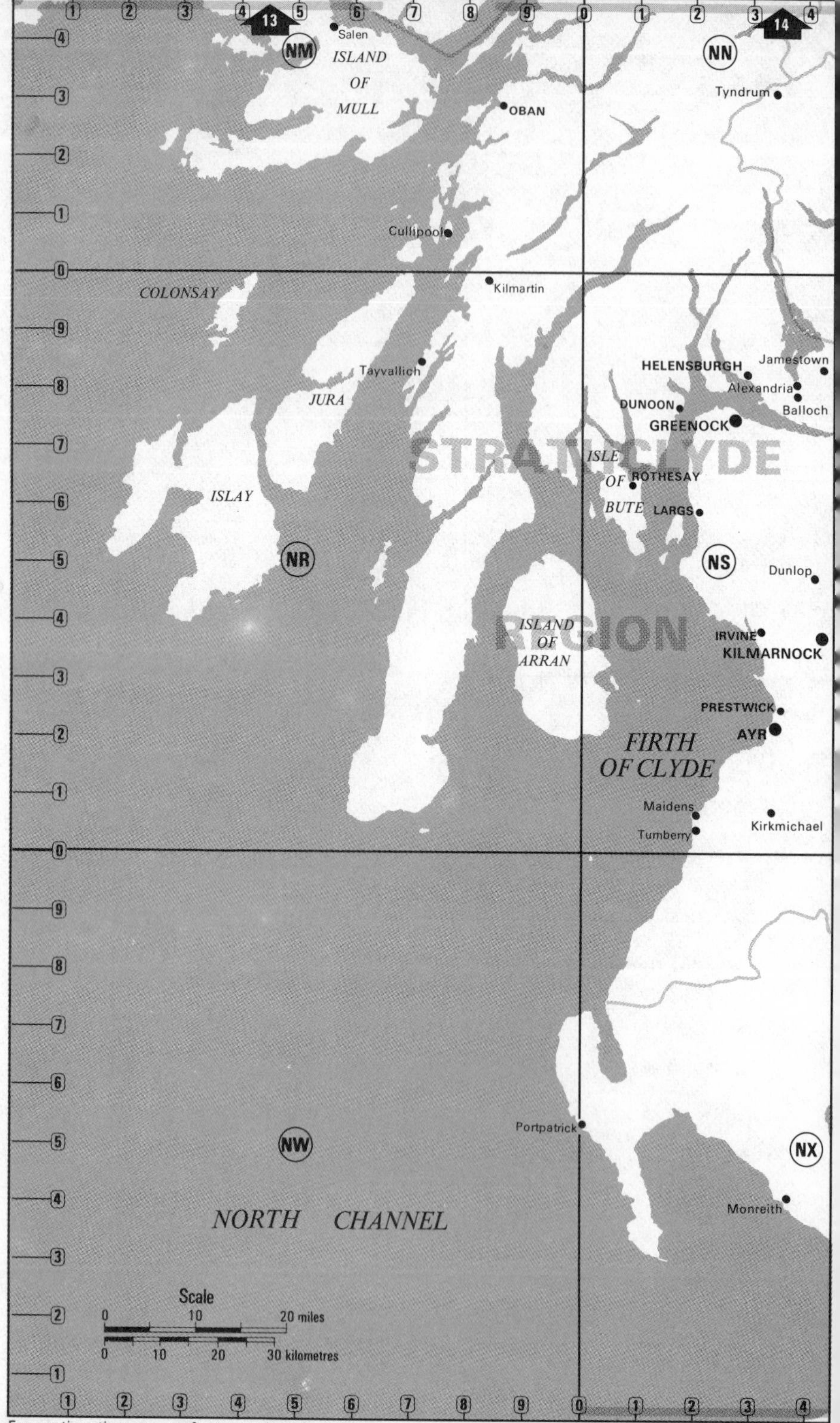

For continuation pages refer to numbered arrows

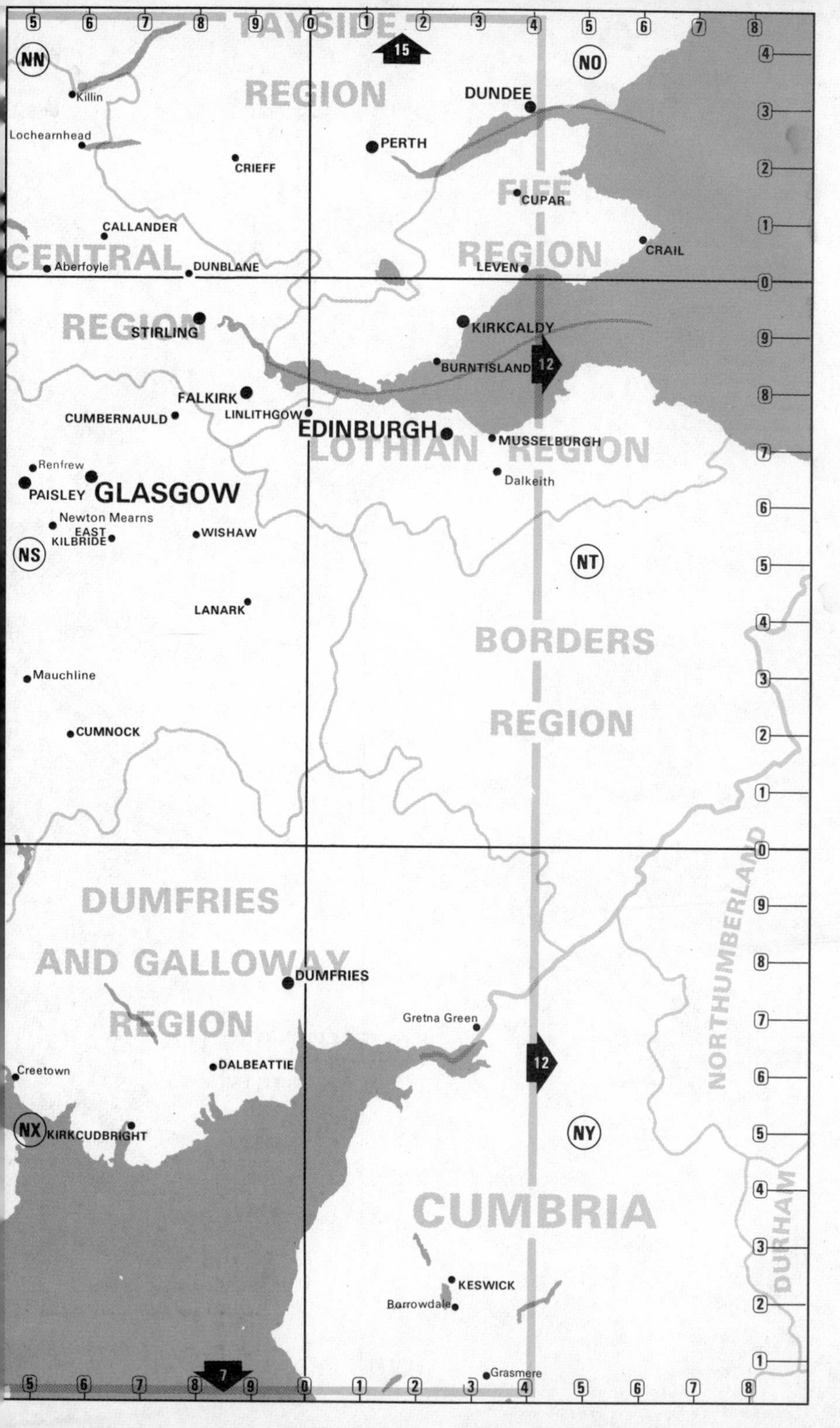
TAYSIDE
REGION
15
NN
NO
Killin
Lochearnhead
CRIEFF
PERTH
DUNDEE
FIFE
CUPAR
CALLANDER
CENTRAL
Aberfoyle
DUNBLANE
REGION
LEVEN
CRAIL
REGION
STIRLING
KIRKCALDY
BURNTISLAND
12
FALKIRK
CUMBERNAULD
LINLITHGOW
EDINBURGH
MUSSELBURGH
LOTHIAN REGION
Dalkeith
Renfrew
PAISLEY
GLASGOW
Newton Mearns
EAST KILBRIDE
WISHAW
NS
NT
LANARK
BORDERS
REGION
Mauchline
CUMNOCK
DUMFRIES
AND GALLOWAY
REGION
DUMFRIES
Gretna Green
NORTHUMBERLAND
12
Creetown
DALBEATTIE
NX
KIRKCUDBRIGHT
NY
CUMBRIA
DURHAM
KESWICK
Borrowdale
Grasmere
7

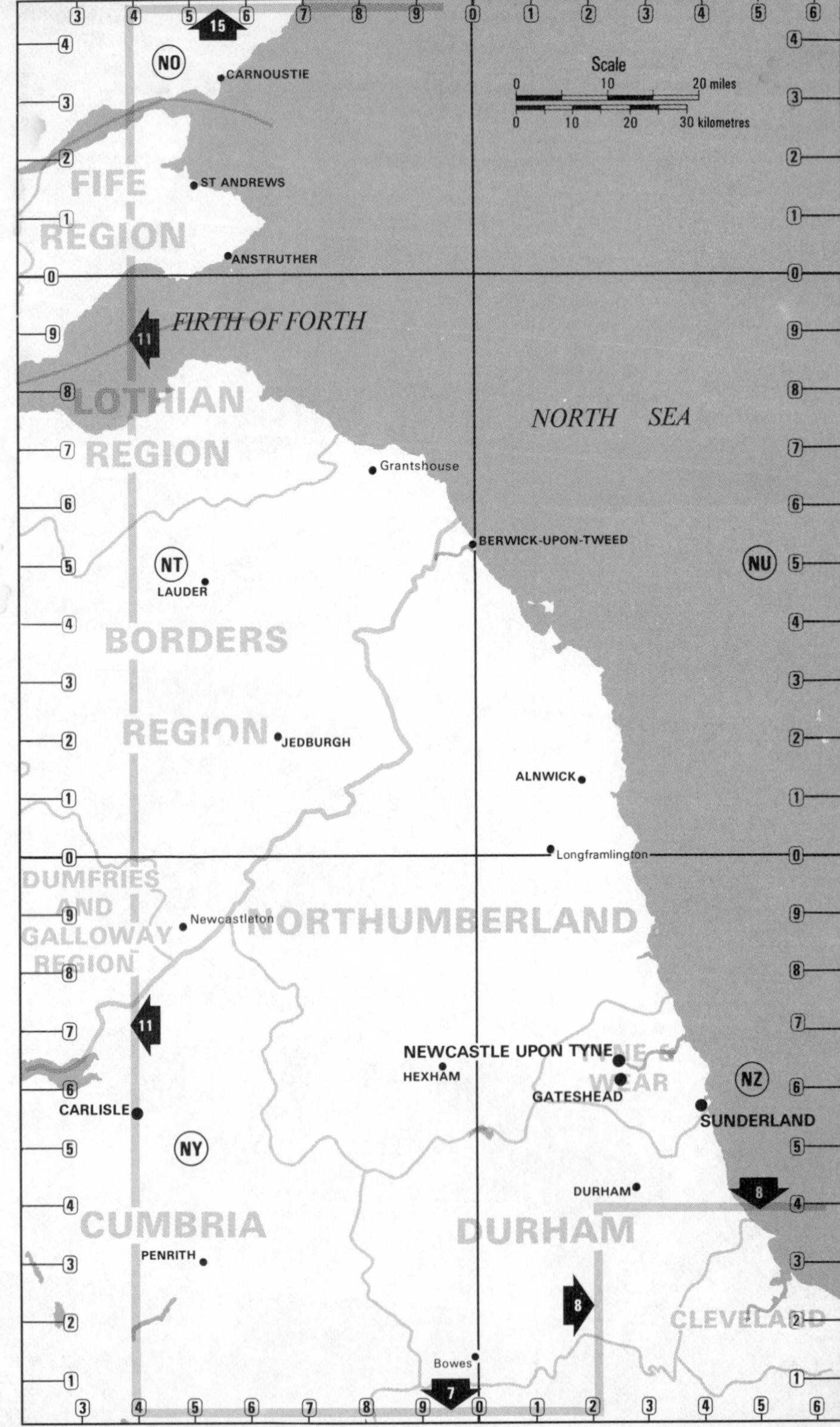

For continuation pages refer to numbered arrows

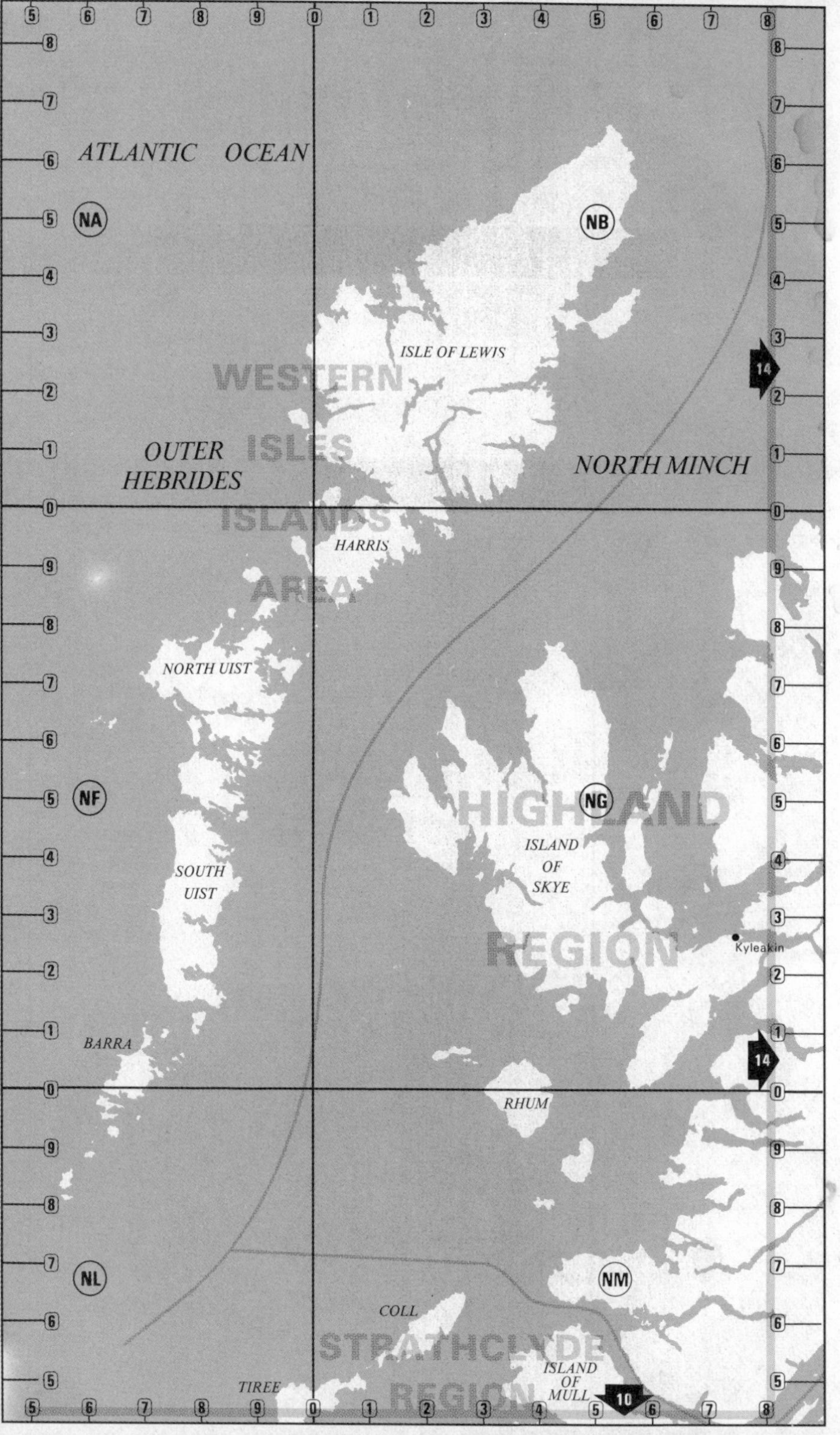
ATLANTIC OCEAN
NA
NB
ISLE OF LEWIS
WESTERN
ISLES
ISLANDS
AREA
OUTER
HEBRIDES
NORTH MINCH
HARRIS
NORTH UIST
NF
NG
HIGHLAND
REGION
ISLAND
OF
SKYE
SOUTH
UIST
Kyleakin
BARRA
RHUM
NL
NM
COLL
STRATHCLYDE
REGION
ISLAND
OF
MULL
TIREE
14
14
10

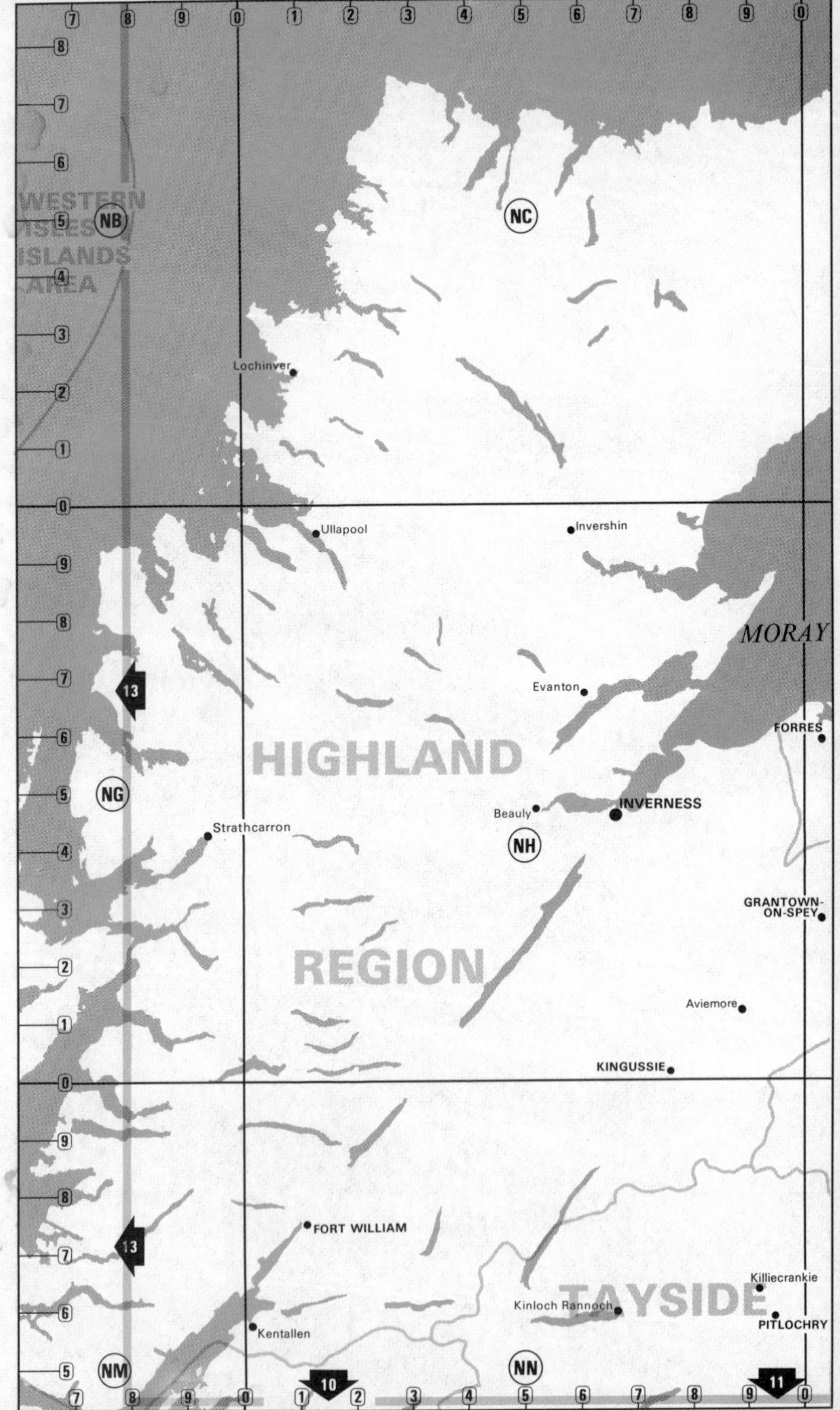

For continuation pages refer to numbered arrows

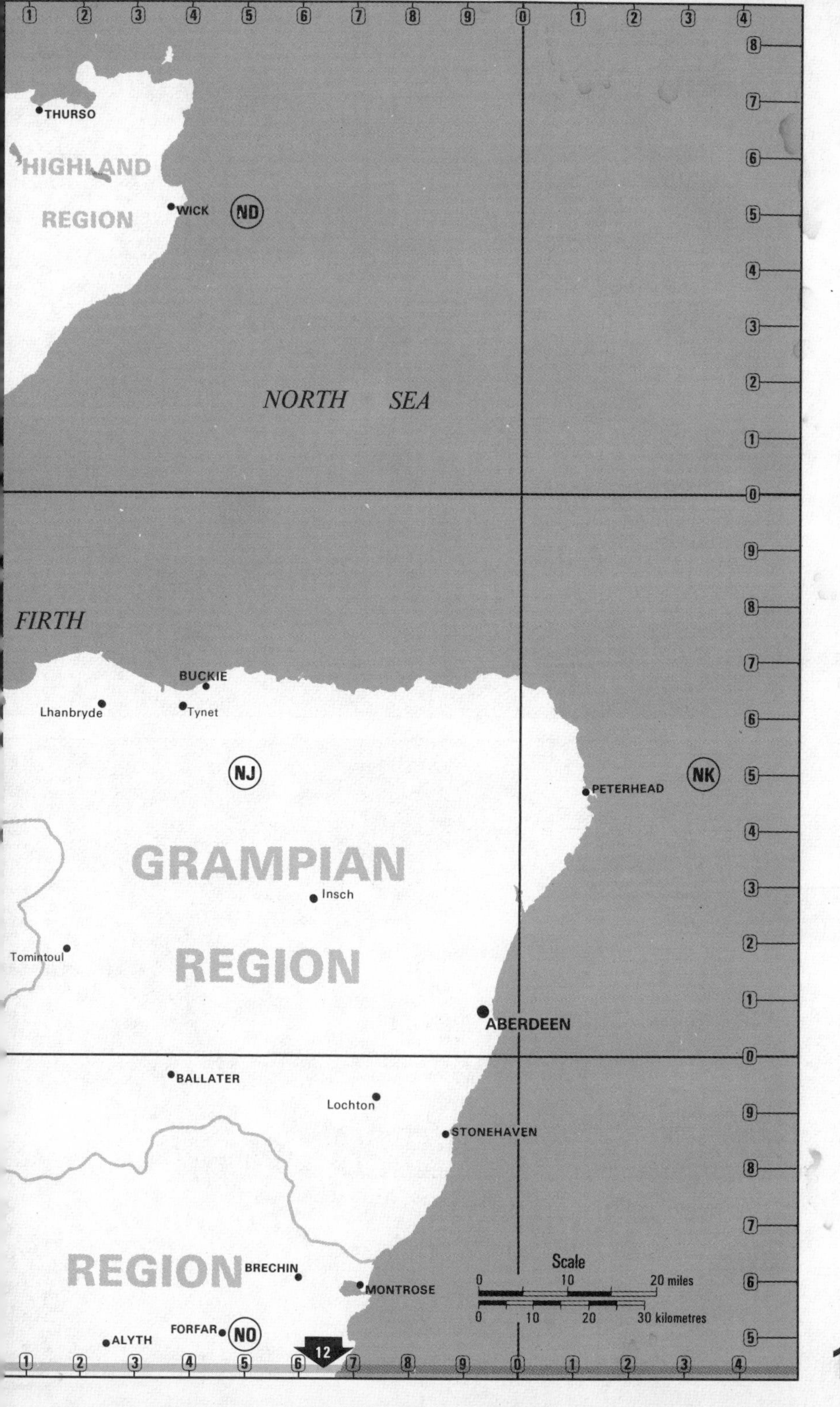
THURSO
HIGHLAND
REGION
WICK
ND
NORTH SEA
FIRTH
BUCKIE
Lhanbryde
Tynet
NJ
NK
PETERHEAD
GRAMPIAN
REGION
Insch
Tomintoul
ABERDEEN
BALLATER
Lochton
STONEHAVEN
REGION
BRECHIN
MONTROSE
FORFAR
NO
ALYTH
12
Scale
0 10 20 miles
0 10 20 30 kilometres

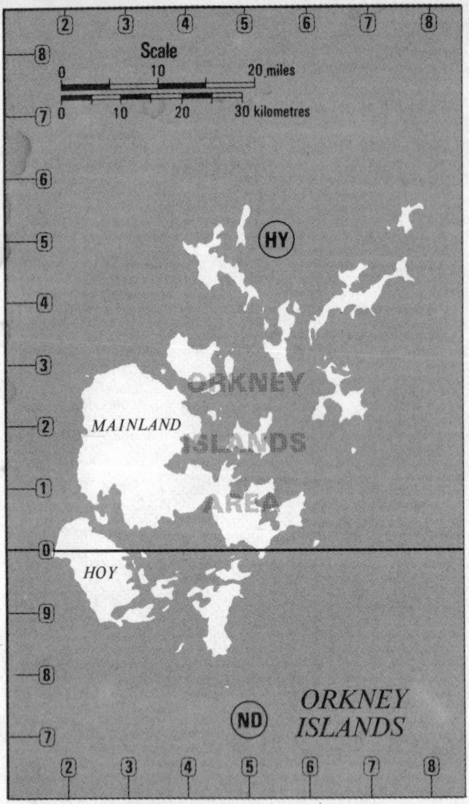

Scale
0 10 20 miles
0 10 20 30 kilometres

HY

ORKNEY ISLANDS AREA

MAINLAND

HOY

ND

ORKNEY ISLANDS

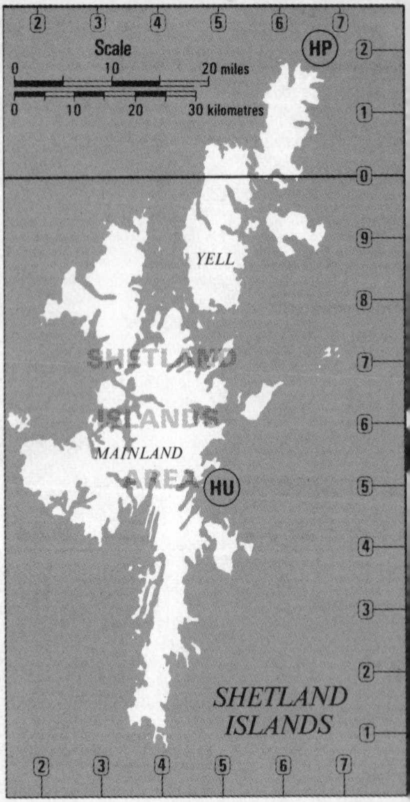

Scale
0 10 20 miles
0 10 20 30 kilometres

HP

YELL

SHETLAND ISLANDS AREA

MAINLAND

HU

SHETLAND ISLANDS

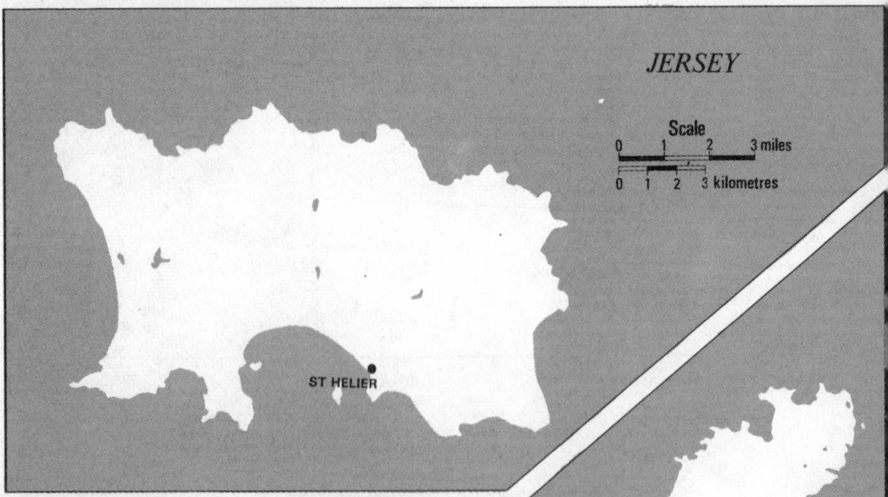

JERSEY

Scale
0 1 2 3 miles
0 1 2 3 kilometres

ST HELIER

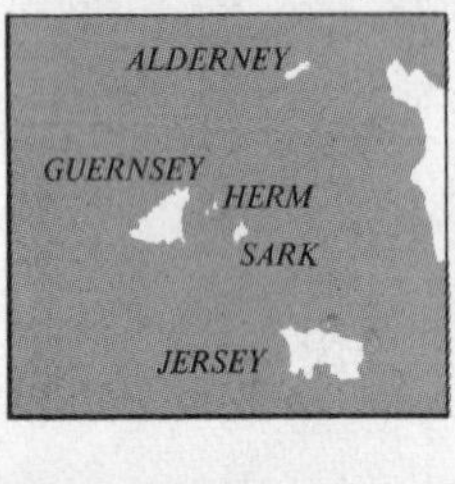

ALDERNEY

GUERNSEY

HERM

SARK

JERSEY

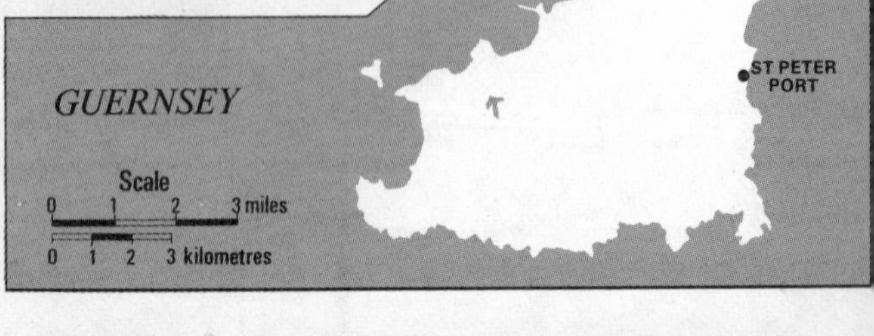

GUERNSEY

Scale
0 1 2 3 miles
0 1 2 3 kilometres

ST PETER PORT